MW01140636

Acknowledgments

With sincere gratitude, I recognize

- my parents for introducing me as a child to Bible stories;
- pastors and professors for cultivating a love for Bible study;
- my wife and son for supporting me with inspiring love;
- family and friends for their trust and encouragement;
- the LORD's yearning grace and faithful care.

****

For Bible Atlas Online go to:
www.anova.org/sev/atlas/htm/index.htm

Preface

"For of Him and through Him and to Him are all things,
to whom be the glory forever" (Romans 11:36).

God's glory shines throughout the Bible; thus, it is also prominent in the Ten Commandments given to Moses, as well as in the Lord's Prayer, the Great Commandment, and the Great Commission given by Jesus. Creation and salvation should glorify the One who brought them into existence. Sadly, man has been rather lax in glorifying God.

The Old Testament, of which this book gives an overview, is a history of (a) God's patient efforts to encourage man to fulfill his intended purpose, and (b) man's mixed response to God's compassionate outreach, a response that was sometimes remarkably hopeful, but often miserably flawed. God's heartache about Israel's poor response was expressed by Jesus when He lamented, *"Jerusalem, Jerusalem, how often I wanted to gather your children together, as a hen gathers her brood under her wings, but you were not willing!"* (Luke 13:34).

However, God did not give up on His people. In spite of their repetitive failures, God patiently continued to reach out to them. He revealed Himself to them in many ways. For instance, His names highlighted different aspects of His being. He revealed to Moses that His name is Yahveh (see next page).

In this study, I was captivated by Yahveh's yearning for His people's trust and love. Does this yearning make God imperfect? On the contrary—it is part of His perfect love. Real love yearns for the loved one. God saw Israel as His "wife." He loved her intensely, and He wanted her to love Him back.

Often Israel ran after false gods ("lovers"), but sometimes her yearning for quality time with the one true God beautifully emerged, as we see in many psalms. The ups and downs of Old Testament history should not distract us from this yearning between God and His people, hence the title of this book.

The Israelites' yearning for God often shifted to things and places that they associated with God, like Jerusalem and the temple. Such associations could affect their faith positively if God remained the focus of their worship; if not, they had replaced God with things. They struggled with this distinction.

God knew that Israel and mankind needed a Savior to enable them to respond with love to His love (Gen. 3:15). The Old Testament shows how God prepared His plan of salvation. When Christ came, He was the ultimate expression of God's outreaching love to Israel and to the world (Acts 1:8). Jesus voiced Yahveh's yearning toward mankind poignantly when He said, *"For God so loved the world that He gave His only begotten Son, that whoever believes in Him should not perish but have everlasting life."* (John 3:16)

About the name "Yahveh"

The Hebrew name of God can be transcribed in English as Yahveh. (The Y is pronounced as in *yes*, a as in *arm*, v as in *view*, e as in *get*, and the h's are soft). In most English Bibles, Yahveh is translated as *the LORD*, and Adonai as *the Lord*.

In ancient Hebrew, the consonants were written and the vowels omitted. Yahveh consisted of four consonants, YHVH. Uncertainty about the vowels in the name Yahveh arose from the post-exile Jewish custom not to pronounce this name of God at all due to the prohibition in the third commandment, "You shall not take the name of Yahveh your God in vain." When they came to the word *Yahveh* in Scripture, they said *Adonai* (Lord) instead. Therefore, the medieval Masoretes added the vowels of *Adonai* to YHVH. This caused non-Jews to mispronounce this name as "Jehovah."

God prohibited the misuse of His name, not the reverent use of it. The name Yahveh is used more than seven thousand times in the Bible. The psalmists and prophets used this name frequently to distinguish the one true God from the many false "gods." Many personal names in the Bible incorporated the short form Ye-, -jah, or -iah, as in Yeshua or Jesus (Yahveh's salvation), Elijah (my God is Yah), and Hezekiah (strength of Yah). Names like these were used daily without fear of God's punishment.

The renowned call to worship, *hallelujah* (praise Yah), uses this name with joy and reverence. The apostles Paul and Peter quoted Joel 2:32 to bring people to faith: "Whoever calls on the name of Yahveh will be saved" (Acts 2:21, Rom 10:13). Psalm 105:1 urges us to do that: "Give thanks to Yahveh. **Call** upon His name."

In Exodus 3:14-15, God links *I am* with *Yahveh*, as both are derived from the verb *to be* (*hayah*). God said to Moses, "**Say** to the Israelites, 'Yahveh ... sent me to you.' God added, *"This is my name forever, the name by which I am to be remembered from generation to generation"* (Ex. 3:15 NIV). God told Moses to reveal His name to the Pharaoh of Egypt as well, "**Say** to him, 'Yahveh, God of the Hebrews, has sent me to you'" (Ex. 7:16). Say Yahveh.

The Pharaoh, the Israelites, and the Egyptians couldn't know that God's name was Yahveh if Moses was not allowed to say it. The Pharaoh referred several times to Yahveh, translated as "the LORD" (Ex. 8:8, 28, 9:27-28). God said that through the plagues "the Egyptians shall know that I am Yahveh" (Ex. 7:5).

There is no command in the Bible that the name Yahveh can be written but not pronounced. Instead God emphasized, "Whoever **calls** on the name of Yahveh will be saved" (Joel 2:32).

1. Touched by Life
Making life possible on earth

Many factors in our solar system are essential for life on earth. The qualities of the sun and the earth's distance from the sun supply enough light and heat. Day, night, and seasons, caused by the tilt and rotation of the earth around its own axis and around the sun, disperse light and heat around the globe.

> January 1
> ~ ~ ~
> Gen. 1

The size, distance, and rotation of the moon regulate tides and sea life. The earth's atmosphere, the distribution of water around the globe, and the nutrients in the earth sustain plants, animals, and humans long enough to secure survival by reproduction.

The presence and balance of these and other life-sustaining factors are critical for life as we know it. If some of these factors would change enough life on earth could cease to exist. The possibility that this fine balance could have come into existence by chance is virtually nil. When left on its own, the natural direction of change on earth is toward decay and chaos, not development. The Bible gives the reason for that: The fall into sin subjected earth to the "bondage of corruption" (Rom. 8:20-21).

In spite of this trend, the intricate structure and functioning of the micro- and macro-cosmos point to powerful, intelligent **design**. The survival of so many life-forms, in spite of many factors against them, points to powerful, intelligent **sustenance**. Genesis 1 and John 1 tell us in non-scientific terms how God created and fine-tuned the universe to make life on earth possible. He started with light, water, land, and plants. Then He got the sun, earth, and moon in the right distance and rotation. After that, He made sea life and birds, land animals, and humans. As He proceeded, He enjoyed His own work.

When believers get out into nature, they too enjoy the handiwork of the Creator. They know He is still touching all creation in loving care because they can see His fingerprints all over the breathtaking beauty of this planet. They don't take it for granted; they don't think for a moment that all this beauty and sensitive ecological balance happened by chance. They know He made it and has sustained it with loving care, and they praise His name.

When believers observe the harm humans have done to this beautiful habitat the Father created for us, they are dismayed at our failure and ask forgiveness for our collective sin. They also take decisive steps to restore what is broken and to prevent further damage. The Creator and His creation yearn for the renewal of all things (Rom. 8:19).

A prayer: Thank You, God, for Your beautiful creation.
A thought: What can I do to counteract damage to the environment?

2. Touched by Love
Let Us make humans in Our image.

<table>
<tr><td>

January 2

~ ~ ~

Gen. 1:26 - 2:25

</td><td>

With regard to the origin of man, we have to deal with the views of creationists (who view life through God's Word) and evolutionists (who view life through Darwin's theory). The first is based on faith, the second on assumption.

</td></tr>
</table>

Genesis 1 tells us that God systematically created the right conditions for life on earth, and then He created life-forms in a certain sequence. Now, which makes more sense: that an intelligent, almighty Being made all these complicated interdependent systems, or that an inexplicable big bang occurred in an inexplicable lump of matter that developed by mere chance into complex life and reality?

God's book tells us that human beings were made in a special way. Although their bodies have organs similar to those of mammals, God added emotional and spiritual components to their beings, making them totally different from mammals. The triune God (Father, Son, and Spirit) decided: "Let Us make man in Our image... male and female He created them."

God made the first person's body from *soil* (Hebrew: *adamah*); therefore, He called him Adam. In the Bible this word is mostly used to indicate humans of both sexes; therefore, the decision *let Us make man* actually means *let Us make humans*. It is stressed by the sentence, *male and female He made them*. In Genesis 1 this fact is stated, and in Genesis 2 more detail about the separate creation of man and woman is given.

Adam's body was made from elements of this planet, and then God instilled the emotional and spiritual components of his being. Eve was made from a part of Adam, indicating the close bond and similarity between the two. Eve was not a clone—she had a chromosome difference.

Eve's creation was also preceded by a decision of God: *"It is not good that man should be alone; I will make him a helper comparable* (suitable NIV) *to him."* The emphasis is on companionship and equality. It was confirmed by Adam when he beheld her with jubilation: She is bone of my bones and flesh of my flesh; I am a man (Hebrew: *ish*), so she is a woman (Hebrew: *ishah*).

If you have been stranded on an island for years, and then suddenly your sweetheart arrives! An electrifying reunion! The unity of husband and wife became a symbol of the unity between God and His people (Hos. 1-3, Eph. 5).

A prayer: Thank You, Lord, for this wonderful, mysterious reality.
A thought: Are we products of evolution or images of our Creator?

3. Touched by Discipline
The challenge of boundaries

Genesis 1 and 2 confronted us with difficult questions on the origin of the universe and the origin of man. Genesis 3 puts us checkmate with questions on the origin of evil. God is holy, loving, omniscient, omnipotent, and omni-present. How could evil have entered His universe? The Bible does not tell us how some of the angels rebelled against God, only that it happened.

January 3
~ ~ ~
Genesis 3

While Adam and Eve still enjoyed perfect harmony with God and His creation, the devil was preparing his ambush. Some ask: Why did God not prevent it? Why didn't He annihilate the devil and his gang immediately? The Bible does not answer these questions because they shift the blame for sin onto God. The fact is that when humans were still sinless, evil already existed. Therefore, God mercifully put up boundaries to protect them (Gen. 2:16-17). Within those boundaries, they would be safe.

God wanted voluntary cooperation (as from His children), not forced obedience (as from slaves). Thus, He gave them a free will to stay within the boundaries voluntarily. It included the possibility of overstepping the boundaries at a high price.

How did Satan try to lure them out of the safety fence? He focused his attack on a natural human need. The drive to explore, discover, invent, and develop was part of the intellectual capabilities God gave to humans. God asked man to know, name, control, and protect plants and animals (Gen. 1:26-29, 2:15, 19). **The challenge was to expand their intellectual boundaries without overstepping God's moral boundaries.** The devil decided to confuse them on this distinction and led them into a trap.

First, he instigated doubt regarding God's boundaries: Has God limited your freedom? When he got Eve to think and talk about it, he had his foot in the door. Then he threw out the bait: You will be like God to KNOW good and evil; you will expand the boundaries of your knowledge!

He kept their focus on intellectual gain, and they overlooked moral loss. He confused them about intellectual and moral boundaries. They doubted God, believed Satan, broke through the fence, and fell into the depth of sin.

The devil still confuses humanity on this issue. The scientific age became the amoral age. Many people think that the expansion of knowledge gives them the freedom to ignore God's moral boundaries. Science and technology face crucial ethical questions on these two kinds of boundaries.

A prayer: Lord, as my knowledge increases I will stay within Your boundaries.
A thought: Did I get confused on the two types of boundaries in the past?

4. Choices and Consequences
Spiritual death due to broken relationships

January 4
~ ~ ~
Gen. 3:7-4:12

The first humans were warned that they would die if they chose to disobey God and step over His protective boundaries. When they did disobey, they did not drop dead right away. Adam died at the age of 930 years (Gen. 5:5), so he saw the eighth generation. He had enough time for remorse and repentance. The death that set in immediately was spiritual in nature: broken relationships with God, others, creation, and self.

Instead of enjoying loving fellowship with their Maker as before, they now feared Him and tried to hide from Him. All their descendants till today would come to know this estrangement from God, this inner guilt that awakens the desire to flee from God. Like the prodigal son (Luke 15), they think that they can only find true freedom and pleasure far away from the Father.

The relationship between Adam and Eve changed too. They covered up their shame with fig leaves. When God held them accountable and started to ask questions, they indulged in finger pointing: Adam blamed Eve, and Eve blamed the serpent.

As soon as Adam and Eve had two children, the process of broken relationships proceeded to the next generation. The interests, temperaments, behavior, and faith of the two boys differed so much that sinful human nature soon let differences escalate into resentment and hate. Tragically, the first person born on earth also became the first murderer.

Their sin also brought distance with nature: They were driven out of the garden. Eve would suffer in the process of childbearing and child rearing, and Adam would suffer in providing for his family. The earth, too, would suffer under the curse of sin: It would yield not only food, but also thorns and thistles. Until God makes everything new again, the whole creation groans in pain and in yearning for the renewal of creation (Rom. 8:18-22).

There was another estrangement—maybe the worst of all: Humans became alienated from their true selves, the image of God in their innermost beings. The conflict between good and evil, light and darkness, invaded their souls. They would be torn apart between a desire to do the good (to be their true selves) and the desire to do the bad (to succumb to their sinful nature, the world, and Satan) (See Rom. 7, Gal. 5).

In Christ, though, victory can be achieved (Rom. 8:8-11, Gal. 5:22-25).

A prayer: Good Shepherd, thank You for coming to us in spite of our failure.
A thought: How can these broken relationships be healed?

5. Grace Amid Catastrophe
Salvation made possible

God set a process into motion that would show the unity between His love and justice, His wisdom and power. The mere fact that man, after violating God's law, did not die physically on the spot already shows the infinite grace of the loving Creator. In His hurt, He did not become revengeful; He reached out to the guilty in their shame. Yahveh yearned for their repentance and reconciliation.

January 5
~ ~ ~
Gen. 3:15,
3:21-24,
4:6-15

Temporary relief efforts would not solve the long-term problem; therefore, God first of all made provision for their salvation. He promised that eventually Someone, born from Eve's descendants, would destroy the devil's power completely and make true reconciliation with God a wonderful reality. After this "mother-promise," God reminded His people repeatedly of His plan of salvation that would become a reality in the "fullness of time" (Gal. 4:4).

Then God attended to their immediate needs. He replaced the fig leaves (which would have given them a nasty rash) with soft garments made of animal skin—the first animals that died for the benefit of mankind, pointing to the Lamb of God who would give His life for the sin debt of humanity.

The perfect Father tempered His discipline with much love and grace. If they had eaten from the tree of life, they would have lived forever in their sinful state. The removal of man from the Garden of Eden was therefore more mercy than punishment. If they would make peace with God in time, death would become a blessing in disguise: It would end their sinful and cumbersome existence on earth. Death would not be a punishment anymore, but a stepping-stone from this life into the next.

This mercy for the guilty was extended to Cain as well. God warned him about the seriousness of the situation when he became envious toward his brother and his resentment started to grow into hate. He ignored the warning and killed his brother anyway. God disciplined him by forcing him to face the consequences of his evil deed. He would remain a fugitive for the rest of his life—a curse that comes on every murderer.

Although Cain's remorse was full of self-pity, God had mercy on him: He put a sign on Cain that would make people refrain from killing him. We do not know what the sign was. It could have been a deformation in his body that would have instigated pity, rather than revenge, in others.

A prayer: God, thank You that Your discipline is filled with grace and wisdom.
A thought: Do I use or abuse God's grace?

6. Two Kinds of People
Serving God or serving Satan

<table>
<tr>
<td>
January 6
~ ~ ~
Gen. 4:17 - 6:4
</td>
<td>
The line between good and evil runs through hearts and through society. Although all knew this inner conflict, Cain and his offspring gave free rein to their evil desires, while Seth and his descendants fought against evil by trusting and serving God (Gen. 4:26).
</td>
</tr>
</table>

Two of them, Enoch and Noah, lived so near to God that it was said of them that they walked with God. Both of them witnessed to the ungodly people of their time (Jude 14-15, 2 Peter 2:5). By faith, Enoch received assurance that he pleased God before he was taken away by God without tasting death (Heb. 11:5). When Noah was warned by God of the coming judgment, he believed God and moved with godly fear to prepare the ark of redemption (Heb. 11:7). Thus, he received righteousness by faith.

Cain's offspring became increasingly independent of and defiant toward God. They glorified themselves with successes in agriculture, music, and technology (4:20-22). Lamech boasted that if Cain would be avenged sevenfold, then he would avenge himself seventy-seven times on his enemies. Thus, he claimed that he could protect himself completely and that he did not need God's protection anymore, as Cain did. In our time, nations also arm themselves to the teeth, ready for retaliation.

Then things took a turn for the worse. The "the sons of God," the offspring of Seth, started to marry with "the daughters of men," the offspring of Cain. Instead of pulling the bad people up to their level, many good people were pulled down by the bad. (The phrase *sons of God* probably does not refer here to *angels* (Job 1:6), but rather to *children of God* (Ps. 82:6). The fact that angels are spirits (Heb. 1:14) who can't have physical intercourse with women argues against *angels* in this context.)

As the blood of good and bad mixed, physical strength and spiritual weakness resulted. This boosted their inflated egos to such an extent that they taunted God more and more by living out their sinful desires without restraint. In our time, the free will is also abused to the extreme.

At the same time, the numbers of people declined at an alarming rate. Eventually only one family of eight was left. God would use them to make a new beginning, while He would wipe out the rest with a flood. In His mercy though, God postponed the judgment to give them time for repentance (2 Pet. 3:9). The same scenario will be repeated in the end time (Luke 17).

A prayer: Father, at great speed we are approaching the same situation again.
A thought: Do I take my stand fearlessly with God, as Enoch and Noah did?

7. Miracles Amid Decadence
Noah finds grace in the eyes of the LORD.

God's creation was in crisis. In the beginning, God enjoyed His creation for it was very good. Now He saw evil increasing rapidly, and it caused Him intense grief. He thought of destroying man and beast. But then His love made a miracle happen—Noah found grace in the eyes of the LORD. Of course, Noah was not sinless, but God's Spirit did accomplish something good in him. Like a devoted pilgrim, he stumbled occasionally, but he was heading in the right direction.

> January 7
> ~ ~ ~
> Gen. 6 - 8

God's grace made a second miracle happen. His mercy toward Noah would be extended to some people and to some animals. That could only happen through another miracle, the miracle of faith in Noah's heart. If he would believe God about the coming flood and build this huge wooden ship in spite of all the mockery of the wicked, then his family and some animals would be saved. Noah's perseverance in faith and his obedience over many years were indeed miracles. He must have had his moments of doubt too.

The ark itself was a miracle. To build a structure of that size with the tools of the day was already a fantastic achievement. Also, the fact that the structure stayed intact on the water, in spite of its load and in spite of heavy winds (Gen. 8:1), was nothing short of a miracle. What a cargo! Land animals and birds of all kinds coming by themselves to the ark, stacked up three stories high with food for one year—a miracle indeed! Think of the work on such a vessel. The daily removal of dung alone would have exhausted them. That year of surviving in the ark was only possible by the grace of God.

What happened outside the ark was just as miraculous. Apparently, a massive amount of water was still trapped in the earth's crust at that time. Suddenly cracks appeared and massive volumes of water were forced out under immense pressure, *"the fountains of the great deep were broken up,"* spouting high into the sky and causing torrential rainfall everywhere. For forty terrible days it continued until the flood submerged everything. Two-thirds of the earth's surface is today still covered by water, up to four miles deep at many places. Maybe a flatter seabed at that time helped to inundate the land more quickly.

The end of the deluge and the disappearing of the water were further miracles. The sinking of the earth's crust at some places, and its rising at other places, could have accelerated the drying process. Eventually those who had been saved stepped out into a new world for a new beginning.

A prayer: Lord, help us to see Your many miracles in and around us.
A thought: Do I proceed in faith and obedience as Noah did?

8. A New Deal
A covenant between unequal partners

<table>
<tr><td>

January 8

~ ~ ~

Gen. 8:20-9:17

</td></tr>
</table>

By many graceful miracles, God saved a few humans and a few of many species. When they came out of the ark, the symbol of salvation, God watched them to see how they would respond. After a year of confinement, animals and birds surely would have shown their relief by boisterous bouncing and joyful sounds. Noah's sons and their wives danced and sang. Tears of gratitude flowed over the cheeks of the two old people. In name of all, Noah brought burnt offerings to God, indicating their thanksgiving, dependence, and commitment.

Seeing this, God reached out to them with more grace and love. Although He knew that Noah and his family were not perfect and would sin again, God decided He would not punish creation in the same way again. The rhythm of the seasons would go on undisturbed. He reassured Noah and his family that they did not have to live in fear of another flood. He declared the rainbow to be a symbol of that promise. For the sacraments too, God used existing realities (water, bread, and wine) to symbolize certain truths.

The commission God had given to Adam, He now also gave to Noah and his descendants—to multiply and to be custodians of God's creation. However, the disturbed relationship between man and beast would become evident in the fear of the animals for man and in the fact that man himself would become a predator. God gave humans permission to eat the flesh of animals on condition that they did not eat blood. Speaking about blood, God added that whoever murders a human being would have to pay with his/her own life for that. These two principles, which were for man's own protection, would later be explained in more detail in the Law of Moses.

In His mercy, God stooped to man's level in this covenant. As the sovereign God, He did not have to make a contract with His creation. Yet in His mercy He did. He talked about Himself in human-like terms. He smelled the aroma of Noah's burnt offering. It sounds as if He would enjoy a barbeque with Noah. He would see the rainbow and remember His covenant—as if the omniscient God needed a reminder.

Actually, it was the other way around: The aroma of food and the colors of the rainbow would remind Noah and his descendants of God's goodness and friendship. He first gives to us so that we can give our thanks and devotion back to Him. He does not ask what He has not given, like our tithes.

A prayer: Merciful Father, thanks for reaching out to us.
A thought: Do I keep myself aware of God's many mercies?

9. The Birth of Nations
God confuses their language.

The genealogy of Noah's sons, as well as the birth of different languages at the Tower of Babel, heralds the dawn of distinct cultures and nations. The genealogies of Shem, Ham, and Japheth are concluded by pointing to the distinctions in families, nations, lands, and languages (Gen. 10:5, 20, 31). Genesis 10 states the fact while the next chapter describes how it happened.

> January 9
> ~ ~ ~
> Gen. 9:18-11:9

The Bible links the breaking up of humanity into nations with man's sinful nature. It started with Noah's inebriety. The man who persevered in faith and obedience to build the ark, who survived the flood and who helped others to survive it, the man who walked with God drank himself into oblivion after the whole ordeal was over. Even today there are many who persevere through severe tests but collapse after they have reached the peak. Yes, people who live near to God also have their moments of weakness. But no one can afford to gloat over their stumbling.

Ham's insensitive response to his father's weakness was severely punished. Israel's victory over the Canaanites centuries later was already predicted in Noah's curse. At the same time, the blessing of the Messiah was promised to Shem (the Jews). Japheth (the Gentiles) would share in that blessing.

One of Ham's descendants was Nimrod, a man of ambition and violence, a mighty warrior and hunter. He built several fortified cities and became the king of Babel (Gen. 10:10). Maybe the construction of the Tower of Babel started under his rule. The people's assertiveness and arrogance were limitless. They wanted to build a tower that reached into heaven. They thought of themselves as equal to God. As with Adam and Eve, the devil tempted them to be like God. This trend has continued till our time. There is a profound difference between self-glorifying and God-glorifying ambition.

Their tower became a monument of humility! Just one move by God and they could not proceed because they could not communicate. It still happens at international meetings. They got so frustrated that they abandoned the work and dispersed in all directions. However, there was mercy in God's punishment. They were enriched by the diversity of cultures, and so are we today.

Unfortunately, the process of globalization blends cultures and tries to reverse the fact of Babel. We have to respect God's order (Acts 17:26). It curbs man's megalomania.

A prayer: Father, keep me on guard against the snares of the devil.
A thought: Am I inclined to the sins of Noah, Ham, and Nimrod?

10. The Promise
In you, all nations will be blessed.

<table>
<tr><td>January 10
~~~
Gen. 11:27-12:10</td></tr>
</table>

Yahveh's yearning now turned to one specific nation. Abram and his descendants had to be a light to other nations. God called Abram first in the city of Ur* in the south of Mesopotamia (Iraq). His whole family moved with him to Haran in the northwest of that region. What was meant as a temporary stop became a long stay. So God called him again in Haran and added that he had to leave his family behind. In spite of the clear command, Abram took his nephew Lot with him. No, Abram did not become a firm believer instantly. It would be a long, painful process.

God linked His command to an awesome promise. Abram would be blessed by God in several ways: His descendants would become a great nation and from them blessings would flow to all nations. This promise also points to Jesus (Gal. 3:16). Abram knew little about God at this point, but God spoke so vividly to him that he did not have any doubts. He obeyed without hesitation (Heb. 11:8). Later his faith would falter many times, but as he struggled, his faith gradually grew. He would become a very human role model for believers.

When Abram arrived in the Promised Land, it was already inhabited and it was also in the grip of a severe drought. It had to be a disappointing anti-climax for him after he had started off with such a wonderful promise. In the short term, God's promises and provisions do not always make sense to us. We see only a tiny bit of reality while God see the whole picture. It is like driving on a winding road through the mountains: We don't know what new scenery is just around the bend.

God would later inform Abram that the iniquity of the present inhabitants had to be completed before Abram's descendants would emerge from Egypt to claim what God had promised to their ancestors (Gen. 15:12-16). Each generation has only a small share in God's agenda for the ages.

Sometimes we get our hopes up high because of promises in God's Word, only to see them shattered to pieces by unexpected disappointments. Like Abram, we have to keep faith in spite of temporary setbacks. As Abram moved on from place to place, he built altars and worshiped God openly in spite of the sinful inhabitants and in spite of the choking drought. For a while, he anchored his faith to God's promise, not to circumstances.

A prayer: Lord, I want to keep faith in spite of disappointments.
A thought: Is my faith a persevering faith?
* Gen. 15:7, Neh. 9:7, Acts 7:2.

11. A Blessing or a Curse?
The Lord plagues Pharaoh's house.

Because the land was inhabited and because they had to find grazing for their flocks and herds in a drought-stricken region, Abram had to adopt a nomadic lifestyle similar to that of the present day Bedouin in the Negev, the southern arid part of Israel.

January 11
~ ~ ~
Gen. 12:10-20

In these adverse circumstances, Abram was sliding down to his first low point in his relationship with God. Instead of trusting God, seeking and obeying His will, Abram shifted his trust from God's promise to his own plans. He thought he could improve on God's meager provisions by leaving the Promised Land and finding a better life for himself in Egypt. Thanks to the abundant waters of the Nile River, Egypt was a place of plenty.

As Abram approached Egypt, the possibility dawned on him that Egypt might bring him death instead of life due to the custom of the time that the pharaoh (king) had unlimited power over all in his domain, including visiting strangers. It did not bother Abram that Pharaoh could take all his possessions, but he was deeply worried that the emperor might take his life to acquire his beautiful wife. That would turn his bright plan into a disaster.

So he had to come up with a second plan of his own to save God's promise to him. If Sarai would say that she was his sister, Abram might not only survive but also receive some gifts from the pleased sovereign. Abram soothed his conscience with the fact that Sarai was indeed his half-sister (they had the same father, but were born from different mothers). Apparently neither Abram nor Sarai was bothered by the adultery that would ensue from their plan.

Initially, the plan worked wonderfully. Abram's life was spared, Sarai moved into the king's harem, and Abram got richer by the day as the pharaoh showered him with gifts consisting of livestock and slaves. Abram smiled in his beard and thought, "What a fantastic deal I carved out for myself—it's far better than those old dusty plains of the Promised Land."

Then the Lord put a swift stop to his folly. Instead of being a blessing to other nations, as the promise said, Abram brought a curse of disease on Pharaoh and his household. The man who should have introduced the true God to the Gentiles was reprimanded by a heathen king for being untruthful. With shame, Abram had to leave Egypt. His shortcut to the promise had failed miserably. And amongst the slaves he got as a present was Hagar, who would become a snare to Abram and a threat to the promise.

A prayer: Lord, I want to stay obedient to You when I do my share.
A thought: Where have I replaced God's will with my own plans?

12. The Broad and Narrow Way
Abram and Lot separate.

January 12

~ ~ ~

Genesis 13

When Abram and his household returned to Canaan, their increased livestock and money caused problems. Although Abram's nephew Lot was part of the household, his animals and slaves were kept separate from Abram's. It would simplify matters when they would decide to part company. And that day arrived sooner than they had anticipated. Friction arose between the two groups of herdsmen with regard to watering and grazing rights.

The way they handled this crisis brought the true characters of the two men to the surface. Abram had learned a lot from his mistakes in Egypt, while Lot had not. Abram had gotten his priorities right again. God was again first of all, and material things were downgraded to their rightful place. Lot was not cured of his greed; on the contrary, Egypt increased his appetite for more.

Abram suggested that they go in different directions in search of water and grazing to keep the peace. They were standing on the hill country north of Jerusalem and had a good view of both the green Jordan valley to the east and the arid hills to the west. Lot did not show his uncle the courtesy of letting him have the first choice. He grabbed the chance to choose the best part for himself. The fact that the greater riches meant exposure to a more sinful lifestyle did not bother Lot. Soon his tents would stand near Sodom, and shortly afterward he lived in that infamous place. Lot was unmasked as a mere conformist. He had been in Abram's camp for several years, but he had not shared in Abram's faith and values. He was not happy among the sinful people either (2 Pet. 2:6-8). Lot was sitting on the fence between church and world, and he could not make up his mind where he really belonged.

Abram was back on track. He did not focus on the unattractive land he got, but on the Lord's presence and promise. After they went their separate ways, God spoke to Abram, not to Lot, confirming that He would give that whole land to Abram's descendants. The meek will inherit the earth. Yahveh showered Abram with blessings so that he could bless others.

The Lord commanded Abram to travel through the land as if it were his already. Abram moved to the south again and made Hebron his headquarters for a time. There he bought a piece of land as a graveyard, the only real estate in the Promised Land that the patriarch would ever have in his name. Once again, he built an altar and worshiped the one true God openly.

A prayer: Lord, help me to keep my priorities right.
A thought: On what principles do I base my important decisions?

13. Abram Becomes a Blessing
to the nations around him.

We are informed in detail about some typical military operations of that time. Small kingdoms put their small armies together to raid and subdue other city kingdoms. With one of these raids, many of Sodom's people, including Lot and his family, were taken captive and their possessions looted. Probably it was one of Lot's slaves who fled to Abram with the bad news.

January 13
~ ~ ~
Genesis 14

Now another side of Abram's character emerged. Up to this point he had followed the path of the least resistance. He did his best to maintain peace with the Canaanites, with the Egyptians, and with Lot. But now it was no longer his own life and property that were at stake but the lives of his family and friends, or rather people who could become his friends.

Abram rose to the occasion and became a shrewd and determined commander who inspired his troops and scared his enemies. However, we can be sure that Abram did not undertake this mission with trust in himself, but with trust in God—his Egypt experience was still fresh in his memory. Abram surprised the enemy with a night attack. God used his small force to create confusion amongst the unprepared armies. Abram drove them out of the land, freed all captives, and regained all property and livestock.

On their return, Abram had two important meetings near Jerusalem. First, he met Melchizedek, the priest-king of Jerusalem. Like Abram, this man worshiped the one true God. Both called God the "Most High." Melchizedek traveled to Abram to meet and bless him. Abram responded by honoring him as his superior and entrusted to him a tenth of the loot as thanksgiving to God. Psalm 110 and Hebrews 7 portray Melchizedek as a type of Christ who would also be a priest-king.

Then the king of Sodom, who had been hiding when his people were abducted, came to thank Abram. When he suggested that Abram keep all the property as reward for his services, Abram flatly refused. He did not want anything for himself from Sodom, but he allowed his army and allies to benefit from it. Abram prayed for Sodom, but he did not associate with them (Gen. 19).

In this episode, Abram became a blessing to the nations of Canaan. Although it was not yet a spiritual blessing, the promise of Genesis 12:1-3 was becoming a reality. Abram had won over the goodwill of the local inhabitants. He was no longer an unwelcome stranger, but an appreciated neighbor.

A prayer: Lord, I want to be a blessing to others.
A thought: How can I become an appreciated neighbor?

14. Grace and Faith
Another covenant between unequal partners

<table>
<tr><td>

January 14

~ ~ ~

Genesis 15

</td><td>

Maybe Abram feared revenge from the kings he drove out of Canaan. God reassured him in a vision not to fear. God Himself would shield him against attacks, and He would reward him exceedingly. Abram's response was that all the riches in the world would be meaningless if he remained childless. God took him out of his tent by night

</td></tr>
</table>

for a practical lesson. His descendants would be as many as the stars. While he was looking up into the glittering firmament, God filled his heart with faith— faith that God who made the heavens would fulfill His promise. And God declared Abram righteous (right with God) because of the faith God laid in his heart (Rom. 4, Eph. 2:8).

When God repeated that Abram's descendants would inherit the land he was standing on, Abram asked for a sign that would strengthen his faith. In effect, he cried out, "Lord, I believe; help me with my unbelief!" (Mark 9:24). Abram was indeed a very human role model for believers. In his moment of justification by faith, unbelief was still yapping at his heels. And in His infinite mercy, God did not blame him for that but helped him in his weakness, just as Jesus grabbed the hand of his sinking disciple (Matt. 14). God then used another object lesson to show Abram that there was a covenant between them.

It was the custom of the time to seal covenants by blood. An animal was killed, divided in two equal parts, and the two parts were then laid over against each other. The two people confirmed the covenant by walking through the opening between the two parts of the carcass. By this action they said, "May the one who breaks this covenant become like this animal."

The next day, God instructed Abram to divide several animals like that. While he waited for the Lord, vultures descended on the carcasses, so Abram scared them off. The devil always tries to jeopardize God's redemptive work. At nightfall, Abram fell asleep and had a terrifying dream. God told him in the dream that his descendants would be enslaved for four centuries before they would be liberated by God and led to the Promised Land.

Then Abram woke up and noticed with awe how a fire moved through the space between the two sets of carcasses. God knew that Abram could not guarantee this covenant; therefore, God alone moved through to confirm the covenant. It was a one-sided covenant between two unequal partners. Yahveh's yearning makes Him generous toward believers.

A prayer: Lord, You hold me like a baby and teach me to walk.
A thought: Do I trust this compassionate Father?

15. A Dangerous Detour
They get tired of waiting.

After ten years in the Promised Land, Sarai thought they had waited long enough for God to fulfill His promise. Her time for childbearing was over. The only way the promise could be fulfilled, she thought, was to use a surrogate mother according to the custom of the time. Trying to help God fulfill His promise, Abram slept with Hagar, who conceived immediately.

> January 15
> ~ ~ ~
> Genesis 16

Hagar's pride about her pregnancy developed into arrogance. With gloating smiles and body language, she reminding Sarai that she, Hagar, was going to give to Abram what Sarai could not. Eventually, Sarai's already poor self-image could not take it any more, and she angrily complained to Abram. He kept himself out of this dispute by reminding Sarai who the boss was and who the slave. Sarai tried to cool her jealous anger by treating Hagar badly. Hagar could not stand that and decided to run away. A nasty piece of interpersonal history was in the making—in the household of God's friend!

While the exhausted, pregnant Hagar rested at a well in the desert, a man approached her. Soon she realized that he was a messenger of God. With one penetrating question, he made her realize who she was (a slave), where she had come from (the plenty of Abram's household), and where she was heading (lonely childbirth in an inhospitable desert). He urged her to go back and apologize for her behavior. Then she and her baby would be safe. He promised that her son would become the father of a great nation.

Hagar probably already had second thoughts about the wisdom of her flight in her condition, so she took the advice and returned in humble spirit to Abram's camp. She realized that God had compassion on her, so she named that well "The Living One sees me." All who heard her story honored that name. When the baby was born, Abram called his son Ishmael ("God hears") as the angel had commanded Hagar.

The sovereign God allows bad things to happen that by their nature are not His will, but He uses them for His own good purpose (Rom. 8:28). He also has compassion on people caught up in the sinful processes of life. Even if Abram and Sarai did not bother much about a misused, insubordinate runaway slave, God had mercy on her and her unborn child. God would not change His plans because of Abram's and Sarai's mistakes, but neither was He indifferent to those who suffered as a result of those mistakes.

A prayer: God, forgive me my impertinence of thinking I know better than You.
A thought: Do I sometimes try to move ahead of God?

16. A New Beginning
Symbolized by new names and a new sign

<table>
<tr><td>

January 16

~ ~ ~

Genesis 17

</td><td>

After thirteen uneventful years, God reappeared to Abram. If Abram and Sarai thought their plan was working and that Ishmael was accepted as the promised heir, God put a sudden stop to their fallacy. The emergence of new names for God, themselves, and the coming heir pointed to a new beginning.

</td></tr>
</table>

God called Himself El-Shaddai, God Almighty, to let Abram know that nothing was impossible for Him. God might have appeared to Abram here in human form for when He finished speaking, God "went up" from him (17:22). (When God reappeared in human form (Gen. 18), Abram recognized Him immediately.) Abram bowed with his face to the ground. God changed Abram's name to Abraham (father of nations) for his offspring would be many. Sarai became Sarah (princess) for kings would stem from her.

When God said that Sarah would bear a child, Abram laughed. Knowing they were too old to have children, he said, *"O, that Ishmael might live before You!"* In other words: "Lord, make Ishmael the heir and bless him." Then God announced another new name: Isaac (laughter) would be born from Sarah and he would be the heir. God meant, "When he is born, Abraham, you will laugh again, not in disbelief as you do now, but in overflowing joy."

God reaffirmed His covenant with Abraham, and He gave him a new sign of the covenant: the circumcision of all males belonging to Abraham's household. It is repeated that all his male slaves, whether bought by him or born in his service, had to receive the sign of the covenant too. Here is an early indication that the blessing of the covenant would be for the Gentiles too. On that same day, Abraham obeyed this command and had all males in his household circumcised, including himself and his son Ishmael.

Although circumcision was a known practice in those days, God gave a new meaning to it for His chosen people. This sign to the male reproductive organ affirmed that the offspring would belong to God. Likewise, He had given a new meaning to the rainbow in his covenant with Noah. The sacraments also gave new meaning to known objects.

With the new names and the new sign, God was setting the scene for the next phase of His revelation: the birth of the miracle son born from two old people who outlived their hope, but whose faith would be wonderfully restored. In spite of Abram and Sarai's detour, El-Shaddai's plan was back on track.

A prayer: Lord, I'm willing for Your correction and a new beginning.
A thought: Have I given up hope on God's promises?

17. A Caring Host
entertains mysterious guests.

The Bible does not explain exactly how God's sovereign grace meets with human responsibility but confirms with practical examples that it is happening all the time. Genesis 18 is another excellent illustration of this interaction between God and man.

> January 17
> ~~~
> Genesis 18:1-15

While Abraham was easing the heat of the day in the shade of his tent beneath the Mamre trees at Hebron, he saw three men approaching. Realizing that they had to be exhausted by traveling at that hour of the day in the hot, dry Negev, he put his hospitality into action. As he approached the men, Abraham recognized El-Shaddai and addressed Him as Adonai (Lord), one of the names for God in the Bible. He offered his hospitality without enquiring about their identity or traveling plans. The Bedouin still practice this courtesy today.

When the Lord accepted his invitation, the elderly Abraham moved as fast as he could to make arrangements for refreshments. While the meal took place in the public part of the tent, Sarah retreated behind a partition. It was clear that Abraham was right: His guests were no other than God and two angels appearing in human form. Although they actually did not need it, they enjoyed Abraham's hospitality. God treats us similarly when He allows us to honor Him with our offerings, praises, testimony, and services.

After the meal, the LORD casually announced that the next year at the same time, Sarah would have a son of her own. God had informed Abraham about this when He instituted circumcision as the sign of the covenant (17:21). The promise was now repeated for the benefit of Sarah, who overheard the conversation. She found the announcement of a son born from two old people quite amusing and incredible. God interacted with her indirectly by expressing His amazement by asking, "How can Sarah laugh in disbelief? How can she think that anything is impossible for God?" In this way, Yahveh invited Sarah to trust Him. In His sovereign power, God could do whatever He chose to, but He wanted to include Sarah's trustful cooperation as well.

God uses means to reach His goals, and we can be part of those means. It includes our time, efforts, money, testimony, missions, and evangelism. We have to do these prayerfully. However, the essence of prayer is not to persuade God to do what we ask, but to praise Him, to embrace His will, and to commit ourselves as instruments into His hands. We have to wait in faith for His time, guidance, and provision.

A prayer: Lord, I want to be part of Your plan and team.
A thought: How do I reconcile providence and human effort?

18. A Caring Intercessor
pleads on behalf of a wicked world.

<table>
<tr><td>

January 18

~ ~ ~

Gen. 18:16-33

</td></tr>
</table>

When his guests decided to move on, Abraham accompanied them for a while. Maybe he hoped for some more information or encouragement. The angels proceeded to Sodom while the LORD talked to Abraham about the imminent judgment of the sinful cities. God presented Himself in a human-like way to Abraham by His physical appearance, His decision to share His thoughts with Abraham, and listening patiently to Abraham's response. Yet in the conversation, God's omniscience and sovereignty are not compromised. He knew exactly how many righteous people lived in Sodom.

When Abraham heard God's plans for Sodom, his caring attitude moved from hospitality to intercession. A while ago, God expressed amazement about Sarah's unbelief; now Abraham vented his amazement about God's plans: "Lord, would You destroy a city if there are fifty just people living there? No, You would not; it is not like You!" God must have smiled at Abraham's openness and honesty. He said, "You're right, Abraham. I will not destroy the cities if there are fifty just people living there."

The thought that Sodom might fall short by only five or so haunted Abraham. Encouraged by God's mercy, he dared to move the bottom line just a little bit. He shared his concern with God, who agreed with him. Once the forty-five mark had been established, the same argument took hold of Abraham, and God made another concession. God's mercy awakened Abraham's compassion, and together they proceeded down Grace Avenue, the one inspiring the other. Yahveh must have enjoyed Abraham's yearning for God's grace. Abraham's compassion made him bold and generous, but he did not want to overplay his hand either. With each request, he apologized for his audacity to push the limits down further, feeling guilty at the same time that he had not put in a better bid the previous time.

This interaction between God and man was far more than a merchant and a customer quibbling in the marketplace. While God's holiness demanded justice on the wicked cities, His merciful love inspired a human being with compassion to wrestle with Him on the balance between His love and justice.

On Calvary, God's Son would absorb all God's justice so that all God's love could become available to sinful humanity. Abraham's intercession pointed to Christ standing in for us and praying for us (Luke 22:32, 23:34 and Rom. 8:34).

A prayer: God, mercifully You include our prayers in Your plans.
A thought: Can my prayers change God, or only circumstances and me?

19. Compromised Believers
Saved by the skin of their teeth

Because there were not ten righteous people in Sodom and Gomorrah, God decided to destroy these cities. Yet, in His mercy, thinking of Abraham's pleading with Him (19:29), God decided to rescue the less-than-ten "righteous" people out of these evil cities.

| January 19 |
| ~~~ |
| Genesis 19 |

Although it looks as if the angels arrived in Lot's house by Lot's hospitality, which he might have learned from Abraham, it is clear from the whole story that Lot's rescue was construed by God and not by Lot himself. Lot and his family were rescued in spite of themselves.

As we have seen on page 12, Lot tried to enjoy the better of two worlds. The Sodomites' sinful lifestyle deeply concerned him and he tried to influence them in the right direction (19:1-9), but he was sinking deeper into this quagmire himself. His tents were no longer standing near Sodom—he was living in Sodom, where he had acquired a high position (19:9).

His two daughters were engaged to men of the city (19:14). To save his guests, Lot was willing to surrender his daughters to the lust of the pressing mob. In spite of the urgent calls of the angels to hurry, Lot still lingered. The angels had to take him by the hand and drag him out. He did not want to flee far—he wanted an easy way out—so he got permission to go to nearby Zoar.

His wife was so attached to their life in Sodom that she disobeyed the command of the angels not to look back to (or long for) the life in Sodom.

When Lot later heard of the complete destruction of the cities, he decided to take the advice of the angels and to move to the mountains. Zoar was just too close to Sodom's ruins. In the isolation of the mountains, the eroded values of Lot and his daughters were further exposed by drunkenness and incest.

The two nations, Moab and Ammon, which descended from them, became idol worshipers, and as such they were thorns in the side of Abraham's descendants for centuries to come. The moral and natural consequences of sin may proceed over many generations if they are not stopped by God's grace. It happened, indeed, in the case of Ruth, a far-off descendant of Lot. King David and Jesus were among her descendants.

Lot and his family portrayed to us the sad picture of lukewarm believers who do not realize the grave danger of their compromises with the world, and who are quite reluctant to change their views and practices. This sad history also proclaims to us the good news of God's grace (Luke 17:28-37).

A prayer: Lord, I want to trust and love You with all my heart.
A thought: How may today's believers be contaminated by the world?

20. A Promise Fulfilled
At the appointed time, Sarah has a son.

<table>
<tr><td>
January 20
~ ~ ~
Genesis 20,
21:1-7
</td></tr>
</table>

There were several low points in Abraham's history, like the Egypt blunder and the Hagar affair. We have also noticed his progress in becoming a blessing to others, as God had promised (12:3). God reaffirmed His covenant with Abraham three times: by a dream, by circumcision, and by divine visitors. Then Abraham stumbled again and lied about his wife. This time it was the Philistine king and his people who suffered under Abraham's sin.

It is something that may happen to every believer, a relapse into an old sin shortly after new peak experiences. It may result from overconfidence and insufficient vigilance against the attacks of the devil. It may also come from an inner conflict that tries to restore the balance between ideals and instincts. In Abraham's case, this episode provided a dark backdrop for the brilliant moment when the promise of a son born from Sarah was fulfilled.

We watched with Abraham how twenty-five years slowly ticked by. The promise of a son was repeated several times, but it had not materialized. When at long last it did happen, this joyful occasion is casually described in only one short sentence. It is as if they found themselves in an emotional vacuum, as we do immediately after an occasion we have looked forward to for a long time. Suddenly it's all over. From God's perspective, the birth of Isaac was something "normal," something they should have expected because God said it would happen. Genesis 21:1 reiterates that twice: *"And the LORD visited Sarah as He had said, and the LORD did for Sarah as He had spoken."*

It happened exactly as God had promised.

After Israel had waited for the coming of the Messiah for ages, His birth also was described in only one sentence (Luke 2:7). It happened as God had promised. When He rose from the dead, the angels were amazed that the women sought the Living with the dead—He had risen as He said He would. And so He will return on the clouds and make everything new, just as He said He would. We can bank on that.

The stability of God's Word is sharply in focus against the blurry background of our instability. For two thousand years after Abraham, God's plan of salvation continued in spite of Israel's many failures. In spite of all the flaws in the genealogies of Jesus (Matthew 1, Luke 3), *"when the fullness of time had come, God sent forth His Son"* (Gal 4:4).

A prayer: Your Word is a lamp to my feet and a light to my path. (Ps. 119:105)
A thought: Is my faith based on God's word of honor?

21. God's Timely Provisions
Apparent disasters become clear victories.

After twenty-five years of highs, lows, and long stretches in between of uneventful nomadic lifestyle, it looked as if the original promise of God to Abraham (12:3) was coming true after all. The patriarch had become a blessing to others on various occasions and the promised son was miraculously born from two elderly

January 21
~ ~ ~
Genesis 21:8-34

people. Then the positive trend was interrupted by an apparently sad chapter in Abraham's history. He had to send Hagar and Ishmael away.

There was a close relationship between father and son, and it had to be a heartbreaking experience for both of them. However, from God's perspective, it was for the long-term good of both Isaac and Ishmael. Hagar got her freedom, Ishmael got his manhood, and God guaranteed their protection. Ishmael was at least sixteen years old at this point. He had to become independent from Abraham's camp.

Years before Hagar and Ishmael thirsted in the wilderness of Beersheba, God had provided for them by letting people dig a well in that region. It might have been the well that had been dug by Abraham's servants. In the next passage (21:22-34) we are told how Abraham resolved a dispute with king Abimelech over the well of Beersheba, "Well of the Oath."

From the human perspective, it looked like a recipe for disaster when Hagar and Ishmael departed with bread and water that could last them only a few days. From God's perspective, their table was set already. At the right moment both mother and child cried out to God for help, and at the right moment the well was pointed out to them. Ishmael did not develop a phobia for the desert, but instead he became a desert survivor and a desert warlord. Gradually God's promises to Ishmael also materialized (Gen. 16:11-12; 17:20; 21:18). However, the competition between Isaac's and Ishmael's descendants continues till today.

Short-term setbacks can rob us of long-term gains if we focus on the problems and not on God. Four centuries after Abraham, his descendants could have entered the Promised Land immediately after the year at Mount Sinai, but because they focused on problems and not on God, they had to roam the desert for forty years. The early church did the opposite when the first persecution started: They fled to God, and He empowered them to accelerate the spreading of the gospel. As believers were scattered, they took the good news with them (Acts 4:18-31, 11:19-21). The disaster became a victory. God is good!

A prayer: Lord, I will focus on You and on Your provisions.
A thought: With God's help I will transform problems into challenges.

22. The Sacrifice
Bring your only son as a burnt offering.

January 22

~ ~ ~

Genesis 22

Abraham's darkest hour became his brightest moment. It leaves us, though, with difficult questions. God detests human sacrifices—why then did He subject Abraham and Isaac to this severe test? As part of God's unfolding revelation, it demonstrated true faith and faithfulness to Israel and to the church. It also symbolized what God and His only Son would do on the same spot on Mount Moriah (2 Chron. 3:1).

God knew what both Abraham and He would do. Why then did He say, *"Now I know that you fear God"*? (verse 12). God was speaking in human terms about Himself. Maybe the deeper meaning was: "Now I know that you know where your faith stands." When God tests us, it is for our edification, not His. God knew how much faith Abraham had for He does not test us above our ability (1 Cor. 10:13), but Abraham had to discover and show the faith God had built up in him over many years (Eph. 2:8, Heb. 11:17).

Why didn't God tell Abraham that it was only a symbolic ritual? Then it wouldn't have been a real test, and they wouldn't have felt the pain. Going through this ritual, believing that it was real, let Abraham show his trusting obedience and let him feel something of what God the Father would feel when He would sacrifice His only Son.

Likewise, Isaac felt something of what Jesus would feel when He gave Himself as a sacrifice for the sins of man. We can only guess what went through the boy when his father bound him, put him on the altar, and laid the knife on his throat. Maybe he pleaded, "Please, Daddy, please! How can you do this to me?" For a moment Abraham hesitated. The angel called, and Isaac was replaced by the ram. A close call.

Two millennia later, God decided to put His Son on the altar. In the garden of Gethsemane, His Son pleaded with Him three times, *"O My Father, if it is possible, let this cup pass from Me."* He was not replaced by a ram because He Himself was the Lamb provided by God as Abraham had prophesied, *"God will provide for Himself the lamb for a burnt offering."*

When He suffered hell in our place, He groaned, *"My God, My God, why have You forsaken Me?"* How could God do this? What motivated Him? Jesus gave the answer to Nicodemus: *"For God so loved the world that He gave His only begotten Son, that whoever believes in Him should not perish but have everlasting life."* It would be the ultimate expression of Yahveh's yearning for reconciliation with man.

A prayer: Father, in response to Your love, I offer You mine.
A thought: Do I give to God the best of myself, my time, and my efforts?

23. The Closure of a Tested Life
and the start of a new generation

Thirty-seven years after Isaac's birth, Sarah died. Abraham's close companion in all his hardships was gone. He wanted to bury her body in a safe place. He negotiated with the local community at Hebron, and, with their support, Abraham became the owner of a piece of land that included the cave of Machpelah. The entrance could be blocked off, and Abraham could have peace of mind that the dead would rest in peace.

> January 23
> ~ ~ ~
> Genesis
> 22:20-25:28

Sarah's death made Abraham aware that his own time was running out and that there was still some unfinished business to attend to. Isaac had to marry a girl from his family in Haran without returning to Haran himself. Like Abraham, Isaac had to stick to the Promised Land through thick and thin, although the land would not become theirs in their lifetime. And so, the detailed story of how Rebekah became Isaac's wife emerged (Gen. 24). God's leading hand in the whole process was recognized by all involved. After mourning his mother three years, Isaac was comforted by Rebekah.

Their young love stirred up amorous feelings in old Abraham too. He took another wife, Keturah, and she bore him six sons. Abraham remained faithful to God's command that Isaac was the heir in whose offspring the promise would be fulfilled, so when Keturah's sons were old enough, Abraham gave gifts to them and sent them to the east.

While Abraham had one son after the other, Isaac and Rebekah were childless. With aching hearts, they watched Abraham and Keturah's playing children. Eventually God heard their prayers, and Rebekah conceived. It felt as if the babies jostled with each other in her womb. She went to God with the problem and He gave her the prophecy that two nations would emerge from the two boys and that the eldest would serve the youngest.

When Esau and Jacob were born, Isaac was sixty-years old and Abraham one hundred and sixty, so Abraham could see his grandchildren grow up for fifteen years (Gen. 25:7). It must have given him the joyful assurance that God was true to His word and that the whole promise would eventually be fulfilled.

When Abraham died with peace of mind, he was buried next to Sarah in the cave of Machpelah by his sons, Isaac and Ishmael. God had subjected Abraham to the tough test of waiting. Though he sometimes stumbled, his faith grew and prevailed. Now the waiting was over, and he went to the God he trusted.

A prayer: Please, God, help me pass the waiting test.
A thought: Do I wait on God, or do I spoil things with rushing?

24. God's Promise Endures
amid the games people play.

January 24
~ ~ ~
Genesis
25:22-28:9

Like history books, the Bible sometimes goes back and forth in time as it tells one story to a certain point and then picks up another one at an earlier stage. Genesis 26 actually took place before the second part of chapter 25. Before the birth of Esau and Jacob, Isaac had experiences similar his father's. He received the same promise from God, he coped with a severe drought, and he was repudiated by a heathen king for telling lies about his wife. If she had children already, it would not have happened.

In spite of his stumbling, God blessed Isaac's efforts regarding livestock, agriculture, and the digging of wells. The Philistines envied his prosperity and played nasty games to drive him away. As a guest in a foreign land, Isaac played a submissive role. However, the saying came true for him as well: *"Blessed are the meek for they shall inherit the earth"* (Matt. 5:5). Isaac honored his father's work by opening the wells his father had dug and restoring their names. We too have to open up old "wells" which the devil has blocked in order to rob them of their beneficial influence.

The birth of Esau and Jacob followed, causing a split in the household. On one side, there was the alliance of Isaac and Esau (bonded by their similar appetites) and on the other side the alliance of Rebekah and Jacob (bonded by the promise that the eldest will serve the youngest).

Although Jacob is seen as a cheat by most preachers, he cheated only once, under the influence of his mother. For the next sixty years, others cheated him, first his uncle Laban and then ten of his sons. Esau should have rejected Jacob's offer regarding birthrights if he really cared about it.

Jacob and his mother tried to secure God's promise by their games, but God would reach His goals with His own timetable, methods, and means.

Due to poor health, Isaac thought his death was imminent. He would still live another fifty years! Isaac and Esau's plan was an attempt to violate the promise God had given to Rebekah. She decided to intervene with her own scheme. Jacob could have refused, but then he might have lost the goodwill of the only one who cared about him so he went along with his mother's game.

He would pay dearly for this sin, but in His grace, God would use it in the unfolding of His plan. Esau played his own games (such as blaming, pleading, threatening, and people-pleasing) in an effort to recapture what he had lost.

A prayer: Lord, I trust You to do Your share and to help me with mine.
A thought: What games have I played to manipulate others?

25. Finding Our Niches
in God's all-inclusive plan

Compared to Abraham and Jacob, little of Isaac's life was recorded. However, as carrier of the promise and its responsibilities, he was honored on the same level as his father and his son. God is often called the "God of Abraham, Isaac, and Jacob." Isaac is taken up in the gallery of believers (Heb. 11). Being ordinary does not disqualify us from fulfilling our purpose in the kingdom of God. The church consists of ordinary people (1 Cor. 1:26).

> January 25
> ~ ~ ~
> Genesis
> 27:41-28:22

When Rebekah heard of Esau's plan for revenge, she urged Jacob to flee to her family and to stay there until Esau's fury had cooled down. She did not want to burden Isaac with Esau's threats, so she used the irritation caused by Esau's Canaanite wives to persuade Isaac to send Jacob to her family so that he could marry within the family clan. Isaac concurred, cautioned Jacob not to marry a Canaanite, blessed him, and sent him to Rebekah's family.

Rebekah's role as the go-getter came to an end when Jacob secretly left one night. She apparently died before he returned twenty years later. When we add up all the years,* Jacob was about seventy-seven years old when he left. The life span of the patriarchs was twice that of ours, so we can accept that at seventy, Jacob had the strength of a thirty-five year old man.

After traveling several days on foot, Jacob was tired and slept in the field with his head on a stone. He had the famous dream of "Jacob's Ladder" that connected earth and heaven. Angels went up and down the ladder, and God was standing on the top. In the dream, God gave the same promise to Jacob that He had given to Abraham and to Isaac.

To meet God face to face like that, with his heart burdened by guilt and worries, made a lasting impression on Jacob. He really needed the reassurance that God would be with him and would bring him back to the Promised Land. However, he did not surrender himself to God yet. He still bargained with God by making conditional promises. But it was a step in the right direction. God got his attention—Jacob would never forget Bethel.

The ladder symbolized the Mediator (1 Tim. 2:5) who God would provide to bridge the gap between holy heaven and sinful earth. This contact is dependant on divine grace and not on human merit—like Jacob, we have none. Do you have a Bethel in your life where you met God? Do you connect with Him daily?

A prayer: Lord, we are under Your care everywhere.
A thought: Do I bargain with God, or do I surrender to Him?
* Gen. 30:25; 31:41; 41:46, 53; 45:6; 47:9.

26. Blessings Amid Hardships
The foundation of a nation is laid.

<table>
<tr><td>
January 26
~ ~ ~
Genesis
29:1 - 31:18
</td></tr>
</table>

Empowered by his Bethel experience, Jacob proceeded to Haran. He met his niece and future bride, Rachel, at a well in the desert. It was love at first sight. He opened up his heart to her, unloaded the burdens of his past, and shared his bottled up feelings.

Her greedy dad, Laban, was glad to see Jacob, and his devious mind began to put some plans together right away. He still remembered all the golden gifts they had received many years ago when his sister, Rebekah, became Isaac's wife. And now, Rebekah's son was standing hat in hand before him. If he played his cards well, he could gain a lot.

Laban noticed the growing affection between Jacob and Rachel. After Jacob had been his guest for a month, Laban threw out the bait and Jacob took it. He had nothing else to give to Laban except himself and his expertise as a herdsman, so Jacob offered to work for Laban for seven years to marry Rachel. Laban was delighted. The riches would stay in the family.

When the great moment eventually arrived, the shrewd Laban cheated Jacob with Leah and thus forced him into another seven-year contract. Whenever Jacob felt resentment about this deceit, his guilty conscience probably reminded him of the day he deceived his father. For the next seven years, there was not much time for regrets as Jacob had twelve children with his two wives and his two concubines.

When Joseph was born, Jacob wanted to pack up and go home. But Laban could not let go of such a loyal employee and fruitful son-in-law. Laban's farming had been flourishing since Jacob had taken control of it, and the twelve grandchildren would make a handy, cheap workforce. So he lured Jacob into another contract by which all the speckled animals would be Jacob's pay. The ritual Jacob performed with the streaked rods (Gen. 30:37-43) has to be read with what God said to him in a dream (Gen. 31:10-13). Jacob was not cheating Laban. God was doing justice to Jacob in spite of Laban's cheating. Whenever Laban saw that the rules favored Jacob, he changed the rules in his own favor, only to find that the outcome was again to Jacob's benefit.

After another six years of utter frustration and testing hardships, Jacob decided enough was enough. While Laban was gone for a few days, Jacob explained his position to his wives, and with their consent, he fled with his entire household and all their possessions.

A prayer: Father, in Your hands I am safe.
A thought: Do I put my trust in God or in myself?

27. Great God, Small People
Conflicting personal and social self-images

When Laban heard of Jacob's desertion, he was furious: "How can he dare to do this to me after all the good I've done to him?!" He organized a posse and set off in pursuit of his renegade son-in-law. Just before Laban caught up with Jacob, God put the brakes on Laban's plans by warning him in a dream not to bribe Jacob with either threats or promises.

January 27
~ ~ ~
Genesis 31

Laban realized he should not try to lure Jacob back into his service, but that did not stop him from reprimanding Jacob for leaving without a proper farewell and for stealing one of his idols. Unaware of Rachel's sin, Jacob challenged Laban to search their tents. A humorous scene evolved. Put off by the true God, Laban fervently searched for his false god. Rachel, who still practiced idolatry secretly, had to protect her god by sitting on him.

After Laban's fruitless search, it was Jacob's turn to rebuke Laban for his false accusations and for all the hardships and cheating Jacob had suffered under him for the past twenty years. This confrontation gave Jacob the opportunity to vent his long suppressed resentments in the face of the culprit.

They reacted to each other's accusations by trying to look good. Laban maintained that all Jacob's possessions were actually gifts from him, Laban, while Jacob pointed out that God gave them to him, Jacob, in spite of all Laban's dishonesty. Both painted themselves as blameless saints while they portrayed each other as despicable cheats. They were small people who, like scared cats, tried to look big.

After they had spoken their minds, hurting each other deeply, they realized that they needed a truce to protect them from each other. They erected a monument and swore not to attack each other. They swore by the God of their fathers because neither of them knew Him personally yet. Twice Jacob referred to God as the "Fear of Isaac." Maybe that was Isaac's view of God after Abraham almost sacrificed him on Moriah. He transplanted that idea in Jacob's mind: God is Someone to be feared.

Both Jacob and Laban needed a real encounter with God, as well as with their true selves and with their fellow human beings. We don't know if Laban got this chance, but for Jacob it was just around the first corner. Yahveh was setting up the scene to reveal Himself more personally to the bearer of the promise. He yearns for that moment in our lives too.

A prayer: God, I need peace with You, with myself, and with others.
A thought: How do I portray God, others, and myself?

28. Jacob Becomes Israel
Victory through surrender

<table>
<tr><td>January 28
~ ~ ~
Genesis 32</td><td>God reassured Jacob of His protection by showing him his guardian angels, but when Jacob heard that Esau was on his way with four hundred men, he started to focus on the danger rather than on God. He was overcome with fear. In his panic he put several self-protecting plans into motion.</td></tr>
</table>

First, he divided his company into two main groups in the hope that if one group was destroyed, the other one might survive. The next day, he prepared five gifts for Esau and sent them ahead to temper his brother's anger. Each gift consisted of different kinds of animals to ensure that at least one group would satisfy Esau's taste. The third day, he divided his family into four groups, each mother with her children, first Bilhah and Zilpah, then Leah and Rachel. By scattering his possessions and his people, it would take Esau longer to destroy all, and there was the hope that Esau's anger would be cooled before he could destroy everybody and everything.

However, all Jacob's shrewd plans did not rid him of his panic, so he begged the God of his father and grandfather for mercy. But he himself had not yet accepted God as his God. He could not enjoy God's gifts any longer without making peace with the Giver.

That night, God came to Jacob in human form and wrestled with him. It was a physical, emotional, and spiritual struggle. God could have knocked him out right away, but He wanted Jacob to surrender voluntarily. Jacob refused. He resisted the pressure all night long. Then God applied the age-old grip: If you don't listen, you will feel the consequences. He dislocated Jacob's hip joint. As soon as his physical strength was broken, his emotional and spiritual resistance were broken too (Ps. 51:19).

He held on to God—not in struggle anymore, but in dependence. He asked God for a blessing, not realizing that he had received it already. After his surrender to God, he would be a different person with a different attitude and a different name. Jacob became Israel, the "Victor of God." Victory through surrender—a proven, paradoxical truth of the Bible (see Acts 9:3-6).

Because of his close encounter with God, Jacob named the place Peniel, "Face of God." When the sun rose that morning, Jacob limped into a new day and into a new future. He would soon learn this truth: When we are weak in ourselves, we are strong in the Lord (2 Cor. 12:10).

A prayer: Lord, I surrender to You so I may be victorious with You.
A thought: Do I rely on my own strength or on God's power?

29. Two Surprised Brothers
They expect the worst; they get the best.

The last time Jacob and Esau had seen each other, Esau had murder in his heart and Jacob fled in fear. After twenty years had elapsed, they prepared themselves to face each other again. Apparently nothing had changed. Esau approached with four hundred well-armed men—obviously not a welcome party—and Jacob reverted to panic plans to soothe his brother's anger.

> January 29
> ~ ~ ~
> Genesis 33

Esau remembered Jacob as a selfish cheat who always wanted the best for himself. In Esau's mind, Jacob was a grabber, not a giver. However, as he approached for his long awaited revenge, he met with one great gift after the other, all from this "selfish" brother, accompanied by kind words and a humble attitude. Then his brother appeared, limping and bowing.

God turned Esau's bitterness into sympathy. By God's grace, Esau realized that all this was not another trick by a deceiver, but genuine goodwill of a changed person. God gave Jacob the grace to ask forgiveness, and He gave Esau the grace to grant it. A surprised Esau embraced an equally surprised Jacob, who had expected a stab, not a kiss. They expected the worst but got the best thanks to God's grace. Yahveh smiled on them.

Then the two reconciled brothers became really generous toward each other. Esau felt awkward accepting all Jacob's gifts while he had nothing with him to reciprocate. He said he had enough of his own. Maybe he did not want to look bad in the presence of all Jacob's riches, or maybe when Jacob had left twenty years ago, Esau had taken all Jacob's flocks for himself and was now rich too. Jacob persuaded him to accept his gifts. Then Esau offered to supply an escort to Jacob to protect him in Canaan, but Jacob cordially declined, using the small children and animals as an excuse. When Esau and his men rode off in a cloud of dust, Jacob probably uttered a sigh of relief and a prayer of thanksgiving.

Now that he got Laban and Esau off his back, he gave himself a break by settling where he was. He built a house for his family and shelters for his livestock at Succoth, not far from Peniel. He might have visited Peniel often to worship at the spot where God turned him into Israel. Eventually, he moved to Shechem, where he bought a piece of land which he later gave to Joseph (Gen. 48:22). When Israel invaded the Promised Land four centuries later, Joseph's bones were buried there (Josh. 24:32). Two millennia after Jacob, Jesus met the Samaritan woman at Jacob's Well on that piece of land (John 4:5).

A prayer: Lord, reconcile people with You and with one another.
A thought: Do I highlight the negative in people I dislike?

30. Sorrow Upon Sorrow
Blessings amid tribulations

January 30

~~~

Genesis 34-35

Jacob had made peace with God, Laban, Esau, the people of Shechem, and himself. He and his family were settling quite nicely into their new circumstances in the Promised Land. Then disaster struck. The one tragedy followed the other until they wondered when the calamities were going to stop.

Dinah, Jacob's only daughter, visited girls in Shechem. A young man also named Shechem, the son of the town's mayor, developed a fatal attraction for Dinah. Instead of following the social customs for marriage, he raped her. Then he fell in love with her and wanted to marry her.

Dinah's brothers were deeply offended, and with revenge in their hearts, they made a deal with Shechem and his father. The men of the town consented to circumcision in view of possible future benefits. When they were in pain the third day, Simeon and Levi lead a gang who massacred all the town's men and looted their possessions, including their women. Jacob, filled with anger, feared possible reprisals from other towns.

God called Jacob to Bethel to renew the covenant He had made with him long ago. Jacob ordered his camp to destroy all idols in their possession. Then they moved to Bethel, where they worshiped God. He appeared to Jacob again at Bethel and gave him His blessing. The misconduct of Shechem and of Jacob's sons did not destroy Jacob's relationship with God.

At Bethel, his mother's much loved nurse, Deborah, died. Her death was deeply mourned. Jacob and his company moved further south. Near Bethlehem, he suffered another severe blow when his beloved Rachel died giving birth to Benjamin. They moved on, and Jacob saw his father again shortly before Isaac's death. While they were still mourning three deaths, Reuben added to Jacob's pain by having sex with Jacob's concubine Bilhah.

Amazingly, in spite of the string of sad experiences, there were still many blessings to count. They got rid of the idols that some people in the camp still had clung to. God reaffirmed His protection and provision for them at Bethel and proved it by giving them safety in a foreign land. They could be comforted at Deborah and Isaac's deaths by looking back on the long and meaningful lives of these two veterans. Rachel died, but her baby gave the aging Jacob much pleasure. The Lord gives and takes; let His name be glorified (Job 1:21). God uses our physical and emotional pain to cultivate our spiritual gain.

A prayer: Thank You, Lord, for blessings amid troubles.
A thought: Do I really notice the silver linings of the dark clouds?

31. Favoritism Breeds Hatred
A dream becomes a nightmare.

Sharing some of our feelings with people we can trust is good for our emotional health. However, making all our feelings, especially our likes and dislikes for people, known to everyone is not wise. Jacob showed his favoritism for Rachel and her children openly and thereby caused much unhappiness and resentment for Leah and her children (Gen. 29 and 30).

January 31

~ ~ ~

Genesis 37

Joseph was very aware of his special position. He snitched on his brothers to make himself look good and his brothers look bad. He irritated them with his fancy clothes and infuriated them with his dreams, which they saw as arrogance. As he could not do hard work while he was wearing that beautiful garment, it would just increase his brothers' resentment. The family became divided, and there was tension in the air. However, God would reach His goals by using the nasty games of small people in His plan.

Joseph visited his brothers in Dothan, far from his father's watchful eyes, and most of them greeted him with murder in their hearts. Reuben saved his life by putting him in a dry well, and then Judah saved his life by suggesting they sell him to passing merchants. Though they were as hard as rock on the outside, they would never forget Joseph's anguished cries as the merchants tied him to a camel and drove off to Egypt with him. Many years later when they were in agony, they confessed, *"We saw the anguish of his soul when he pleaded with us, and we would not hear"* (Gen. 42:21).

Callously, they dipped his garment in blood and suggested to their father that Joseph had been killed by a wild beast. For twenty-three years, they suppressed their guilt and lived with this lie. Eventually, the truth caught up with them with a vengeance. This is how sin works: First they thought it, then they said it, then they did it, and then they suffered the guilt and consequences. It is the best for all involved to stop this chain of events as early as possible.

Three families with major problems started the chosen people: Abraham's, Isaac's, and Jacob's. Each generation seemed to be worse than the previous one, but the Potter did not discard the clay. When one vessel failed, He formed a new one (Jer. 18:1-6). Jacob erred by favoring Joseph. Joseph erred by irritating his brothers. His brothers erred by allowing their resentments to boil over into mean reprisals. And in His grace, God would use their mistakes to shape the future of His chosen people.

A prayer: Father, please reach Your goal with me in spite of my shortcomings.
A thought: Do I treat all people with respect and fairness?

32. Character and Conduct
Do people really change?

February 1
~ ~ ~
Gen. 38, 39

There are passages in the Bible which decent folks tend to avoid and page over. The episode of Judah and Tamar is one of them. How come such a piece of "filth" was taken up in God's Word? Well, the Bible tells us about God's interactions with sinful humanity; therefore, it does not hesitate to expose the sins of man. The purpose is not to let us enjoy the wicked, but to let us see the salvation God prepared for us. There is gospel (good news) on every page of the Bible.

The characters of Judah and Joseph are sharply contrasted in Genesis 38 and 39. By denying her the levirate marriage with his youngest son, Judah violated the rights of his daughter-in-law Tamar. He did not hesitate, either, to make use of prostitution to satisfy his sexual needs. In contrast, Joseph conscientiously looked after his master's business and firmly declined the attentions of his master's sexy wife.

In spite of his prosperity, Judah was drifting away from God, while Joseph was moving closer to God in spite of his slave status. Their different **relationship with God** caused their difference in **character**, which caused their difference in **conduct**. These are the main links in the moral chain.

Genesis 38 also serves as the dark background for Judah's change of heart in Genesis 44. God would use Joseph's interactions with his brothers to bring them to insight, repentance, and forgiveness. The self-centered Judah would become the compassionate mediator who pleaded on behalf of his young brother and his elderly father.

God was changing Joseph, too. His father's favoritism had inflated his ego, but God was stripping him of all haughtiness in Egypt. In spite of his temporary success in the service of Potiphar, he was soon further degraded from slave to prisoner. He learned to trust God in spite of circumstances. His life pointed to Christ, who also would reach glory through humiliation.

Genesis 38 reflects on the genealogy of the Messiah. His lineage would run through Judah and Tamar to David and to Jesus. The gospel is indeed on every page of Scripture. As all people are sinners (Psalm 14), God had to reach His goal of salvation through them and in spite of them. God's mercy endures forever (Psalm 136). Before we page over Genesis 38, we have to answer some searching questions about our own relationship with God and how that affects the development of our own character and conduct.

A prayer: Lord, mold me into a useful tool in Your hand.
A thought: Do I resist or yield to God's pruning?

33. Trust and Work Ethics
Joseph is a successful manager.

When Joseph was plucked from his father's house and thrown into the foreign culture of Egypt and into a foreign role of a slave, he found refuge in the faith of his father. Joseph had been well informed about the promises that God had made to Abraham, Isaac, and Jacob, and about their faith in this one true God. In his crises, Joseph anchored himself firmly to God.

February 2
~ ~ ~
Gen. 39:1-6,
20-24

In his innermost being, Joseph knew that his emotional survival was dependent on his spiritual life. He reaffirmed his choice daily to trust in God and to remain faithful to Him in thoughts, words, and deeds. And God rewarded his faith by blessing him in what he did. These are the ingredients of biblical work ethics that inspire one to much greater heights than any man-made code of conduct.

When Joseph was in Potiphar's service, he did his work well, although he was just an unpaid slave whose only reward was meager food, shelter, and clothing. He believed that God would bring justice to him if he trusted and served God and did his daily work to the satisfaction of his employer.

This recipe worked well for Joseph and for many others through the ages. His excellent work was recognized and rewarded. He was placed in charge of all the other slaves and all the work they had to do. Joseph inspired them to follow his example, and soon the business of Potiphar was flourishing in all departments. Joseph was a blessing to his workplace.

Everybody was delighted except Satan. He decided to throw a spanner in the works and break up this happy, successful organization. God allowed Satan to degrade Joseph even further so that God's salvation for Joseph could shine even brighter against the dark background of Satan's evil.

Joseph was falsely accused of harassing his master's wife and was thrown into prison without a trial. Joseph could have sulked and moaned, "Is this my reward for doing good?" Instead, he just proceeded with his unwavering trust in God and with his admirable service to his fellow human beings who were in the same misery as he was. And again, this recipe worked and pushed Joseph up to the highest position in his lowly circumstances.

Jesus said, *"He who is faithful in what is least is faithful also in much; and he who is unjust in what is least is unjust also in much. And if you have not been faithful in what is another man's, who will give you what is your own?"* (Luke 16:10, 12).

A prayer: Lord, help me to trust in You while I do my best.
A thought: What determines the quality and quantity of my work?

34. Dreams and Reality
God reveals the future to Joseph.

February 3

~ ~ ~

Gen. 40 - 41

While Joseph was managing the prison for the warden, God provided the first step for his liberation. Pharaoh was displeased with his butler and baker and imprisoned them. One night both of them had dreams that intensely puzzled them. Joseph sensed their distress and encouraged them to tell him about it.

When he heard the butler's dream, God revealed the meaning of the dream to Joseph. The three branches of the vine resembled three days. The serving butler pointed to his restoration in Pharaoh's service. The butler smiled and hoped Joseph's words were true. For the baker, the three baskets also resembled three days, but the destruction of the loaves by birds pointed to his demise. The baker grinned and hoped Joseph's words were not true.

Within three days, the prophecies were fulfilled. Joseph hoped for a break, but he had to wait for another two years for God's perfect timing.

Then Pharaoh dreamed about the fat and thin cows, and the fat and thin heads of grain. Although the meaning of the dreams was rather clear, God hid the obvious from Egypt's wise men. Then God refreshed the memory of the butler, and he told Pharaoh about Joseph. In no time, the shabby prisoner was shaved, bathed, and dressed to enter into Pharaoh's presence.

The humor of the situation was that the one on the throne was completely powerless before God, and the prisoner at his feet was empowered by God to save Pharaoh's kingdom from starvation. Likewise, Jesus stood before the rulers of His time. After he had heard the meaning of his dreams, as well as Joseph's advice, Pharaoh appointed Joseph as second in command over Egypt.

God gave Joseph quick insight into the dreams of others, but insight into his own dreams only dawned on him when his brothers came to Egypt to buy grain. When his brothers bowed before him, Joseph suddenly understood the meaning of the bowing sheaves and stars that he dreamt of years before.

While God did sometimes use dreams to convey a message, the Bible surely does not teach that all dreams are messages from God. In Joseph's time, the Bible did not exist yet. As God inspired people to write down His Word, He expected His people to seek His will in Scripture, not in dreams.

If our "dreams" (hopes, expectations, plans) are realistic and if we take realistic steps to make them come true, while trusting in God, then God can use that to develop our potential and make our "dreams" come true.

A prayer: Lord, help me to understand and to fulfill Your dream for me.
A thought: Do I share my "dreams" with God?

35. Facing the Truth
Joseph puts his brothers to the test.

As God had predicted, Egypt enjoyed seven years of plenty, and Joseph stored all extra grain in well-guarded silos. Then the seven years of drought arrived, and Joseph provided for the people from his well-organized system. Surrounding nations also suffered. Soon they heard of Egypt's bounty. Urged by their father, ten sons of Jacob joined other caravans on route to Egypt to buy food for their families.

February 4
~ ~ ~
Gen. 42-43:14

Joseph couldn't believe his eyes when he saw them in the lineup of foreign buyers. He put them to the test to see if they showed any change of heart. He put intense pressure on them by accusing them of spying. They could be executed for that, so they just had to start talking in self-defense.

They soon came up with all the basic facts without giving details about the brother who "is no more." Joseph put them in jail for three days to simmer in their fear and guilt. Their long suppressed guilt ruptured like an abscess. They first recalled the anguished cries of their younger brother when they had sold him into slavery. Joseph realized they had passed the first test, and he went aside and wept—tears over his own hardship, tears over their sin and guilt, tears of gratitude for a possible new beginning.

He sent nine of them back with their money hidden in their sacks of grain while he kept Simeon hostage. When the others arrived home, they were very open with their father, whom they had deceived with lies about Joseph for two decades. Joseph had squeezed out of them all appetite for cover-ups.

Jacob listened and made his conclusions. Joseph and Simeon were already gone, and now they wanted to take Benjamin from him as well. Over his dead body, he decided. Stalemate.

They rationed themselves with the grain to make it last longer. They enjoyed the gift, but they were not yet reconciled with the giver. For a few months, they were silent. They wrestled with their own thoughts, trying to get out of the tight corner. As they began to run low on grain, their tension rose and they started to argue.

They realized they had no choice. For their own sake and for Simeon's sake, they had to go back to Egypt. And they could not dare to go back without Benjamin. Even Jacob had to agree with that at long last. They had to face the man who had the bread of life. Eventually, all will have to face Christ too, the only One with the bread of life (John 6:48-51, Phil. 2:9-11).

A prayer: O God, help me to face the truth—Your truth.
A thought: What important decisions do I put off?

36. Facing the Person
I am Joseph, your brother!

February 5

~ ~ ~

Gen. 43:11 - 45:8

When Jacob told his sons to return the money they found in their sacks and to take a present to the man who was in charge of the grain in Egypt, he was not relapsing into cheating. God renamed him Israel because there was a real change in him. Jacob's gift just displayed goodwill and good manners.

Joseph accepted the gift brought by his brothers and reciprocated by inviting them to dinner. In spite of his brothers' fears and suspicions, they were well treated. They had passed the second test for honesty and integrity. Now they had to face the third test for compassion. All eleven were sent on their way, unaware of the surprises hidden in their sacks. Joseph's police overtook them and accused them of stealing. When the silver cup was found in Benjamin's sack, they were shocked and returned to intercede for him.

Judah spoke for all of them. The same people who had ignored Joseph's anguished cries when they sold him into slavery now pleaded for Benjamin that he would not become a slave. They were not concerned for him only, but especially what Benjamin's arrest would do to their father. Years ago they did not care what effect Joseph's disappearance would have on their father. When Joseph saw that his heartless brothers had become compassionate intercessors, willing to go into captivity themselves to spare their brother and father, he knew that the time had come to reveal himself.

For Joseph, it was a moment of tremendous relief; for his brothers, it was the shock of their lives. The man whose mercy they were pleading for was none other than their brother for whom they had had no mercy years ago!

They expected the worst. Instead, they got the best: wholehearted forgiveness. For Joseph, it was perfectly clear that God had sent him ahead to provide for his entire extended family. As there were still five years of famine ahead of them, Joseph right away made arrangements for his father and brothers to come to Egypt with their families and livestock.

Pharaoh backed him up with the necessary means. Seventy more people would not hurt Egypt, and then Pharaoh could rest assured that he would keep his wise governor to lead the country through those difficult years.

All sinners enjoy God's gifts while they keep the Giver out of their lives. Those who have met Him in Christ realize that He is not to be feared, but trusted and loved as Father, Savior, and Comforter.

A prayer: God, open the eyes of sinners to accept Jesus as their Savior.
A thought: How have I reacted toward the Savior God provided?

37. The End of the Beginning
Conclusion of the patriarchal era

Genesis tells of the first generations of mankind and the first generations of God's chosen people. Pioneers usually struggle to establish themselves in new circumstances. They have to survive and find their way without the help of a map or a manual. Naturally, there are successes and failures.

> February 6
> ~ ~ ~
> Gen. 47:13-
> 50:26

The patriarchs of Israel lived as nomads in a foreign land that belonged to others but was promised to them. Someday in the future, when their offspring would have become a nation, they would conquer the land. God took them to Egypt to multiply fast in a good land. The book about the beginning ends with Jacob's prophecies about the tribes of Israel.

As was the case with Jacob and Esau, the younger Ephraim would be more blessed than the older Manasseh. Although Ephraim later became a strong tribe in Israel, it played no significant role in the unfolding of God's revelation. Jacob's favoritism would not determine history.

Regarding his own sons, Jacob did not have much praise and good news. Maybe he was stern with them because he had suffered unnecessarily for many years by their deception about Joseph. Reuben lost his rights as firstborn because of his relationship with Bilhah, his father's concubine. Simeon and Levi were reprimanded for the Shechem massacre. The main blessing came on Judah, from whom kings and the Messiah would descend.

Joseph received material and spiritual blessings. The other sons received an indication of the circumstances of their descendants. However, fate doesn't have to be final. Four centuries later by a positive decision at Mount Sinai, the tribe of Levi became a spiritual blessing to Israel (Ex. 32:26, Num. 3:6-9). Several centuries later, the tribe of Dan would choose idolatry and lose their inheritance (Judg. 18). Dan is omitted in Revelation 7.

Jacob commanded his sons to bury him in the cave of Machpelah in the Promised Land. So when he died, Joseph had Jacob's body embalmed and, with a great cortege, went to Canaan and fulfilled his father's wish. His brothers feared that Joseph would take revenge on them after their father's death, but he reassured them that he still believed that his coming to Egypt was a godsend.

The curtain is drawn on Genesis with the prospect that the descendants of Israel would leave Egypt as a nation and would take Joseph's remains with them for burial in the Promised Land. God remained in control.

A prayer: Lord, I want to do Your will for my generation.
A thought: How do I see my past, present, and future?

38. Preparation for Liberation
Egypt's benefits turn sour.

February 7

~ ~ ~

Exodus 1 and 2

In Egypt the twelve sons of Jacob became the tribes of Israel. Amid the plenty of Goshen, they thrived and multiplied. Eventually, the Egyptians began to feel threatened by this nation within a nation and decided to curb their prosperity. After a few centuries, all the good Joseph had done for Egypt was forgotten.

The pharaoh issued one decree after the other to bring down the birth-rate of the Hebrews and to mobilize them into a cheap workforce. They became slaves in bitter bondage—part of God's plan to get them out of Egypt and into the Promised Land. Oppression prepared them for liberation.

The killing of male newborns reminds of the Bethlehem massacre (Matt. 2). Both were cruel endeavors of Satan to prevent the coming of the Savior who would crush Satan's kingdom (Gen. 3:15). God intervened and thwarted the evil plans repeatedly. He is the almighty Creator and Sustainer of the universe. He stays in control in spite of Satan's subversive activities.

Israel's oppression was already taking place when Moses was born, but their liberation came when Moses was eighty years old (Ex. 7:7). Why did God allow the suffering of Israel to proceed for so long? God was waiting for them to become willing to let go of the plenty of Egypt, which they enjoyed at an ever-increasing cost to their own well-being. Moses tells us how many times the Israelites yearned back for Egypt when the going got tough in the desert, showing how glued they were to Egypt. Usually it is God who is waiting for us to get to the right point and not the other way around.

While God was waiting for Israel to get ready for the exodus, He was preparing Moses for his task. The liberation of Israel from Egypt started with a baby in a basket, and the deliverance of humanity from sin started with a Baby in a manger. Israel's liberation from slavery became an eternal metaphor of the Christian's salvation from the enslavement to sin.

Until age forty, Moses enjoyed royal privileges in Egypt. He gained intimate knowledge of the monarchy's thinking and doing (Acts 7:20-23). During his next forty years, Moses acquainted himself with the Sinai desert, where he would mold disgruntled slaves into a well-organized nation. God used the knowledge and experience He had given to Moses to fulfill his task in God's kingdom. Likewise, He used Paul's knowledge of the Greek culture and language in the expansion of the early church. God prepares His instruments for their task.

A prayer: Lord, make me willing to be sharpened for the next step.
A thought: Do I drag my feet while I'm praying for a miracle?

39. Moses Meets God
and discovers the purpose of his life.

In God's unfolding revelation, Moses fulfilled a key role. Although other people also made unique contributions, Moses has had more influence on the daily lives of Jews for the past three and a half millennia than any other person of the Old Testament.

February 8

~ ~ ~

Ex. 3:1-6

Moses fulfilled many roles during his lifetime: prince, shepherd, visionary, prophet, miracle worker, liberator, organizer, legislator, mediator, intercessor, writer, friend of God, father of his people, and patient leader—who lost his cool only once and paid dearly for it. His diverse gifts enabled him to fulfill his complicated task.

His life had already taken a few drastic turns: his adoption by Pharaoh's daughter, the killing of an Egyptian, his flight to Midian, becoming Jethro's son-in-law, and adapting to a shepherd's lifestyle in the Sinai desert. However, his burning bush experience at Mount Horeb, where he met God, had the most profound influence on his life and destiny. This occasion also brought a new revelation about God.

To Abraham, Isaac, and Jacob, God revealed Himself as God Almighty (El-Shaddai), but to Moses He also revealed Himself as "I AM" (Ex. 6:3). The name Yahveh, translated as LORD, comes from "I am." This name emphasized God's eternal existence (Heb. 11:6), as well as His unchanging integrity: *"I am what I am."* Although God first revealed this name in Exodus 3:14, Moses used this name in Genesis because he was the author.

The unity between the "Angel of the Lord" (Ex. 3:2) and God Himself (Ex. 3:6) is obvious in this passage, indicating that this "Angel" is God appearing in human form just as He appeared to Abraham. God's true Being cannot be seen by humans (Ex. 33:20, 1 Tim. 6:16). However, on some occasions He did appear in visible, human form (Gen. 18, John 1:18). This was the Second Person of the Trinity, the Son of God, revealing Himself in the Old Testament.

It was not the burning bush that changed Moses, nor is it a sensational experience that will change us. Moses was transformed while he was in contact with God. He was honest with God and shared with Him his unworthiness and even his unwillingness. As he interacted with God, something happened inside of him. He did not know that this was only the beginning of many interactions with God and that these interactions would improve in glory as he proceeded.

Yahveh and Moses demonstrated the yearning between God and man.

A prayer: Lord, I want to communicate with You.
A thought: Is my silent time quality time with God?

40. Revealing Questions and Answers
Learning the truth about self and God

February 9
~~~
Ex. 3:7-22
</div>

Fools rush in where angels fear to tread. Wise leaders don't. Their insight into the difficulties of leadership makes them modest and cautious. Moses, Gideon, Isaiah, Jeremiah, and Peter were unwilling candidates who later became good leaders.

When God told Moses that He had heard the cries of His people in Egypt and was going to liberate them from slavery, Moses must have been overjoyed. But when he heard that he, Moses, was going to be God's instrument to deliver God's people, Moses was overwhelmed. One insurmountable obstacle after the other suddenly rose up in his mind.

His first reaction was, "Who am I?" He wanted to remind God of his disqualifying past and of his insignificant present. His reasoning was something like this: "Don't You remember, God? I'm wanted in Egypt for murder! Going back will be suicide. And regarding the Israelites—they didn't want me as leader. They told the Pharaoh about my crime, and I had to flee. Remember?"

God made this objection null and void by assuring Moses that He, the Almighty God, would be at his side: "Last time you tried to liberate Israel by your methods; this time you will do it My way." God also assured him that He had already dealt with his persecutors—all in Egypt who had wanted him dead were now dead themselves (Ex. 4:19).

His next question was, "God, what is Your name?" Moses knew the problem the Israelites battled with during their stay in Egypt: All the gods of Egypt had names, but their own God was nameless. They knew He was the God of Abraham, Isaac, and Jacob, but that was not a name, only a reference. They would ask, "Who sent you?"

What God had refused to Jacob (Gen. 32:29), He now granted to Moses by revealing His name and being: I am Yahveh (see notes on page iv). God did not give up His descriptive name but repeated several times that He is the God of Abraham, Isaac, and Jacob. His self-revelation to Moses was not detached from His self-revelation to the patriarchs. Israel had to know that the same God who had dealt with their ancestors was dealing with them. They should not think for one moment that there were other gods besides the one true God.

Moses would spell it out to them later: *"Hear, O Israel: the LORD our God, the LORD is one"* (Deut. 6:4). Moses used the name Yahveh (LORD) in Genesis because he wrote Genesis after the burning bush event.

*A prayer: God, help me to know You and myself better.*
*A thought: When God calls me for a task, what are my questions?*

# 41. The Inescapable Task
## He has to fulfill the purpose of his life.

The first problems that Moses had foreseen were removed. He had more certainty about himself and about God. As he tried to imagine the practical situation he would face, he could hear more difficult questions thrown at him by a suspicious slave-nation: "How do we know God has sent you?"

|        |
|--------|
| February 10 |
| ~ ~ ~ |
| Ex. 4:1-17 |

Moses knew words are cheap. When one claims to be someone special, one has to prove that. God gave Moses three signs and made him practice the first two right there. His staff could be changed into a snake and back, and he could contract leprosy in a few seconds and then be healed of it in a few seconds too. The sign of changing water into blood, Moses had to accept in faith. Moses was impressed by these deeds of power, but the talking part bothered him.

"Who will do the talking?" he asked. Moses knew he was not eloquent. He searched for words, sometimes even stuttered, and during all those years of isolation as shepherd in the desert, it only had gotten worse. He was sure this stumbling block was a hundred percent legitimate: "A good leader must be a good speaker too—surely, God, this disability disqualifies me completely!"

For God, that was not a problem at all. He created man's intricate systems for vision, hearing, and speaking, and He can make any one of these functional or dysfunctional. He can give vision to the blind, hearing to the deaf, and speech to the mute. Centuries later, this would be wonderfully done by God's Son when He would become a human being (Matt. 11:4-5). However, Moses did not have the New Testament. He had to trust God on this matter of speech. After him, many poor speakers who trusted God were equipped by God to bring His Word powerfully and effectively.

Having been put in checkmate, Moses disclosed the real reason for his reluctance: "Why don't You send someone else?" He did not want this job. God was honoring him by offering him a wonderful ministry, and he declined the offer. He returned the gift to the Giver.

God became angry with Moses, talked tough to him, and refused his resignation. There was no backing off from this assignment. God had been forming Moses from his mother's womb for this work. If he would not do it, he would miss the whole purpose of his life.

Jesus would find Himself in the same situation shortly before His crucifixion. He had to complete the task He had come for (John 12:27).

*A prayer: Lord, I will do what you want me to do.*
*A thought: Do I try to talk myself out of my God-given duties?*

# 42. Back to Egypt
### Pretty words, bad results

February 11
~~~
Ex. 4:18-6:30

After his encounter with God, Moses got Jethro's permission to visit his people in Egypt. When Moses set off with his wife and kids for Egypt, who would have believed that God would use this single man to deliver an oppressed nation? Many years later when Joseph took his wife and Baby to Egypt, who would have believed that this Baby would become the Savior of the world?

At a caravan stop along the way, Moses got acutely ill. Zipporah suspected that God threatened her husband's life because one of their sons had not been circumcised. When she obeyed God's command, Moses was healed. God shapes His workers. At this point, Moses apparently sent his wife and children back to Jethro (Ex. 18:1-4). God's announcement that the Pharaoh's firstborn would die might have convinced Moses to keep his family out of harm's way.

The traditional locality of Mount Horeb or Sinai (Ex. 3:1, 4:27) is in the south of the Sinai Peninsula. However, it looks like a long detour from Midian to Egypt. Jethro's camp was east of Horeb. After Moses had briefed Jethro about his mission, he had to pass Horeb again on his westward journey to Egypt. That is where he met his brother Aaron. Moses briefed him about their assignment as they proceeded on their way to Egypt.

Arriving in Egypt, they put the facts, including the signs of snake and leprosy, before Israel's tribal leaders, who were overjoyed that at long last God had heard their cries and would liberate them from their bitter bondage. So far so good—now what would Pharaoh think of their bright ideas?

As could be expected, Pharaoh was not impressed at all. To him, it was clear that the whole plan was concocted to provide a holiday for lazy workers, so he increased their work by withholding straw from them while expecting them to deliver the same amount of bricks. To stress his point, he had the Hebrew foremen flogged. Seeing the immediate results of Moses' intervention, Israel blamed him for their worsening circumstances and distanced themselves from him. Once again, Moses was the rejected leader.

Moses had to be deeply disappointed. God's beautiful promises at Mount Horeb had not materialized. Instead of liberating Israel, he aggravated their plight. Moses did not hide his feelings. As he communicated his frustration to God, God assured him that Pharaoh's resistance would become part of the plan. God would use it to show His power to Egypt.

A prayer: God, empower my faith when I get the wind in the face.
A thought: How do I react when plans go wrong?

43. The Contest Starts
God versus gods

Pharaoh said he did not know Yahveh; therefore, he would not listen to Him (Ex. 5:2). "Well, your majesty, then it's time you get to know Him," Moses thought. He and Aaron returned to the palace. Their expectations were more realistic now, having been forewarned by God about the monarch's hardened heart.

February 12
~ ~ ~
Ex. 7 - 8

Each of God's signs was aimed at Egypt's belief in false gods (Ex. 12:12). Yahveh would prove that He was in control of river, land, animals, humans, insects, plants, and weather and that the idols were lifeless products of man's sinful imagination. The battle was between reality and fiction.

The sign of the stick that changed into a snake did not impress Pharaoh because his magicians could do the same "trick." God showed that His snake was not produced by a trick. His snake swallowed the other snakes and was then turned back into a staff. Knowing how easily the magicians could cheat with the leprosy sign, Moses skipped that one and proceeded with the changing of water into blood. Because all water in Egypt was affected, this sign became the first plague. For seven days the people were without drinking water.

As Pharaoh did not change his attitude, the first Nile plague was followed by the second one: Myriads of frogs emerged from the river, spreading all over the land, even intruding into their food and beds. What a slimy mess! Not even the king could take it, and he pleaded for mercy. When the plague was over, they had to cope with the millions of stinking dead frogs. The magicians could also produce bloody water and slimy frogs—there were enough of both around to borrow from! However, they could not stop the plagues. Only Yahveh could do that. The gods of the Nile had been proven to be nothing but lifeless idols. Egypt's source of life, the Nile, became a source of death.

Pharaoh had heard the command of God several times: "Let my people go!" He had seen the consequences of his wrong choices. And yet, he stubbornly refused to comply. This time two plagues from the land would bug him to the point of despair: gnats (mosquitoes/lice) and flies (stinging flies). Whatever the right translation might be, the irritation of these plagues must have been horrific. The magicians themselves were so exasperated that they gave up the contest and recognized the plagues as signs by "the finger of God." Now there was a distinction between Goshen and the rest of Egypt. Only Yahveh could make a plague so geographically selective.

A prayer: Lord, You are in control of the good and the bad times.
A thought: If not convinced by God's grace, I might be by His judgment.

44. Mercy Amid Judgment
Calls to repentance

February 13

~ ~ ~

Ex. 9:1 - 10:20

The next four plagues were aimed at the pride of Egypt—their livestock and harvests. The idols, including the bull, which were supposed to protect these investments, would suffer a severe blow due to Pharaoh's resistance against the true God.

Before the animals would suffer for the sins of their masters, God gave Pharaoh ample time to reconsider. Moses went personally to him and spelled it out to him. God postponed His judgment to give them time for repentance. Unfortunately, they did not grab the opportunity. The next day the bull of Egypt and all the livestock it represented bit the dust. Once again, Goshen was protected from this pestilence.

Jesus said to Nicodemus that God wants all people to be saved; therefore, He gave His only Son to make salvation possible for them (John 3:16-18). The apostle Peter stressed the same point when he wrote that God does not want people to be lost, but He postpones judgment day to give people the opportunity to repent (2 Pet. 3:9).

Because the Pharaoh and his people did not have compassion on their livestock but stubbornly gave them up to the pestilence, they now would feel the wrath of God in their own flesh. Sores and boils appeared on their skin. The livestock they had acquired from Goshen and other sources also suffered from this skin disease. The magicians were so sick that they could not stand with Pharaoh to face Moses and his God. Moses informed them that God did not kill them for then there would be nobody to observe His mighty deeds (Ex. 9:15-16). God remained merciful even in His judgments.

Five times Pharaoh hardened his own heart by choice. Now God hardened his heart. Centuries later, Isaiah and Jesus reiterated that when people refuse repeatedly to listen to God, eventually they cannot hear Him (Matt. 13:14-15).

In spite of that, God did not stop speaking to the Egyptians through His mighty works. The irritation of their skin did not convince them, but maybe the irritation of hunger in their stomachs would. First, their plants were destroyed by hail and what was left was devoured by locusts some weeks later. Although it is not always mentioned, the region of Goshen where Israel lived was apparently exempt from all the plagues except for the first three. Jesus prayed (John 17:15) that God's children would not be taken out of the world but be protected in the world, as were Daniel and his friends.

A prayer: Lord, I want to thrive in Your will.
A thought: Do I see God's mercy in my tribulations?

45. Tragedy and Triumph
The high cost of freedom

The battle against the gods of Egypt was heading toward a climactic finale. Yahveh had proven Himself to be in full control of all aspects of life: water, land, humans, animals, insects, diseases, plants, and weather. The false gods of these domains were defeated (Ex. 12:12). Next in line were the sun god and the Pharaoh.

> February 14
> ~~~
> Ex. 10:21-11:10
> 12:29-30

However, in spite of the overwhelming evidence, Pharaoh and his people refused to obey Yahveh's command to let His people go. Slavery has been one of the most persistent social evils through all centuries. Today this injustice to fellow human beings is still being committed, like in the sex and drug trades. The Exodus was God's statement about all slavery.

Pharaoh tried to compromise several times. First, he said the Hebrews could go but not far away. Then he gave permission to the men only. His next move was to hold back their livestock. Pharaoh tried to lure Moses into second best options. On God's command, Moses could not give an inch. For salvation from sin, halfway measures don't work either. Christ had to pay the price.

God's final word to Egypt was preceded by three days of darkness. This gave them enough time to think. The darkness also symbolized the spiritual darkness in which they lived. The children of God have been called out of this darkness to God's wonderful light (1 Pet. 2:9).

Then came the knockout blow—Egypt's firstborn died so that Israel could be freed. It was a terrible night. By this time, Israel knew that what God had predicted had happened. So when He said that all firstborn would die that night except those covered by the blood of the lamb, they knew it would come true. They must have prepared for the Passover meal with mingled feelings of fear and joy. Many firstborns might have wondered if the blood on the doorposts would really protect them. However, God's protection was not linked to their subjective feelings but to the objective reality of the blood on the doorposts. The blood protected those who trusted God as well as those who had doubts and fears. The latter could have had peace of mind too if they had accepted God's word of honor.

As the anguished cries and heartbreaking lamenting spread from one Egyptian house to the next, Israel realized that their freedom was costly. However, before each plague the Egyptians had the choice to obey God and reap the benefits or to disobey God and suffer the consequences.

A prayer: Jesus, You are the Lamb who died so that we may live.
A thought: Why shall I live in uncertainty while I can be sure?

46. The Passover
Saved by the blood of the lamb

February 15
~ ~ ~
Ex. 12:1-28
12:43-13:16

The Bible focuses on the triumph of God and His people, not on the tragedy Pharaoh brought on his country. The spotlight was on the firstborn saved by the blood of the lamb and on the Passover feast, which was instituted to remind Israel once a year about their deliverance.

The Passover contains meaningful symbolism for both Jews and Christians. The name itself has reminded Israel of the occasion when the grace of God made the angel of death "pass over" them so they could pass over from death to life, from slavery to freedom. For Christians, this event points to Christ, who paid our sin debt so that the wrath of God could pass over us and we could pass over from eternal death to eternal life, from sin slavery to spiritual freedom.

The main elements of the Passover feast were bitter herbs, a lamb, and unleavened bread (Ex. 12:8). The bitter herbs signified the bitter bondage they were saved from, the lamb symbolized the means they were saved by, and the unleavened bread pointed to the new life they were saved to.

The lamb had to be a year old male without blemish, which meant a perfect, young full-grown sheep or goat. One or more families shared. The entire lamb had to be spit-roasted over fire (not cut up or cooked in water) and all leftovers burnt to ashes. The blood of the lamb saved their firstborn from certain death during Egypt's tenth plague. The painting of the blood on the doorposts would not later be repeated with the yearly Passover Feast.

For Christians, the Passover lamb points to Christ. He died so we can live. He gave Himself as our substitute when He was a young adult without blemish. He suffered the fire of God's wrath in our place. Not one of His bones was broken (John 19:31-37, Ps. 34:20). The good news that God passes over our sins for Christ's sake has to be shared in and between families. His blood is applied only once for our salvation (Heb. 9:12).

As leaven permeates bread, sin permeates the lives of sinners. Unleavened bread symbolizes a new life in which sin is forgiven and conquered. The week of unleavened bread starts with the Passover. It means: When we have been saved by the Lamb of God, we live a new life out of gratitude by the power of His Spirit. Immediately after He had observed the Passover, Jesus instituted the Lord's Supper. He was the unique Passover Lamb. Because the old symbols were fulfilled in Him, He replaced them with new ones.

A prayer: Jesus, I accept You as my Passover Lamb.
A thought: Do I commemorate this salvation by partaking of the Lord's Supper?

47. Consecrating the Firstborn
They belong to the Lord.

The death of Egypt's firstborn was a serious matter to God. He delayed it as long as possible. He gave the Pharaoh and his people nine other wake-up calls before He broke their resistance with this terrible catastrophe. God wanted Israel to remember the fallen firstborn of Egypt so they could praise God for their own spared firstborn. For this, He instituted special rituals.

> February 16
> ~ ~ ~
> Ex. 13:1, 11-16
> Num. 3:11-13,
> 3:45-48,
> 8:16-18

The one true God is the source of life. When He created life on earth, He gave living organisms the ability to reproduce. The firstborn "opened the womb" and showed the life-producing ability of the parents; therefore, the firstborn were special to God.

After God had taken the lives of all firstborn in Egypt, the firstborn of Israel, who were saved by God's grace, were even more special to Him. They should have died too. He bought them free by the blood of the lambs. They belonged to Him twice: as being the first from the womb and as being bought free by the blood of the lambs.

God, therefore, commanded that all firstborn from humans and livestock had to be consecrated to Him. The firstborn of "clean" animals had to be sacrificed, and the firstborn of "unclean" animals had to be replaced by a lamb. The firstborn of humans had to be redeemed by paying five shekels to the priests. Later, on God's command, the males of the Levi tribe stood in for all the firstborn of Israel to perform duties in the Tabernacle (Num. 3:45-48).

As Jesus was a firstborn, his parents brought Him to the temple for His consecration to God (Luke 2:22-23). It was on that occasion that Simeon and Anna prophesied about Him. He was the Firstborn who would not be redeemed by lambs or shekels. He would go into the Most Holy in heaven with His own blood to redeem all who believed in Him (Heb. 9:12). He even redeemed the lambs. Shortly after His death, animal sacrifices stopped when the temple was destroyed in A.D. 70.

The memory of the Egyptian firstborn who died and of the Israeli firstborn who were saved was kept alive by the Passover, by the consecration of the firstborn of man and beast, and by the services of the Levi tribe. The Passover was fulfilled in the Son of God and all who believe in Him become firstborn saved by the blood of the Lamb. Those who do not believe in Him find themselves in the same danger as the firstborn of Egypt.

A prayer: Praise God! I'm redeemed by the blood of the Lamb.
A thought: What can I do for those who are not yet saved by His blood?

48. Limited Freedom
A free but fearful nation

February 17
~ ~ ~
Ex. 12:31-42
13:17-14:14

When two to three million slaves suddenly packed up and left in the middle of the night, it could have caused a chaotic situation. Strangely enough, they marched off in orderly ranks after they had first "robbed" their masters by asking farewell gifts.

They knew they were going to Canaan, but the specific route to their destination was uncertain. To spare their families unnecessary dangers of combat, they avoided Philistia in the southwestern corner of the Promised Land. Had that road been available to them, they could have reached their goal within a few weeks. Now they had to take a more southern course through the Sinai Desert. For the immediate future, they had exchanged slavery in the lush of Egypt for freedom in a scorching desert. Some questioned the wisdom of the move.

To make the doubtful deal many times worse, Pharaoh and his people had second thoughts about setting the slaves free. Their generosity while grieving gradually turned into selfish anger. They decided to rectify their mistake before the slaves got too far away and swiftly called the Egyptian army into action. As the Israelites camped on the Red Sea shore, the roar of approaching horse hoofs and chariot wheels became louder and louder until it filled them with choking panic. What they feared was not going back into slavery, but being wiped out in a bloody massacre. Their joy about liberation was replaced by fear for death. They blamed Moses for their plight.

Christians find themselves in the same predicament many a time. After they have been liberated from sin slavery, the going may get rough, and they may be overwhelmed by fears and doubts. They may even question God's faithfulness and the wisdom of their conversion. God's encouragement for us is the same as for Israel: *"Stand still, and see the salvation of the Lord!"*

While we run around in panic, our fears become worse; when we surrender to God, we get peace of mind. Often we try to create salvation for ourselves instead of embracing the salvation God has prepared for us.

The Angel of the Lord appeared as a cloud by day and as a pillar of fire by night. He moved in between Israel and the enemy. For Israel, He gave light in darkness, and for the enemy, He made the night even darker. Before God provided a solution, He protected them in the waiting period. When Yahveh stands between Satan and us, the evil one cannot touch us.

A prayer: Father, when I look back I thank You for Your fantastic provisions.
A thought: Does my trust in God calm down my panic for problems?

49. Salvation Demonstrated
The choice between life and death

God concluded His mighty signs in Egypt with one that was extremely awful to the Egyptians and at the same time extremely awesome to Israel. To show that He was working through Moses, God commanded him to lift his staff over the sea. God divided the water and created a path

| February 18 |
| ~ ~ ~ |
| Ex. 14:15-31 |

for His people where nobody thought a path could be made, for He is Yahveh, the Almighty. He controls the laws of nature. The path of life for His people was also a deathtrap for their enemies.

Israel probably crossed the sea on dry ground with mixed feelings. On the one hand they would have been overwhelmed by awe for God's power and by gratefulness for His mercy. On the other hand they might have feared the wall of water on either side of them, not knowing when natural forces would kick in again and make the water return to its place. They also did not know yet if the Egyptians would be allowed to use the same path to pursue them. At first the Egyptians were so bold in their anger that they thoughtlessly followed the Israelites onto the road through the sea. When they were about halfway, the wheels of their chariots started to fall out (or to sink in), the way got blocked and they could not make progress anymore. Their bold anger gave way to bewildering panic. Too late they realized they were caught in a trap. As they started to flee back on foot the Lord commanded Moses to lift his staff over the sea once more. The walls of water collapsed and roaring waves rushed in to fill the cavity. When supernatural law was lifted, natural law resumed.

The path that brought life to some brought death to others. The same is true of the gospel. To some it is the aroma of life unto life and to other it is the aroma of death unto death (2 Cor. 2:16). To those who accept the Son of God as their personal Savior the gospel has indeed brought the good news of eternal life. For those who ignore or reject God's gift of love, His only Son, the gospel brings the bad news of eternal suffering. If Christ does not bear your sins you will have to bear them yourself.

This most spectacular rescue of all ages deeply impressed the Israelites. They praised God for their deliverance, and they accepted Moses as His servant. Unfortunately, their adoration and gratitude would not last long. Only a few days later, when God tested their faith with thirst, they forgot about God's care of the past and started to complain about the problems of the present.

A prayer: Father, thank You for the wonderful salvation You provided.
A thought: I will remember God's past provisions when I face current problems.

50. Desert Pains and Joys
Problems and provisions on the way

<table>
<tr><td>
February 19
~~~
Ex. 15 - 16
</td></tr>
</table>

To sustain a few million people moving on foot through the Sinai Desert required miracles. They could not take much food and water with them and the places where they could get these were far apart. Soon they ran out of both.

After three days, they came to Mara, a small oasis. With a shock, these thirsty, exhausted people discovered that the water was too bitter to drink. They complained to Moses, who passed it on to God. God used the situation as an object lesson. He showed Moses how to cure the water with wood. Then He urged them to trust Him every step of the way. As He healed the water so He wanted to heal them in body, soul, and spirit. Some of today's resources like sport, entertainment, media, and the Internet also need to be cured and filtered to make them usable to Christians.

Israel proceeded on their journey, and after another few days they reached Elim, an oasis with twelve springs and seventy palm trees. What a relief to have enough water in a dusty desert! God provides Elims along our journey through life too—places of rest and refreshment like Bible study, prayer, church, family, friends, scenery, fun, and recreation. Do we notice, use, and appreciate these, or do we hurry along, too busy to make a stop and enjoy the good of life?

They probably stretched their food supplies with grains and dried fruits, but eventually they ran out of everything. Again they confronted Moses with the problem and flavored it with their usual blaming. Again Moses took it to God. He took God on His word that He would provide, although he did not have the faintest idea how God would do that.

Millions of migrating birds from Europe and Asia use the route via Sinai to Africa and back, usually avoiding the sea in case they become exhausted. Ages before the Exodus, God had already put this system in place to provide for His people. Now He showered them with exhausted birds from the sky.

He also provided for them supernaturally lest anyone explain away His miracles with natural phenomena. They needed four to six million liters of manna per day! It could not have come from trees in the region because there just were not enough of those trees to feed a few million people every day during all seasons for forty years. They knew they could not live from bread alone, but only by the Word of the Lord (Deut. 8:3). The manna became an eternal metaphor of our spiritual daily bread (John 6:35, Matt. 6:11).

A prayer: Our Father, give us today our daily bread.
A thought: Israel had to do their part to enjoy God's provisions.

51. Rock of Ages
cleft for me

Yahveh had been providing water, meat, and bread. What would they do the next time they thirsted? Instead of pleading with God, they quarreled with Moses again and threatened to stone him. He took his problems to God as before, and God did not disappoint him. God wants us to do what Moses did.

February 20

~~~

Ex. 17:1-7

</div>

The trekking nation was spread out over many square miles; therefore, Moses took some eyewitnesses with him so they could tell the people how a fountain was opened to them in the desert. As God had told him, when Moses struck the rock with his staff, the rock cracked in two and a stream of fresh, clear, cool water burst from it. The people and their livestock could quench their thirst. Soon every person saw the water flowing from the rock and heard the story behind it. A similar event is described in Numbers 20. God could have provided water to them by means of rain, and maybe sometimes He did, but then they could ascribe the relief to natural causes. They had to learn to trust God for all their needs, knowing that He alone could sustain a nation for so long in hopeless desert conditions.

If the water from the rock were just a trickle, it would not be enough for the whole nation and their animals. It had to be a substantial stream. When the psalmists reflected on God's provisions for Israel in history they sang about the stream from the rock (Ps. 105:41, 114:8). Paul showed the meaning of the rock: *"That rock was Christ"* (1 Cor. 10:4). On the cross, He was struck and cleft so that a stream of living water could flow to the entire world. At the Feast of Tabernacles, where the Jews commemorated the journey of their ancestors in the wilderness, Jesus presented Himself as the rock from which spiritual blessings flowed: *"If a man is thirsty, let him come to Me and drink. Whoever believes in Me, as the Scripture has said, streams of living water will flow from within him"* (John 7:37-38, NIV).

This episode became an ageless lesson for believers of all times. Like Israel in the desert, the situation of sinners is also hopeless. They thirst for God's blessings but cannot provide for themselves. When sinners turn to God in complete dependence, He provides for their spiritual needs with real answers, not with the false answers of the world.

We should drink from this stream daily ourselves and then share the living water with others too. We have to channel the water from the Rock to others who are dying of spiritual thirst.

A prayer: Lord, I drink this water myself and share it with others too.
A thought: Do I recognize God's provisions in my life?

52. Persevering Intercessors
They support Moses' arms.

When God had satisfied the physical needs of His people, Satan changed course and took aim at their emotional and social needs. He tried to instigate fear with an attack by the Amalekites. On many occasions, Satan tried to wipe out the people of God so that the promise of the Seed who would crush his head could not be fulfilled. Now he sent the Amalekites against them.

Nobody likes to be rejected or attacked. Knowing this, Satan likes to use this onslaught against Christians. The social problem (rejection) creates an emotional problem (fear). People try to get out of this situation in various ways. Some try to negotiate a truce with compromises. Some try to buy friendship by people pleasing. Some try to avoid confrontation by isolation. Others try to ignore the problem and wish it would go away by itself. The best policy is always to face the problem with realistic solutions.

Israel had to stand up for themselves. There was not even time to blame Moses. They took up the weapon and defended themselves under Joshua's command. While the army was fighting, Moses prayed for them as he watched from a hill. He was practicing spiritual warfare while Joshua and his men engaged in physical warfare.

Soon it was clear that Israel was winning as long as Moses lifted his hands up to God in prayer. However, as his arms tired and he lowered his hands, the enemy got the upper hand. Aaron and Hur, who were with him, made a quick practical plan. They let Moses sit on a stone, and they stood on either side of him and supported his arms. They kept up the intercession until that evening to ensure a complete victory for Israel.

This episode became an object lesson for intercessors. While some do the fighting and the work, others have to persevere in prayer. Paul urged us to "pray continually"—to engage in continuous, trusting dependence on the Lord while we are busy with our daily work (1 Thess. 5:17). All who work for God need this prayer attitude to empower them.

Moses was a type of the coming Christ: Many of his actions pointed to Christ. Jesus assured Peter before he denied Him that He would keep praying for him (Luke 22:32). Later that same night, He made His intercessory prayer for His disciples (John 17). Since His ascension, He has been interceding for us at the throne of grace (Rom. 8:34). He wants us to follow His example and to pray for others (James 5:16). His indwelling Spirit inspires us to do that (Rom. 8:26-27).

A prayer: Lord, please make me a faithful intercessor.
A thought: How do I handle rejection and attacks?

53. Easing the Burden
by sharing feelings and delegating tasks

When Israel was approaching Mount Horeb, Moses'
father-in-law, Jethro, visited them. He brought Moses' wife
and their two sons along. Moses and Jethro treated each other
with courtesy. Jethro told Moses that he was coming, and
Moses went out to meet him, bowed before him, and escorted

February 22
~ ~ ~
Exodus 18

him into the camp. They talked at length about each other's well-being before
they got to business. The Bedouin still honor this custom.

Moses told him about all the great signs God had done in Egypt, how
God had persuaded Pharaoh to set the slaves free, and how He had provided
for them in the desert. Overjoyed, Jethro savored every bit of detail and
eventually broke out in praises to Yahveh, whom he recognized as above all
other gods. He realized that the plagues were aimed at the gods of Egypt,
which were completely powerless to protect against the one true God.

After Moses and Jethro had exchanged their stories and feelings, Aaron
and the elders of Israel got their chance to feast with Jethro. Undoubtedly, all
the stories would have been retold and enjoyed from different angles and
perspectives. Here was an opportunity for the leaders to look back, relive,
evaluate, share, and rejoice. It was and still is an important way to work
through good and bad experiences and to come out on top of it all.

When Moses resumed his work as judge for Israel, Jethro realized that
Moses would wear himself and the nation down. The process was too slow and
too heavy for one person. Jethro advised Moses to select wise men from the
nation and appoint them as judges over groups consisting of a thousand,
hundred, fifty and ten people. If they could not solve the problem, then Moses
could take it to the Lord. In practice, this system consisted of lower and higher
courts. Moses was relieved of a heavy burden by making community leaders co-
responsible for law and order and for solving social disputes.

This common sense administrative method is practiced today on all levels
of church, business, and government, yet some leaders still hesitate to delegate
responsibilities in the belief that only they can do the job properly. Often they
are brought back to reality with a shock. They harm their health, or they are
criticized for falling behind, or they are seen as being autocratic. And when
they eventually agree to share responsibilities, they are usually pleasantly
surprised by the efficient way others can do the job too.

A prayer: Lord, I want to share my feelings with You and with fellow believers.
A thought: Do I sometimes try to pull the wagon all by myself?

54. Preparing for Worship
God invites, sanctifies, and meets them.

February 23
~ ~ ~
Exodus 19

Three months after they had left Egypt, Israel arrived at Mount Horeb (Sinai). God's promise to Moses was fulfilled—the liberated nation would worship Him at the same place where God had appeared to Moses in the burning bush (Ex. 3:12). The people had to be properly prepared for worship.

This meeting was God's plan. In His love, He wanted to come close to them, but not too close lest His holiness devour them in their sinfulness. A respectful distance had to be maintained. Moses mediated between God and people, as Jesus does for us today (Rom. 8:34, 1 Tim. 2:5, 1 John 2:1).

God first sent a message of love to His people. He reminded them of what He had done to the Egyptians and how He had cared for them during the plagues and during their journey to Mount Sinai: *"I bore you on eagles' wings and brought you to Myself."* God was glad to have them there. All nations belong to God, but Israel would be His special instrument to bless the nations (Gen. 12:3) if they would be faithful to Him. Moses brought this message of Yahveh's yearning to the people, and he took their positive response back to God.

Sanctifying the nation was the second stage of preparation. During the next two days, they had to be cleansed physically and spiritually. God had provided the water. To observe a respectful distance, the mountain was fenced off. They had to kill any trespassing person or animal from a distance.

On the third day God descended on the mountain in a cloud of smoke accompanied by lightning, thunder, and trumpet sounds. While the mountain quaked and the people trembled, Moses led them to the foot of the mountain. Moses spoke to God, and God answered him in a loud voice that could be heard clearly by the massive crowd. Once again, the people were warned not to set foot on the mountain. Only Moses and Aaron were allowed to ascend.

Then a whole nation heard the most impressive sermon ever delivered to mankind. Jesus delivered the Sermon on the Mount as the Son of God in His humility. At Mount Sinai, God delivered the Ten Commandments in glory. The rumbling mountain was His pulpit and Israel was His congregation. His voice was so awe-inspiring that the people pleaded with Moses to bring God's Word to them for they could not bear to listen to God Himself (Ex. 20:19). They were so overwhelmed by God's holiness that they did not notice His outreaching love.

A prayer: Lord, You've carried me too on eagles' wings.
A thought: Do I prepare seriously for worship?

55. Undivided Loyalty
The first commandment

Although we will never fathom the full depth of God's Word, including the Ten Commandments, we should always try to improve our understanding of revelations from God's mind and heart. Remember, *"God spoke all these words"* to His people. He reached out to them and identified Himself as "I AM."

> February 24
> ~ ~ ~
> Ex. 20:1-3
> Deut. 5:4-7

Before asking anything of them, He first reminded them of what He had already done for them: "I am Yahveh, your God. I brought you out of Egypt, out of the place of slavery." God's law was not a way to earn salvation but a way to thank God for salvation already received as a gift. Likewise, He frees sinners from sin, their "place of slavery" (John 8:34), by the atoning death of His Son. Yahveh yearns for the salvation of sinners and for their response of thanksgiving, doing His will because they trust and love Him (John 14:15).

God expects saved sinners to obey His commandments on ground of what He DID, creating and saving them, and on ground of who He IS—Yahveh, the eternal "I am" (Ex. 3:14). The first commandment demands undivided loyalty to Him: *"You shall have no other gods before Me."* No other gods in His presence (and He is omni-present). Out of love and respect for Him—no other gods.

Although nine of the commandments are given in negative form, "you shall not," each implies things we should **avoid** and things we should **do**.

The first commandment demands that we avoid all idolatry, magic, occult, superstition, and worshiping of creatures, including living or deceased people. An idol (false god) may be more than a statuette; it can be anything or anybody we trust in place of, or alongside of, the one true God.

The positive side of the first commandment urges us to acknowledge, trust, love, respect, serve, and praise the one true God in accordance with His Word. In humility and patience, we should look to Him alone to provide all our needs. We should worship Him as caring Father, saving Son, and comforting Spirit. Although we will never fully understand His Being and His Persons, we should accept Him as He revealed Himself in Scripture.

Yahveh's first commandment demands that we accept Him for who He is and shape our lives accordingly. The commandment is loaded with grace and love, but also with awesome holiness and authority. God is not asking us; He's telling us. He put our awful sin debt on His Son. Therefore, He demands wholehearted dedication by grateful citizens of His kingdom.

A prayer: Father, Savior, Comforter, You deserve my full dedication.
A thought: Who or what have been my idols?

56. Word and Image
The second commandment

February 25
~ ~ ~
Ex. 20:4-6
Deut. 5:8-10

God's voice made the earth quake and the people tremble. To the first commandment (no other gods) He added the second: no images of God and no images of anything else used as an object of worship or as a channel of worship. God knew humanity's ability to rationalize, giving itself excuses to bend the rules. If God had stopped at "no other gods," people would still make images and convince themselves that they worshiped the one true God through those images. God blocked that avenue immediately.

We should not exonerate ourselves too easily regarding this command. Although we may not make physical images of God, we do make images of God in our imagination. A false belief system about God may be such an image. People who think of God as only a God of wrath are guilty of making a false image of God. Likewise, those who think of God as a God of love only who will never condemn sinners to hell are also guilty of making a false image of God. All theories about God and Christ (God incarnate) that are not in line with Scripture violate the second commandment.

God backed up this command with a self-revelation, with a threat, and with a promise. He revealed Himself as a jealous God—He yearns for our undivided love and is not willing to share our devotion with anybody or anything else. He is also patient and merciful, waiting for several generations before He executes justice, giving ample time for repentance. And on those who do serve Him wholeheartedly, He pours out His blessings for many generations. Children learn by example. Just as bad examples can jump over from one generation to the next, so good examples can be handed down from generation to generation.

What is the positive side that we should do? We should worship God in the way He prescribed in His Word. To do that, we have to study His Word and so acquaint ourselves with His will. He wants the gospel to spread by the preaching of His WORD (Rom. 10:14-17). Jesus was the true image of God (John 14:9, Col. 1:15), but it pleased God to leave us only word pictures of Him.

We may use visual means to explain God's Word. Jesus used object lessons like seed and leaven in His parables. People may not worship images on a screen, but permanent statues or paintings in church may eventually serve that purpose. The first commandment says: Worship God, not gods. The second says: Worship God according to His Word, not through images.

A prayer: Lord, keep my ideas about You in line with Your Word.
A thought: Do I try to bend this rule with a yes-but game?

57. God's Name
The third commandment

After God had spelled out to His people **who** they must worship and **how**, He shifted the focus to His NAME and to His DAY. God wants His name to be honored and respected, not disgraced and degraded. Jesus put God's name first in His model prayer: *"Our Father who is in heaven, hallowed be Your name."*

February 26
~~~
Ex. 20:7
Deut. 5:11

The Bible uses various names for God like Yahveh (LORD), Adonai (Lord), Elohim (God), and Abba (Father). Each one of His names describes an aspect of His character. To abuse any one of His names slanders His character.

The phrase "You shall not misuse the name of Yahveh" convinced post-exile Jews not to say this name ever. When they came to this name in Scripture, they said "Adonai" instead. The medieval Masoretes added the vowels of Adonai to Yahveh, and so Yahveh came to be pronounced as Jehovah. However, the prophets did not hesitate to declare, "Thus says Yahveh." God only forbids the misuse of His name. God wants His people to remember Him by the name Yahveh from one generation to the next (Ex. 3:15).

To honor God's name, we have to avoid any negative remarks about God, as well as using any of His names for cursing, perjury, and even unnecessary oaths. Oaths should be used sparingly and seriously. When authorities demand it from citizens or when it is needed to confirm truth and trustworthiness, it has to be used in a way that will honor God and serve others. By an oath, I am calling upon God to witness to my truthfulness and to punish me if I swear falsely. Therefore, such an oath has to be taken in the name of the one true God, for no creature is worthy of such honor.

A short but fierce threat is added to this commandment: God will not leave anyone unpunished who misuses or dishonors His name. Immediately we are all guilty, for all of us have sinned and sin dishonors God's name.

However, by accepting God's Son as our Savior and allowing God's Spirit to change our hearts and lives, we start to glorify God's name. There is nothing more glorifying to the name of God on earth than the salvation of sinners. Therefore, God went to great lengths to open the way of salvation to them. He urges saved sinners by the Great Commission to carry the gospel to the ends of the earth so that other sinners can be saved too.

God is merciful in His divine discipline—His condemning Law drives us to His saving Son (Gal. 3:24).

*A prayer: Father, I want to honor Your name by what I think, say, and do.*
*A thought: Do I insult the Father by rebelliousness?*

# 58. God's Day
## The fourth commandment

<table>
<tr><td>

February 27

~~~

Ex. 20:8-11

Deut. 5:12-15

</td><td>

Israel had to serve God daily, but they had to use every seventh day to make loving contact with God and with other believers. Yahveh yearns for inter-action with His children. On that day, they and their children, servants, strangers, and animals had to stop ordinary work. After creation, God had rested on the seventh day and blessed and sanctified it.

</td></tr>
</table>

God tells His people to work for six days and fulfill all their duties so that they can give their undivided attention to God and to His kingdom on the seventh day. It brings them in touch with God, others, self, and creation.

The day of rest is not meant for laziness. We have to stop our work in order to attend to our Father and His interests. We have to assemble to worship Him together. That includes expressing praises and thanksgiving, listening to His Word, partaking of the sacraments, and bringing prayers and offerings for the expansion of His kingdom and for helping the poor. The Sabbath pointed to the eternal Sabbath after death when believers will forever cease sinning and will glorify God forever for the salvation He provided in His Son (Heb. 4:9-11).

When God's Son walked on earth as a human being, He clashed with the religious leaders repeatedly regarding the Sabbath. The leaders were fixated on what they should NOT do on the Sabbath to maintain purity. Jesus focused on what they should DO to show love for God and for others. Therefore, healing on the Sabbath was completely wrong for the leaders, while it was completely correct for Jesus. He pointed out to them that they looked after their animals on the Sabbath. The rules for needs, emergencies, charities, and worship override the rules of the Sabbath. Jesus concluded: *"The Sabbath was made for man, and not man for the Sabbath."* (Mark. 2:27). God knows man's needs and provided for them.

On the one hand, we must guard against disrespect for the day of rest ordered by God. On the other hand, we must guard against legalism about it, thereby obeying the letter of the law but forgetting the spirit of it.

Jesus summarized the first four commandments by saying, *"You shall love the LORD your God with all your heart, with all your soul, and with all your mind, and with all your strength"* (Mark 12:30). That is the true spirit of the fourth commandment, as well. God wants quality time with His children, who should have the same yearning toward their heavenly Father.

A prayer: Father, show me how to use my day of rest.
A thought: Do I ignore the God-given rhythm for mankind?

59. Respecting Authority
The fifth commandment

This commandment forms a bridge between the first and the second table of the Law. God appointed authorities to look after our relationships with God and with fellow human beings (Rom. 13:1-7).

February 28

~~~

Ex. 20:12

Deut. 5:16

Parents are the first authority children know. However, long before discipline starts, children enjoy the **loving care** of their parents (or parent-figures). This care should remain the main role of parents during their children's development, the umbrella under which their authority receives its rightful place. God's discipline is wrapped in love. Other authorities, from local to international, should follow this example and exercise their discipline under the umbrella of care.

Children honor their parents when they express love, trust, and respect for them. They can do this by spending quality time with them, affirming their feelings with words, deeds, attitudes, gifts, caring, and sharing. They honor their parents by maintaining lifestyles that do not shame them and by helping them when needed. Show love to God in the same way.

The fifth commandment also addresses a negative attitude that started with Adam and Eve and that is experienced by all human beings. It is the propensity to rebel against authority and to "throw off the chains" (Ps. 2:1-3). People rebel in many ways, but when driven to extremes, rebellion usually leads to dreadful injury to people and to unnecessary damage to property.

God is certainly not against our right to express our complaints, but He warns us to be cautious lest we hurt others and ourselves by undermining community authorities. *"Honor your father and mother"* is a figure of speech that includes all legitimate authorities in spite of their imperfection. No parent or other authority is perfect, but we have to honor them.

God used the "stick and carrot" approach. He issued the death penalty for those who curse their parents (Ex. 21:17), but He added a promise of a long life to those who honor their parents. It also applies to our relationship with the heavenly Father. Those who reject His salvation will suffer hell; those who accept His salvation will enjoy eternal life.

Although not stated explicitly here, it is implied and emphasized in other parts of Scripture that parents/authorities should act in a way that will make it possible for their children/citizens to honor them (Eph. 6:1-9). Authority figures who abuse those in their care forfeit their privilege to be honored.

A prayer: Lord, help parents and authorities to be honorable.
A thought: How do I behave toward my parents and my authorities?

60. Respect for Life
The sixth commandment

February 29

~ ~ ~

Ex. 20:13
Deut. 5:17

This commandment opens up many questions. For some, it is okay to kill humans in war and for certain crimes, to kill animals for food, or to combat pests that threaten our livelihood. For others, all life is sacred and should be protected, even when huge damage is done by rodents and insects. Some are pro-life in certain areas and pro-death in other areas.

Does the sixth commandment prohibit all killing or just some killing? Does it prohibit destructive attitudes as well? It demands life and death decisions from us on abortion, euthanasia, stem-cell research, justice, war, attitudes, and eating habits. The commandment itself does not provide all the answers. We have to look at the rest of Scripture for direction.

God allowed man to eat certain animals (Gen. 9:3, Lev. 11). He ordered that certain animals be sacrificed to signify forgiveness of sin. He abhorred murder and human sacrifices so much that He prescribed the death penalty for such crimes. He wiped out several communities because of their sins. God is the source of life—He gives life to all and He takes it back from all.

Jesus gave new meaning to the sixth commandment when He warned against angry heart attitudes (Matt. 5:21-26). Anger in the heart may first spill over as abusive verbal or non-verbal messages before it is expressed in aggressive deeds. These may become fatal if allowed to escalate.

"Wars" between groups and individuals are fed by hatred and fueled by revenge upon revenge. Eventually, it is impossible to determine who is most guilty and who should make the first move to end the cycle of violence. In spite of international conventions on war, the ethics of war is subjectively interpreted by every warring group. And what is okay for strong countries is not always okay for weak countries, like having nuclear weapons.

"*You shall not kill*" commands us to avoid any thought, word, or deed that can harm others or ourselves and to activate those thoughts, words, and deeds that will protect others and ourselves and promote the safety and well-being of all. Blessed are the peacemakers—they will inherit the earth.

The golden rule, "*Do to others what you would have them do to you*" (Matt. 7:12 NIV), and the Great Commandment, "*Love your neighbor as yourself*," are included in the sixth commandment. It covers body, soul, and spirit of self and others—even those that we do not like (Luke 10:25-37, Matt. 5:44-45).

A prayer: Lord, help me obey this command in letter and in spirit.
A thought: Are my pro-life and pro-death viewpoints in line with Scripture?

61. Sexual Morality
The seventh commandment

After the need for air, water, and food, sex probably has the strongest influence on human behavior. Although it is not a physical necessity, its link with social and emotional needs makes it quite difficult to ignore. The Creator built it into our systems. He made Adam and Eve in such a way that they needed closeness with each other. Yahveh also yearns for the exchange of love with His people.

March 1
~ ~ ~
Ex. 20:14
Deut. 5:18

This mutual fulfillment is not achieved all at once, and it does not stay that way by itself, either—as many honeymoon couples have discovered with a shock. The relationship can only become and remain fulfilling with continuous fine-tuning of the give-and-take process through many subtle verbal and non-verbal interactions. Because of this sensitive process, you can't have a fulfilling relationship with everyone. You have to search for a mate who is willing to persevere with you on a long-term journey.

Because God made us this way, He knows what is good for us and what will destroy us. He commanded that we neither harm the relationships of others nor harm ourselves with wrong relationships. We must avoid adultery and immorality and strive for good marriages. Whether married or single, we must maintain our bodies as temples of God (1 Cor. 6:18-20).

God did not give His Law to spoil our fun, but to secure our joy. He knew that the pleasure of immorality would destroy the joy of a good relationship with Him and with a spouse, and maybe even the joy of a healthy body. By putting up a fence, He protects us against falling into an immoral abyss.

Jesus told us to eradicate the sinful inclination at its roots: the sinful desire in the heart. Those who lust after a person (regardless of that person's sex or age) have already started with immorality (Matt. 5:27-32). When Jesus advised that we should pluck out the evil eye and chop off the sinful hand, He did not mean amputation—that would harm the temple of God. He showed us that what is brought in by the senses (eye) is processed in the heart (by mind, feelings, and will) and is then put into action (hand). We have to focus our senses on the right things, purify our thinking-feeling-willing processes, and steer our actions in the right direction.

Jesus knew how our physiology and psychology influence spirituality. He did not separate these three aspects of our being as we often do.

A prayer: Lord, purify my senses, heart, and actions.
A thought: Do I like to play near the edge of the abyss?

62. Honesty and Kindness
The eighth commandment

March 2

~ ~ ~

Ex. 20:15
Deut. 5:19

The spirit of each commandment represents much more than the letter of the Law. *Father and mother* stands for all legitimate authority, *kill* symbolizes all animosity, and *adultery* typifies all sexual immorality. In the same vein, *steal* epitomizes all material harm done to others by deed or neglect.

As we study the laws God gave to His people through Moses, we will find that the Ten Commandments were explained later in more detail. We can only read into each commandment what Scripture allows us to read into it. *"You shall not steal"* includes taking from others in a dishonest way (such as stealing, overcharging, fraud, or illegally withholding just goods, wages, debts, rent, taxes, or offerings). We violate this command when we allow others to suffer loss by not looking out for their interest (for instance, when I see someone in need or being robbed or attacked and do nothing about it).

Through the prophet Malachi (3:8-10), God said we can rob Him by withholding our tithes and offerings. We may also overstep this commandment when we harm our families by overspending or being stingy.

The positive side of the eighth commandment calls on us to do all we can to protect the property of others and ourselves by courteously cooperating, being kindly alert, supporting law and order to keep our roads and neighborhoods safe, and supplying the needs of the less fortunate.

Jesus issued stern warnings to those who hold back on charity when they see someone in need, and He promised great rewards to those who open up their hearts to the needy. *"Come, you blessed of My Father, inherit the kingdom ... for I was hungry and you gave Me food ..."* (Matt. 25). His parable of the Good Samaritan is a timeless example of what we should do or avoid regarding human need and suffering. The priest and Levite in this parable refused to help, while the Samaritan offered himself, his time, and his means (Luke 10).

Sometimes we try to maintain an artificial border between Sunday and the rest of the week, between the spiritual and the material. The eighth commandment tells us clearly that God is King over everything and everybody and that He lays down the rules for money and possessions, too. What others and we have was granted to us by the Owner of the universe, and as stewards and custodians, we have to use it to His glory and for the common good.

A prayer: Lord, I want to serve You and others with what I am and have.
A thought: Where do I "steal" from the Lord or from others?

63. Truth and Love
The ninth commandment

All people love and hate truth. They love to hear the truth about others—especially the juicy stuff—and many love to pass it on, too. However, they hate nasty truth about themselves, especially when it is dispersed by gossip. In order to promote their own positions, people from all walks of life are inclined to highlight their own merits and the faults of their competitors, while they minimize their own faults and the merits of their competitors.

<table><tr><td>March 3
~ ~ ~
Ex. 20:16
Deut. 5:20</td></tr></table>

The finger pointing that started in Paradise (Gen. 3:12-13) flourished with many other defense mechanisms as man waded deeper into the marsh of sin. The ninth commandment is an antidote for all the deception that blinds man to the truth about self, others, God, and creation. The Trinity is strongly associated with truth (John 14:6, 17; 17:17) and Jesus identified Satan as *"the father of lies"* (John 8:44).

Prohibiting false witness or testimony against one's neighbor reaches much farther than the court of law. It includes any dispersing of information and the daily interactions with fellow human beings. There, too, we must stand for truth and against deceit in all its subtle forms like gossip, framing, twisting someone's words, withholding or over-emphasizing information to create false perceptions or suspicions, phrasing statements to create vague innuendos without clear charges, condemning anyone without a fair hearing based on reliable information, and harming someone's reputation with lies or with twisted information. Jesus said our *yes* must be *yes*, and our *no, no.*

Speaking the truth in all circumstances can also hurt other people, and then one has disobeyed the essence of the second table of the Law, namely to love one's neighbor. For example: When one gives correct information to the enemy in time of war, resulting in the killing of one's own people, then one has overstepped the law of love. When Samson told the truth to the enemy about his strength, he lost his eyes and later his life (Judg. 16).

Truth without love can be very cruel. If telling nasty truth about others does not serve justice, but only hurts those who made mistakes, then I may serve the Great Commandment of love better by shutting up. The apostle Paul warns Christians against the cycle of vindictiveness (Gal. 5:14-15), and he urges them to speak the truth in love (Eph. 4:15). Our debates about doctrine must never become loveless battles. The law of truth must stay part of the law of love, which characterizes the second table of the Ten Commandments.

A prayer: Lord, help me to stay truthful and loving.
A thought: How do I reconcile truth and love?

64. Contentment
The tenth commandment

<table>
<tr><td>

March 4

~ ~ ~

Ex. 20:17
Deut. 5:21

</td><td>

The first nine commandments implied that sin starts in the heart; therefore, the tenth is not a summary of the first nine. It is a separate commandment in its own right. It points to a state of mind that is discontented with what one has, an attitude that wants what others have.

</td></tr>
</table>

This attitude may spawn actions of greed that rob others of what is dear to them. The ninth commandment seems to be an extension of the eighth, which also deals with property. But covetousness is not focused on property only. It goes beyond house, wife, servants, and animals and includes envy regarding position, honor, talents, achievements, and relationships. It is not just a desire to have a wife similar to my neighbor's, but to acquire my neighbor's wife so that he will not have her anymore.

If coveting is to be avoided, then we should go for the opposite: an attitude of contentment that is grateful for what we are and have and an attitude of generosity that grants to others what they are and have. Then we can be proud about our successes and enjoy the talents and achievements of others without pushing them out of their privileges. This attitude will bring new dimensions into competition between persons, companies, and countries. They will seek ways to promote their own interests without walking over others.

In His Word, God shows us the evil of covetousness and its dreadful consequences. King David's adultery with Bathsheba robbed Uriah of his wife and his life, and it brought misery to David's family (2 Sam. 11-13). King Ahab's coveting of his neighbor's vineyard robbed Naboth of his vineyard and his life, and the king lost his throne and his life (1 Kings 21-22). Achan's love for gold and silver brought defeat to Israel and death to him and to his family (Josh. 7). God warned Israel many times by the prophets not to be enticed by the immoral sexual desires associated with idolatry. However, they would not listen, and eventually He sent them into exile.

Jesus warned that adultery starts with lusting after someone (Matt. 5:28) and that the worshiping of mammon (money) starts with worry about material things (Matt. 6:24-34). He showed us the futility of winning the whole world but losing one's soul (Mark 8:36). He underlined this truth with the parables of the "Rich Fool" (Luke 12), the "Prodigal Son" (Luke 15), and the "Rich Man and Lazarus" (Luke 16). God wants us to be grateful, not greedy.

A prayer: Father, fill me with gratitude for Your many gifts.
A thought: Do I enjoy what I have, or do I fret over what I don't have?

65. Footnotes to the Law
Applying the Law to everyday life

A book can be written on each of the Ten Commandments without exhausting the wealth of truth stored up in
them. All the other laws God gave to Moses can be seen as
detailed interpretations and applications of the Ten. God
immediately followed the basic Ten up with some footnotes
to show the people how the Law had to be practically applied
in their lives.

> March 5
> ~ ~ ~
> Ex. 21-23

The people were in shock when they heard God's Law spelled out in God's
own voice. God knew that in this awe they would try to worship Him;
therefore, He gave them the basic rules for worship, reiterating the first table of
the Law. Again, He strictly forbade worship through images. God is not
impressed by human luxuries; thus, their altars had to be very plain. No
precious metals or works of art could be used—just common soil or stones from
God's earth, indicating that the whole earth belongs to Him.

The seventy laws that followed were comments on the second table of the
Law. They showed in detail how respect for authority, life, marriage, property,
truth, and persons should be applied in real-life situations. The Book of the
Covenant referred to in Exodus 24:7 consisted of the Ten Commandments plus
these seventy footnotes.

Although circumstances differ from century to century and from culture
to culture, the issues addressed in the Book of the Covenant are still current. It
addressed the fair treatment of workers; the curbing and handling of violence;
taking responsibility for the behavior of one's animals; the handling of theft
and damage to property; rules for borrowing and for care-taking; sexual abuse
and perversions; idolatry and sorcery; caring for widows, orphans, and the poor;
blasphemy and slander; tithes and offerings; truth and justice; and strangers
and enemies. The Book of the Covenant concluded with directions about the
Sabbath year and three annual feasts.

God promised to lead them by His Angel to survive the desert and to
conquer the Promised Land. He would send fear and hornets before them to
scare and confuse their enemies. However, the conquering of the land would be
a gradual process so that wild beasts could be kept in check. God warned them
strongly against mixing with the nations of Canaan lest those nations lured
them into those sins for which God was judging those nations. God offered
them His love and protection on condition that they stayed true to Him.

A prayer: Father, Your rules are for our own protection.
A thought: Do I resist or embrace God's will as revealed in His Word?

66. The Sinai Covenant
They see the glory of God.

March 6
~ ~ ~
Exodus 24

The covenant had been made in spoken form. Moses knew, though, how easily people forget; therefore, he wrote down in the Book of the Covenant what God had said and what Israel had answered. Next, He prepared a ceremony for the covenant between God and His people to be visually ratified.

As God had not yet appointed the Levites to serve as priests, Moses chose young men, presumably one from each tribe, to build a plain altar of stones and erect around it twelve rocks that represented the twelve tribes. He then had them bring oxen as burnt and peace offerings on the altar.

Moses acted as mediator between God and Israel. He sprinkled half of the blood on the altar and read to them the Book of the Covenant. That was God's part of the covenant. Then the people had to do their part by accepting again the Ten Commandments with the seventy footnotes. Moses sprinkled the other half of the blood on the people (or maybe on the twelve rocks around the altar that represented the people). He said, *"This is the blood of the covenant which the Lord has made with you according to all these words."* When Jesus instituted Holy Communion He said, *"This is My blood of the new covenant"* (Mark 14:24).

After the covenant had been ratified by this ceremony, God called Moses, Aaron and his two sons, and seventy elders higher up on the slopes of the mountain. God revealed some of His glory to them. Most probably, they were so awestricken that they fell flat on the ground and hid their faces. All they could see from that position was the platform beneath God's feet, and even that was so glorious that they could not describe it in words. God had mercy on them, for instead of dying, they feasted in God's presence.

God then sent them back to the people, except for Moses and Joshua, whom He called higher up on the mountain. God wanted to give Moses the stone tablets on which God Himself had written the Ten Commandments. Moses had to prepare himself for six days before God called him into the fiery cloud on the mountaintop. The awe-inspiring way in which God gave the Ten Commandments, first in His own thundering voice and then written in stone, emphasized their importance from God's perspective. Therefore, He expected parents to teach them daily to their children (Deut. 6:4-9). But in our time, in countries where the Bible is still the holy book for the majority, the Ten Commandments of God have been banned from schools!

A prayer: Lord, I accept Your moral law and Your merciful covenant.
A thought: Do I take my covenant with God seriously enough?

67. Mosaic Law and the Church
The old and the new covenants

Let's take a short detour for the sake of better perspective. God made several covenants with man, although He knew that sinful man would break each one sooner or later. That's how much He wanted to have a close relationship with mankind. Major covenants so far were those with Adam, Noah, Abraham, and with Israel at Sinai. The essence of these covenants was the same: trust, love, and obey God in order to enjoy His blessings.

March 7
~ ~ ~
Rom. 3:20-28
Gal. 2-3

The Bible shows how God progressively revealed His will to man. He did not give man all information all at once. In the time of the prophet Jeremiah, when first Israel and then Judah went into exile because of their sins, it was abundantly clear that man was not capable of doing God's will completely. Then God announced the coming new covenant (Jer. 31:31-34) through which He would change man's heart in order to change his deeds. The night before His crucifixion, Jesus announced at the Last Supper that this new covenant was becoming a reality at that moment (Mark 14:24). His death would pay our sin debt, and His resurrection, ascension, and the outpouring of the Holy Spirit would make triumph over sin possible.

In Paul's letters, especially in Romans and Galatians, he explained that the old covenants of works-in-human-power had been replaced by the new covenant of grace-in-Christ (Gal. 4:21-31). The old ceremonial laws (like sacrifices, feasts, and circumcision) were fulfilled in Christ and had come to an end. The moral law remained in power, not for justification, but for sanctification. We cannot save ourselves by fulfilling the law, but after we have been saved by grace in Christ alone, then we begin to live in line with the moral law out of gratitude for free salvation. The moral law consists of the two tables of the Ten Commandments, namely love for God and for other human beings. Jesus said that not one iota of this law would be abolished (Matt. 5:17-19).

The expression "You are not under the law but under grace" (Rom. 6:14) has to be understood in this context. It refers to our salvation. As to our sanctification (the new life after we have been saved), the moral law stays in effect. Only the ceremonial laws have been fulfilled and abandoned. The Ten Commandments that were given at Sinai are still applicable to us today, and they should not be pushed aside, as was the case in recent years in most Western countries. God's moral law has not changed.

A prayer: Lord, give me insight into the old and the new covenants.
A thought: Have I underestimated the importance of the Old Testament?

68. The Golden Calf
Israel relapses into idolatry.

March 8
~ ~ ~
Ex. 32:1-16

While Moses was forty days on Mount Sinai in God's presence receiving specifications for the sanctuary and the priests, the nation tired of waiting. Their impatience got out of hand and pushed them back into the idolatry of Egypt (Josh. 24:14) with tragic consequences.

Before people sin, they usually give themselves, as Adam and Eve did, good reasons for their action. Israel blamed their decision to make an idol on the long absence of Moses. They demanded that Aaron make something visible onto which their faltering faith could cling. Aaron sympathized with their cause for he too was probably tired of standing in for Moses. He rationalized that he would help the people to worship God with the help of an object lesson. *"Tomorrow is a feast to the LORD,"* he said.

When Moses later repudiated him, Aaron called his brother *"my lord"* (to soft-soap him) and reminded him that *"the people are set on evil"*—they could have killed him! He tried to make his part in sculpturing the golden calf look innocent, *"I cast it into the fire, and this calf came out."* He mentioned nothing of the painstaking work of making a clay model, then a clay mold, and eventually melting the gold and casting the idol.

Defenses cannot cover sin. God saw through all the excuses. God was disgusted that they tried to do the very thing that He explicitly had forbidden, that is, to worship Him by means of graven images.

God shared His feelings with Moses and said that He was ready to destroy Israel right there and to start all over with Moses. Moses pleaded for his people in the same way Christ is pleading for us. Moses knew his offspring would not be better than the descendants of Abraham. They would also land in the same predicament, and the idea of a nation dedicated to God would be delayed for centuries.

God knew what Israel had done, what He would do, and what Moses would do, but He wanted Moses to portray the interceding Messiah. God would grant forgiveness, but first the culprits had to suffer the consequences of their actions.

God sent Moses down from the glorious mountaintop to the disgusting orgy in the valley. When Moses saw with his own eyes what was going on, the compassionate intercessor became a furious authority. In his anger, He smashed the tablets to pieces because Israel had broken the Law that was written on them. Then he set the process of discipline into motion.

A prayer: Father, help me not to fool myself about the wages of sin (Rom. 6:23).
A thought: What excuses have I used to bend the rules?

69. Choices Have Consequences
Reward and punishment in God's discipline

How does one destroy idolatry and the behaviors spurned by it? Moses had to get rid of the golden calf in such a way that nobody would use the gold again. The defiled gold was not good for anything. He probably melted the idol into smaller pieces and then set people at work to grind the

<table>
<tr><td>March 9</td></tr>
<tr><td>~ ~ ~</td></tr>
<tr><td>Ex. 32:17-29</td></tr>
</table>

pieces to powder. He scattered the gold powder over the stream flowing from the rock. The gold would be dispersed by the stream into the sand.

It is not easy to calm down mass hysteria. The orgy did not suddenly stop when Moses appeared on the scene. Once the indulgence into immorality got going, the golden calf was not the center of focus anymore. The calf was just the catalyst that brought the repressed drives to the surface and set them into motion. The restless, lustful, drunken movement in the camps continued despite Moses' strong objections and repudiations.

He circulated a message that those who were on the LORD's side had to distance themselves from the rest and stand with Moses. The tribe of Levi, to which Moses belonged, came forward and stood with their leader. Moses commanded them to draw their swords and kill those who continued with their immorality, even if they were brothers, companions, or neighbors.

Centuries before, Levi helped massacre the people of Shechem for defiling his sister Dinah. He was strongly reprimanded by his father, Jacob. Now Levi's descendants drew their swords again, not in ego-driven revenge, but to execute God's judgment on those who insulted God to His face. The tribe's faithfulness to God was richly rewarded. God appointed them to serve in the temple and teach the nation the Word of God. The tithes that people had to give to God, He gave to the Levites (Num. 18:21-24).

Many people believe today that children should only be taught by positive conditioning (rewards for desired behavior) and not by negative conditioning (punishment for undesired behavior). They argue that rewards build good self-esteem while punishment breaks down self-esteem. God's Word and real life do not agree with them. While continuous negative feedback will surely harm anybody's self-esteem, the absence of consequences for negative behavior will surely also harm a person's development. It is a life lesson we all have to learn as early as possible in life: If we do what is good (trusting and loving God), we will be rewarded; if we do what is wrong, we will face unpleasant consequences.

A prayer: Father, I stick to Your rules, rewards, and discipline.
A thought: Do I fearlessly stand with God, even when I land in a minority?

70. Contact With God
Increasing and decreasing closeness

March 10

~ ~ ~

Ex. 32:30-35
Ex. 33-34

By faith and obedience, Moses got increasingly nearer to God, while Israel in their unbelief and disobedience drifted farther and farther away.

After Moses had personally seen and dealt with Israel's sin, he returned to the mountain to plead for God's forgiveness. If God could not forgive, then He should blot out Moses' name from the book of life.

God heard his prayer, replying that Israel would be punished but not destroyed. Moses had to lead them to the Promised Land. God's Angel would protect and guide them, but God Himself would not go with them lest He consume them for their sins.

Israel was immensely saddened by this news. They showed remorse by removing all decorations from their bodies. To symbolize the gap between them and their God, Moses put up a tent outside the camp where God met with him. This tent served as a temporary sanctuary where the pillar of cloud and fire rested. God's love now reached His people through Moses. God spoke "face to face" with Moses. From the next passage, it is clear that Moses did not see God's face. Maybe God appeared to him in human form as He had appeared to Abraham (Gen. 18, Num. 12:8). "Face to face" may also mean "up close," hearing God's voice only (Num. 7:89).

Moses pleaded that God would give them a sign of His presence. If not, they could not dare to proceed with their journey. Once again, God granted his request. His successful intercessions encouraged Moses to ask for more. He expressed his deepest desire, *"Please, show me Your glory."* God answered that He would show him His goodness. God's holiness would kill Moses; God's mercy would bless him. God prepared Moses for the greatest moment of his life by telling him in advance how it would happen. God told him to get two tablets of stone ready and to ascend the mountain again.

God put Moses in a cleft of a rock and covered him with his hand, while God passed and proclaimed His name and His character of love and holiness. Then He allowed Moses to see His back. That sight was so glorious that Moses' face radiated some of that glory when he returned to the people. Yahveh's interaction with man peaked in this encounter. Since the burning bush, God had showed more and more of His glory to Moses until Moses' face shined with God's glory. When we experience God's presence, we too will shine with the fruit of the Spirit: love, joy, peace ... (Gal. 5:22).

A prayer: Lord, show me Your goodness so that my face will shine.
A thought: Am I moving nearer to or farther from God?

71. Joyful Volunteers
Giving and working for God's kingdom

Moses stayed with God on the mountain twice for forty days, before and after the golden calf episode. The first time Israel got tired of waiting and fell into sin; the second time they kept in line, knowing the terrible price of disobedience.

March 11

~ ~ ~

Ex. 35-36

When Moses returned after the second period of forty days, he directed the nation to start building the sanctuary, which would be called the Tabernacle or tent. First, there was an ingathering of material. When God prescribed to Moses the kinds of material needed to make the tent and its contents, He knew that those materials were scattered in thousands of households throughout the camps of Israel. Now God worked in the hearts of those owners to bring the materials to the crafts people who would mold it into the right form. Some brought wool and skins, some brought linen and wood, others brought precious metals and stones. Soon there was more than enough of everything, and Moses had to stop the gathering of material.

The second phase of the project was to organize the crafts people under supervision of Bezalel and Aholiab, to whom God had given the wisdom, talents, and skills to shape the Tabernacle and its contents into the form God had shown to Moses on the mountain. Again many volunteers were involved. Some wove, colored, or stitched, while others melted, cast, or carved metals. Others worked on wood or polished stones—an enthusiastic team effort.

In this way, everybody felt part of the project because all had contributed in some way by giving, serving, helping or encouraging. What a change! Instead of serving the devil with idolatry and orgies, they were now serving God together by giving and working for His cause. Serving the devil left them empty, remorseful, and punished. Serving God filled them with joy, purpose, self-respect, and praise. Yahveh must have smiled.

Jesus invited people to exchange Satan's hard yoke for His light yoke (Matt. 11:28-30). What a difference for the demon-possessed, like Mary Magdalene and Legion of Decapolis, to sit with a sound mind and a serene heart at Jesus' feet instead of being haunted and trampled by evil spirits!

By tasting the difference between the gods of Egypt and the God of Israel personally, Israel had a learning experience that would give them a strong push in the right direction. Yes, they would stumble again, but they would never forget the difference between the golden calf and the Tabernacle experiences.

A prayer: Lord, I want to be on Your team.
A thought: Do I repeat the same mistakes or learn from experience?

72. The Sanctuary
Designed for a journey

March 12
~~~
Ex. 25:1-9
Ex. 26, 27:9-19

While Israel multiplied in Egypt, the God of their fathers faded and they began to worship the gods of Egypt (Josh. 24:14; Ezek. 20:6-8). Therefore, God defeated the gods of Egypt with the ten plagues, led Israel out of bondage, sustained them in the desert, and made a covenant with them at Mount Sinai.

On the mountain, God showed Moses how He wanted Israel to worship Him. The people supplied the material for the sanctuary. God had first given to them so that they could give back to Him. *"The earth is the LORD's and all its fullness, the world and those who dwell therein"* (Ps. 24:1).

God showed Moses in detail how he should make the sanctuary and its contents. Like an architect, God gave detailed blueprints and specifications to the master builder (Ex. 25-31, 35-40). We do not go into all the details but focus on the meaning of the main components. They would soon be moving on from place to place in the wilderness; the sanctuary and everything in it had to be portable. Christians, too, have to remember that this world is not our final destination. We're only moving through.

The Tabernacle had a court (100 x 50 cubits or roughly 52 x 26 yards), which consisted of a fence of linen (5 cubits high) held upright by pillars. The court was the public part of the sanctuary and could be entered by people who wanted to bring a sacrifice to the bronze altar near the gate of the court. Inside the court was a tent with a holy part (20 x 10 cubits) and a most holy part (10 x 10 cubits). The holy part could be entered by sanctified priests, and the most holy part could only be entered once a year by the high priest on the Day of Atonement. The priests were descendants of Aaron.

The three parts of the Tabernacle represented different degrees of closeness to God. Like the court, God's general revelation and grace, displayed in nature, is open to all people. Jesus said that God lets the sun shine and the rain fall on good and evil people (Matt. 5:45). Like the holy part, God's special revelation and grace is available only for His children whom He has called to Himself (Eph. 2:13). Like the most holy part, God's immediate presence is only reachable by His Son, who has atoned for our sins with His own blood (Heb. 9:12).

In our hearts too, there is a public space where we allow almost everybody, a holy space where we only allow some privileged family and friends, and the most holy space where we are alone with God (Matt. 6:6).

A prayer: Jesus, with You I may enter the most holy place.
A thought: Do I visit the three parts of my sanctuary regularly?

73. Symbols in the Sanctuary
The meaning of the contents

Drawings of the Tabernacle are available in study Bibles.* In the far end of the court was the tent with its holy and most holy sections. In the open part of the court, near its entrance, was the bronze altar on which the sacrifices were brought (Ex 27:1-8). Between the altar and the tent was a container with water where the priests had to wash their hands and feet before they served at the altar or entered the tent (Ex. 30:17-21).

| March 13 |
| ~ ~ ~ |
| Ex. 25:10-40 |
| 30:1-10 |

God wants us to make contact with Him, whatever the reason may be. The altar symbolized forgiveness of sins, pleas for help with problems, intercession for others, thanksgiving for answered prayers, and praises to God for who He is and for what He does. The water basin for the priests underlines that those who serve God in His sanctuary should be purified. Respect for God is strongly emphasized in the worship style He prescribed to Israel.

In the holy part of the tent there were, to the right, the table with showbread (25:23-30), and to the left, the lampstand with seven lamps (25:31-40). In the middle close to the veil that separated the Holy from the Most Holy, stood the altar of incense (30:1-10). The table with showbread symbolized our thanks to God for our daily bread. The lampstand symbolized God's light shining through His people to the world (Matt. 5:14, 16; Rev. 1:10-20). The altar of incense represented the prayers of God's people. Our prayers should be like a pleasant aroma rising before God (Rev. 8:3-4).

In the Most Holy was only the ark of the covenant. In it were the stone tablets with the Ten Commandments. It underscored their importance in the eyes of God. A jar with manna and Aaron's staff were later added (Heb. 9:4). The lid of the ark was called the "mercy seat" from where God spoke to Moses (Num. 7:89). It was also called the "lid of atonement," where the high priest sprinkled blood once a year to atone for the sins of the nation. No one could touch the ark and live (2 Sam. 6:6-7). When they moved to a new place, priests had to cover the objects of the Holy and the Most Holy before Levites carried the objects by poles attached by rings (Num. 4). The ark represented God's holy presence in the midst of His people. The twelve tribes camped around the Tabernacle, three tribes on each side. Yahveh was back among His people, but they had to keep a respectful distance.

A prayer: Father, bring my worship in line with Your will.
A thought: How can I make the Tabernacle atmosphere part of my worship?

* Spirit Filled Life Bible For Students, Thomas Nelson. Thompson Chain-Reference Bible, Zondervan.

74. Serving in the Sanctuary
Teaching God's Word to the nation

March 14
~ ~ ~
Ex. 28-29
Lev. 8-9

The essence of worship is two-way contact between God and His people. That was the meaning of the Tabernacle and its symbols. God chose the priests and Levites to mediate in this regular meeting between Him and Israel. By performing their duties at the six focal points of the Tabernacle, the priests conveyed Israel's worship to God and God's grace to Israel.

Furthermore, by teaching God's Word to the nation, the Levites would also bring God and His people nearer to each other. This mediating role pointed to the Messiah, who would be the unique Mediator between God and man (1 Tim. 2:5).

Moses and Aaron belonged to the tribe of Levi. Their tribe stood with them when others turned against them. Because of the tribe's dedication, God appointed them as leaders in the nation's religious life. In the Promised Land, they would not receive a province as the other tribes would. Instead, forty-eight cities scattered over the whole country were allocated to them so that they could fulfill their teaching ministry to the whole nation.

Six of their cities were appointed as cities of refuge for those who killed someone accidentally (Josh. 20). Such a person had to stay in the city of refuge until the death of the high priest. It protected the person against revenge and exposed the person for a long time to the teachings of the Levites. It was meaningful "house-arrest" that promoted the person's rehabilitation.

Only male descendants of Aaron could become priests and serve at the altar, the basin, the showbread, the lampstand, the incense altar, and the ark. The Levites had to assist them in handling thousands of sacrifices at the burnt offering altar. When Israel broke up camp in the wilderness, the Levites had to carry the components of the Tabernacle to the next camp. This process was governed by strict rules so that the Levites would not touch the holy objects and be killed by God's holy wrath (Num. 4).

While serving in the Tabernacle, the priests and Levites had to avoid ritual impurity, such as touching a corpse. Maybe that was the reason Jesus said in the parable of the Good Samaritan (Luke 10) that the priest and Levite avoided contact with the apparently dead man. For Jesus, however, compassion for the needy was more important than ritual purity; therefore, He touched impure people like lepers, sinners, and tax collectors. Jesus said to the lawyer that the law of love overrides all other laws, traditions, and customs (Matt. 22:34-40).

A prayer: Lord, show me how You want me to serve You.
A thought: Is my religion dead formalism or living gospel?

75. Sacrificing to God
Blessing the people

Yahveh's purpose for worship was not to spoil people's fun but to give them real joy. By sacrifices, the priests reconciled Israel to God and blessed them in God's name (Num. 6:22-27). The work of the priests pointed to Christ, our unique High Priest, who sacrificed Himself for us, who intercedes for us at the right hand of the Father (1 John 2:1), and who showers us with spiritual and material blessings (Eph. 1:3).

> March 15
> ~ ~ ~
> Ex. 29:38-46
> Ex. 30

God did not flood the priests with a long list of sacrifices right away, but He gradually introduced them to their daily, weekly, monthly, and annual duties. He started off with the daily morning and evening burnt offering on the altar in the court (Ex. 29:38-46). It symbolized Israel's dedication. After the burnt offering, Aaron had to go into the Holy to fill the lampstand with pure oil every morning (Ex. 27:21). He also had to burn incense on the incense altar every morning and evening directly after he had serviced the lampstand (Ex. 30:7-8). Every Sabbath the showbread was replaced (Lev. 24:5-9). Once a year on the Day of Atonement, Aaron had to sprinkle blood on the ark's lid.

However, most of the activity in which the people could share was focused on the altar in the court of the Tabernacle. Apart from the mandatory sacrifices that had to be offered to God in the name of the people on annual feasts, people could bring voluntary sacrifices to God for various reasons. Burnt offerings had to be totally incinerated on the altar to symbolize the person's complete dedication to God. Other offerings were usually divided into three parts: The first part was offered to God on the altar, the second part was given to the priests as food, and the third part was eaten by the person and his family to symbolize communion with each other and with God (Lev. 7:11-38).

The names of sacrifices revealed either the purpose of the sacrifice, like sin offering, or the substance of the sacrifice, like grain offering (Lev. 1-7). Cattle, sheep, goats, doves, grain, flour, oil, and wine were used as offerings. The central idea was that the person or the nation gave something of God's blessings back to Him. When Israel had settled in the Promised Land, many animals were sometimes sacrificed on one day (1 Kings 8:63).

Israel's sacrificial worship symbolized what God's Messiah would do for them. This kind of worship was meant for an interim period until Messiah comes. Animals had to be unblemished—like the sinless Messiah.

A prayer: Father, let me understand the meaning of Your symbols.
A thought: Am I indifferent or excited about the symbols of the church?

76. The Annual Feasts
The four feasts of spring

March 16

~ ~ ~

Lev. 23:4-22
Num. 28:16-31

During their sojourn in the desert, the Israelites were probably scattered over a large area in order to graze their animals. In the Promised Land, they would disperse over a far larger area. The sanctuary was a focal point where the nation could congregate for the annual feasts.

Yahveh wanted to feast with them. He instituted seven feasts for Israel. These feasts were arranged like the seven lamps of the lampstand: three in early spring, one in late spring, and the last three in autumn. We studied the first two, Passover and Unleavened Bread, with Israel's liberation from Egypt (page 46).

In the Promised Land, the first Sunday in the week of Unleavened Bread would be the Feast of First Fruits. Barley ripened before wheat (Ex. 9:31-32); therefore, a sheaf of barley from the coming harvest would be presented to God to honor Him as the Giver of food to man and beast.

All religious activities including the annual feasts pointed to the coming Messiah. On Passover, Jesus died as the Lamb of God who took the sins of the world onto Himself (John 1:29, 1 Cor. 5:7). He was also the unleavened bread that had to be pierced, striped, and broken according to Jewish custom. At the Last Supper, Jesus took unleavened bread and said, *"This is My body which is broken for you"* (1 Cor. 11:24). On Sunday morning, the Feast of First Fruits, He rose from the dead as *"the first fruits of those who have fallen asleep"* (1 Cor. 15:20, 23). He will raise the bodies of believers on the last day.

Due to the Promised Land's climate, the end of the wheat harvest was celebrated in late spring by the Feast of Pentecost, fifty days after the Feast of First Fruits. At Pentecost, leavened bread made from wheat was presented with thanks to God as a heave offering and then eaten by the priests. It honored God for His blessings on the harvest. Unleavened bread was only used at Passover and for the following week. Leavened bread showed God's presence in everyday living and was used year round.

Jesus said, *"I am the bread of life. He who comes to Me shall never hunger, and he who believes in Me shall never thirst"* (John 6:35). The "bread of life" became a wonderful reality on the day of Pentecost when the Holy Spirit was poured into the followers of Jesus in Jerusalem. They started to testify fearlessly about Jesus, and on that day three thousand people accepted Him as their personal Savior. They represented the spiritual harvests of the future.

A prayer: Father, let me understand the meaning of Your feasts.
A thought: How can God's feasts enrich me personally?

77. Cleansing and Rejoicing
The three feasts of autumn

The first four feasts pointed to the redemptive work of Christ in His first coming. The last three feasts pointed to the practical application of that salvation in this life and the next. In the fall, they had the feasts of Trumpets, Atonement, and Tabernacles.

March 17
~ ~ ~
Lev. 23:23-44
Num. 29

The first day of the seventh month was "Day of Trumpets". (Later it became the Jewish New Year in their civil calendar.) It was kept like a Sabbath. No ordinary work could be done, and the nation had to congregate for sacrifices and instruction from the Torah. The ram's horn was blown during the day reminding people of the coming Day of Atonement on the tenth day of that month. The Day of Trumpets was a wake-up call for God's people to start a ten-day period of self-search and repentance and honor God as King and Judge. For Christians, this day may point to a wake-up call of the Holy Spirit to bring them to new dedication and the lost to rebirth, and to prepare all for the return of Christ when the heavenly trumpet will sound (Matt. 24:31, 1 Cor. 15:52, 1 Thess. 4:16).

The Day of Atonement, Yom Kippur, was a day of fasting, repentance, and forgiveness. In the Most Holy Place, the high priest covered the Law in the ark with blood sprinkled on the ark's lid, the mercy seat. The sins of the nation were symbolically laid on a scapegoat that was sent off to the desert. The blood and the goat resembled Christ, who took our sins onto Himself.

The painful period of repentance ended with the joy of forgiveness. The church facilitates atonement by teaching God's Word and by trusting God's Spirit. The church should also look forward to the day of Christ's return when all sin will be eliminated forever.

Five days after Atonement, the Feast of Tabernacles, Sukkoth, started. It commemorated Israel's sojourn in the wilderness. It was a time of rejoicing— for atonement received on Yom Kippur, for blessings on the harvest of grain and fruit, and for being rescued from bondage to the land of milk and honey.

This feast urges Christians to be grateful for all the material and spiritual blessings they receive from their caring Father in heaven. We also celebrate Thanksgiving that part of the year. It also directs our eyes to heaven, where all tears will disappear and where God's children will have complete joy forever. There we will not live in temporary booths but in the place Jesus prepared for us (John 14:1-3), *"a building from God ... eternal in the heavens"* (2 Cor. 5:1).

A prayer: Jesus, thank You for atonement and a place in heaven.
A thought: Do I sound the trumpet faithfully and clearly?

78. New Beginnings
Periods of rest and restoration

<table>
<tr><td>
March 18
~ ~ ~
Lev. 25
Num. 28:11-15
</td></tr>
</table>

Some feasts were introduced later. The Purim feast originated in the 5th century B.C. when Esther and Mordecai thwarted a plot to kill all Jews (Esther 9:26-28). The Hanukkah feast (John 10:22) points to the rededication of the temple in the 2nd century B.C. after it had been desecrated by the Syrians.

With the Exodus, God instituted several sabbatical events. Although they were not feasts in the same sense as the ones described in the preceding lessons, the sabbatical events were joyful occasions with tremendous impact on the nation. We looked at the **weekly Sabbath** when we studied the fourth commandment (page 58). It instituted a weekly cycle of work and rest.

On the first day of the month with a **new moon**, silver trumpets were blown (Num. 10:2, 10). That day, starting at sunset, was set aside as a Sabbath (Amos 8:5) with special offerings and meals (1 Sam. 20:5). Apparently, the purpose of the new moon feasts was to dedicate the new month to God and to ask for His blessing on their activities. Yahveh wanted to be part of their daily, weekly, and monthly schedules.

In His mercy, God commanded that every seventh year in the Promised Land had to be a **Sabbath Year** and every 50th year a **Jubilee Year**. The land had to rest. Then they could not prepare or harvest their fields, vineyards, and orchards. Whatever sprouted naturally was for the poor and for the animals. God promised to give them in the sixth year a threefold crop that would supply for them from the sixth to the eighth year, just as He provided a double share of manna on the sixth day to provide for the Sabbath. Israelites who had sold themselves as slaves were set free in the Sabbath Year.

In the Jubilee Year, all land had to be returned to the original owners or their descendants. God told them straight that the land belonged to Him. They were only stewards and custodians of the land. When they sold land, the price had to be based on the number of harvests left before the next Jubilee Year. In other words: They could sell the harvests, but not the land.

The purpose of this law was to prevent oppression of the poor by greedy landlords. It gave a new beginning to those who were impoverished or enslaved either by their own mistakes or by circumstances beyond their control. Surely, the heart of the law was mercy (Matt. 9:13). The Jubilee Year looked forward to the new earth and the new heaven (Rev. 21).

A prayer: Lord, I want to be a better steward of Your earth.
A thought: How can we share our privileges with needy people and countries?

79. Spiritual and Physical Hygiene
Maintaining and restoring purity

Long before scientists discovered the link between diseases and microscopic organisms like germs, bacteria, and viruses, the laws of God had taken this fact into account and had prescribed cleansing rituals that prevented contamination.

March 19
~ ~ ~
Lev. 11-15

These laws contained detailed lists of "unclean" animals that were forbidden as food, as well as lists of "clean" animals that could be used as food (Lev. 11). Meat had to be cooked. Touching contaminated objects like corpses and carcasses made people and things impure, and steps had to be taken to restore purity. This rule was also applicable to people, clothes, and houses tainted by skin diseases (Lev. 13-14) and people fouled by unnatural discharges (Lev. 15). Women were declared "impure" for a time after menstruation or childbirth, probably to protect them against men (Lev. 12).

All these laws about physical impurity stressed that the body was part of God's domain and that His people had to be holy in body, soul, and spirit.

Impurity had to be prevented as far as possible, but when it had occurred, purity had to be restored by means of a quarantine period, by washing, and sometimes also by offerings (Lev. 11:32). It highlights God's forgiveness.

People could become contaminated without knowing it; therefore, many washing rituals emerged just to be on the safe side. When Jesus was accused by His enemies that He neglected hand-washing rituals, He pointed out to them that dirty hands do not make one morally impure, but that a dirty heart does (Mark 7). Jesus was not against hygiene, but against superficial morals.

With today's medical knowledge about contamination, we know why we wash our hands before eating and why we keep up other hygienic practices. Unfortunately, many have become rather *don't care* about moral contamination. Before the disturbing wake-up call of sexually transmitted diseases, people got increasingly casual about sexual immorality.

However, we can "catch" spiritual illnesses in many ways. Mixing with the wrong company can contaminate our views, faith, and lifestyle. God warned us about unholy mixing by symbolic prohibitions such as mixed breeds, harvests, or clothes (Lev. 19:19). Israel was also sternly warned against the mixing of religion (Ex. 23, 34). The apostle Paul warned us, *"Do not be unequally yoked together with unbelievers"* (2 Cor. 6:14).

A prayer: Lord, purify me from evil ideas and fill me with Your ideas.
A thought: Are my Christian values tainted by worldly standards?

80. Blood and Fat
The importance of a sound diet

<table>
<tr><td>March 20
~ ~ ~
Lev. 7:22-27
Lev. 17</td></tr>
</table>

The Creator knows what is best for us. He prohibited the eating of blood and fat for religious and health reasons. The blood carries food and oxygen to the cells of the body and picks up waste material like carbon dioxide so that organs like the lungs, liver, and kidneys can get rid of them.

Heart and blood vessels circulate the blood through the body; injury to either one of them can be fatal. No wonder God said the life of man and beast is in their blood. For this reason, God reserved blood for religious purposes and prohibited the eating of it.

After Peter received the vision of unclean animals and heard the voice saying that he should not regard anything as unclean (Acts 10), the first church council decided not to prohibit the eating of any animal to Gentile Christians but to uphold the rule of not eating blood (Acts 15). The fact that Jesus gave His blood for our salvation was emphasized by the church and may have determined this decision (Acts 20:28, Rom. 5:9, 1 Pet. 1:18-19, 1 John 1:7).

The prohibition of fat as a food is meaningful and somewhat surprising. In Moses' time, people knew nothing about cholesterol; therefore, the use of fat as part of food was a general practice in other nations. Even in our time, in spite of all the research results, we still enjoy bacon, sausage, hamburger, and steak, which all contain a lot of animal fat. Once again the Creator showed His knowledge of the physiology of His creatures by prohibiting fat as a food. All visible fat had to be removed and burnt whether the animal was killed for offering or for normal use.

In spite of the best precautions, not all blood and fat cells could be removed from meat. That did not bother God. He is holy but not unreasonable. He made, knows, and maintains the smallest particles in physics, but He does not view His people through a microscope. Therefore, the form that is read in many churches before Holy Communion states that "sin which remained in us against our will" should not deter us from the sacrament.

When baptism water is sprinkled on a person, the water symbolizes the blood of Christ (1 Pet. 1:2). In the worship God prescribed through Moses, people and things were purified by the sprinkling of blood, not by submersion in blood. Baptism by submersion symbolizes that the person becomes one with Christ's death, burial, and resurrection (Rom. 6:3-4).

A prayer: Lord, You made us and sustain us. You know what is best for us.
A thought: God already knows what man still has to discover.

81. Respect for Boundaries
The morality of relationships

The Bible is primarily a book about relationships. It tells how the relationship between God and man was derailed and how it can be restored. It also tells how this relationship affects the relationships among people, as well as their relationships with creation.

March 21
~ ~ ~
Lev. 18-20

The Ten Commandments and their footnotes dealt with these relationships (pages 54-69). The sanctuary with its contents and activities, as well as the feasts and resting periods, were instituted to develop these relationships (pages 70-78). God's prescriptions for personal hygiene (pages 79-80) put the spotlight on our relationship with ourselves. Moses and Jesus referred to it when they said, "love your neighbor as yourself" (Lev. 19:18, Matt. 22:39).

Leviticus 18-20 has stern warnings regarding all four relationships. Besides sexual perversions like incest and bestiality, it also deals with general human inclinations such as gossip and cheating. Idolatry and immorality are rejected in the same breath, while the honoring of parents and the Sabbath is commanded in the same sentence. The four relationships are woven together into a pattern of love and respect for God, self, others, and creation. The way they harvest their fields should show their mercy for the poor. Their self-respect should become visible in their respect for the elderly, the deaf, the blind, and the stranger. To make sure they did not miss a point, Leviticus 20 reiterated God's will regarding parents, perversions, idols, occult, adultery, and hygiene.

As God had put up boundaries for Adam and Eve for their own protection, so He put up boundaries here for the protection of His people. God encourages us to expand our intellectual boundaries without breaking through the moral boundaries He instituted for our protection (page 3).

How we handle social boundaries (e.g. between husband and wife, parents and children, brothers and sisters, teachers and students) determines whether relationships are functional or dysfunctional. When boundaries are too thick, people become isolated; when boundaries are too thin, people's personal space is violated. The right amount and type of contact is of vital importance. For example, there should be agape love between father and daughter but not erotic love. God wanted contact with His people, but He repeatedly warned them not to overstep the boundaries (Lev. 10:1-2). We must reach out to one another, respecting each other's signals, lest we violate the boundaries and personal space of that person and so ruin the relationship.

A prayer: Lord, I respect the limits and boundaries You erected for me.
A thought: Which of my boundaries are too thick or too thin?

82. Nazirite and Nazarene
God's blessing on our devotion

March 22
~ ~ ~
Num. 6

The Nazirite vow was apparently already in use and was only better defined here. People used it to devote themselves to God for supplication, thanksgiving, or spiritual growth. The Nazirite had to avoid wine, haircuts, and corpses. This voluntary abstinence had symbolic meaning. The uncut hair made the Nazirite's position known to others. Avoiding wine and corpses was applied to priests, too, when they served in the Tabernacle. To devote themselves to God, they had to shun both parties and funerals.

When the Nazirite period came to a close, the person had to cut his/her hair at the entrance of the Tabernacle and give the hair to the priest, who had to burn it on the altar with the offering of the person. The apostle Paul cut his hair in Cenchrea because he took a vow (Acts 18:18). We don't know if he did it at the end of a Nazirite period.

The Bible tells us of only three lifelong Nazirites: Samson, Samuel, and John the Baptist. Jesus was not a Nazirite, but a Nazarene (Matt. 2:23)— He grew up in the town of Nazareth. Jesus said that John the Baptist did not drink wine and the leaders called him demon-possessed; Jesus drank wine and they called Him a drunkard (Matt. 11:18-19). Jesus refused to take sour wine when He was paying the price for our sins on the cross (Matt. 27:34). When that task was finished, He wet his mouth with wine from a sponge before He declared loudly that His mission was accomplished (John 19:30).

The chapter on the Nazirite vow ends with the blessing of the nation by the priests. God honors our devotion with undeserved blessings.

In Hebrew, the blessing consists of three sentences, each containing the covenant name of God, Yahveh. Besides this name, the first sentence contains two other words, the second contains four other words, and the third contains six other words. Twelve words of blessing from Yahveh to the twelve tribes.

The blessing is repeated three times to emphasize its certainty and that it comes from the Trinity. The blessing underlines God's love and protection, His closeness and mercy, and His power and peace. The Hebrew word "shalom" describes a comprehensive peace—to be at peace with God, with others, with creation, and with one's self.

The blessing reflects the true nature of God. He is full of love, mercy, and goodwill. He is a loving Father who wants good things for His children.

A prayer: Father, let Your blessing increase my devotion.
A thought: Have I invested time in special devotions like courses and retreats?

83. Direction and Protection
The pillar of cloud and fire

Now that Israel was about to depart from Sinai, Moses wrote more about the pillar of cloud by day and the pillar of fire by night. It had directed and protected them from Egypt to Sinai (Ex. 14:19-20), it rested on the "tent of meeting" outside the camp before the Tabernacle was erected (Ex. 33:9-10), and eventually it rested on the Tabernacle when it was finished (Ex. 40:34-38). As they

> March 23
> ~ ~ ~
> Num. 9:15-23
> Ex. 13:21

journeyed farther from Sinai to the Promised Land, the pillar of cloud and fire showed them when and where to go and to stop. It was their guide and shield. It was the visible sign of God's presence and protection.

Vision and hearing are our major channels of information. Although God had forbidden Israel to worship Him through images, He knew how important vision was in the learning process, so He gave them many object lessons like the sanctuary and its contents and activities, as well as the feasts and resting periods. Likewise, the pillar of cloud and fire gave visual assurance that He was there in spite of their many sins and shortcomings.

When Israel took possession of the Promised Land, they spread out over a large area; therefore, the pillar of cloud and fire disappeared and the manna stopped falling. The cloud reappeared momentarily when Solomon's temple was inaugurated five centuries later (1 Kings 8:10-11). However, they had to start believing without seeing. That is the natural way of existence for God's children in this life. Jesus said to Thomas, *"Thomas, because you have seen Me, you have believed. Blessed are those who have not seen yet have believed"* (John 20:29).

The parables of Jesus were word pictures that enabled His followers to visualize, understand, and remember the truths He conveyed to them. The sacraments He instituted were audiovisual explanations of the gospel. When the church is planted in new areas, miracles happen to convince the people of the truth and power of God's Word (Mark 16:20). Afterward the signs diminish because *"the just shall live by faith"* (Rom. 1:17).

That does not mean that miracles do not take place anymore. Many things that we see as natural are actually fantastic miracles. The body with all its specialized cells is a miracle in itself. Just think of the processes by which the senses pick up stimuli and convert them to electrical impulses that are conveyed by nerves to the brain where they are analyzed as vision, sound, smell, taste, or touch. Think of the miracle of multiplying food for the whole world every year.

A prayer: Father, I will not fear—for You are with me.
A thought: Do I stay aware of the many signs of God's presence?

84. Doubts about God
Can God prepare a table in the wilderness?

When Israel moved on from Mount Sinai, the moaning about food soon resumed. They were sick and tired of eating the same old manna day after day. Though one can sympathize with them, boring food is still better than no food. Even today, boring diets are still a fact of life in many parts of the world. For billions, the staple food comes from rice, corn, wheat, or potatoes.

March 24
~~~
Num. 11

</div>

Their attitude infuriated both God and His servant Moses. Then Moses started to vent his frustration on God. We can sympathize with Moses too. He was sick and tired of his "miserable" job but could not resign. God knew that after all the highs and lows at Mount Sinai, Moses needed a break.

On Jethro's advice, judges were appointed to assist Moses with his judicial work (page 53). God now told Moses to appoint seventy elders to assist with his spiritual duties. God empowered them by His Spirit. All of them started to prophesy, even two who were not at the sanctuary. When Joshua wanted to stop these two, Moses prophesied about the outpouring of the Holy Spirit on Pentecost: *"Oh, that all the LORD's people were prophets, and that the LORD would put His Spirit upon them"* (See Acts 2).

Regarding the cry for meat, God promised to give them so much meat that after a month they would find it repulsive. In disbelief, Moses said that herds of cattle, flocks of sheep, and schools of fish were not enough to feed the nation. They thought, *"Can God prepare a table in the wilderness?"* (Psalm 78:19). Their doubts about God were so much more insulting when seen against the background of recent events. They had commemorated after one year their liberation from Egypt by celebrating the second Passover (Num. 9). They would have recalled all that had happened, including the provision of meat in the form of migrating birds before they reached Sinai (page 50).

God responded to their doubts by saying His arm is not too short to help. Then He brought the wind and the exhausted migrating birds, and they had to work their way through a layer of birds, three feet deep, as far as the eye could see. In their greed, they ate the birds without cooking them properly and thus stepped over the rule of not eating blood. The guilty ones paid with their lives. Israel's joy was ruined by their greed and grief. They got what they wanted for their bodies, but their souls remained hungry (Ps. 106:15). They left many graves behind and called the place "Graves of the Greedy."

*A prayer: Lord, empower my faith by Your provisions of the past.*
*A thought: Do big problems sometimes limit my great God in my mind?*

# 85. Futile Uprisings
## God disciplines them severely.

God severely punished the people who rose up against Moses and Aaron because primarily these rebellions were aimed at God Himself. It was not just discontent about food and water. The rebels made deliberate attempts to push Moses and Aaron out of their God-given leadership positions.

> March 25
> ~ ~ ~
> Lev. 10
> Num. 12, 16-17

The first challenge came from Nadab and Abihu, two sons of Aaron. They brought incense offerings before the Lord that He had not ordered. God was so offended by their arrogance that they died instantly, and their father was not allowed to mourn their death. By this tragic event God said loud and clear that worship in Israel was not a human invention that people could change as they liked. Worship was a God-given contact between God and man, a contact that took place because of God's grace, not man's merit.

The next challenge to Moses' authority came from his sister, Miriam. Aaron supported her. They argued that God did not speak to Moses alone but also to them. God summoned them to the entrance of the Tabernacle, and the pillar of cloud descended there. In an audible voice God told them that He spoke in a much more personal way to Moses than to prophets. Moses could hear His voice and see His form. Moses did not see God's face (Ex. 33:20-23) but an appearance of God in human form (Gen. 18). Miriam was infected with leprosy. Aaron and Moses prayed for her. God told her to stay seven days outside the camp like a daughter who was severely reprimanded by her father.

After the return of the spies (page 86), Korah, Dathan, and Abiram rebelled against Moses and Aaron. The earth opened and the rebels disappeared into the pit. The 250 unauthorized people who burnt incense before the Lord died instantly in the Tabernacle. Their pans were hammered into covering plates for the altar as a reminder to the nation. Two kings, Saul and Uzziah, centuries later committed the same sin (1 Sam. 13, 2 Chron. 26).

God ordered the leaders of the twelve tribes to present a staff to be laid in front of the most holy place. Aaron's staff, representing the tribe of Levi, was the only one that blossomed the next morning, showing without any doubt that he and his male descendants were chosen by God for the priesthood. God commanded that his staff be kept at the ark of the covenant as proof of their calling. As Creator and Ruler of the universe, God has been in control from the beginning. People rebel, but He remains sovereign.

*A prayer: Father, You are my sovereign King.*
*A thought: Where have my rebellions brought me?*

86

# 86. When Fear Crushed Faith

**They miss a golden opportunity.**

March 26
~~~
Num. 13-14

When Israel approached the southern border of the Promised Land, God told Moses to explore the land and to gather information on the enemy. God already had given the land to them, but they still had to take possession of it. God's grace did not eliminate their action; in His grace, He would use their action.

The spies came back with good and bad news. It was a fertile land with developed fields, orchards, and vineyards, as evidenced by the fruit they had brought with them. However, ten spies exaggerated the physical and military power of the inhabitants, thus instigating fear in the nation. Only Joshua and Caleb were convinced that they could conquer the land.

Fear and faith influence perception. The fear of ten spies made them see themselves as "grasshoppers" and their enemies as "giants." Their fear robbed them of confidence in self and God, so they decided, "We cannot." The faith of two spies gave them a totally different view of themselves and the enemy: "We are well able... they are our bread... their protection has departed from them." Their faith made them focus on God; therefore, they said, "We can because God can." The apostle Paul phrased it this way, *"I can do all things through Christ who strengthens me"* (Phil. 4:13).

The nation's faltering faith surfaced many times in the form of discontent. Now it made them identify with the fear of the ten negative spies. Because of their own weak faith, they could not identify with the faith of Joshua and Caleb. So they wept and started to make plans to return to the wonderful slavery of Egypt. They longed back for the privileges of Egypt because of selective recall, thinking only about the good things of the past and blocking out the bad.

When they heard what their punishment was for not trusting God, they tried to make a fast U-turn. But some sins and their consequences are irreversible, like murder and insulting God. These sins can be forgiven, but what was done can't be undone, and the consequences can't be avoided.

Israel had to live in the desert until all soldiers who were older than twenty years would have died, except for Moses, Joshua, and Caleb. But God is merciful in His punishment. Although Moses recorded very little about those years in the desert, Israel learned in that time to trust and obey God. When they stood on the border of the Promised Land again thirty-eight years later (Deut. 2:14), the new generation accepted the challenge. Yahveh's discipline had worked.

A prayer: Father, I can do all things by Your power.
A thought: Are my decisions governed by fear or faith?

87. Purified from Death
by the ashes of a red heifer

Israel had seen many deaths lately, and they would see many more on their sojourn in the desert. God commanded Moses to institute a ritual to purify the sanctuary and the nation from death and its consequences. The symbolism of the red heifer pointed to Christ, who saved us from eternal death to eternal life (Heb. 9:13-14).

March 27
~ ~ ~
Num. 19

Israel had to give an unblemished red heifer that had never been yoked. The human nature of the Messiah also came from Israel. He was unblemished in character and never under the yoke of sin. His blood would be the red sacrifice to rid us from sin and death. As the heifer was killed outside the camp, Christ died outside Jerusalem (Heb. 13:12). As the entire heifer was burnt to ashes, so Christ gave Himself completely unto death.

The blood of the heifer had to be sprinkled seven times in the direction of the entrance of the Tabernacle, thereby purifying the sanctuary from the death of the rebels (page 85) and dedicating it as a source of life. Likewise, the church became a path to eternal life through the blood of Christ.

The ashes had to be mixed with spring water. Whoever came in contact with death had to be sprinkled with this mixture on the *third* and the *seventh* days. If not, the person had to be expelled from God's people. When Christ's redemption is mixed with the Spirit's "streams of living water" (John 7:37-39 NIV), it saves us from eternal death by giving us eternal life. We were cleansed from death when Christ rose from death on the *third* day, and the process will be completed on the *seventh* or *last* day when Christ returns to take us home.

People who have not been purified from sin this way are cut off from God's people until they undergo this cleansing experience. Jesus said to Peter, *"If I do not wash you, you have no part with Me"* (John 13:8).

The choice of a heifer might have been for practical and symbolic reasons. Because there were surely more unblemished, unyoked red heifers than bulls, it would be easier for Israel to come up with such a heifer.

After Christ's ascension, the church was called His bride on earth (Eph. 5:25, 1 Cor. 12:27). The bride of Christ has to bring His redemption (symbolized by the ashes of the heifer) and the work of the Holy Spirit (symbolized by the spring water) to people so that they can escape eternal death and can receive eternal life—*"For the wages of sin is death, but the gift of God is eternal life in Christ Jesus our Lord"* (Rom. 6:23).

A prayer: Jesus, You died so that we can have eternal life.
A thought: Have my sins been washed away by Jesus?

88. Moses Stumbles
and his dream is shattered.

God had given Moses great victories up to this point. The mighty Pharaoh and his gods had been crushed by ten plagues and by the Red Sea miracle. The hungry and thirsty nation had been fed by bread and birds falling from the sky and by water bursting from a rock. God had revealed Himself to Moses in wonderful ways at Mount Sinai. Several rebellions had been squashed.

Had all these victories gone to his head? At Kadesh, an old problem recurred—the desperate lack of water. As usual, the nation moaned and blamed Moses for their suffering. To make things worse, Moses' sister, Miriam, died. His grief made him more vulnerable.

When God told him to speak to the rock to open up water to the nation, a little voice might have whispered in his ear, "It's stupid to talk to a rock, man! Rather smash it with your stick as you did the last time and so vent your frustration too." Moses' anger flared up and he yelled: *"Hear now, you rebels! Must we bring water for you out of this rock?"* He hit the rock and water came out, but Moses lost something very precious to him.

God did not blame Moses for his anger. God too got angry with that stiff-necked people many times. It was the word "we" that offended God. If Moses had said, "Must *God* bring water for you out of this rock?" there would not have been a problem. By replacing "God" with "we" Moses had stolen God's glory. He was disciplined immediately. He would not enter the Promised Land. Moses could have replied: "Now, is that a way to thank a man for his hard work?" But Moses wisely shut up, knowing he had erred.

There were more disappointments for Moses just around the corner. The Edomites, descendants from Jacob's brother, Esau, would deny Israel passage over their land, thereby forcing Israel to make a long detour that would break the spirit of many. Moses would also lose his brother, Aaron, who had stood with him for many years except for two occasions. Moses knew the forty years in the wilderness were almost done. As he would not enter the Promised Land, he knew that his own death could not be far off.

Moses must have entered the last part of his ministry with a heavy heart. However, he knew that the successful conquering of the land was not dependent on human power and ingenuity, but on a merciful, almighty God. What he didn't realize was that God had a big surprise in store for him. He would go to a far better Promised Land to be with God forever.

A prayer: Our Father, hallowed be Your name.
A thought: Where have I stolen God's glory?

89. Speaking Serpents
The snakes drive them to God.

It was not only the snake in the Garden of Eden that spoke to man. When Israel had to trek around Edom, they became weary and rebelled against the Lord. God punished them with snakes whose bites were fiery and fatal. In pain and agony, they called on God for mercy. The snakes drove them back to God.

March 29

~ ~ ~

Num. 21:4-9
John 3:14-18

God told Moses to make a bronze snake and to put it on a pole. Because of the large camp, people would have carried the snake-on-a-pole through the camp so all could see it. All who looked up in faith to the bronze snake were healed from the poison of the fiery serpents. Centuries later this bronze snake was still in Israel's possession. They began to worship it as an idol; therefore, King Hezekiah destroyed it (2 Kings 18:4).

Jesus showed us the true meaning of the bronze snake. He told Nicodemus that just as the bronze snake had been lifted up, so He would be lifted up on the cross. Just as people who looked up in faith to the bronze snake were healed, so those who would look up in faith to Him would be saved. The bronze snake was a symbolic prophecy about the Messiah.

How could the Son of God be represented by a snake? Isn't Satan, *"that serpent of old"* (Rev. 20:2), the exact opposite of Jesus? Actually, the bronze snake was not an effigy of Jesus but of the sins Jesus was carrying as our substitute. The snake-on-a-pole portrayed Satan's power over us. Jesus turned that negative symbol into a positive one. Jesus-on-the-cross portrayed His victory over Satan, sin, and death. Jesus nailed our debt to the cross and wrote "paid in full" over it (Col. 2:14).

With all His miracles, Jesus turned hopeless situations into joyful ones. He turned the sad picture of crowds who looked like sheep without a shepherd into the glad picture of a plentiful harvest (Matt. 9:36-38).

Moses and his people had no idea that God was using snakes to prophesy to them about the Messiah, the Savior of the world. They thought they were forgotten people in a forsaken desert. Little did they know how bright the light of the gospel was shining on that spot at that moment.

Do our afflictions drive us to God? Do we trust God to turn our "forsaken desert" into a gospel opportunity? Do we take Jesus to people who are dying spiritually, as the bronze snake was taken to the suffering? We must bring the message to them: "God so loved the world that He gave His only begotten Son, that whoever believes in Him should not perish but have everlasting life."

A prayer: Jesus, I look up to You as my only Savior.
A thought: Do I recognize the blessings hidden in my afflictions?

90. Friend or Foe?
Identify the real enemies.

<table><tr><td>March 30
~ ~ ~
Num. 21
Deut. 2-3</td></tr></table>

God forbade Israel to go into war at this point with Edom, Moab, and Ammon because they were related to Israel. The Edomites were descendants of Esau, and the Moabites and Ammonites were Lot's offspring. Many years later there would be war between Israel and these nations, but for now they had to avoid fighting with relatives, in spite of the fact that these relatives denied them passage, food, and water.

The same policy was not followed with King Sihon of the Amorites and King Og of Bashan. God told Israel to engage them in battle, to wipe out people and idols, and to take their land and property. And so it happened. God warned Israel not to take credit for triumph—it was God who secured the victory because of the sins of these nations (Deut. 9:4-6).

The territory of these nations east of the Jordan River was given to the tribes of Manasseh, Gad, and Reuben. They had to promise that their soldiers would help the other tribes conquer the rest of the Promised Land while their wives and children would continue farming in that region.

As it is important for a country to identify its real enemies and to take appropriate steps to guard against that threat, so Christians, too, have to make sure who the real enemies are, to guard against them, and to avoid needless battles with fellow believers.

The Bible says our real enemies are Satan, the "world," and the "flesh." Satan uses the temptations of the world to lure us into sin. He sets up the opportunity. To be successful, he needs the cooperation of our sinful nature. Then the temptation from outside becomes a temptation from the inside. When opportunity and desire coincide, the temptation may work. Even then, we can resist it by prayer and the power of the Holy Spirit.

Instead of fighting these real enemies, Christians can waste a lot of spiritual energy on fighting brothers and sisters for social or theological reasons. We should never forget that the ninth commandment about truth is part of the second table of the Law, which deals with love for one's neighbor. That is why Paul urges us in Ephesians 4:15 to debate the truth in a loving attitude.

Of first importance is our personal relationship with Christ, not our theological viewpoints. However, when we have been saved by Christ, we should humbly try to keep our views in line with God's Word.

A prayer: Lord, show me who my real friends and enemies are.
A thought: Do I get along with fellow Christians from other churches?

91. The Blessed are Protected
How shall I curse whom God has blessed?

Israel's victory over Sihon and Og scared Moab to death. In a desperate effort to protect themselves, their king, Balak, asked a heathen prophet, Balaam, to come and curse Israel to secure victory for Moab over Israel. God allowed Balaam to go on condition that he only said what God told him to say.

> March 31
> ~ ~ ~
> Num. 22-25

Although Balaam complied with his lips, he had other plans in his heart. God sent an angel to block his way and change his mind. At first Balaam did not see the angel, but his donkey did, and three times she avoided the angel. Each time Balaam hit the donkey. Then God opened the donkey's mouth, and she complained about the way her master was treating her. She spoke on behalf of millions of other animals that had been mistreated by their owners over the centuries. When God opened Balaam's eyes and ears to see and hear the angel, he realized that he had been saved by his donkey and warned by God.

Balak took Balaam to three different mountains to look over the camps of Israel and curse them. Each time seven bulls and seven rams were sacrificed and Balaam consulted the Lord and came up with a wonderful blessing for Israel. Balak was furious and sent him away empty-handed. Before he left, Balaam gave a fourth prophecy about the distant future of Israel and One special person from Israel: *"A Star shall come out of Jacob, A Scepter shall rise out of Israel ... Out of Jacob One shall have dominion."* It looks like prophecies about David and Jesus (compare Micah 5:2-4).

We don't know how Moses got hold of Balaam's prophecies. Maybe when Balaam was later killed with the Midianites (Num. 31:8), the soldiers of Israel found his written prophecies on his body. God made sure that the prophecies He gave to Balaam were recorded and saved for all generations.

God blessed His people through heathens more than once. The patriarchs were well treated by the inhabitants of Canaan (Ps. 105:13-15). Melchizedek, priest-king of Jerusalem, blessed Abraham. Jacob, his sons, and their families were well received in Egypt. The kings of Phoenicia helped David and Solomon construct the temple. Kings of neighboring nations made peace treaties with David and Solomon. King Cyrus of Persia helped Judah return to their country. Wise men of the east worshiped the Christ-Child. Gentile Christians dispersed the Bible over the world, including the Old Testament, making Israel's history known worldwide.

A prayer: Lord, continue to speak to those who are not yet your children.
A thought: Should Christians note the wisdom of the secular world?

92. Satan's Favorite Weapon
Israel is seduced to immorality.

<table>
<tr><td>

April 1

~ ~ ~

Num. 25, 31

</td></tr>
</table>

When Balaam had spoken, by God's command, blessings over Israel four times in a row, he returned to his original plans in order to get his pay. He advised Moab and Midian to weaken Israel by seducing them to immorality (Num. 31:8; 2 Pet 2:15). Balaam had heard of Israel's holy God, Yahveh, and of Israel's unholy inclinations. He knew what trap to set for them. By falling into sin, they would lose God's blessing. The same person who said good things about God's people now turned against them. Beware when the world praises you.

In the commercial world, many believe that "sex sells." Balaam believed that too. On his advice, women from Moab and Midian lured men from Israel to the feasts for their favorite idol. Baal was the god of the clouds that fertilized the goddess of the earth. To encourage Baal to do his job, his followers indulged in sexual orgies around his altars. Some men from Israel thought that was real fun, so they eagerly accepted the invitations of the sexy women.

God knew about the plot and put a swift stop to it with a plague. When Phinehas, son of the present high priest, Eleazar, pierced an Israeli man and a Midianite woman with his spear, the plague stopped. This man and woman were both from high status. This kind of sin attracts people from all walks of life. Nobody is immune against Satan's favorite weapon.

God commanded Israel to punish Midian for their despicable deed. Each tribe gave a thousand soldiers for the expedition. They killed all the men, including Balaam, but saved the women, children, livestock, and loot. Moses was angry at them for saving the very women who lured them into sin. He had these women put to death, except for the virgins who obviously had not taken part in the Baal feast. The livestock and loot were carefully divided among the tribes, including the Levites and priests. The principle that those who went to war shared equally with those who guarded the home front was later affirmed by David when he was still a fugitive (1 Sam. 30:21-25).

The power of sinful sex displayed on this occasion was repeated many times in the history of Israel. Satan never gave up this weapon. In some periods of history, it became more overt or covert. In our time, it is becoming public again. God made sex as something holy and beautiful in marriage. Satan distorts it and turns loving, God-honoring couples into lusting, God-insulting sinners. Yahveh hates casting pearls to swine.

A prayer: Lord, please protect me from Satan's favorite weapon.
A thought: Am I strict or permissive with these assaults of Satan?

93. Moses' Bible School
The importance of revision

As Moses was not allowed to lead Israel into Canaan, he gave a series of farewell messages to his people to help them to stay on track. These messages were recorded in Deuteronomy ("second law"). It gives a review of some historical data and of some aspects of the Law, but it is more than a repetition or a summary. It reflects the insights Moses gained over time into the meaning of history and into the meaning of the law.

April 2
~ ~ ~
Deut. 1-10
14-16

The importance of the fifth book of Moses is underscored by the fact that when the Son of God was tempted by the devil, He used three quotations from this book to defeat the evil one (Matt. 4; Deut. 6:13, 16; 8:3).

Moses would later return to other sins of Israel, but as a departure point he used the inexcusable national sin of refusing God's gift by turning their backs on the Promised Land (Deut. 1). That was the goal of leaving Egypt and crossing the desert—to take possession of the Promised Land—but when they had to take the gift, they refused. Jesus said that the main reason for missing heaven will be the refusal to accept God's gift of salvation, which His Son earned for us by His death: *"He who believes in Him is not condemned, but he who does not believe is condemned already, because he has not believed in the name of the only begotten Son of God"* (John 3:18).

By reminding the nation how the territory east of Jordan was captured, Moses encouraged them to keep on trusting God for conquering the rest of the land (Deut. 2-3). For the new generation, the circumstances in which the Law was given forty years ago at Mount Sinai might have been vague; therefore, Moses refreshed their memories with the details (Deut. 4-5). Then he put the first table of the Law in a nutshell: *"You shall love the LORD your God with all your heart, with all your soul, and with all your strength"* (Deut. 6:5). Jesus quoted these words when asked what the greatest commandment was.

Moses repeated two words like a refrain: **love** and **obey** Yahveh. Jesus did the same when He said farewell to His disciples (John 14:15). The two are the same: "obeying God's commandments" = "loving God and neighbor." Moses reminded them what happened when they did not do that by pointing to the episode of the golden calf (Deut. 7-11).

He urged them again to serve God by faithfully keeping up the worship and feasts God had instituted for them (Deut. 14-16). They had to teach God's Law daily to their children (Deut. 6:7).

A prayer: Lord, let the lessons of the past make me wise in the present.
A thought: How can I use the past without getting stuck in the past?

94. The Unity of the Trinity
Your God Yahveh is one.

<table>
<tr><td>

April 3

~ ~ ~

Deut. 6:4

</td><td>

When Moses wrote "Yahveh is **one**," he used the Hebrew word *echad* for *one*. And when he wrote that man and wife *"shall become **one** flesh"* (Gen. 2:24), he also used the word *echad* for *one*. In Hebrew, *echad* is used to describe the unity of parts. Therefore the phrase "Yahveh is one" does not preclude the Trinity.

</td></tr>
</table>

Many passages in Hebrew Scripture affirm the existence of the Triune God. Genesis 1:1-3 introduces us to God, His Spirit, and His Word (compare John 1:1-3). Before creating mankind God said, *"Let Us make man in Our image ... male and female He created them"* (Gen. 1:26-27). God talked about Himself in the plural and created a plural image. One of the names of God in the Old Testament is *Elohim,* which is a plural Hebrew word.

God the Father said to Moses that he could not see His face (Ex. 33:20), yet God the Son appeared to Moses in human form (Num. 12:8), as He also did to Abraham (Gen. 18) and Jacob (Gen. 32:24-30). This human appearance of God is called the "Angel of the LORD" in the Bible (Ex. 3:2-6). When God called people to a special task, He put His Spirit on them, like the elders in Numbers 11. The Triune God revealed Himself in the Old Testament.

The oneness of God is also stressed in the often repeated prohibition not to worship idols. Because God is the one and only true God, all counterfeit gods had to be avoided and destroyed (Ex. 20:3-6).

To protect the worship system God had given through Moses, God commanded that in the Promised Land they should have only one place for communal worship (Deut. 12 and 14). That place would be where the Tabernacle would be. Centuries later God used David and Solomon to make the temple in Jerusalem that one place of worship. The nations who lived in Canaan before Israel had many gods, and they worshiped them on every hill and under every tree. To prevent Israel from doing that, one place of worship was instituted.

Sadly, the history of Israel became a record of many relapses and many reforms. The reasons may be many and complicated. They did not wipe out the native populations completely. These people lured Israel to idolatry with their sensual practices, which were more attractive to human nature than the strict laws and rules of Moses. However, in the long-term these pleasures destroyed their joy. First they lost their land for seventy years, and when they rejected the Messiah, they lost their land for nineteen centuries.

A prayer: Father, Son and Holy Spirit, You are my one and only God.
A thought: Do I accept God as He revealed Himself in His Word?

95. God's Word
has to be their map and compass.

The main goal of Deuteronomy was to exhort the nation to stay true to God. God's great deeds and words, as well as man's right and wrong choices, were recorded in the five books of Moses. These books were the beginning of God's written Word, the Bible. It would be their map and compass to stay on track.

April 4

~~~

Deut. 8, 30-31

In Deuteronomy 8:3 Moses explained to Israel that God had sustained them with manna in the wilderness so they could learn *that man shall not live by bread alone; but man lives by every word that proceeds from the mouth of the LORD."* Jesus quoted this passage at the beginning of His ministry when tempted by the devil to change stone to bread (Matt. 4:3-4). Shortly afterward, He started to heal people physically, emotionally, and spiritually by His healing words. In the synagogue of Capernaum (John 6), He told people that He was the true manna from heaven who gave them eternal life. In Him, God's Word became God's bread. The feeding of the multitudes symbolized that.

Moses exhorted the nation (Deut. 8) not to forget God when they became prosperous in the Promised Land. In times of plenty, they had to remind themselves of the times of scarcity in the desert and of God's provision for them. For forty years their clothes had not worn out, nor had their feet been swollen, because God had sustained them. To refresh their memories from time to time, the books of Moses had to be kept next to the ark in the Most Holy Place and read to the whole nation every seven years (Deut. 31:1-13, 26). A copy of God's Word had to be made for the king so that he could study it daily and rule accordingly (Deut. 17:18-20).

Because the Levites had to teach God's Word to the nation all over the country, we can assume that they too needed copies of the books of Moses. Nobody could say that God's Word was too far away to gain knowledge of it (Deut. 30:11-16). Paul quoted these words in Romans 10 to show that God's Word and the salvation it brings have become available to all through the gospel. The hearing of the Word brings faith in the heart.

Christians are so much more privileged than Israel was in the time of Moses. We have the whole Scripture in our homes. We too have to feed ourselves spiritually on the life-giving Word of God. Devotional books explain Scripture, but they cannot replace the Bible. Psalm 119:105 remains true for believers: *"Your word is a lamp to my feet and a light to my path."*

A prayer: Lord, I enjoy Your Word as a meal for my soul and spirit.
A thought: Does God's Word propel and steer my life every day?

96. Future Leadership
In religion and politics

<table>
<tr><td>

April 5
~ ~ ~
Deut. 17

</td><td>

Moses realized that the sanctuary with its worship and feasts, as well as the laws for daily living spelled out in the Torah, could only stay effective when the leaders of the nation supported the system and when they encouraged the nation to follow their example. Therefore, Moses gave

</td></tr>
</table>

direction to future religious and political leaders.

Judges had to be appointed for all regions. They had to rule justly in view of sufficient evidence and without regard for the status of the guilty. When regional judges could not come to a conclusion, they had to refer the case to the priests at the tabernacle/temple. They were the highest court and their judgment was final. Because judgment was based on the Law of Moses, the Levites and the priests fulfilled the task of the judiciary.

Four centuries before the nation of Israel would ask for a king, God gave some basic rules for kings to ensure their politics do not clash with the religion of the nation. The king had to be an Israelite, and he had to be chosen by God. He should not acquire many horses, wives, or riches. He should study a copy of the Law every day of his life to enable him to rule wisely in accordance with God's will. All these rules were later ignored by most of Israel's kings.

Since the fourth century, when Christianity became the official religion of the Roman Empire, many power struggles erupted between state and church. Most modern democracies accepted a system of 'separation' between state and church. Each of the two is supposedly sovereign in its own domain. However, in recent times, church institutions have been increasingly forced to break their own laws in favor of secular state laws. For controversies regarding scriptural values, the separation of church and state is going in a direction that is obviously not in the best interest of the church.

For countries where the vast majority of the population still regard themselves as affiliated with the Christian faith, their values should be taken seriously by their elected representatives in local, provincial, and federal government. If these representatives presume not to know what the values of their electorate are, they should hold a referendum. Voters should make their views known in any legal way, e.g. in polls, in election campaigns, and at the ballot box.

Wouldn't it be great if the Great Commandment of God could be the benchmark for all man-made laws, bylaws, and regulations?

A prayer: Our Father, Your kingdom come, Your will be done.
A thought: Do I function as salt and light in my community?

97. Mercies of the Law
Love your neighbor as yourself.

To have enduring and endearing value, the Law had to be of practical use for ordinary people. To serve that purpose, Moses lifted out some of the commands they had received already and added some practical applications as well.

> April 6
> ~ ~ ~
> Deut. 19-25

The poor were allowed to glean on fields and in vineyards. Laborers had to be paid daily so that they could feed their families. When a poor person's cloak was taken as a pledge, it had to be returned before nightfall. Widows, female captives, and unloved and divorced wives were given certain rights and freedoms. Harlotry, perversions, and incest were strictly forbidden. Strayed and suffering animals had to be looked after. Even birds had to be freed when their eggs were taken. Oxen could not be muzzled on the threshing floor.

Defendants were protected against false witnesses by the "eye for an eye" principle. The guilty could not receive more than forty blows with the lash. To stay on the safe side, judges allowed only thirty-nine blows. That's why Paul said he received from the Jews forty stripes minus one on five occasions (2 Cor. 11:24). The bodies of hanged offenders had to be removed before nightfall. Those who caused death by accident could flee to cities of refuge where avengers could not touch them. Guidelines were given for unresolved murders.

Boundaries could not be moved, and every fifty years properties were returned to their original owners. People could taste some of their neighbor's fruit or grain, but they could not take any of it with them. To prevent injury, people had to put up parapets around the flat roofs of their houses. The people of Israel were forbidden to ask interest on loans from each other, but they could take it from foreigners. In certain situations, men could be excused from serving in war. Guidelines were given on war ethics.

Wearing clothes of the opposite sex or clothes made from different materials was forbidden. They could not plant different seeds together or yoke an ox with a donkey (1 Cor. 6:14). Intermarriage with Gentiles was forbidden. These prohibitions urged them to avoid the blending of religions.

God's mercy for His people was beautifully illustrated by the image of the eagle that forces her young out of the nest to teach them to fly and then dives beneath them and carries them on her wings back to the nest (Deut. 32:11-12). Likewise, Yahveh practiced tough love with Israel to teach them His will and strengthen their faith, yet carried them in mercy all the time.

A prayer: Lord, Your commandments are for my protection.
A thought: Does God's will spoil my fun, or does it enhance my joy?

98. Reward and Punishment
The two sides of discipline

<table>
<tr><td>April 7
~ ~ ~
Deut. 27-30</td></tr>
</table>

God told Moses to help Israel make a choice. He had to prepare twelve curses and twelve amens. Four of these curses dealt with sexual sins and the rest with idolatry, parents, honesty, charity, justice, violence, integrity, and obedience. The Levites had to say one curse at a time, and the whole nation had to affirm it together with a loud "Amen!" This ceremony had to take place at Mounts Ebal and Gerizim after entering the Promised Land.

Then God showered them with great promises of blessing if they would stay true to Him. They and their children, livestock, and harvests would be blessed with rain and fertility. From Deuteronomy 28:21-22, we can assume they would also enjoy good health if they followed God's commands. They would conquer their enemies, have peace in their urban and rural areas, and among the nations they would be the head and not the tail.

To rivet the nails, God painted a horrible picture of the curses that would befall them if they became unfaithful to God. In place of every blessing came the opposite as a curse. But many more were added. It makes one sick just to read it—people eating their own children, and women their own placentas, due to hunger when their enemies would besiege them. The diseases they would suffer would exasperate them before killing them.

In his mercy, however, God ended with some good news again. If they would repent, He would bring them back to their land. Seven hundred years before Isaiah, God already gave a prophecy through Moses about the return of Israel from exile.

God's blessings and curses came to other nations too. Amalek would be wiped out for attacking Israel after leaving Egypt (Deut. 25:17-19, 1 Sam. 15:2-3). Israel should abhor neither Edomites, for they were "brothers," nor Egyptians, for Israel stayed in their land for 430 years (Ex. 12:40). People from Moab and Ammon would never be taken up in Israel because they refused food and water to Israel on their way to the Promised Land (Deut. 23:3-8).

In His mercy, God later made an exception for Ruth. Although a Moabite, her faithfulness to Naomi and to God was rewarded. She became the wife of Boaz and the great-grandmother of King David.

God's holiness and love are in perfect harmony as was demonstrated by Jesus' atonement on the cross. He took the punishment for sin so that sinners could be saved.

A prayer: Jesus, You took the punishment so that I can receive the blessings.
A thought: Do I take both God's holiness and God's love seriously?

99. A New Leader for a New Era
Moses gives the reins over to Joshua.

Moses had concluded his last instructions to Israel as they camped east of Jordan. Now it was time to give the reins over to the new leader, Joshua, who had assisted Moses for forty years.

April 8
~ ~ ~
Deut. 31-34

Moses molded his final farewell into the form of a song and a blessing. The Creator of man knew that the roots of learning go much deeper when cognitive left-brain input is accompanied by emotional right-brain input. When truths are put into easy-to-remember slogans and songs, they stick for a lifetime. So God commanded Moses to end his lectures with a song that the whole nation could learn by heart. One of the things they would sing about was that the Lord carried Israel as an eagle carries her young on her wings—a refrain that every small child would learn to sing.

Much evil has been carried into the minds of young people by means of popular music and songs. Just as we fight evil with good in the media, so we must fight evil music and songs with good music and songs.

Moses blessed eleven tribes of Israel, omitting the tribe of Simeon. Their territory would be inside Judah's, with whom they would merge eventually. Moses had warned Israel many times with curses, so now he just concluded with something sweet. Parents too have to be on their guard against the trend to give only negative instructions to their children—don't do this, don't do that! Instead of focusing only on what they should not do, focus more on some nice things they may do.

Moses not only inaugurated the new leader, but he also prophesied about the Messiah, the leader of the future (Deut. 18:15-19). Actually, all the laws and worship Moses had instituted pointed symbolically to the Messiah.

Moses placed his hands on Joshua, hugging his friend for the last time. He waved to the crowds, turned, and started his walk up the foot of the Pisgah Mountains to the Nebo peak. He was relieved of the heavy burden of bringing Israel to the Promised Land. Yet, as father of the nation, he was still concerned about them. He tore himself away. He was going home now.

Although they had been angry at him many times, the nation now looked at the departing servant of God with heavy hearts. How would they survive without Moses? God had kept him strong through all the difficult years. With a slow but steady pace, he ascended the mountain until they could see him no more. God took care of him as He had done since he was a baby in a basket on the Nile.

A prayer: Lord, make me faithful till the end.
A thought: Do I use song and music to lift up my spirit?

100. Be Strong
God empowers Joshua for his task.

<table>
<tr><td>
April 9
~ ~ ~
Joshua 1
</td></tr>
</table>

On God's command, Moses had appointed Joshua as his successor in the presence of the nation. For a month Israel mourned Moses' death. In that time Joshua might have felt inadequate to step into the shoes of his formidable predecessor. Then he got his assignment and empowerment directly from God.

God calls different people for different tasks in different times. The Moses-era had ended and the Joshua-era had started. Joshua had to shift his focus from the past to the present. Many centuries later, another Yeshua (Jesus) said, *"No one, having put his hand to the plow, and looking back, is fit for the kingdom of God."* (Luke 9:62). The apostle Paul said: *"One thing I do, forgetting those things which are behind and reaching forward to those things which are ahead"* (Phil. 3:13).

Joshua's task for the present was the conquering of the Promised Land. God guaranteed the victory, but they still had to make the effort. Israel's liberation from Egypt, like the Christian's justification, was entirely God's work. However, their survival in the desert and their taking of the Promised Land were accomplished by a combination of God's grace and human effort—like the Christian's sanctification and glorification respectively.

To empower Joshua for his task, God showered him with encourage-ment and promises. Three times God spurred him on to be strong. Instead of sinking into a loser attitude, he had to maintain a winner attitude. Thirty-eight years before, in contrast with ten negative spies, Joshua and Caleb had displayed a winner attitude. Joshua had to proceed with that attitude because God would support him, as God had supported Moses.

God nurtured the winning attitude in Joshua with at least ten promises that covered God's presence, the land, the enemy, Israel's inheritance, and their prospering. These promises were conditional. They depended on Joshua's study of, meditation on, and obedience to God's Word. If Joshua stayed true to God's Word, God would stay true to His promises.

Although Joshua might have been overwhelmed by his enormous task after Moses' death, surely this encounter with God would have brought a bounce into his step. At once he gave orders to make preparations to cross the Jordan within three days. The tribes who had received their land east of Jordan pledged their military support to Joshua until the job was done.

God made Joshua ready to take the Promised Land.

A prayer: Lord, with You I want to look forward and to go forward.
A thought: How do I react to new challenges?

101. Mercy for Sinners
Saved by a red rope

In view of the disaster caused by the negative spies thirty-eight years earlier, Joshua now sent two scouts secretly to Jericho to gather intelligence about the city and the mood of its people. God led the scouts to a woman whose heart He had already prepared for this occasion. She was the most unlikely candidate in Jericho to be on the side of Yahveh, the holy God of Israel. She ran the town's brothel, which usually was near a bar. At such public places people met to chat, so the spies could pick up the atmosphere, gossip, and news of the day.

> April 10
> ~ ~ ~
> Joshua 2

Archaeology has shown that ancient cities were small towns encircled by stone walls. People knew each other well; therefore, the scouts did not remain unnoticed. Rahab realized the peril the scouts faced and ushered them into her house, which was up against the city wall. She hid them on the flat roof under drying flax. When the king sent guards to arrest the spies, she told the guards that she didn't know they were spies and that they had left already. She urged the guards to pursue them immediately. When the guards had left, the city gate was closed and the scouts were trapped.

Rahab returned to the scouts on the roof and told them that Israel's miraculous crossing of the Red Sea forty years ago, as well as their recent victories east of the Jordan, had filled the Canaanites with fear. She professed her faith in Yahveh as the only true God and asked for mercy, not only for herself, but also for her father, mother, brothers, and sisters.

While she got ready to lower the scouts outside the city wall by means of a red rope, they promised to grant her request on three conditions. When the city was taken, she had to identify her house to the armies of Israel by hanging the red rope from her window. She had to gather her family in her house, and then they would be saved by the red rope, as sinners are saved by the blood of Christ. She had to keep silent about the scouts and about their agreement. Then the scouts climbed down—saved by the scarlet rope.

On Rahab's advice, they hid in the mountains for three days before they returned to Joshua. They shared with him the good news that the hearts of the Canaanites had melted and that God had already secured Israel's victory. They also told Joshua of their deal with Rahab. They were men of integrity.

Rahab is mentioned in the genealogy of Christ and in the gallery of believers (Matt. 1:5, Heb. 11:31, James 2:25). God turned the harlot into a heroine.

A prayer: Lord, please open the right doors and roads for me.
A thought: Have I escaped from hell with God's Red Rope?

102. Crossing the Jordan
Setting foot on the Promised Land

<table>
<tr><td>
April 11
~ ~ ~
Joshua 3-4
</td></tr>
</table>

The positive report of the scouts, on top of God's personal encouragement, spurred Joshua into action. He gave the command to prepare to cross the Jordan, which was in flood that time of the year. Instead of a stream only thirty yards across as usual, it was now more than a mile wide. Dark circumstances form a perfect backdrop for bright miracles.

The priests led the procession with the ark. As soon as their feet touched the water of the river, an invisible wall cut the stream off. Upstream a massive dam formed while downstream the water flowed away. The priests proceeded with the ark to the middle of the riverbed. Then Joshua let the nation pass in awe. He erected two monuments to commemorate this incredible occasion: One heap of stones was placed where the ark stood in the river; another was placed in Gilgal. Both consisted of stones taken from the riverbed.

Most of the people who had witnessed the dividing of the Red Sea were not alive anymore. God now performed a similar miracle for the new generation to show them that the rescue from slavery and the inheritance of the Promised Land were both gifts of God. They could never ascribe these to their own ingenuity or efforts. Lest they forget, monuments were erected.

This fantastic event was of paramount historical importance for the nation of Israel. The often repeated promises of God to Abraham, Isaac, Jacob, and Moses had become a reality at long last. It had been five centuries since Abraham first set foot in Canaan until his descendants returned to claim their God-given inheritance. Although it seems as if the wheels of God's vehicle turn very slowly, His clock is always right on time.

Just as the liberation from Egypt points to salvation and the life in the wilderness to the hardships of believers in this life, so Israel's crossing of the Jordan became a metaphor of passing over from this life into the next. That is where we make the metaphor end, conveniently forgetting about the great task Israel still had ahead of them—the conquering of the land.

Those who think of heaven as a never-ending time of leisure may be in for a big surprise. Stagnation was never part of God's plan for His creation. He enjoys putting up new challenges for Himself and His loved ones. What looks like the end of the road to us is usually the beginning of a new era. Staring back at "the good old days" may blind us to present and future opportunities.

A prayer: Lord, open my eyes for the opportunities of today.
A thought: Do I hesitate to take possession of my inheritance?

103. The Covenant Restored
Circumcision and Passover resumed

Israel did not practice circumcision while wandering in the wilderness. No reason is given, but it could have resulted from their refusal to enter the Promised Land, a failure that broke their covenant with God. For the same period, the Passover is not mentioned either. Probably it was not observed for the same reason. The church also withholds the sacraments from those who break their covenant with God.

> April 12
> ~ ~ ~
> Joshua 5

Now that the disobedient generation had perished, God restored His covenant with the new generation when they entered the Promised Land. All males were circumcised, and the whole nation participated in the Passover. Repentant sinners are likewise restored by the church to partake of the sacraments. Broken relationships displease our heavenly Father intensely; restored relationships delight Him exceedingly. The whole Bible is about God's plan of salvation—the restoration of humanity's relationship with Him and with one another.

By bringing His people into Canaan and by restoring the signs of His covenant with them, God *"rolled away the reproach of Egypt"* from them. Up to this point, the Egyptians mocked Israel by saying that their God led them out of Egypt to perish in the wilderness because He could not lead them into the Promised Land. They could not say that anymore. Yahveh was fulfilling His promises to His people, and He was restoring them in the eyes of the world.

As God had planned Israel's crossing of the Jordan for the time when the river was in flood, so He planned their arrival in Canaan when the harvest was ripe. When their enemies heard of their victories east of Jordan and saw their miraculous crossing of the Jordan, they panicked and locked themselves up in their fortified cities while Israel reaped their harvests for themselves. Because they now ate the produce of the Promised Land, the manna ceased to fall. The supernatural was replaced with the natural.

There is a wonderful promise, as well as an awful warning, embedded in this history. When we keep our covenant with God, He maintains a blessing relationship with us, providing all our needs even when we go through difficult times. When we are unfaithful to Him, we lose His blessings and suffer His discipline. That does not mean that we have to earn God's grace. Our faithfulness is the result of the gracious working of His Spirit in our hearts, while our unfaithfulness is the result of our own negative choices.

A prayer: Father, thank You for Your generous gifts.
A thought: Do I enjoy the privileges of restored relationships?

104. Crumbling Walls
The fall of Jericho

April 13
~ ~ ~
Josh. 5:13-15
Josh. 6

When the covenant with God had been restored, Joshua met the Commander of the LORD's army. The Angel of the LORD, in the form of the pillar of cloud by day and the pillar of fire by night, had led and protected Israel in the wilderness. Now He took on another form to suit the circumstances. Israel had to conquer the Promised Land. By the appearance of His Commander, God let them know that He would be fighting with them.

In principle, God had given them the whole land, but in practice they had to take it city by city. Jericho was the first one on the list. However, God's Commander let Joshua know that Jericho would be taken in such a way that it would be perfectly clear that it was God's victory and not Joshua's. They had to walk silently around Jericho once a day for six days. On the seventh day, they had to circle the city seven times. Twelve times they had to engage in this stroll without saying or doing anything. The soldiers of Jericho must have watched them from the walls, puzzled at first, and mocking them later.

This scene illustrated persevering prayer. Often we too have to circle our Jericho many times before the walls start to crack. While we are faithfully doing our "knee-work," the powers of evil mock us for continuing with a ritual that obviously has no effect on the practical problems we are facing. Then we have to continue in faith, as Joshua and his followers did, knowing in our hearts that at the right moment, God will intervene.

After the thirteenth round, they did as Joshua had told them. Joshua shouted, the trumpets resounded, the people cheered, and then the walls came down, crushing the taunting soldiers on the wall. Only one piece of wall remained standing. It had a house attached with a red rope hanging from its window. Rahab and her family were saved by the red rope of grace.

From all sides, Israel's soldiers stormed in and killed man and beast, as God had commanded. Destructible items were destroyed, and precious metals were gathered and handed over to God's treasury in the Tabernacle. As the firstborn of animals had to be sacrificed to the Lord, so the first conquered city of Canaan had to be completely dedicated to the Lord. Unfortunately, one man convinced himself with "good reasons" to disobey God's command. Achan's greed made him steal from God. As a result, Israel suffered an unexpected and unnecessary defeat, and Achan and his family would pay a terrible price.

A prayer: Lord, help me not to give up on my Jericho.
A thought: Do I rob God's money, time, or planet?

105. The Purpose of Failure
Learning from mistakes and successes

Encouraged and delighted by the miraculous victory over Jericho, Joshua sent a small force against the small city of Ai. Unexpectedly, they suffered a humiliating defeat. Thirty-six Israeli soldiers were killed, leaving as many families in mourning.

April 14

~~~

Joshua 7 - 8

</div>

The jubilating nation was suddenly shocked back to reality. Without God, they could not even capture a small town. Their old fears of the Canaanites started to resurface. The confidence Joshua had built up over the past weeks with the crossing of the Jordan, with the renewal of the covenant, and with the dramatic fall of Jericho was completely shattered by the Ai disaster. He was literally flat on his face before God.

God told Joshua to stop whining and get rid of the evil that caused the miserable failure. God knew who the culprit was, but He preferred to use the lot as means. Only after the tribe, the family, and the person had been identified did Achan admit his guilt. He had not stepped forward earlier. Until the last moment, he hoped that he could get away with his crime.

His children had to be adults because they were treated as accomplices. His wife is not mentioned. Maybe she was deceased or condemned Achan's sin. Achan and his children were executed, his livestock killed, his possessions burnt, and the remains covered by a large heap of stones. Achan and all he had were obliterated, yet his sin would be remembered forever by taking it up in the Word of God so that we can avoid the same pitfall.

When the evil was wiped out, Joshua attacked Ai again. With a well-planned strategy, Ai was razed to the ground. Israel's shame was turned into fame once more. The Canaanites could not build their hopes on the Ai defeat for Ai and its people were no more. After Joshua had renewed the covenant between God and His people, they could proceed with their conquest.

Because of sinful human nature, Israel would fail many times in the future. God knew this but did not turn away from them because of future sins. He walked with them one step at a time, as we do with a toddler. We know little ones will fall many times as they grow up; therefore, we don't despair about their ability to make progress.

God looks on His children with even more compassion. When we learn from our mistakes, a step backward can become a step forward—like relapsing into an old sin and rediscovering that the long-term pain far outweighs the temporary pleasure.

A prayer: Father, help me to learn from my mistakes rather than to cover up.
A thought: Do I have the guts of a toddler to stand up after a fall?

106. Deceiving the Gullible
They do not ask counsel of the Lord.

April 15
~~~
Joshua 9
</div>

While most city-kingdoms braced themselves for the onslaught by Israel, the Gibeonites came up with a shrewd plan to trick Israel into a peace treaty. Their story sounded rather fishy. Why would people from a far-off country be anxious to make peace with Israel? And by the looks of their clothes, sandals, and provisions, their country had to be really far away.

Suspicious, the leaders of Israel asked , "How can we be sure you are not living just over the next hill?" Israel's leaders did not listen to their gut feelings; neither did they consult the Lord. They gave in to that human need to have peace at any cost. And if this country was really far away, what harm could it do to have good relationships with their distant neighbors?

So they ratified the treaty with an unconditional oath. In the light of their suspicion, it would have made sense to safeguard themselves with a condition by saying, "If you have given us false information, we will be free from this oath." Abraham had put in such a condition when he asked his servant Eleazar to take an oath regarding a wife for his son, Isaac (Gen. 24:8).

Only three days later, the truth surfaced. The news of the Gibeonites' "victory" swiftly spread to neighbor cities (Josh. 10:1). The Gibeonites just couldn't keep silent about it—they were gloating and feasting about their clever triumph over a strong opponent. Joshua and the elders felt embarrassed over their gullibility, especially when the nation rubbed salt into their wounds. They could not revoke their oath, but they could punish the Gibeonites for their deceit. They were made servants of Israel for ages to come. More than four centuries later, in the time of King Saul and King David, this oath to the Gibeonites led to a tragic piece of history (2 Sam. 21). The Gibeonites have to be distinguished from the Gideonites, the followers of Gideon (Judges 7).

Although the Law of Moses made provision to rectify oaths taken recklessly (Lev. 5:4-6), Joshua did not make use of it here. Maybe they forgot about this law, or maybe they did not want to portray themselves as people whose word of honor was worthless. Because of the seriousness of an oath taken in the name of Yahveh, Jesus urged His followers to avoid swearing. He said our *yes* must mean *yes* and our *no* must mean *no* (Matt. 5:37).

The Bible warns against the flagrant deception of the end time (Matt. 24:4-5, 2 Thess. 2:9-10). If we don't stay vigilant, we will be taken in for suckers.

*A prayer: Omniscient God, protect me from deception and gullibility.*
*A thought: Do I gobble up everything the media dishes up?*

# 107. Finishing the Job
## The danger of incomplete victory

This chapter is loaded with tragic humor. The Gibeonites were still boasting about their smart tactics when they learned that five Canaanite kings were marching with their armies against them to punish them for making peace with the invaders. In panic, they sent word to Joshua and pleaded for protection. It's kind of funny that the deceivers asked help from the deceived and that some Canaanites asked protection from Israel against other Canaanites.

<table><tr><td>April 16<br>~ ~ ~<br>Joshua 10</td></tr></table>

Joshua believed what David later wrote in Psalm 15: *"LORD, who may dwell in your sanctuary? ... He who keeps his oath even when it hurts."* (NIV). Although Joshua could have kicked himself for his stupid deal with the Gibeonites, he held his end of the bargain and rushed to help them in their need. God used these human intrigues to accelerate the conquering of the Promised Land. There was no time for procrastination now. They just had to grab the bull by the horns and take on five armies all at once.

God motivated them by His promise that He would give them victory. He put fear into the enemies and peppered them with hailstones as they ran, but Israel still had to pursue them and put the dispersed regiments to the sword. However, the day was too short to complete the task. Joshua cried out to God to give them some extra hours of daylight. The Creator granted this request with a smile—He gives the poles 24 hours of sunshine for a day every summer, doesn't He? God showed His power and allowed His people to finish the job.

The kings who started off as brave generals of their armies now scuttled like scared rodents into a cave. They were spotted, trapped, and arrested. Joshua brought them out, made them lie down, and had his officers put their feet on the necks of the five kings before the kings were executed. Joshua probably made sure that Gibeonites attended this triumphant ceremony so that the story could spread over all of Canaan. It was a clear statement about Israel's domination to both the enemy and to their own people.

In the following days Joshua led his army to each of the five cities that came against him and destroyed their inhabitants. Unfortunately, Israel did not inhabit these cities, so other Canaanites moved in and Israel later had to recapture these cities (Judges 1). Half measures against our spiritual enemies may cost us dearly. Israel might have had "good reasons." Maybe they did not feel safe enough yet to break up their unity and spread out over the land.

*A prayer: Lord, help me to finish unfinished tasks, hurts, and ideals.*
*A thought: Do I stick to my word even when it costs me?*

# 108. The Primary Goal
## The expansion of God's kingdom

In the conquering of Canaan, we repeatedly read of cities and "their villages." Because of recurring clashes between fortified cities, people living in nearby villages fled into the fortified city when an approaching army was spotted. Although people brought food with them, they soon suffered hardships in such a besieged city. Many had to sleep on the streets, food and water were rationed, and sanitation became a problem. The city could become a death trap.

Joshua's approach was to first conquer the main fortified cities with the combined armies of all Israel and to leave it to the army of each tribe to subdue the villages in its territory. Although the southern cities were captured in a short time, some of them were reinhabited by Canaanites when Israel's army returned to Gilgal (10:43). For example, Jerusalem and Hebron are listed as cities taken by Joshua (12:10), but later they were in Canaanite control again (15:14, 63).

We too sometimes do not follow through on great victories and thus lose the benefits of hard earned progress. Jesus said that if an evil spirit has been driven from a house and the house is left empty, then that evil spirit may return to that house and bring seven evil spirits with it (Matt. 12:43-45).

The northern campaign took "a long time" (11:18; 13:1). Because Hazor was the strongest fortified city in the north, Joshua destroyed and burnt it (11:10-13). Current excavations exposed evidence that a severe fire occurred when Hazor, the double-walled city, was destroyed.

After twenty years or more when Joshua was old (13:1; 24:29), he divided the land west of the Jordan between 8½ tribes. The tribe of Levi did not receive a territory of its own, only 48 cities of which six were called "cities of refuge." Joshua had to spur on the nation west of Jordan to take control of and to inhabit the territories allotted to them. They tried to do that, but rather half-heartedly. They did not eliminate the local inhabitants completely, as God had commanded, but they used them as laborers. These people lured Israel into idolatry repeatedly, as the book of Judges tells us.

Like Israel, we too sometimes make compromises and do not eliminate old sins completely. Subduing every part of our lives to God takes a long time; therefore, we cannot afford to do it half-heartedly or to allow the enemy to regain control over conquered terrain. The expansion of God's kingdom must proceed. Jesus taught us to pray, "Let Your kingdom come."

*A prayer: Lord, spur me on by Your Spirit to expand Your kingdom.*
*A thought: Have I become lax in expanding God's kingdom in my own life?*

# 109. Rewards for Faithfulness
## Joshua and Caleb labor for their inheritance.

God forgets forgiven sins completely (Jer. 31:34), but He remembers unfinished business well. He did not forget the attack of the Amalekites and punished them five centuries later (1 Sam. 15:2-3). He also remembers good attitudes, choices, and deeds. He did not forget about Joshua's and Caleb's faith and courage to stand up against the ten fearful spies long ago.

| April 18 |
| ~ ~ ~ |
| Josh. 14, |
| 19:49-51 |

Like Moses (Deut. 34:7), they had been rewarded already by physical strength to survive the forty years in the desert unscathed. But they would get their share of the Promised Land, too, as the Lord had promised.

The fact that Hebron was retaken by the big guys, the children of Anak, didn't bother Caleb. He was not scared of them forty years ago, and he was not scared of them now. In God he trusted. "Give me this mountain!" Caleb insisted. He still had to fight for his prize, but that was okay with Caleb because all Israel had to conquer their inheritance in order to possess it.

Christians face the same scenario. Our victory over the three "big guys" (Satan, world, and flesh) is promised by God's Word, but we still have to fight to make the promise become reality. Likewise, we have to plan carefully, work hard, and motivate ourselves to make our dreams come true.

Joshua waited for his share until everybody else had been served. Then the leaders asked him what he would like as reward for all his hard work. He chose a city in ruins and rebuilt it. That was his way of conquering his inheritance. In God he trusted. Some people have an eye for the potential of a shabby old building and then renovate it into something extraordinary.

Christians have to develop an eye for the potential of ruined lives. God specializes in restoring broken people: *"He restores my soul"* (Ps. 23:3), *"A broken and a contrite heart—these, O God, You will not despise"* (Ps. 51:17). Sinners can be changed by the Holy Spirit to accept Jesus Christ as personal Savior and to change their lifestyle accordingly. Pick your ruined "city" and rebuild it.

Joshua and Caleb still speak to us about faithfulness and its rewards, about visions turned into reality. The things we really treasure are not those that fall in our laps but those God grants us through hard work. You too have a "city" to conquer or to rebuild. Ask God to show you that "city," and then go for it with all your might, trusting in the Lord.

Make sure your goal is in line with God's Word for Satan will try to lure you to wrong "cities."

*A prayer: Lord, show me the "city" You want me to conquer or build.*
*A thought: Do I grieve about buried dreams, or do I pursue current ones?*

# 110. Set Aside for God's Work
## The inheritance of the Levites

<table>
<tr><td>
April 19

~~~

Josh. 20-21
</td></tr>
</table>

Instead of receiving a province of their own like the others, the tribe of Levi received 48 cities scattered over the entire country. Although the Levites would receive the tithes of the nation to live from, they were not parasites. They had livestock, and they supplied soldiers in times of war (1 Chron. 12:26). Their true inheritance, however, was not material but spiritual in nature. They were dispersed in Israel to teach God's Word to the nation. They also had to take turns assisting the priests in the Tabernacle and later in the temple.

God had reminded Moses several times about the cities of refuge (Ex. 21:13, Num. 35:6, Deut. 4:42). The justice system of the time made provision to punish murder with the death sentence. A family member of the murdered person could act as avenger and kill the murderer. However, God knew that accidents do happen. In His mercy, God provided clemency for unintentional manslaughter.

A person who caused someone's death without premeditation could flee to a city of refuge. There were three such cities east of Jordan and three west of it. These cities were appointed in such a way that any one of them could easily be reached from any part of the country. God's mercy was close.

The elders of the city of refuge had to hear the case, weigh the evidence, and decide if the fleeing person was guilty of murder or manslaughter. If the verdict was in the person's favor, he could stay in the city of refuge. As long as he stayed there, the avenger was not allowed to kill him, but if he left the city of refuge, the avenger had the right to kill him. These rules would be applied until the high priest's death. Then the person who caused death by accident was free. For the time of his stay in the city of refuge, he would be subject to the teaching of the Levites there.

All sinners deserve the death penalty (Gen. 2:17), but God provided a refuge for us in His Son. Christ is our city of refuge. In His protection, we are safe. If we move out of His protection, we are exposed to the attack of the avenger, Satan. Jesus is not only the city of refuge but also the unique High Priest. When we accept Him as personal Savior, His death sets us free from the avenger.

A clinic for addicts near Cape Town was named after one of these cities, Ramoth, which means "peaks." The clinic is a refuge for addicts; with the help of the clinic, patients may reach new peaks in their lives, and the death of Christ can set them free. This should be true of every church.

A prayer: Lord, under Your protection, I am safe.
A thought: Do I stay in my refuge or wander off to dangerous places?

111. Mission Accomplished
The trans-Jordanian tribes return to their land.

When the tribes of Reuben, Gad and Manasseh had asked Moses to give them land east of Jordan, Moses made them promise that their soldiers would assist the rest of Israel conquering the Promised Land west of Jordan. They had fulfilled their promise over many years, and now that the land had been conquered, they could return to their

| April 20 |
| ~~~ |
| Joshua 22 |

inheritance. The Bible does not tell us how they managed to stay away from their homes for many years. Maybe they had a revolving system that allowed some to return home for certain periods while the others kept on fighting. Now that the job had been done, they could all go home.

God had also kept His promise to give Canaan to the descendants of Abraham, Isaac, and Jacob. Israel had not taken possession of every square mile yet, but for all practical purposes, they were in control of the country.

The Bible takes promises seriously. Whether it is God's promises to us, our promises to Him, or our promises to one another—promises have to be kept as sacred agreements. What has happened to our promises when we became adult members of a church, or when we got married, or when we baptized a child, or when we became citizens of a country, or when we comforted a friend in need? Have we kept our promises and stayed a friend in deed? Do we feel and show gratitude for the fulfilled promises of God and for those of our friends?

When the trans-Jordanian tribes had fulfilled their promise and returned home, they were afraid that their loyalty would soon be forgotten and that eventually they would not be seen as part of Israel any more. The river Jordan looked like a line of division to them that could easily become a border of estrangement. To confirm their unity with the rest of Israel, they built an altar on the eastern banks of the Jordan.

It was completely misunderstood by the other tribes. They thought the trans-Jordanian tribes were seceding from Israel and from the central worship at the Tabernacle. They prepared for war, but first they sent a delegation to make sure their perception was correct. When the tribes east of Jordan assured them that the altar was only a symbol of unity with Israel and that no sacrifices would be brought on the altar, peace was restored.

This incident shows how easily different perceptions can lead to misunderstandings. Instead of acting on our perceptions as if they are infallible, it is wiser to get more information first in order to make an informed decision.

A prayer: Lord, help us to deliver on promises, as You do.
A thought: Do I make informed decisions, or do I act impulsively?

112. Joshua's Farewell Address

As for me and my house, we will serve the LORD.

April 21

~ ~ ~

Joshua 23-24

When Joshua was a hundred and ten years old, he knew that his death was near. He first summoned the leaders of the nation to him to hear his last will. He admonished them to stay true to their God, Yahveh, and to proceed to drive out the remaining Canaanites. He stressed that they should not mix with these nations socially or religiously, lest they became a snare to Israel. If they remained faithful to God, they would be richly blessed. If they strayed from God, they would be harshly punished.

Probably the leaders felt that this important message should be heard by as many ordinary citizens as possible. The people assembled at Shechem where the blessings and curses of Moses had been recited by the twelve tribes shortly after entering the Promised Land (Deut. 27:12-13, Josh. 8:33).

Joshua reminded the nation of their history: how Yahveh had called Abram out of idol worshipers; how God had revealed Himself to the patriarchs; and how God had shown His power and mercy to Israel and to the nations by the plagues in Egypt, by the miracles in the desert, and by the conquering of the Promised Land. God had made their victories easy by putting fear into the hearts of the enemy and by tormenting them with hornets. In the light of God's record, Israel had to decide who they wanted to worship—the true God who had carried them thus far or the idols of the nations who had fled before them.

When he put this choice before Israel, Joshua added his personal testimony, which has become a banner in many Christian homes: *"But as for me and my house, we will serve the LORD."* LORD with capital letters in the Bible always means Yahveh, the God of Abraham, Isaac, Jacob, and Moses (Ex. 6:2-8). Joshua identified himself and his family completely with the LORD. Nobody is neutral to the one true God, Yahveh, who is Creator of the universe and Savior of His people. One stands either with Him or against Him. Those who refuse to make a choice for Him are seen by the Bible as being against Him.

The nation followed Joshua's example. Although some of them would stray repeatedly, God would always keep a remnant true to Him (1 Kings 19:18). The book started off with Joshua, *"Moses' assistant,"* but ends with Joshua, *"the servant of the LORD,"* the same title used for Moses (1:1). Like Moses, Joshua had completed his last effort to keep Israel on track. He laid down his head in peace, knowing that his mission had been accomplished.

A prayer: As for me and my house, we will serve the LORD.
A thought: Do I plead enough with my people to stand with the LORD?

113. Sliding Back
The new generation does not know the LORD.

In the first few chapters of Judges, the author moves back and forth in history before and after the death of Joshua. God had told Moses that the conquering of the Promised Land would be gradual (Ex. 23:29-30, Deut. 7:22) so that the sudden removal of all inhabitants would not create a vacuum in which wild animals would multiply and become a safety hazard.

April 22
~ ~ ~
Judges 1 - 3

The remaining pockets of enemy land were thus acceptable in the early years of the conquest, but as time went by, it became disobedience to the command of God to wipe out the inhabitants because of their idolatry and sinful lifestyles. To the sin of neglect was then added the sin of deed: Israel started to assimilate with the remaining Canaanites by intermarriage and by the blending of religions—the very thing God had prohibited through Moses and Joshua (Deut. 7:1-5, Josh. 23:12-13).

God even sent His Angel, maybe in the form of the Commander who had appeared to Joshua at Jericho (Josh. 5:14), to remind the nation of their task and to motivate them to obey the LORD.

Sadly, it had to be recorded that most of the tribes west of Jordan did not finish the job, leaving Canaanites in their midst. They used them as laborers at first, but later they became in-laws and fellow worshipers of idols. Eventually, the tables were turned and Israel's former servants became their oppressors. It was God's punishment for Israel's unfaithfulness.

When the nation cried out to God for help, He inspired a judge to throw off the yoke of the enemy, to reinstitute worship of the true God, and to govern the nation for several decades. In the book of Judges, this cycle is repeated like a refrain as it describes the contributions of twelve judges over a period of about three hundred years.

God included material in the Bible that is essential for the edification of believers (1 Cor. 10:11). Israel's history is an object lesson about the trials, tribulations, and victories of believers. Christians too often suffer backslides for taking halfway measures in their sanctification. Paul said we have to "work out" our salvation with fear and trembling (Phil. 2:12). We cannot save ourselves, but we have to apply to our daily lives the free salvation we have received. We have to conquer those pockets of resistance. The more we surrender of our lives to God, the more we are filled with His Spirit. The fruit of the Spirit is genuine love for God and for His creation, including human beings, animals, and nature (1 Cor. 12-13, Rom. 5:5, Gal. 5:22).

A prayer: Lord, inspire me to conquer those pockets of resistance in my life.
A thought: Do I fight Satan steadfastly, or do I play games with him?

114. Mighty Man of God
Othniel connects past and present.

April 23
~ ~ ~
Judges 3

The first foreign power that conquered Israel was from Mesopotamia, the region from which Abram had come and to which Israel would later go into exile. There was a strong message in this affliction about their origin and their destiny. If they strayed from God, they would lose the Promised Land and become slaves in their country of origin.

After Israel had been oppressed for eight years, God's medicine took effect: They cried out to the LORD, Yahveh. He inspired Othniel, son of Kenaz, Caleb's younger brother, to judge and liberate them. He first judged them; that is, he first led them to repentance, forgiveness, and reform. They had to be purged from the inside before they could be delivered from the outside. When they were reconciled with the LORD, He inspired them to throw off the yoke of the enemy. This first reform lasted forty years.

Othniel linked the old era with the new. As a young man in Joshua's army, he helped his uncle, Caleb, to conquer the city Debir and thus won Caleb's daughter, Achsah, as wife (Josh. 15:15-19). She urged Othniel to ask her father for fountains, but apparently Othniel was a doer and not a talker so Achsah had to ask her father for the favor herself. This incident is repeated in the book of Judges (1:12-15). However, when the Spirit of the LORD came on Othniel, he judged Israel for forty years, which would have included a lot of listening and talking. When God calls you for a special task, He will enable you to do it.

The book of Judges states that the new generation did not know the LORD, and they did not know war (2:10, 3:2). As a survivor of the old generation, Othniel did know war, and he did know the mighty works of God. In his position as inspired judge of Israel, he could teach the new generation from his own experience. Senior citizens may retire from occupations, but they should never retire from the task of sharing their experience with the new generation. Their integrity as persons is as important as their knowledge and experience.

Through the ages there was always a generation gap, a tug of war, between views of the past and views of the present. Some people want to hang on to the "good old days" while failing to meet new challenges; others discard the proven methods of the past too easily while they don't know yet if the new approaches will stand the test of time. Othniel lived up to his name, "Mighty Man of God," by trusting God and using the good of the past as foundation to build on in the present to secure a better future.

A prayer: God, inspire me to fulfill my task for my generation.
A thought: How do I reconcile the good of past and present?

115. A Man with a Plan
Ehud prepares for victory.

When Israel slid back into idolatry after Othniel's death, God disciplined them with eighteen years of Moabite rule. On their way to the Promised Land, God had forbidden Israel to attack Moab, although Moab had refused them passage through their land. The bad blood

| April 24 |
| ~ ~ ~ |
| Judges 3:12-30 |

between the two nations peaked during Moab's dominance over Israel.

Eventually Israel got the message again and repented. This time God called Ehud, a left-handed warrior from the tribe of Benjamin (which means "son of the right hand"), to lead them. After he had delivered Israel's tribute to King Eglon of Moab, he sent the rest of the delegation home while he returned to the king, pretending to have a secret message for him.

The obese king was resting in a cool upper room. He ordered everyone out, showing that he knew and trusted Ehud. The hidden dagger on Ehud's right side was not detected by the guards. Ehud's "message from God" was to thrust the eighteen-inch dagger into the king's belly. Fortunately for Ehud, the doomed king didn't utter a sound. Ehud's escape showed his acquaintance with the layout of the building and the customs of the king. By the time the guards realized something was wrong, Ehud was long gone.

While Moab was still reeling from the shocking news about the assassination of their king, Ehud launched a surprise attack by Israelite forces. They took over all the crossings of the Jordan River, thus cutting off all Moabite soldiers on the west side of the Jordan. Moab lost ten thousand men, and Israel was freed from their domination. With this swift campaign led by Ehud, God gave Israel eighty years of rest from their enemies—double the time they had had peace under Othniel. Had they learned their lesson this time ...?

Later many fighters from the tribe of Benjamin were left-handed (Judges 20:16). Was it a characteristic of the tribe, or was it a result of their adoration for Ehud? Like him, they changed their apparent drawback into their forte. From the little we know about Ehud, we get the impression that he first patiently acquainted himself with the enemy and with their setup. When the time was ripe, he acted swiftly and decisively. God can use such people today again to overthrow the enemies of His kingdom.

We must remember, though, that Jesus saved us by giving His life, not by taking someone's life. We have to follow His example (Phil. 2:5, Col. 3:13).

A prayer: Lord, help me to plan wisely and to act decisively.
A thought: How can I turn my drawback into victory?

116. Women of Valor
Deborah and Jael shine in God's victory.

<table>
<tr><td>

April 25

~ ~ ~

Judges 4-5

</td></tr>
</table>

The viewpoint that women could not be leaders in biblical times is not quite true. Scripture tells of many women who influenced history remarkably, some for the better and some for the worse. We have noticed the influence of Eve, Sarah, Hagar, Rebecca, Leah, Rachel, Miriam, and Rahab. Now the names of Deborah and Jael are added to the list.

Deborah was already judging Israel when she and Barak were called by God to free Israel from Canaanite oppression. When Ehud had passed away, Israel started to stray again, the lessons of the past forgotten. This time God disciplined them with an embarrassing situation: Their former servants, the Canaanites, became their rulers. The new regime rebuilt Hazor, the city that Joshua had utterly destroyed (Josh. 11). From this fortified city, the Canaanites oppressed Israel—surely with anger for injustices done to them.

When Israel eventually admitted their unfaithfulness to God and repented of their sins, Deborah received a message from God that Barak, from the tribe of Naphtali, had to lead Israel to victory over the Canaanites. Instead of putting his trust in God, Barak had more faith in Deborah's presence. She complied with his wish to accompany him but warned him that the honor of the victory would be taken from him and given to a woman.

Barak mustered his ten thousand soldiers at Mount Tabor, and Sisera immediately rushed to them with his nine hundred iron chariots to quench the rebellion. Again Barak apparently hesitated, and Deborah had to spur him on.

As he engaged the impressive army of horses and chariots, God unleashed the awe-inspiring forces of nature against the enemy. A severe thunderstorm disrupted and confused them—some were swept away by the floodwaters and others got stuck in the mud. In those circumstances, the chariots the Canaanites depended on were suddenly worthless. They dismounted and fled on foot. Their general followed their example and splashed along through the mud and rain.

Because of their good relations with the Kenites, Sisera fled to their camp. In normal circumstances, Jael's false hospitality and gruesome killing of Sisera would have been despicable. War changes rules, though. She was hailed as a heroine when Deborah and Barak sang about the dramatic end of Sisera and about the tragic anxiety of his waiting mother. In Genesis 3, God promised that the Seed of the woman would crush the head of the serpent.

A prayer: Lord, make me brave and firm to combat evil.
A thought: In what way can a Christian imitate Jael?

117. Mighty Warrior...?
Gideon has doubts about his calling.

Like the rest of the Bible, the book of Judges places
the spotlight on man's sinfulness, God's salvation, and the
victories that flow from the combination of faith and
mercy. Consequently, Judges says little about the good
times, which were about twice as long as the bad times.

April 26
~~~
Judges 6:1-16

</div>

That does not mean that the book is negative in its focus; on the contrary, it
highlights the gracious redemption God provided to His people when they
repented and turned back to Him.

After another good period of forty years under Deborah's leadership, Israel
slid into the ditch again. This time God used a nation that had been conquered
by Israel shortly before they entered the Promised Land (Num. 31). The
Midianites were apparently nomads who swarmed Israel every year at harvest
time, robbing Israel of their grain, fruit, and livestock. When this enemy
covered the land like locusts, Israel hid in the mountains to escape the
plundering. After seven years, Israel cried out to God to forgive and to redeem
them. God first sent a prophet to remind them of all God's mighty works in
the past and to scold them for their unfaithfulness. God wanted a change of
heart before He would give political and material relief.

When they were ready, God sent His angel to call and prepare a leader for
them. When the angel greeted him with the words *"The LORD is with you,
mighty warrior"* (NIV), Gideon did not know what to make of it. Gideon did not
even bother to react to the "mighty warrior" part, probably thinking it was
sarcasm, for here he was—threshing a small amount of wheat in the winepress
for fear of the enemy. He did voice his skepticism, though, to the words, "The
LORD is with you." For goodness sakes, how could the LORD be with them if it
was going so badly? He did not realize how close the LORD was at that
moment.

As we have seen before, when God appeared in human form He was called
the Angel of the LORD (Ex. 3). Verse 14 states, *"the LORD turned to Gideon"* and
looked at him in a way that sent chills down Gideon's spine. Then God gave
him the firm command, *"Go in this might of yours, and you shall save Israel from the
hand of the Midianites. Have I not sent you?"*

Like Moses at the burning bush (Ex. 3), Gideon was intensely aware of his
inadequacy for such a task and tried to use it as an excuse to back out of this
assignment. God swept his argument away with the fact that God Himself
would go with him. Yahveh had mercy on His people again.

A prayer: Lord, with You on my side I will be successful.
A thought: What are my excuses when God gives me a task?

118. Searching for Reassurance
Gideon needs signs to support his faith.

<table>
<tr><td>April 27
~~~
Judges 6:17-38</td></tr>
</table>

When Gideon got the impression that the person he was talking to was more than a man, he asked for a sign to confirm his impression. He also wanted to bring an offering, a request that was graciously granted. For someone who was short on food, Gideon's offering was quite lavish. God used his generous offering to give him the sign he had asked for. The angel made fire emerge from a rock, consuming the offering in a second. When the angel disappeared, Gideon realized with awe that he had seen the Angel of the LORD. He thought he would die. God reassured him not to fear.

Gideon built an altar where the Angel had appeared to him and called the altar "Yahveh Shalom" (LORD of Peace) to celebrate the fact that God wanted to make peace with Gideon and with Israel. To establish peace with God, they had to break with idolatry. They could not serve God and idols. Gideon had to take the lead by destroying the symbols of Baal worship that his father had erected.

He still did not have the confidence to do it in daytime, so he and his helpers did it under cover of darkness. He must have been quite surprised when his father protected him the next day when the enraged townsfolk demanded his head. It was actually another sign that God was fulfilling His promise.

Inspired by God's Spirit, Gideon blew the trumpet to call the nation to combat. Thirty-two thousand men from four tribes answered the call and assembled near the valley of Jezreel where the enemy was camping amidst their thousands of camels—a noisy, dusty, smelly multitude.

Even at this point, Gideon was still struggling with his faltering faith. He decided to ask God to confirm again that He was indeed calling him for this mission. If the fleece was saturated with dew the first night and absolutely dry the second night, he would be sure that he had not misunderstood God. His experiments worked out perfectly, and Gideon had no other choice than to do as God had commanded him.

Gideon's calling reminds us of the calling of Moses (Ex. 3). They were both very unwilling to accept the task the LORD was giving them. Both used every possible excuse they could think of to back out of their mission. God handled both of them patiently but firmly and refused to accept "no" for an answer. When God gives an assignment, no excuse is good enough because the outcome is not dependent on us, but on Him who calls (1 Thess. 5:24).

A prayer: Here I am Lord; use me in the way You see fit.
A thought: How many more signs do I need to convince me of my calling?

119. God plus a Few
are on the winning side.

God had been building Gideon's faith step-by-step, preparing him for a situation that he could not handle without trust in God. Gideon was probably grateful for the 32,000 men who stood with him. Then God ordered the fearful to go home. While Gideon looked at the departing 22,000 with a lump in his throat, God increased the pressure even further by diminishing the remaining ten thousand to three hundred. Amazingly, we hear no complaint from Gideon. He had no other choice than to put all his trust in God alone.

April 28
~ ~ ~
Judges 7-8:21

God had some more faith-boosters in store for Gideon. God sent him and his servant to spy on the Midianites. Gideon's faith was reinforced by what he overheard in the enemy's camp. Someone told his dream to a friend: A loaf of barley bread tumbled down the hill and demolished his tent. His comrade interpreted the dream as an omen about Gideon's victory over them. Gideon right away thanked God for the message. He returned to his small army and prepared them for the onslaught.

Centuries ago, father Abraham also had made a successful night attack with a small force on a mighty army (Gen. 14). Gideon must have thought about that for he had grown up with those stories of the patriarchs.

Suddenly the silence of the night was broken by a nerve-racking noise when three hundred men smashed their clay jars, blew their horns, waved their torches, and shouted their war cry, *"The sword of the LORD and of Gideon!"* The cry affirmed Gideon's trust in God as the real commander of the small force.

The sleeping Midianites awoke with doomsday fear in their hearts. One look at the waving torches convinced them they were being attacked by a large army. In the poor light of the campfires, dimmed by smoke and dust, they could not see well. Thinking that their attackers were already among them, they started to attack each other. Others decided to get out of there while they could, and they fled in panic and in disarray.

Gideon called the forces he had sent home to back him up. A massive pursuit of the fleeing Midianites and Amalekites resulted. Some of their kings and princes were captured and executed. Gideon punished the cities that refused food and water to his army. The man who had started off as an insecure and unwilling leader had grown into a hero with faith and confidence—under the shaping hand of the One who called him.

A prayer: Lord, You can accomplish much with few and with little.
A thought: Am I willing to become a Gideon for the Lord?

120. A Sad Ending
Gideon's life takes a tragic turn.

<table>
<tr><td>

April 29

~ ~ ~

Judges 8:22 -
9:57

</td></tr>
</table>

After Gideon's historic victory, the soldiers wanted to crown him as king. He refused this honor, reminding them that God was their king. "If you want to reward me," Gideon said, "give me the earrings you looted from the enemy." The soldiers eagerly obliged. Gideon used the gold to make a golden ephod, that is, a cloak that was used to seek divine guidance—a continuous need in Gideon's heart.

Gideon had received several signs from God to reassure and to guide him. He wanted to proceed on that road. The ephod was meant to be a tool through which God could guide him.

Though Gideon wanted to serve God, he used a method that was not in line with God's Word. According to the books of Moses and Joshua—the only part of the Bible that existed at that time—God had commanded an ephod to be worn only by the high priest (Ex. 28). Gideon tried to satisfy his spiritual needs by man-made instead of God-given methods. He forgot that God's Spirit never leads us contrary to God's Word.

Whatever good purposes Gideon had in mind with the ephod, the people soon saw it as something with magical powers. When Gideon died after forty years of judging, the nation soon resumed their worship of idols.

It went from bad to worse. Gideon's son, Abimelech, who was born out of wedlock, murdered Gideon's seventy sons, except for one, and made himself king in Shechem. His only surviving brother, Jotham, warned the people of Shechem with a parable that they and Abimelech would devour each other.

After Abimelech had ruled for three years, God stirred up ill will between the people of Shechem and their king. Abimelech quenched the rebellion in a cruel way, killing most of the inhabitants by the sword and burning the rest alive in a tower. When Abimelech tried to do the same to the people of Thebez, ten miles northeast of Shechem, a woman killed him by dropping a millstone from the tower on Abimelech's head.

This sad piece of history could have been prevented if Gideon had not fathered this son with a woman he did not want to marry. He already had many wives, so one more wouldn't have mattered. Choices have consequences, and often we pay dearly for wrong choices. Tragically, the man who tried so hard to make right choices eventually made many others suffer because of a few wrong choices he made after his moment of glory.

A prayer: Lord, help me to keep up my guard against evil.
A thought: Do I rest on my laurels?

121. From Disgrace to Honor
Jephthah survives in extreme conditions.

Like Abimelech, Jephthah started his life on the wrong foot—born from a harlot and rejected by his father's family. Such children can't be blamed for the mistakes of their parents, but their own choices in life determine their destiny. Abimelech was destroyed by the life he had chosen. Initially, Jephthah headed in the same direction.

April 30
~ ~ ~
Judg. 10:6-
12:7

Driven out by his half-brothers, he went abroad and became a gang-leader. The kind of followers he assembled showed that they lived by the sword, either raiding others for their own gain or serving as mercenaries. Jephthah could thus act out his anger for the injustice done to him. He made a name for himself as a brave leader and a shrewd strategist.

Israel had been straying again, and this time God punished them by the Ammonites. The consequences of their sin made them cry to God for help. This time God refused their plea. He sent them back to their idols for help. Israel discarded all their idols and waited in humility for God's grace.

Eventually, Yahveh had pity on them and mustered them for war against Ammon. The soldiers checked in, but—there was no leader! The only person who could lead them in battle was in exile. They swallowed their pride and send a delegation of elders to Jephthah.

The bandit now proved himself to be an excellent negotiator too. He discussed problems and solutions before he went into action. He got the elders to admit the wrong done to him. Then he got them to agree to make him their leader after the enemy had been destroyed.

Then Jephthah negotiated with the Ammonites, giving them a lesson in history. The land they claimed had been given to Israel three hundred years ago by God. They took possession of the land in a war that was started by their enemies. According to the custom of the day, that land then belonged to Israel. The Ammonites did not agree with Jephthah's reasoning, so the war between the two nations started with disastrous results for the Ammonites.

When the tribe of Ephraim criticized Jephthah excluding them, he negotiated with them before punishing them harshly for their stubborn opposition. Unfortunately, Jephthah also bargained with God before the war with Ammon, making a dangerous promise if God would grant him victory. His daughter honored her father's vow. Human sacrifice was forbidden, so we can assume she never married and dedicated her life to God's service.

A prayer: Lord, I make Psalm 139:23-24 my prayer for today.
A thought: Do I discuss problems and solutions before I act?

122. The Order of the Ordinary
The 'small' judges do a great job.

May 1

~ ~ ~

Judges 3:31,
5:6, 10:1-5,
12:8-15

Jephthah was preceded and followed by the so called "small" judges. Little was recorded about Shamgar, Tola, Jair, Ibzan, Elon, and Abdon except for their names, the tribes they belonged to, and the number of years they judged. Unlike the other judges, they did not liberate Israel from an oppressor.

Although Shamgar killed six hundred Philistines with a stick, he did not throw off their yoke completely because in his time, the highways were still deserted (Judges 5:6). About Jair, Ibzan, and Abdon, the number of their children and their donkeys is recorded. One may ask: Is that all you can tell me about them?

The "small" judges have a message about the ordinary people and leaders of all times. Like most of us, they did their work, fulfilling their duties faithfully, but never did anything so extraordinary that they were acknowledged in history books. And yet, these ordinary people and leaders are the backbone of society, the salt of the earth, and the light of the world.

This fact of life could also be noticed among the disciples of Jesus. We hear often of Peter, John, and James. A few times Andrew, Matthew, Philip, and Thomas are mentioned. Judas became the notorious traitor. But from the other four, we know little more than their names. And yet, they were there all the time, witnessing what Jesus said and did and spreading the good news to all nations after Pentecost. The same goes for all the unnamed people who were helped by Jesus: a blind or deaf person, someone with an evil spirit, a woman with blood flowing, a mourning widow, and a centurion with a sick servant.

The "small" judges encourage us to do our small but important part in family, church, and workplace. Daily contributions of ordinary people may not be important for history, but they are vitally important for their own time. The input of parents for their children, teachers for their students, pastors for their parishes, and workers for the economy all help shape a healthy society where all members can flourish. If we do our share properly, the next generation can build their future on the foundation we have laid.

The all-seeing Eye will notice, and the all-knowing Mind will remember. One day we will hear from His lips the most beautiful of all acknowledgments: "Well done, good and faithful servant; you have been faithful over a few things, I will make you ruler over many things. Enter into the joy of your Lord."

A prayer: Lord, help me to do my part in a way that will please You.
A thought: Do I serve for external recognition or internal satisfaction?

123. The Playful Strongman
Samson's incredible feats

Samson and John the Baptist were both born from
childless parents after an angel had announced their birth.
Both had to stay Nazirites for all their lives (82). Both were
killed in a tragic way. The difference between them was that
John remained faithful to God till the end, while Samson
played with sin repeatedly.

<table><tr><td>May 2
~ ~ ~
Judg. 13:1-
15:8</td></tr></table>

When Samson became interested in the opposite sex, he
preferred Philistine girls. As it was against the Law, his parents objected, but
the Bible says that God allowed that in order to create confrontation with
Israel's oppressors. Eventually he and his parents journeyed to Timnah, a
Philistine town, to set up betrothal with the girl he had fallen in love with. On
the way Samson turned off into the bushes. Suddenly facing a charging young
lion, he wrestled the predator to the ground and ripped it apart with his bare
hands. Apparently he walked off without a scratch and proceeded with his
parents as if nothing had happened, keeping the secret to himself.

Some months later during the wedding feast, Samson, the boisterous
bridegroom, challenged his friends with a riddle as part of the fun. The riddle
was about the honey he got from the lions carcass, but he formulated it in a
mysterious way to conceal the answer even more. While he enjoyed the
puzzling faces of his friends, as well as all their wild guesses, he was also
plagued by his bride to reveal the answer to her, not knowing that she was
being blackmailed by his friends. Blindly in love, he eventually revealed the
answer to her. To his utter dismay, he discovered that she betrayed him. He
had lost the bet and had to give thirty suits for his friends. He went in anger to
a Philistine town, killed thirty men, and took their clothes to pay his debt.

Disgusted by his bride's disloyalty, he returned home without her. When
his anger had subsided, he paid his "wife" a visit, only to find that she was now
married to his best man! The playful strongman then engaged in a costly
mischief. He took the time to trap three hundred foxes, tied them up two by
two at the tails, fixed a burning torch to their tails, and then set them loose in
the ripe grain fields of the Philistines, thus destroying their annual food supply.

Now the game had become deadly serious. The Philistines avenged their
losses by burning his ex-wife and her family to death in their home. Samson
reacted with a fierce assault on the culprits, most likely leaving many maimed
or dead. For the Philistines, he was now enemy number one.

A prayer: Lord, help me to use Your gifts to Your glory.
A thought: Do I use my talents to serve God or myself?

124. Playing with Fire
Samson moves ever closer to danger.

<table>
<tr><td>

May 3

~ ~ ~

Judg. 15:8-
16:14

</td><td>

Samson realized that his relationship with the Philistines had turned sour, so he withdrew and lived in a cave at Etam. If he had taken the time to think about the way he had used his special gift, he would have realized that he had been playing with fire. Deep inside he knew that his strength was God-given and that it was linked to his Nazirite lifestyle. Yet he willfully exposed himself to

</td></tr>
</table>

situations that threatened his status as being set aside for God.

Nazirites had to avoid corpses and carcasses, but Samson ate honey from the lion's carcass—that's why he didn't tell his parents where the honey came from. Marrying or even socializing with someone from a foreign culture was forbidden by law, but Samson sought the intimate company of one Philistine girl after the other. He killed thirty Philistines and robbed their corpses of their clothes, another violation of his Nazirite vows.

His playing with fire reached a dangerous level when he caused the Philistines considerable agricultural losses by setting their grain on fire with the help of foxes. He played with evil fire when he slept with Philistine prostitutes, not only defiling him physically and morally, but also putting his life in grave danger. On one such occasion, he escaped during the night by pulling the town gates from their hinges and dumping them on a nearby hill. This contempt for his enemies made him increasingly vulnerable.

Samson put his life in jeopardy again when he allowed his own people to bind him and hand him over to the enemy. Someone could have put a spear through his heart! Just in time, he broke the ropes, grabbed a jawbone from a donkey's remains, and crushed the skulls of a thousand Philistines with this simple weapon. In his thirst and exhaustion, he cried out to God, who opened a fountain for him. The invincible was vulnerable after all.

Long before Samson met Delilah, he had already begun his fatal slide to self-destruction. However, even Delilah would not have subdued Samson without his own help. As she kept on fishing for the secret of his strength day after day, Samson should have seen the real reason. Delilah herself gave him the clue repeatedly: *"The Philistines are upon you, Samson!"* Every time when he woke up, there the guards were, ready to grab him!

He took an extreme risk when he told Delilah to weave his hair into the web of the loom. His hair? He was coming awfully close to the real secret.

A prayer: Holy Spirit, open my eyes to self-deceit.
A thought: In what ways have I played with "fire"?

125. The Tragic End of a Gifted Person
Samson loses his sight, freedom, and life.

The game Samson and Delilah played with each other was intriguing but dangerous. Like two self-confident spies of two opposing countries, they thought they could separate their private pleasures from their political duties. They made physical love to each other while hating each other's country.

May 4

~ ~ ~

Judges 16 - 17

Then Delilah was bribed by her countrymen to use her love affair with Samson to bring about his downfall. Samson still thought they could have fun without putting themselves or their countries at risk. While Delilah kept on pressing for his secret, Samson's self-confidence kept growing. Probably he thought, "Maybe my strength is not linked to my hair. Maybe my parents made up the story to make me comply with the rules."

In his over-confidence, he eventually shared his secret with his callous lover. This time he woke up to a rude reality. He thought, "I will free myself as before." Instead he ended up as a blind, powerless slave, pushing a millstone in an endless circle in prison. The shock to his body and soul was terrible. The throbbing pain in his forehead and the constant darkness reminded him that it was not a passing nightmare but a horrible, permanent reality. His dismal future as a blind slave in a Philistine prison pushed him into hopeless depression. His remorse toward the One he had failed made him long for death.

This tragic history became a metaphor of the sinner's fatal attraction for sin, as a moth is attracted to a flame. In overconfidence, the sinner thinks, "I will save myself." God says, "No, you can't. Only I can save you. Come to Me and exchange the heavy yoke of Satan for the light yoke of Jesus."

Samson's suffering drove him back to God. He is mentioned in the gallery of great believers (Hebrews 11). Like many others before and after him, he learned that we have to be broken before we can be made whole.

When God relieved him from his misery, He also granted him the greatest victory of his life. The Bible ended Samson's story with the note that *"he had judged Israel twenty years."* It brings long-term perspective over his career. Samson's life consisted of much more than the few anecdotes recorded in the book of Judges. The long good times when nothing extraordinary happened are skipped. The focus is placed on the lessons God wants to teach us. However, the short note on his long ministry puts everything into perspective. Likewise, we too can make meaningful contributions in spite of our shortcomings.

A prayer: Lord, keep my eyes open for Satan's traps.
A thought: I want to proceed with my life without Samson-mistakes.

126. When Whims Go Wrong
All do as they want.

<table>
<tr><td>
May 5

~ ~ ~

Judges 17-21
</td></tr>
</table>

The book of Judges ends with two stories that illustrate the whimsical attitude of the time. The first story shows how easily some Israelites replaced God's Word with their own religion. A man named Micah stole his mother's money. She cursed the thief, unaware it was her son. Fearing the curse may come true, Micah admitted his guilt and returned the money. In an effort to cancel the curse, his mother used some of the money to make two idols and an "ephod" or cloak. When a wandering Levite visited them, Micah hired him as his personal priest.

The tribe of Dan could not drive the Canaanites from their territory, so they searched for a place that was easier to conquer. When they migrated to the north of Israel, they grabbed Micah's idols and priest and started their own religion. Apparently the tribe of Dan never returned to the worship God prescribed to Israel through Moses. In the last book of the Bible, Dan is not mentioned as one of the tribes (Rev. 7).

The second story describes the gross immorality and cruel violence that occurred in that time. An unfaithful concubine fled to her parents. After a few months, her husband visited her. He feasted with her father before he brought her back. On the return journey, he slept over in a Benjaminite town. When the men of the town demanded to practice sodomy with him, he gave them his concubine to save his own skin. After she had been raped and abused all night, she died and they dumped her body at the house where her husband was.

In anger, he cut her body into twelve pieces and sent one piece to each tribe with the facts about the tragedy. It shocked the nation to such an extent that they mustered their soldiers against Benjamin and demanded that they hand over the culprits. When Benjamin refused, the war started.

Because Israel wanted to punish Benjamin in self-righteous arrogance, God let them suffer defeat. When they turned to the Lord with all their hearts, they won the battle but almost wiped out the foolhardy Benjaminites. Realizing they had gone too far, they had to resort to further violence to find wives for the six hundred men from Benjamin who survived the ordeal.

Both stories show that man-made rules do not work for religion, for morals, or for law and order. Too often hidden agendas and political gains jeopardize the best options. Man needs the compass of God's Word, the objective norm that is not swayed by man's subjective motives.

A prayer: God, keep our law and order in line with Your Word.
A thought: Are my actions directed by whims or by God's Word?

127. Preference and Providence
They emigrate and take foreign wives.

From the national and religious viewpoints, it was treacherous for an Israelite family to move to a neighbor country. Although the patriarchs roamed as foreigners in the Middle East, the situation changed when God gave the Promised Land to Israel. Then Canaan was their God-given inheritance, and they had to stay loyal to their God and their country.

| May 6 |
| ~~~ |
| Ruth 1:1-5 |

In those days, gods and country were closely linked. Moving to another country was equal to moving to the gods of that country. When Elimelech (*My God is king*) left Bethlehem (*house of bread*), he denounced both names by seeking bread from the god of Moab because his God had not provided bread in Israel. One mistake led to another. When his sons married Moabite women, the planned short visit became an unforeseen long stay.

Most likely, Elimelech and his family were forced by Moabite law to attend human sacrifices to their idols. Often the victims were small children. Every time they unwillingly attended such a senseless public killing, they got sick in the stomach and sad in the heart. "What are we doing in a place like this?" they asked themselves. However, these horrible scenes were later overshadowed by the personal grief of death in the family. As she stood at the graves of her husband and sons, Naomi wondered if they had been punished for coming to Moab. Their dreams had turned into nightmares.

From God's viewpoint, the move to Moab resulted from lack of faith, and it exposed them to pagan worship. Nevertheless, Yahveh would weave it into His plan of salvation by bringing Ruth into the ancestry of the Messiah. Satan removed a family from the holy lineage; God replaced it with another.

Emigration is tough. Anxiety about the future is mixed with grief about the losses of the past. The culture shock in the new country—with foreign values, customs, rules, and language—makes immigrants feel alien and aggravates their yearning for the old country. Today the pain of immigration is alleviated by **protections** (like freedom of religion, social security, and health care) and by **contacts** (with expatriates, new friends, and family by visits, phone, and e-mail). When one realizes that the whole earth belongs to the LORD (Ps. 24:1) one can worship the true God anywhere in truth and in spirit (John 4:23-24).

As we try to steer our lives according to *our* goals, God is using the good and the bad in our lives to bring us to the place *He* has prepared for us.

A prayer: God, keep me on the course You have in mind for me.
A thought: Do I ask God to direct my path, and do I obey?

128. Loyal unto Death
Your God is my God.

May 7
~ ~ ~
Ruth 1:6-18

The three widows persevered in the same small house every day. They knew each other's sorrows and struggles. Realizing their words did not really comfort, they supported each other with gestures and favors. Although Naomi felt that God had brought much bitterness into her life, she kept clinging to Him. After she had lost her husband and two sons, there was no one else to cling to.

When the night was at its darkest, the Morning Star rose. Naomi got the news that the drought in Israel had been broken. The harvests were promising. She decided to swallow her pride, return to her hometown, and admit that their emigration to Moab was a total disaster. When she shared her plans with her daughters-in-law, Orpah and Ruth, they decided to go with her. Having been married to Hebrew men, their future in Moab was bleak in any case.

Naomi must have been somewhat at a loss about this reaction. She allowed them to accompany her while she searched her heart and mind for the words to handle the situation. She did not expect a hearty welcome for herself in Bethlehem—but how would people react if she brought two Moabite widows with her? When they approached the border, they rested for a while, and Naomi spoke her mind while her eyes swam in tears.

She thanked Ruth and Orpah for their love and support, urging them to return to their land and culture. When this argument did not convince them, Naomi shifted to a personal and practical level: their chance for remarriage. Time was against them. Naomi was too old to have more sons, and even if she could, Orpah and Ruth could not wait for them to grow up. Orpah realized the truth of Naomi's words, kissed her farewell, and turned back.

But Ruth would not give in. When Naomi encouraged her to follow Orpah's example and return to her people and her gods, it brought Ruth to profess her loyalty to Naomi, her people, and her God: *"Wherever you go, I will go; and wherever you lodge, I will lodge; your people shall be my people, and your God, my God. Where you die, I will die, and there I will be buried."* Faithful unto death.

Naomi could not argue with Ruth's devotion. They looked into each other's eyes with genuine love, hugged, and proceeded on the long uphill road from the Jordan valley to Bethlehem. Although Naomi appreciated Ruth's loyalty, she had no idea about the exhilarating events ahead of them. The flickering Morning Star would be followed by a brilliant dawn.

A prayer: Lord, I want to be loyal to You unto death.
A thought: Am I loyal to family, friends, and God?

129. Call Me Mara
Views determine attitudes and actions.

Naomi and Ruth moved slowly with their pack-donkey through the little town of Bethlehem. To the one, the scene was nostalgically familiar; to the other, it was scarily foreign. After some second looks, Naomi and the townsfolk began to recognize each other. They greeted with exclamations of excitement and amazement. Then Naomi was showered with questions about her family and their experiences. In the process, Ruth was introduced, and her support of Naomi adored.

> May 8
> ~ ~ ~
> Ruth 1:19-
> 2:2

Apparently there were no ill feelings about Naomi's moving away ten years ago, only gladness about her present return. After all, who would trample on a poor widow who had gone through so much bereavement? But Naomi could not suppress her ill feelings about those hardships. She would not blame the dead—let them rest in peace. She would not blame herself either, so she put it on God: "Don't call me Naomi, the lovely one, anymore. My skin is wrinkled and my heart is bleeding. Rather call me Mara, the embittered one, for the LORD has over-burdened me with terrible losses." Focused on her personal pain, Naomi didn't notice the many blessings that Yahveh had already sent her way: the broken drought, the safe return, the welcome by old friends, and the loyal support of Ruth, who gave up everything to be with her. And more blessings were coming. We often stare with tearful eyes into the tomb, like Mary Magdalene, unable to recognize the risen Lord behind us who can change our sorrow into jubilation (John 20).

While Naomi and her friends shared and savored stories of the past ten years, Ruth gazed beyond the town to the surrounding hills and valleys. The barley fields were in golden brown attire, ready to be harvested, while the wheat was beginning to change color from green to yellow. It was shortly after the Feast of First Fruits. She got a plan. She had learned from Naomi about the gracious God-given law that farmers should leave some grain on the edges of their fields for the poor. She decided to start gleaning early the next morning. She would be part of the Gentile first fruits.

Naomi's focus on the bad of the past depressed and embittered her, unable to recognize the many mercies of the present. Ruth's focus on the opportunities of the present made her hopeful about the immediate future. Naomi's views and attitudes got her stuck in passive sulking; Ruth's views and attitudes motivated her toward constructive action.

A prayer: Lord, lift up my eyes to see the ripe harvests.
A thought: How do my views influence my attitudes and actions?

130. Faith and Mercy Meet
The industrious Ruth meets the generous Boaz.

May 9
~ ~ ~
Ruth 2:1-17

Naomi returned to her neglected home. When Ruth wanted to go gleaning for the day, Naomi let her go without giving her any directions. Naomi would rather work through her emotional pain by cleaning up after ten years of absence.

Ruth set off without any clear plan in mind. She would test the attitude at each field until she found one where they would accept her. However, in a small town everybody knew everyone else, and news spread fast by gossip. So when she arrived and asked permission to glean, they already knew who she was. Without her knowledge, her goodwill toward Naomi had kindled the goodwill of the local population toward Ruth.

Even more remarkable was the fact that she unknowingly came to glean at the field of Boaz, a relative of Naomi. Strangely, he had not yet come so far as to make up his mind about a wife. The almighty and all-knowing One let the paths of these two unlikely lovers cross in a sweltering barley field.

Even Boaz had heard about Ruth, though he had not met her yet. He enquired about the woman gleaning over there, and his foreman informed him. Boaz assured her safety by giving orders to his workers. He went to her and invited her to keep gleaning on his field. Ruth bowed gratefully and thanked Boaz for his kindness to a stranger. He responded by acclaiming what she had been doing for Naomi, and he expressed his hope that God would reward her.

During lunch break, Boaz extended courtesy to Ruth by offering her some of his food and drink. When she resumed work after a break, Boaz ordered his reapers to let some extra ears of grain fall for Ruth to pick up. Twice he warned them not to harass her. With this help from Boaz, Ruth did well. That evening she went home with several kilograms of barley.

This endearing love story directs our eyes to an even greater love story—the love of Jesus for each believer. As Boaz, the redeemer, was kind and merciful towards Ruth, the foreigner, so Jesus, our Redeemer, is kind and merciful toward us who have been foreigners to His kingdom (Eph. 2:12-13). He wants us to stay on His "field" where we will be protected. He commands his angels to drop some "ears of grain" deliberately for us, but we still have to make the effort to pick them up. At His table, He shares His bread and wine with us, reminding us that He gave His body and blood to save us and to make us children of the heavenly Father. Yahveh reaches out to us through Yehshua His Son.

A prayer: Thank You, my Redeemer, for Your kindness and mercy.
A thought: Do I go to the right field and pick up what God provides?

131. My Redeemer Lives!
Ruth learns about God's merciful Law.

When Ruth arrived home, tired but excited, and showed the results of her hard day's work, Naomi was amazed and curious. With grateful tears, Ruth shared her experience of the day. Naomi's face lit up with a knowing smile. Sensing there was something she did not know, Ruth now became the curious one.

> May 10
> ~ ~ ~
> Ruth 2:18-23

Naomi explained to her the family tree and those parts of God's Law that deal with "redemption" when a family got into trouble and the clan came to their rescue (Lev. 25:25). This law ensured that tribes, clans, and families would not lose their land permanently (pages 78, 97). The Law also provided for family marriages to secure the survival of the family lineage (Deut. 25:5-6). Although Moses had not linked the two—redemption of land and levirate marriages—they probably were linked in the time of the judges.

Within this context, Boaz was a near relative who could both redeem Naomi's land and marry her late son's childless widow. Maybe Ruth looked at Naomi with big, puzzled eyes, and stuttered, "You mean ... uh... Boaz and I ...?" Naomi nodded with a smile.

Ruth followed the advice of Boaz and Naomi to keep gleaning on Boaz's fields in order to prevent harassment by workers on other fields. When the barley harvest was done, she continued gleaning during the wheat harvest as well. As Boaz watched her and talked to her occasionally, God was preparing him for an important decision in his life. He liked her a lot.

In this book, we see the merciful side of God's Law. Even in the time of the judges when cruel injustices sometimes occurred, God's Law protected the less fortunate. They could glean on the edges of the fields, and clan members could act as redeemers to secure land and care for widows. Naomi said God had caused her much bitterness—yet compassion in the book of Ruth contrasts sharply with cruelty in the book of Judges. As they proceeded with their daily work, Yahveh turned sad losses into joyful gains.

Some people only see God's wrath in the Bible and in real life, and they cannot make peace with such a "cruel" God. If they would read the Bible properly and look at life honestly, they would recognize that God showers us with many undeserved blessings. He uses the whip only when people have rejected and insulted Him repeatedly. Even then, Yahveh is quick to forgive if they turn to Him with wholehearted repentance (page 98).

A prayer: God, Your mercies are fresh every morning. (Lamentations 3:22-25).
A thought: Do I rejoice like Ruth and Job that my Redeemer lives? (Job 19:25).

132. The Risk of Faith
Ruth asks Boaz to be her redeemer.

<table>
<tr><td>

May 11

~ ~ ~

Ruth 3

</td><td>

Naomi knew that Boaz shied away from women. When she returned to Bethlehem after ten years of absence, Boaz was amazingly still unmarried. However, the way Boaz interacted with Ruth convinced Naomi that Boaz found Ruth attractive but that he just could not muster the courage to propose to her. Naomi took the role of matchmaker.

</td></tr>
</table>

The sheaves of ripe grain were stacked at the threshing floor. When the wind was right, they spread some sheaves over the floor and let cattle trample it underfoot to release the grain. Then they flung the chaff into the air with winnowing forks so that the wind blew the chaff sideways onto a heap while the grain fell back to the floor from where it was scooped up into containers. In this time, men slept at the threshing floor at night to guard the fruits of their labor. They enjoyed food and wine before they dozed off on their chaff-beds.

Naomi's plan would be tested in this harvest setup. Ruth waited until the men had finished eating and drinking and were fast asleep. As master, Boaz probably slept some distance from the others. Ruth sneaked up to him and crept in under his blanket at his feet. The wine made him sleep deeply, so it was already after midnight when he discovered with a shock—there's a woman at his feet! They whispered their true feelings toward each other.

Ruth risked her reputation by going to Boaz at night and by asking him to be her redeemer. He or an observer might have seen it as an attempt to seduce him. Boaz honored her boldness by praising her support to Naomi, as well as her coming to him first. For her own safety, he let her stay till daybreak. Before the others woke up, he sent her home with as much barley as she could carry. We have a generous Redeemer too.

Arriving home, Ruth excitedly shared the romantic story with her mother-in-law. Naomi was sure that Boaz would address the problem of the other redeemer that very same day. They had taken the risk in faith and hope, and now they had to wait upon the Lord to show the way.

Have you laid yourself down at the feet of your Redeemer? When we come to Jesus and ask Him to save us, there is no risk of being rejected by Him. He promised that whoever comes to Him, He will in no way cast out (John 6:37). The risk of faith for us is when we proclaim Jesus as our Savior and when we change our lifestyle accordingly—then the world may reject us.

A prayer: Lord, help me to take the risks of faith wisely and boldly.
A thought: Do I passively wait for miracles, or do I do my fair share?

133. Servants of the Lord
The survival of the messianic lineage

Being so close to Ruth that night brought Boaz in touch with his real feelings for her. This awakened in him the desire to marry her. He vowed that he would redeem her if the other redeemer would back off. When people started to proceed with their daily activities in Bethlehem that day, Boaz was already at the city gate where the town elders gathered on weekdays to conduct a people's court.

> May 12
> ~ ~ ~
> Ruth 4

At the right moment, the Lord led the other redeemer, as well as ten elders, to the city gate for an important encounter with Boaz. First, he presented the material side of business to them—the redemption of Naomi's property. The other redeemer was quite willing to buy the land, or rather to buy the number of harvests left till the next jubilee year (Lev. 25:15-16).

Knowing his rival's family setup, Boaz then played his trump: The redemption of the land is linked to the levirate marriage—buying the land will include marrying Ruth to provide an heir for her deceased husband. The other redeemer did not see his way open for this aspect of the deal. He gave his sandal to Boaz, thereby symbolizing that he gave up his right of ownership to both the land and the woman. The elders confirmed the contract and wished Boaz a blessed and fruitful marriage.

The cat was now out of the bag, and we can imagine that for several weeks the people of the Ephrathah region talked a lot about this unexpected romance between Bethlehem's shy bachelor and Moab's bold young widow. Everyone attended the wedding feast and showered the couple with their best wishes.

The author of this very human and romantic story could not leave out the fact that young couples celebrate their union by becoming one in body and soul. And from that, of course, usually comes a new generation. Ruth's new friends called the boy Obed, meaning *servant*, because he would not only serve his mother and grandmother, but above all he would also serve the purpose of Yahveh. He was an important link in the messianic chain. He would be the grandfather of king David, and thus a forefather of Jesus, who was also called the "Servant" of the LORD (Isaiah 40:1-4; 53:11).

The bereavement of Naomi and Ruth was blended into God's magnificent painting. The dark shadows in the painting accentuated the colors of the trees and flowers. We can trust the omniscient and omnipotent Artist to blend the good and the bad of our lives into His great plan for us and for His kingdom.

A prayer: Father, I trust You with every aspect of my life.
A thought: Do I yield to the hand of the heavenly Artist?

134. Lonely Pain
Hannah weeps and does not eat.

Hannah bore her burden alone. She could not share her emotional pain with her husband, Elkanah, for he believed he meant more to her than ten sons. She could not share her heartache with Peninnah, her husband's other wife, for Elkanah loved Hannah more, and therefore Peninnah taunted Hannah regularly about her childlessness.

Hannah had lost her appetite for food and her zest for life. As she became increasingly skinny in body and morbid in face, she ran the risk of losing her husband's interest in her—something that would rob her of her only joy. She had prayed daily for years about her deepest need, but nothing happened. Eventually, she decided to ask in a completely unselfish way. If God would grant her a son, she would dedicate him to God's service. She wanted to make this promise to God at the tabernacle in Shiloh.

However, this prayer seems to be selfish too. It reflected only Hannah's wishes and disregarded the wishes of God and her son. Wouldn't they have a say in the matter at all? Maybe Hannah reasoned that the mere birth of her son would prove that God accepted the deal, and then He would work in her son's heart to go along with the idea too.

She eagerly awaited their next visit to Shiloh. When that happened, she slipped away from the sacrificial family meal to say her prayer and make her promise at the entrance of God's house. The high priest, Eli, could not help but notice this unusual worshiper. Not only was she praying at an unusual spot, but praying was the husband's duty, not the wife's. Hannah emptied her heart with emotion before the Lord. It made Eli suspicious.

For the uninvolved Eli, her countenance looked like that of a drunken person. When he addressed her about her conduct, she shared her burden with the old priest. He noticed that her speech was not slurred and that her thoughts were clear. Eli changed his diagnosis and gave her his blessing, hoping that God may grant her what she asked so fervently of Him.

Hannah went back to the family and started to eat—her heart relieved, her burden shared with the pastor of Israel. When she had opened her heart to God and to another human being, the bottled up mixture of hurt and anger was released. In His mercy, God then also opened her tubes, and she conceived. The most appreciated pregnancy is that of the childless. Knowing that it was from God, Hannah did not live in fear but started to work on a song of praise.

A prayer: Lord, help me share my lonely burdens with You and with a friend.
A thought: Do I try to cover up my personal hurt?

135. The Blessing of Giving
Hannah gives her best to God.

While Hannah's time of pregnancy was filled with sincere gratitude and with excited anticipation, those first three years with Samuel must have been pure joy for this fulfilled mother. She wished time could stand still so that she could enjoy her baby as long as possible. She spent quality time with him every day, knowing that he was lent to her by the Lord for a short time.

> May 14
> ~ ~ ~
> 1 Sam. 1:19 -
> 2:11

She did not accompany the family on their annual visit to Shiloh while she was still nursing Samuel. Just to see the tabernacle would tense her up with conflicting emotions. That was the place where she received her son, and that was the place where she would have to part with him also. She pushed all thoughts of their eventual separation out of her mind and enjoyed him fully while she still could.

The three years rolled by like a fleeting thought.

By the time she had to wean Samuel, Hannah could not ignore the inevitable any longer. She began to prepare herself and her child for the separation crisis ahead. How could a mother explain to a three-year-old boy that she was going to leave him at the tabernacle and return home without him? All she could promise him was that she would visit him as often as possible. In His mercy, God must have enabled Samuel to make peace with the idea in his innocent little mind.

Sometimes parents are concerned to leave a child at hospital or school. Separation anxiety in a child can be gradually diminished by opportunities to play with other children under supervision and by slowly increasing the time of the parents' absence. Once children start to enjoy the fun of playing together, realizing they will not be completely abandoned, they do not experience temporary separation from parents as a big problem.

The way the small Samuel reacted to Eli, to God, and to the temple setup made it look as if he was quite at home there. When Hannah gave her best to God, this caring Father took care of her and her son.

As the months and years passed, both of them grew stronger. Both of them experienced the blessing of giving, giving your best, giving yourself, to the One who made you and called you to serve His higher purpose.

As in the case with Ruth, Hannah and Samuel's dark moments turned out to be shadows that accentuated the colors in their life painting. The heavenly Artist was at work in Samuel—to become the last of the judges.

A prayer: Here I am, Lord. I want to give my best and myself for Your kingdom.
A thought: Do I experience the blessing of giving often?

136. Scolding the High Priest
Eli talks, but he does not act.

May 15

~ ~ ~

1 Sam. 2

While Samuel innocently played around in the tabernacle, watching Eli going through his daily routine, the sons of Eli wickedly fooled around with the worshipers and with their sacrifices. They even seduced women on that holy ground. People complained to Eli, and he reprimanded his sons for their evil ways, but he did not enforce the rules. His sons probably made promises, laughed behind his back, and proceeded as usual.

In contrast with the despicable conduct of Eli's sons, the Bible repeatedly stressed that Samuel grew physically and spiritually (verses 11, 18, 21, 26, 35). Every year Hannah made a new robe for Samuel to fit his increased stature. After a few years, Samuel was already of such help to the aging high priest that Eli praised Samuel in presence of his parents. Eli expressed the hope that Hannah would have more children as reward for the one child she had given to God. This wish came true: Hannah eventually had five other children. Yahveh is gracious.

Eli had already been warned by the people about the conduct of his sons. Then God warned him through another "man of God." Preachers and teachers of God's Word should help each other stay on the right path. Eli was first reminded of the history, meaning, and privileges of the priesthood. Then he was scolded for his lax attitude towards the sins of his sons, who brought shame on the priesthood. At last he heard what his punishment would be: His family would be cut off from the priesthood. Eli's sons and their descendants would die young. God would call another priest from another family to minister in God's heavenly tabernacle—a prophecy about the Messiah (Heb. 8:2, 9:11).

A third warning would later come to Eli through the young Samuel. It shows that after each warning, God was waiting for a response from Eli. The wrath of God could have been avoided by an appropriate response from the guilty. Many years later, God announced His wrath over Nineveh through Jonah, but when the people of that city repented, God spared them.

Some say that people can only respond correctly to God's warning if the Holy Spirit enables them to. Could Eli say that he could not react correctly because the Holy Spirit would not help him? Would God warn His high priest and then refuse to help him? No. We stand here before the undeniable fact in God's Word that God's sovereign grace is somehow linked to human responsibility. Let us not presume to be wiser than God.

A prayer: Lord, help me to respond correctly to Your Word.
A thought: Have I blamed God for my own unwillingness?

137. Your Servant Hears
Samuel meets God.

The Bible reports that Samuel's parents had visited him every year and that Eli had been warned by a prophet. After this, several years could have elapsed while God patiently waited for the right response from His priest. Samuel was probably about twelve years old by now, time to become "bar-mitzvah." Although Eli would have taught him to read the Torah, Samuel did not yet know God personally.

May 16
~ ~ ~
1 Sam 3

Eli was the second last judge. As was the case with six other judges (page 122), nothing extraordinary had happened in Eli's life up to this moment—no visions or victories. The one prophecy that had come to Eli was a stern warning about his wicked sons who served as priests. God was now going to speak again, but not to the priests who failed Him.

Apparently Eli slept near the Holy Place of the tabernacle (or "temple" as it was then called), while Samuel slept inside the sanctuary. Each night Samuel dozed off in the dim light of the menorah, a few yards from the Most Holy Place where the ark of the covenant was. One night became unforgettable, not only for Samuel but also for Israel and for the church.

Three times God called Samuel by name, and each time he eagerly ran to Eli, thinking that the ailing old man was in need of something. Twice Eli assured Samuel that he had not called him and sent him back to bed. The third time it dawned on Eli that it might be God who wanted to speak to Samuel, so he told Samuel how to respond when he heard the voice again.

Then something awe-inspiring happened: *"The LORD came and stood there, calling as at the other times, 'Samuel! Samuel!' "* (NIV). Apparently God appeared in visible form, as He had appeared to Moses on the lid of the ark (Num. 12:6-8).

In awe, Samuel did not take the name of God on his lips, but only stuttered, *"Speak, for Your servant hears."* At that moment, the young Samuel became a prophet: receiving God's Word to convey it to others. The first message he received from God was horrifying—the death sentence of Eli and his sons. Hearing the message, Eli realized why God had spoken to his student and not to him. He was rejected already. In spite of his failures, Eli taught Samuel to bow in submission when God spoke.

After this incident, God spoke to Samuel regularly, and he brought God's Word to the people. As he matured, Samuel unified the offices of judge, priest, and prophet in one person, pointing to Jesus, our King, Priest, and Prophet.

A prayer: Speak, Lord, for Your servant is listening.
A thought: Have I mistaken God's voice for the pastor's voice?

138. Man Can't Control God
Without God, the symbols are void.

This chapter shows that none of God's words to Samuel remained unfulfilled. Israel prepared for war against the Philistines without turning to God first. They lost the battle. They searched for the cause of their defeat, but did not look for it in their sins. Instead of repenting, they tried to force God to assist them in battle by taking the ark of the covenant to the battlefield so that *"it may save us."* It? They put their trust in the ark instead of in God.

God gave them the shock of their lives. Again they lost the battle—with many more dead and with their prize religious symbol, the ark, captured by the enemy. God clearly distinguished Himself from His symbols. The ark and all the other elements of the tabernacle had no magic power in themselves. Although ordered and sanctified by God, these symbols were simple man-made objects that had no meaning when separated from God. Centuries later, Israel likewise put their trust in the temple instead of in God (Jer. 7:4), and God allowed the temple to be destroyed to teach Israel once more to trust in Him and not in religious things or activities.

Eli's sons were among the dead, but the old man sort of expected that. However, when he heard that the unthinkable had happened, that the holy ark of God was in the hands of unbelievers, it broke his heart. He fainted, fell from his chair, and broke his neck. His son's pregnant wife was overwhelmed by the one tragedy after the other—her husband and his father killed, the ark robbed from Israel—so she went into labor, and while she was dying, she named the child Ichabod, *no glory*. It probably did not refer to Israel's lack of glory, but to the fact that God's glory had departed from them when the ark was gone.

The focus can so easily shift from the Person we worship to the things we use in worship like the building, the pulpit, the sacraments, the customs, the type of music, and the sign of the cross. When we trust on religious symbols instead of on God, then we are again carrying the ark to the battlefield in the vain hope that it will protect us.

Does a child seek safety with his dad or with dad's hat? Do you seek support with a friend or with his/her chair? In distress, do you seek comfort in a person or in things like food or drugs? The Bible teaches relationship worship. God is our Father and we are His children (John 1:12). Jesus is our Friend (John 15:14) and the Holy Spirit is our Comforter (John 14:16).

A prayer: God, I put my trust in You, not in religious symbols.
A thought: Nothing can take the place of our Father, Friend, and Comforter.

139. Merciful Judgment
They are punished but not totally destroyed.

Now we catch a glimpse of God's merciful humor underneath His holy judgment. The Philistines had the same misconception as the Israelites: They thought the God of Israel was inseparable from the ark of the covenant. They thought that by capturing the ark, they had captured the mighty God who had smitten the

May 18
~ ~ ~
1 Sam. 5 - 7:1

Egyptians centuries before. Within a few days, God scared the living daylights out of them by showing them His absolute control.

They put the ark in front of their god Dagon to show that Dagon had overpowered Yahveh. The next morning the Dagon statue lay face down before the ark, as if in worship. They helped their god up, only to find him in the same position the next day, now with severed head and hands.

Their growing concerns exploded into raw fear when the news started to roll in about a rapidly spreading plague. Their fields were devoured by millions of rats, and the whole population fell ill with a strange disease that could have been caused by the rats. Painful, swollen humps appeared on their faces and bodies, and choking panic spread as they saw this curse on others and felt it on themselves. Suddenly the gloating victors became pathetic victims.

They tried to end the plague by sending the ark from place to place. To their utter dismay, the plague spread wherever the ark went. Mercifully, God did not kill those Philistines who saw or moved the ark, as He would do to unconsecrated Israelites who would dare to see or touch the ark (6:19). God judged them lightly for their ignorance about handling the ark, but He judged them harshly for their arrogance in putting their idols above Yahveh.

After they had suffered for seven months, all through fall and winter, they decided to part with the booty and send it back where it came from. They added peace offerings to the God of Israel: golden replicas of the rats and tumors. They showed their respect by using a new cart, and they proved they were doing the right thing by using cows with newborn calves.

The Levites of Beth Shemesh (Josh. 21:8, 16) were harvesting their wheat when the ark arrived by cow cart. In their joy, they ignored the rules about the ark, and many died. Like the Philistines, they then send this dangerous object to their neighbors. The ark never returned to the Tabernacle. Those who treated the ark with respect were richly blessed. Those who did not paid dearly for their mistake (2 Sam. 6:7, 11).

A prayer: Lord, teach me how to combine joy and respect in my worship.
A thought: I will respect God and His symbols without confusing the two.

140. New Times, New Methods
Samuel's approach to the problems of his time

May 19
~ ~ ~
1 Sam. 7

Circumstances and events before and after Samuel's birth are reported in sensitive detail, but his lifelong service to God is described in just a few vague sentences. That was the case with all the judges: For some, a wonderful victory is recorded; for all of them, little is mentioned about the many years that they judged Israel. That goes for all of us: The billions of people who do their duties every day do not reach the headlines or the history books.

For twenty years after their defeat at Ebenezer, apparently nothing changed in Israel. Before this happened, it was recorded that God spoke to Samuel regularly: *"And the word of Samuel came to all Israel."* (4:1). We can assume that Samuel proceeded with his ministry during those twenty years. The change of heart that Israel experienced after twenty years was most likely the result of Samuel's faithful preaching of God's Word. When Samuel noticed that the nation was being moved by God's Spirit, he urged them to repent of their sins, destroy their idols, and turn to the LORD. This dramatic reform culminated at a mass meeting at Mizpah—not at the ark or Tabernacle. Samuel steered them away from trust in things to trust in God.

Their oppressors, the Philistines, thought it was a rebellion and marched on them with their army. Israel was not prepared for war and sought God's protection. Although Samuel was not a descendant of Aaron, and therefore not a priest, he offered a burnt offering to God at Mizpah and prayed for God's help against the enemy. God answered by creating havoc among the Philistines by means of a severe thunderstorm. Israel used the confusion to deal them a heavy blow, probably with their own weapons that they lost in the chaos.

Samuel erected a stone to mark the victory, and thus he gave a new meaning to Ebenezer: *"Thus far the LORD has helped us."* This sentence became a testimony for many afterward to express their thanks for received blessings. Samuel was not a general, but his intervention encouraged Israel to throw off the Philistine yoke and to recapture their territories and cities.

Samuel ministered to Israel at various cities. He lived at Ramah where he was born and built an altar there. The Philistines had destroyed Shiloh, and the tabernacle had been moved to Nob. Samuel did not try to replace the priests. He concentrated on his own unique role as judge, prophet, and "private" priest, and so he still fulfilled his mother's promise to God—to serve Him all his life.

A prayer: Teach me how to approach the unique problems of my time.
A thought: I will do the seeding faithfully and trust God for the harvest.

141. The Cost of Government
Samuel warns Israel against government spending.

Having described Samuel's career in general, the Bible skips about forty years to the time when Samuel was very old. He asked his sons to help him govern Israel, but their wickedness stained his good name. The lack of central government had probably been discussed by the elders of the cities and towns for many years, but now it came to a point where they were ready to grab the bull by the horns.

May 20
~~~
1 Sam. 8

When they conveyed their ideas to Samuel, he was shocked. He took the matter to God, who told him that he should not take it as a personal insult because the elders were not rejecting Samuel as judge, but God as king. From the time God had led them out of Egypt and formed them into a nation, God Himself had been leading them step-by-step, using leaders He had chosen as His instruments. Their main motivation—to be like other nations—pointed in a dangerous direction. The next step would be to mimic other nations with regard to fashions like idolatry too. Yahveh yearned for their loyal trust and love.

Nevertheless, God was going to grant their request in the same way that He had granted the request of their ancestors in the desert when they had demanded meat. He gave it to them ad nauseam. However, in His mercy, He warned them in advance what they could expect of the king they so dearly desired. They would get much more than they asked for: They would get an expensive government system. The state machinery would gradually expand, and to keep it running, the nation would have to produce the people to do the work and the money to pay the bills.

While the government system would create many jobs, the nation would pay a heavy price in the form of taxes, labor, and lives. In those days kings made war, either to defend or to conquer, and they would use the sons of the nation as pawns on their chessboard.

In spite of many ages of central governments since then, there probably is not a nation on earth today that does not complain about excessive government spending paid for by tax money squeezed from their citizens. If taxes were used for good causes and managed by wise and honest administration, people could abide by that, but all too often the people have to hear that some of their tax dollars went down the drain with little or nothing to show for it.

Many governments pay huge annual interest on debt. When such debt has been paid, much good can be done with the money saved on interest.

A prayer: God, please help our leaders to govern honestly and wisely.
A thought: Am I a wise administrator of the money God gives me?

142. From Donkeys to Kingship
God uses small things to reach His goals.

<table>
<tr><td>May 21
~ ~ ~
1 Sam. 9-10:16</td></tr>
</table>

God granted Israel's request for a king with a touch of humor. He chose a shy person for this esteemed position. To convince Saul of his calling, God used a string of events that could not be ascribed to mere coincidence.

He and his servant searched in vain for his father's lost donkeys. As they decided to return home, it was the servant—not the future king—who got the idea to consult a "seer" who happened to be in a nearby town, and it was the servant who produced the gift for the seer. Maidens on their way to draw water directed them to the seer whose name is not revealed until they meet him face to face—no one less than Samuel himself.

Samuel had already received information and directions from God with regard to this visitor. Saul was treated as the guest of honor by Samuel in the presence of the community leaders. He spent that night as guest at the prophet's house, where a lot of serious talk took place (9:19, 25). The next morning, Samuel anointed Saul secretly as king and sent him off with three predictions, which all came true, to convince Saul that it was God Himself who was calling him to this high responsibility. Yahveh reached out to Saul.

As the signs became a reality, God changed Saul's heart, filled him with His Spirit, and let him prophesy with a group of prophets, probably students of Samuel. The sarcastic remarks of uninvolved observers could not undo what God was doing. When a person becomes a prophet, God is his Father, and his earthly background becomes of secondary importance. When Saul's uncle prompted him about his encounter with Samuel, Saul only referred to the donkeys while he modestly kept his silence about the kingship.

It remains the proven way to seek God's guidance: to look for clues inside and outside. On the inside there must be the growing conviction in the heart, and on the outside there must be provision in the circumstances. When we listen to God's voice in our hearts, He will close the wrong doors and open the right ones at the right time.

As God led Saul (by an unsuccessful search) to meet Samuel, so He led the apostle Paul (by closing several doors) to meet Luke in Troas. At this point, Luke, the author of the book of Acts, started to write in the first person (Acts. 16:6-17). Instead of viewing closed doors as disappointments, we must appreciate them as part of the loving care and guidance by our heavenly Father.

A prayer: Lord, open my eyes for Your guidance.
A thought: Have I hurt others or myself by ramming closed doors?

143. Proven Leadership
God confirms Saul's kingship by lot and victory.

God had revealed His will regarding the future king secretly to Samuel and to Saul. The next step was to reveal it to the nation as well. God knew what their problem would be: Although they wanted a king, they would also be skeptical about a king coming from their own ranks. To combat this social paradox, God confirmed His choice of Saul not only by secret vision and anointing, but also by public lot and victory.

> May 22
> ~ ~ ~
> 1 Sam. 10:17 -
> 11:15

God told Samuel to call the nation to Mizpah, where the king would be appointed by lot. First, they were reminded of how God had saved the nation many times through the ages, from Egypt to the present, and that their demand to move from theocracy to monarchy was not God's will. Then the lot was cast to show the tribe, clan, and family from which the king would come. When Saul noticed how each cast of the lot came closer to him, he could not stand the tension any longer and ran for a place to hide. Maybe he hoped that Samuel had made a mistake and that God would choose someone else. Like Moses and Gideon, he started off as a very modest and hesitant leader.

Once again God's will prevailed in spite of the humorous situation. God not only confirmed His choice of Saul by lot, He also told them where this tall king-to-be was playing hide-and-seek. When they led this big fellow to the stage, almost like a captive, everyone was impressed by his sturdy stature and smiled about his modest attitude. While most shouted, "Long live the king!" some whispered, "My, o my, what a jerk! How can he save us?"

That opportunity came sooner than they had thought. Yahveh used the cruel plan of a heathen king and the desperate cry of a besieged city to give Saul the chance to prove himself to both supporters and opponents. God empowered him with His Spirit to seize the opportunity. With authority, he called the nation to action, and soon an army of three hundred and thirty thousand men stood with him. They delivered their besieged friends in Jabesh, and Samuel called them to Gilgal to celebrate Saul's coronation.

When his supporters wanted revenge on his early opponents, Saul again asserted himself with authority and prevented such a folly. This clemency no doubt won over the goodwill of those who almost had lost their heads. When one's leadership is questioned, it is best to ignore the insult and wait for the opportunity to prove oneself by helping those in need.

A prayer: Lord, empower me to live up to Your expectations.
A thought: Don't despair about Mizpah; wait for Gilgal.

144. Samuel's Farewell Message
He retires as judge but not as prophet.

<table>
<tr><td>May 23
~ ~ ~
1 Sam. 12</td></tr>
</table>

When Saul's kingship was firmly established after his victory over the Ammonites, Samuel formally gave the reins over—from the last judge to the first king. Before he closed the "old book," he made sure there was no outstanding debt. He asked the assembly if he had ever done something they regarded as inappropriate. No one voiced a complaint; instead, loud "no's" went up from the crowd, thereby actually admitting that their demand for a king was not due to any lack on Samuel's side as judge.

By means of a short overview of their history, he showed them how God had provided in their needs, how He had punished them for rebellion, and how He had forgiven and saved them when they had repented. The conclusion was obvious: If you and your king stay true to God, you will prosper; if you don't, you will suffer the same consequences that your ancestors suffered.

To drive his point home, he asked God to send a thunderstorm and rain right in the middle of the dry season. To everyone's amazement, it happened. The storm was so severe that they were overwhelmed with fear, realizing that they had angered God with their request for a king. They asked Samuel to intercede for them and to beg God's forgiveness.

Then Samuel opened the "new book." He reassured them that although the kingship was a bad idea, God would not abandon them as long as they didn't stray from God by adopting the idolatry and lifestyle of other nations. He assured them that he would not stop praying for them and ministering to them. In his eyes, that would be a sin against God: *"Far be it from me that I should sin against the LORD in ceasing to pray for you; but I will teach you the good and the right way."* Although he retired as judge, He did not retire as prophet. Until his death, Samuel would still minister to the people and to their kings.

He concluded his message by admonishing them to serve God out of gratitude for what they had received already: *"Consider what great things He has done for you."* If they would not do that, they and their king would be swept away. Samuel's farewell message was a plea to the nation to serve God with faith, love, and gratitude as faithfully as Samuel himself had done. Like Moses (98) and Joshua (112), Samuel's main wish for his people was that they should fulfill their purpose as the people of God. The plea of these great leaders is as urgent today as in their own time.

A prayer: Lord, I choose Your way, for I need Your presence and Your blessing.
A thought: Do I see it as a sin to stop praying for my nation?

145. Dark Times
for Israel and for their first king

During the forty years or so that had expired since
Ebenezer, the Philistines had gained ground and eventually
had taken control of Israel again. The first task of the new
king was to free Israel from this foreign oppression.
However, the situation was desperate.

> May 24
> ~ ~ ~
> 1 Sam. 13

Saul guarded the Michmash pass with two thousand
men, while his son Jonathan was in charge of a thousand men at Gibeah, a few
miles away. Jonathan was a brave commander with firm faith in God. When he
attacked the enemy garrison, he poked a stick into a beehive. The Philistines
mustered their forces in full strength and marched against the small army of
Israel. Saul called for reinforcements, but Israel was not in the mood for war.

Saul had to evacuate his men from Michmash, withdraw to the east, and
redeploy at Gilgal. His men scattered in all directions—they hid wherever they
could, and some of them even fled over the Jordan to Gilead. The reason was
that they did not have weapons to fight with. The Philistines had gradually and
efficiently disarmed Israel and had taken all blacksmiths hostage so that they
could not start to develop weapons secretly.

The enemy was approaching; his own men were deserting; and to make
the nightmare even worse, the one person who could talk some will into his
soldiers, Samuel, was missing. For seven days Saul waited in vain while the
situation deteriorated rapidly. He just had to do something. Unfortunately, he
made a foolish and an unnecessary decision. He took the role of priest and
brought the burnt offering himself.

He could have kicked off his campaign with a prayer meeting just as well.
For those who are losing the substance of religion, the form becomes more
important. Here we see the first sign of a characteristic in Saul's personality
that would drag him into one trouble after the other. He was inclined to follow
his own common sense rather than God's direction, and he did it in an
impatient and impulsive way. His uncertain self-image also began to use big-
ego defenses to assert himself. His trust in self replaced his trust in God.

Samuel scolded Saul for his presumptuous arrogance and informed him
that this impulsive deed would cost him his kingship. One cannot help but feel
some sympathy for Saul—usually his intentions were good, but he used the
wrong methods to achieve his goals. As time went by, his contact with reality
would gradually decrease and let him make grave mistakes.

A prayer: God, help me to think straight in difficult situations.
A thought: Do I sometimes think I know better than the Bible?

146. A Bad Command
can spoil the victory.

May 25
~ ~ ~
1 Sam. 14

The put-down by Samuel and the desertion by his army made Saul uncertain and indecisive. He joined Jonathan with his last six hundred men. Depressed, he sat beneath a pomegranate tree. When he saw his father like that, Jonathan's faith and bravery urged him to try something on his own.

He believed that God could give victory by few or by many. Abraham and Gideon had overcome strong armies with few men. Jonathan decided, "If the Philistines at the outpost challenge us to climb up to them, then it is a sign that God will give us victory; if not, it shows that God does not want us to attack." Jonathan's trust in God was rewarded. They ascended the rock and prevailed over twenty men. The panic it caused in a nearby Philistine garrison was aggravated by an earthquake. Yahveh was on Jonathan's side.

When Saul's spies reported to him about the commotion among the Philistines, he wasted time, first with a roll call, and then with a religious ceremony that he could not finish. It was obvious that he and his men had to back up his son and take advantage of the confusion in the enemy camp. In the consternation, the Philistines started to fight one another, while others dropped their armor to flee as fast as they could. Their Israelite captives grabbed the fallen swords and spears and helped the small army of Saul and Jonathan to slay the Philistine regiments, who were now in total disarray.

In his zeal to wipe out the Philistine army completely, Saul issued a foolish command: Anybody who ate something before sundown would be killed. He did not want his army to waste precious time with looting and feasting. The downside was that their motivation would soon be paralyzed by their fatigue. If they could have grabbed a snack here and there as they pursued the enemy, they could have kept their momentum until the job was done. Jonathan proved that when he ate some honey, unaware of his father's command.

When the famished soldiers gorged themselves after sunset with meat of animals that had not been slaughtered properly, Saul rectified the situation. He wanted to proceed with the pursuit after the meal, but God would not answer them. Jonathan's inadvertent transgression of Saul's unwise command was exposed. Because he initiated the day's victory by his brave faith, the army bought him free from the death sentence, presumably by offering an animal in his place. The pursuit was called off and a complete victory was missed.

A prayer: God, help me to be wise in my zeal.
A thought: Does my faith make me brave?

147. People-Pleasing
can be displeasing to God.

Saul now received his final obedience test. God commanded him, through Samuel, to bring God's judgment onto the Amalekites for their sins of past and present (verses 18 and 33). Just as God had given almost five centuries of grace to the Canaanites (Gen. 15:13-16) before He ordered Israel to wipe them out, so He had given almost five

May 26
~ ~ ~
1 Sam. 15

centuries of grace to the Amalekites since the exodus from Egypt (Ex. 17). Saul had to wipe them out, all people and all animals. In the light of the Jericho history, this command left no room for partial obedience.

Because of their helpfulness to Israel with the exodus, Saul gave a friendly warning to the Kenites to remove themselves from among the Amalekites. It shows the good side of Saul. He then executed God's judgment on God's enemies, but he decided to make a few exceptions: He spared the king and the best livestock. He later admitted that he did it to please his soldiers. Saul rewarded himself with a monument and then proceeded with his army and loot to Gilgal to celebrate, as they had done with his coronation (page 143).

God informed Samuel of Saul's disobedience and the punishment for it. Samuel pleaded the whole night with God for mercy. The next day, he went to Saul to see for himself. What followed was an object lesson about defenses erected by guilt and needs created by poor self-esteem. Saul put up a false face of compliance, knowing he had not exactly fulfilled his mission.

Samuel used the bleating sheep and lowing cattle to bring him back to reality. Saul tried to justify his non-compliance saying that they had saved the animals for sacrifice. With a strong statement, Samuel made it very clear that God prefers obedience above sacrifices. Saul tried to shift the blame to his army, but with that trick he could not escape God's judgment either.

Strangely, Saul was less concerned about God's punishment than about the people's opinion of him. He asked Samuel to accompany him to the meaningless sacrifice so he would save face, a request that Samuel at first refused. Saul tried to hold Samuel back by his shoulder, and in the process tore Samuel's cloak. The prophet used it as a metaphor of how the kingship would be torn from Saul. On second thought, Samuel agreed to go with Saul because he had to do what Saul had neglected—execute the evil king.

Saul's sensitivity for public opinion made him a people-pleaser. On that road he displeased God by partial obedience.

A prayer: Show me where I am disobedient and help me to obey in faith and love.
A thought: Do I water down God's commands with excuses?

148. David's Anointing
The Spirit of the LORD comes on him in power.

May 27
~ ~ ~
1 Sam. 16:1-13
Ps. 23

God told Samuel to stop grieving past losses and start celebrating future victories. Saul's wrongdoing caused God to reject him. It was time to appoint his successor. Though Saul would be king for twelve more years, God wanted to lift Samuel out of his grief and usher the next king onto the road of preparation.

God directed Samuel to a specific family and place: the house of Jesse in Bethlehem. For safety's sake, Samuel kept silent about the real reason for his visit and made it look like a sacrificial meal. After the meal, Samuel apparently visited Jesse to finish the real task he had come for. He let Jesse's sons pass before him one by one. God told Samuel not to be impressed by outward appearances. They must have been surprised and amused when Samuel asked them to go and fetch David, the youngest, the ruddy teenage shepherd-boy.

A puzzled David, not far from home at the time, was soon brought in. In simple shepherd's clothes, he was introduced to the dignified old prophet of God. Samuel heard God's voice clearly in his mind: *"Arise, anoint him; for this is the one!"* Yahveh and David loved each other.

The smiles fell from the faces when Samuel got up, announced the next king of Israel, and anointed him with sacred oil. David later wrote, *"You prepare a table before me in the presence of my enemies; You anoint my head with oil; My cup runs over"* (Ps. 23:5). Maybe Christmas bells started ringing in heaven—a thousand years later, the Messiah, the Son of David, would be born in Bethlehem.

As Samuel anointed David, something wonderful took place in David's heart. The Spirit of the LORD came on him in power. The anointing with oil was a symbol of his anointing with the Holy Spirit. Not only were his natural gifts enhanced, but he also received special gifts to fulfill special tasks.

There is a difference between the indwelling, filling, and anointing by the Holy Spirit. He *dwells* in all God's children (John 14:17, 23; Rom. 8:9, 16). This is also called "baptized" by the Spirit (1 Cor. 12:13). He *fills* God's children when they surrender themselves totally to Him. The main sign of that is agape love (1 Cor. 13, Rom. 5:5, Gal. 5:22). The Spirit also *anoints* God's children with special gifts to fulfill specific tasks in the church (1 Cor. 12:7-11). Jesus is called Messiah, *The Anointed*, because He was anointed by the Holy Spirit to fulfill His unique task as Savior (Luke 4:14-21, Acts 10:38).

A prayer: Lord, show me my task and anoint me for it.
A thought: Do I rest in God's sovereign and compassionate will?

149. Music Therapy
David becomes Saul's musician.

It is stated in one breath: When the Holy Spirit came upon David, He departed from Saul. To make it even worse, God allowed an evil spirit to torment Saul. It made him morbid and aggressive. Nothing his servants did was right in his sight. They conferred and decided to encourage him to get a musician. Instead, they should have suggested a prophet to get Saul back on track.

<table><tr><td>May 28
~ ~ ~
1 Sam. 16:14-23</td></tr></table>

To their amazement and delight, the king accepted the idea. When he asked for names, they had one ready: David, the harp-playing shepherd from Bethlehem. He had additional qualifications too: He was a brave young man who could serve as one of Saul's bodyguards, and his eloquence would be an asset to the king's court. That sounded good enough to Saul to give it a try.

Saul commanded Jesse to send him his son without giving any reasons, causing a lot of tension in Jesse's heart and household. They would have been plagued by many unanswered questions: What is Saul's intention? Has he heard about David's anointing by Samuel? If so, what will he do to David? If not, what else could be on his mind? Jesse did not have much choice, and he decided to respond submissively. He sent his son with a gift to the king. The small gift reflected the simple lifestyle of the time.

When the handsome, friendly young man stood before him, Saul liked him immediately. And when David's fingers glided over the strings of the harp, intermittently accompanied by soothing song, Saul knew that he had found a diamond in the dirt. The music pacified his troubled spirit. Centuries later the Son of David said, *"Come to Me, all you who labor and are heavy laden, and I will give you rest"* (Matt. 11:28). Maybe Saul spoke with his musician occasionally and discovered that he got far more than he had hoped for. David was also a firm believer. He would testify about God's grace to Saul, both in music and in conversation. So after all, Saul did get a prophet as well.

The uncertainty and fears in Jesse's home subsided when they got word from the king that David had been well received and that the king would like him to stay for longer periods. The fact that some time later Saul forgot the name of David's father (17:55) shows that there might have elapsed a considerable time since David's last visit to the palace (17:15).

Music and songs are gifts from God that can bring emotional calm and spiritual blessing. We need this sustenance regularly.

A prayer: Lord, feed us with Your Word and uplifting music and song.
A thought: Do I glorify God with my talents?

150. Training for Triumph
David's victory is not a sudden stroke of luck.

May 29
~~~
1 Sam. 17:1-37

The story of David and Goliath is probably one of the best known stories around the world. It captures the imagination and warms the heart. We may forget, however, that this heroic victory was not a fluke. It happened after the hero had been subjected to tough training—spiritually, emotionally, and physically.

When a young person shows the rock-firm faith that David had, others usually have been instrumental in shaping that young life. We don't know who sowed the first seeds in David's soul, but he surely responded positively to the work of the Holy Spirit. If David did not have the firm belief that God worked miracles for those who trusted Him, he never would have dared to face Goliath. Since God's Spirit had come on him with his anointing by Samuel, his trust in God had been strengthened daily. Yahveh enjoyed David's growing faith.

David's faith made him a positive thinker. He took on his assignments believing that, with God on his side, nothing was impossible for him. With that winner's attitude, he took on predators daring to attack his flock. And in this optimistic spirit, he ventured into the king's house with his harp and changed the king's mood with his songs. This acquaintance with Saul later made it easy for David to speak to the king about Goliath. Not even the put-down by his brother or the doubts of the king could then dampen his zeal.

To pass the long hours of shepherding, he had been practicing with his harp and sling since childhood. Sheep don't have insight or instincts for self-protection. While grazing, some of them easily wander off. With a well-aimed stone from his sling, the shepherd directed straying sheep back to the flock without having to walk all the way to such sheep to bring them back. To improve this skill, David practiced on targets until he could hit accurately like the Benjaminites (Judges 20:16).

This preparation could not be ascribed to human efforts. God had given the right exercise to David at the right time. Yahveh gradually built David up in his faith, his views, and his body. God even arranged David's trip to the battlefield at exactly the right moment. For forty days, the army of Israel had been demoralized by the champion fighter with his tall stature and harsh voice. They had been hoping and praying for a hero to silence the brute.

God usually does not dump us in at the deep end without proper preparation. All our ups and downs are part of His great plan for our lives.

*A prayer: Lord, in Your continuous training I want to do my best.*
*A thought: Today's experience prepares me for tomorrow's task.*

# 151. Warming Up for a Duel
## Your servant will go and fight this Philistine.

Detail in the Bible has a purpose. The armies of Israel and Philistia camped at Elah, some fifteen miles west of Bethlehem. Jesse sent David with provisions for three of his sons who served in the army. On his return, David had to give a physical token to his father to prove that he had indeed made contact with his brothers. It showed a lack of trust in David. Jesse would be ashamed and dumbfounded by the proof his youngest son would bring back to him.

> May 30
> ~~~
> 1 Sam. 17:17-37

As the youngest, David was saddled with the chores the other brothers despised. But this time he didn't mind. He was filled with excited eagerness. He departed long before daybreak, loaded with sixteen kilograms of grain, ten loaves, and ten cheeses, and, thanks to his fitness, covered those fifteen miles before sunrise. He arrived just in time: The armies were already lining up for battle. He dropped his pack at the provisions guard and ran to the battlefield to greet his brothers before the fighting began.

He was just in time for something else too. With the two armies lined up for close combat, Goliath stepped forward again and loudly repeated his insults. Immediately the soldiers of Israel backed off, afraid that the giant may throw his massive spear into their ranks and kill several of them with one shot. David was infuriated by the giant's audacity and disgusted by the army's fear. Then he heard about the grand prize for the one who could silence Goliath forever. David enquired further and made no secret of his feelings about Goliath.

Embarrassed that David had seen his fearful retreat, Eliab, David's eldest brother, projected his guilt feelings onto David, spewing unfounded angry accusations of negligence, pride, slyness, and dishonesty at him. He did not appreciate David's tough trip to replenish their supplies.

One of the soldiers David was talking to took him to the commander, who took him to the king. Saul was probably amused when he realized the "hero" was none other than his musician! David volunteered to fight Goliath, but Saul dismissed the idea as ridiculous. When David insisted, Saul ridiculed him by putting his oversized armor on the smaller David.

God used all the commotion and put-downs to fire David up by His Spirit. God pumped enough holy anger into David's heart, and enough adrenaline into his blood, to make him ready for the fight of his life—the unequal duel that would make him famous for the next three millennia.

A prayer: Lord, let the right things happen to me at the right time.
A thought: Are my mind, feelings, and will involved in spiritual warfare?

152. The Final Showdown
I come to you in the name of the LORD.

<table>
<tr><td>

May 31

~~~

1 Sam. 17:31-51

</td></tr>
</table>

No one stood up for David so he had to stand up for himself. In telling the king about killing a bear and a lion, he didn't brag about his own strength and speed. He testified about the care of Yahveh, the God of Israel: *"The LORD who delivered me from the paw of the lion and from the paw of the bear, He will deliver me from the hand of this Philistine,"* convincing Saul to give the fight to God and David.

One can only imagine what thoughts and feelings went through Saul, the officers, the soldiers, and through David's brothers when David stepped forward to fight Goliath. Most felt that this athletic adolescent didn't have a chance. Yet many silent prayers for a miracle went up.

David used the weapons and the outfit he knew: his shepherd's sling, staff, pouch, and clothes. With that, he could move fast and hit hard. As he selected five pebbles from the dry brook, he might have whispered to himself, *"Yea, though I walk through the valley of the shadow of death, I will fear no evil; for You are with me..."* (Ps. 23). David was not so over-confident that he picked up only one pebble. He gave himself five shots. When Goliath insulted and threatened David, he did not keep silent. He testified loudly and clearly about the power of the one true God: "I come to you in the name of Yahveh!" He added a few sentences that made the big guy so mad that he became careless in his rage.

David surprised Goliath by storming him. The giant reached for his sword to chop his tiny opponent to pieces, not even lowering his visor to protect his face. At the right distance David suddenly stopped, whirled his sling, and let the stone fly. All his might, all his concentration, and all his faith were in that blow. And Yahveh blessed David's best. He guided that pebble-missile to the only unarmored place in Goliath's outfit—his forehead. The pebble penetrated his skull and he plunged facedown into the dust. David quickly finished him off, using Goliath's own sword.

He held up the enemy's head, signifying victory. The Israelites, stunned for a moment, lifted their spears and shields with a roaring war cry. When Jesus crushed the serpent's head on Calvary, He cried, "It is accomplished!"

God teaches us much about spiritual warfare in this passage. We should use the talents, methods, and means we know best. Instead of only one "stone," several approaches may bring more success. We must testify openly, giving the glory to God. He will bless us when we do our best.

A prayer: Lord, with You I will prevail over gigantic problems.
A thought: Do I take challenges on with jubilant faith in Almighty God?

153. Reactions to Victory
David is loved by Jonathan and hated by Saul.

When Goliath fell, there was silence for a moment. Then the Israelites rose to their feet with a loud war cry and pursued the fleeing Philistines, killing many of them up to the gates of their fortified cities. David's victory inspired more victory. The news spread through Israel like wildfire, and people began to celebrate.

> June 1
> ~ ~ ~
> 1 Sam. 17:52 -
> 18:16

In contrast, we hear no word of praise or thanks from Saul or his general, Abner, when David appeared before them with the sword and the head of the giant. All they could say was, "Who is your father?" They were more interested in his background than in him—as if David was only defined by his parents and not by his own achievements as well.

Jonathan, the crown prince, immediately befriended the young hero of the day. He adored David's courage and skill when he defeated Goliath, and when they got to know each other personally, they soon became soul mates. Jonathan gave one of his outfits to David so that the hero could look like an officer. They surely chatted and celebrated till late that night. David took his weapons to his "tent" or house. That meant: He presented Goliath's sword to his dad, who was speechless over the sudden fame of his son. Jesse got the token he required.

David took Goliath's head to Jerusalem, which was still a Jebusite city, five miles from Bethlehem. The border between the territories of Benjamin and Judah ran close to Jerusalem, so Israelites lived around this stronghold. David had grown up in that area and knew it well. Showing Goliath's head to the people in and around Jerusalem conveyed a message about the future. David would later conquer Jerusalem as he had conquered Goliath.

Returning from the battlefield, Saul expected the usual honors for a victorious king. When he heard that the singing women honored David above himself, he was affronted. An ominous thought struck him—was David perhaps the future king that Samuel had referred to when saying that Saul would be replaced? Saul clenched his teeth and cursed David.

From that day, he tried one plan after another to get rid of David. Saul became obsessed with trying to kill this young intruder. Unable to pin David to the wall with his spear, Saul sent him on dangerous missions hoping that the Philistines would kill him for humiliating them. But all Saul's wicked plans for David were turned in David's favor by the God who loved David. Yahveh must have enjoyed this intriguing power struggle.

A prayer: God, help me handle both recognition and opposition correctly.
A thought: Does success or criticism easily go to my head?

154. From Hero to Fugitive
Saul starts to persecute David openly.

<table>
<tr><td>
June 2
~ ~ ~
1 Sam. 18:17-
19:24, Ps. 59
</td><td>
When Saul heard that his daughter, Michal, was in love with David, Saul let him know that the bride price that would please him most was the foreskins of a hundred Philistines. He hoped that David would be killed in the process. David and his men presented double
</td></tr>
</table>

the amount. The young commander became increasingly successful and esteemed.

Then Saul revealed his hatred for David to his son and to his advisors. He expected them to seek with him David's death. Jonathan was stunned. Why on earth would his dad want to kill someone like David? He asked David to hide at a certain place at a certain time. Jonathan took his dad to that spot and asked him why he wanted to kill such a good, brave, and loyal person as David. Whether Saul realized his mistake, or suspected a trap, or just wanted to mislead his son, we don't know, but in any case, Saul took an oath in the name of the LORD that he would not kill David.

For a time the peace seemed to be restored, and David proceeded with his excellent work in Saul's service. When Saul was plagued by the distressing spirit again, David played on his harp for Saul. Instead of calming Saul as before, Saul's irrational hatred for David flared up, and again he tried to kill David by hurling his spear at him. David escaped to his house where Michal alerted him about her father's plans (see Ps. 59). She helped him to flee and delayed pursuit by deceiving the guards with the lie that David was sick.

David fled to Samuel and poured out his heart to the old prophet who had anointed him as the next king of Israel. Soon Saul found out where David was. He sent soldiers to arrest David, but as soon as they saw Samuel and the student prophets, they started to prophesy. After it had happened with two other groups of soldiers as well, Saul went to kill David himself, but he, too, started to prophesy. God's Spirit can take control of people who are actually God's enemies. He did it with Balaam too (Num. 22-24).

While Saul lay in a trance with Samuel, David fled to Jonathan, his only friend besides Samuel. Jonathan could not believe that his dad was breaking his solemn oath, so he and David worked out a plan to make sure what Saul's true intentions were. It began to dawn on David that he was persecuted for his faith. Without any wrongdoing, the most celebrated hero was becoming the most wanted fugitive. But Yahveh protected him in this perilous time.

A prayer: God, You protect Your own against the enemy's schemes.
A thought: How can I survive spiritually when I'm persecuted?

155. David and Jonathan
They vow to stay loyal to each other.

This chapter shows how love and hate work. David and
Jonathan made a covenant, vowing lifelong loyalty to each
other. In view of his narrow escapes from Saul that week,
David knew that one wrong step would cost him his life.
Jonathan was unaware of his father's vile efforts to kill his
friend. He could not believe that his dad was that false. They
decided to test Saul's real feelings toward David.

June 3
~ ~ ~
1 Sam. 20

Although Saul had openly tried to kill David a few days before, he
expected David to attend the new moon feasts on two consecutive days. No
fugitive in his right mind would do that! It showed how sick Saul's mind
already was. When Jonathan used an innocent situation to protect David,
saying he was attending a family meeting in Bethlehem, Saul got into such a
rage that he insulted his son in the presence of others and hurled his spear at
him. Hate makes people unreasonable, demanding, angry, and aggressive.

To avoid detection by Saul's spies, Jonathan warned David in the way
they had agreed to. He shot three arrows over the place where David was
hiding and shouted to the boy to search farther off for the arrows. He sent the
boy back to town and then had a secret meeting with David. They realized that
Saul was determined to kill David and that David had to flee for his life. The
two close friends wept as they said farewell, deeply hurt by the unfair treatment
both of them were suffering and deeply saddened by the sudden interruption to
their short but genuine friendship. They comforted each other by reaffirming
their mutual loyalty. They would see each other only once more.

The friendship love of David and Jonathan made them try not to put each
other at risk. They looked out for one another's well-being and worked to serve
each other. Everything they did was constructive and helpful. They trusted
God. Everything Saul did was destructive and harmful.

Through the ages till this day, positive people have gone far out of their
way to help others, while negative people have done their utmost to harm
others. Among the latter are those who use their brilliant minds to develop
computer viruses that can damage computers and destroy data that are used for
the common good of society. Others use their intelligence to plan theft, murder
or terrorism. How can anybody get a kick from harming others? And yet, who
can claim not to have hurt a loved one with sharp words? Our sinful nature
urges us to do things that make us untrue to our real selves.

A prayer: Lord, help me act always in love, even when I'm hurt or angry.
A thought: How does competition affect my desire to help others?

156. The Point of No Return

When Saul turns against God, he is doomed.

<table>
<tr><td>
June 4
~~~
1 Sam. 21-23
Ps. 34, 52, 56
</td></tr>
</table>

The Tabernacle was David's first stop when he became a fugitive. David found refuge in God's tent (Ps. 27:5). He hid the truth from the high priest in order to fulfill his urgent need for food, weapons, and guidance (1 Sam. 22:10). Unfortunately, his visit to the Tabernacle was noticed by one of the enemy.

Panicked, David fled to Philistine country. Recognizing him immediately, they alerted their king. David was now in the late Goliath's hometown, and it could be expected that the townsfolk would cry for revenge. In a frantic effort to save his own skin, David acted the mad man (see Ps. 34, 56). The king decided to send him away instead of killing him. David fled to the cave of Adullam, twelve miles west of Bethlehem. Fearing Saul's vengeance, his family came to David, as did four hundred "wanted" men. Suddenly David was not alone. Instead of sulking over his own predicament, he now had to plan for the safety and sustenance of others.

Being a descendant of Ruth, a Moabitess, David took his parents to Moab, east of the Dead Sea, for safety. They were well received. David and his men stayed in a nearby mountain stronghold. Gad, the prophet, advised David not to stay there but to return to Judah, probably to stay in touch with his tribe. Because of Saul's spies, David and his men could not stay long at one place.

Frustrated in his horrible obsession to kill David, Saul blamed his guard that they had not done enough to help him to reach his goal. Then Doeg, an Edomite, tried to win Saul's favor by telling Saul about David's visit to the Tabernacle (Ps. 52). Saul summoned all the priests for a hearing. In spite of their innocence, Saul ordered his guards to put them to death. The guards refused, but when Doeg started to execute the king's cruel command, the guards did nothing to stop this insanity. Even the families and livestock of the priests were killed. Saul could not bring himself to wipe out the Amalekites, but now he did it in cold blood to the priests of Yahveh. With this massacre, Saul reached the point of no return. God would never speak to him again, just as Jesus gave Herod no answer after Herod had killed John the Baptist (Luke 23:7-9).

Only one priest, Abiathar, escaped. He joined David and his men and would serve them with vital advice. While David now had a prophet and a priest of the LORD with him, Saul had none. Because Saul rejected God, God abandoned him. David trusted God and God protected him.

A prayer: Precious Lord, take my hand.
A thought: I must not focus on my enemies, but on my friends.

157. A Few Sweet Drops
in a bitter cup

David's recent visits to Philistia and Moab could have been seen as disloyalty to Israel. So when the Philistines attacked Keilah in Judah, David saw it as an opportunity to clear his name. However, to ensure he did not put his foot in a trap, David first consulted God through the priest Abiathar.

June 5

~~~

1 Sam. 23
Ps. 63

</div>

Apparently the ephod (cloak) used by the priest gave a "yes" or "no" answer to a single question. It happened twice that David had to ask two questions to get to a more precise answer. The fact that God told them to free Keilah from the Philistines was not enough for David's men; they wanted assurance that they would win the fight, too. After they had gotten this assurance, they dealt the enemy a heavy blow and recaptured the loot. For a while, David and his men were the heroes of the town.

When Saul's spies informed him of the situation in Keilah, he saw in it an opportunity to besiege David and his men. In his delusion, Saul audaciously thought that God had given David into his hand—forgetting that he had murdered God's priests recently. When David's spies told him of Saul's plans, David consulted God again with two questions: Will Saul come against them? And if so, will the people of Keilah turn David over to Saul? A "yes" to both questions set David and his men on the run again.

Jonathan's quick visit to David was another sweet drop in David's bitter cup. Jonathan *"strengthened his hand in God"* by encouraging David to keep his faith in spite of the adverse circumstances—God would eventually exonerate him and make him king. Jonathan was willing to serve under David. Renewing their covenant, they said farewell for the last time.

David and his men kept moving from place to place to elude Saul. The Ziphites served David another bitter cup by not only giving intelligence about his whereabouts to Saul, but also by guiding Saul to the exact place (Ps. 63). Saul tried to encircle David. The two regiments were separated only by a ridge. At that critical moment, Saul received the news that the Philistines had invaded Israel. Intensely frustrated, he had to turn back.

This timely divine intervention was another sweet drop in David's bitter cup. In gratitude, they named that ridge the Rock of Division. It showed how God protected His children from harm by putting His hand between them and danger. It also pointed to the division between believers and unbelievers.

A prayer: Thank You, Lord, for the silver linings of the dark clouds.
A thought: Do I sulk about the bitter cup, or do I rejoice about the sweet drops?

158. Goodwill Disarms Hatred
David spares Saul's life.

<table>
<tr><td>

June 6
~~~
1 Sam. 24
Ps. 57, 142

</td></tr>
</table>

While Saul's army drove the Philistines back, David moved to En Gedi on the west side of the Dead Sea. Springwater and goats sustained them. They started a new service to local farmers: They protected their flocks and shepherds against predators and invading gangs (1 Sam. 25:15-16). To render this service, they probably split up in smaller groups.

When the Philistine invasion had been repelled, Saul resumed his pursuit of David. His spies directed him to En Gedi. David and some of his men were fulfilling their self-imposed duty of guarding flocks and shepherds when the sentinel warned them that Saul and his army were close by. David and his men hurried into a cave. Some caves had sheep pens at the entrance as the caves provided shelter in extreme heat or cold.

Unaware of David's presence, the tired king entered the cave alone to rest. He sank into a deep sleep. David's men urged him to kill Saul, but David flatly refused to kill the anointed king of God. He sneaked up to Saul, cut off the corner of his robe, and retreated back into the darkness of the cave. The bleating of the sheep and the shouting of the shepherds at the entrance could have muffled David's stalking.

When Saul had left the cave, David called him from a safe distance and bowed to show his respect. He asked Saul why he tried to kill him and who was inciting the king in this matter? If Saul had answered this question honestly, he would have realized that his hatred for David was from the devil. In contrast with Saul's motives and actions, David presented the proof of his motives and actions—the corner of Saul's robe. A quick glance at the bottom of his robe convinced Saul that David indeed got close enough to kill him. David urged Saul to attend to more urgent matters of the state rather than wasting his time chasing after one single "flea."

Realizing the contrast between his and David's attitude, Saul felt so guilty that he burst into tears. He admitted that he was wrong. He even expressed his view that David would become king, and therefore he asked David to vow that he would not wipe out Saul's family. As David had already promised that to Jonathan, he granted this request to Saul as well.

This incident demonstrated in a tense real-life situation what it means to love your enemy (Matt. 5:44, Rom. 12:20).

*A prayer: Help me to show goodwill even when others get mean.*
*A thought: Am I revengeful or forgiving?*

# 159. Friendliness Calms Anger
### Abigail prevents bloodshed by David.

It was not easy to feed six hundred men, many with families (1 Sam. 30:3), in the dry southern part of Israel. They tried to earn their food by doing favors for local farmers, such as protecting their flocks and herdsmen. This relationship was a goodwill gesture rather than a formal contract. David and his followers had to keep moving from place to place to stay out of Saul's clutches. While they were in Carmel, they extended the same friendship to the shepherds of a rich man called Nabal.

> June 7
> ~ ~ ~
> 1 Sam. 25

It was customary for farmers to treat their shearers to a party when the shearing was done. Having guarded Nabal's flocks against predators and gangs, David sent a deputation to him with a cordial request that Nabal kindly return the favor by sharing some of the food with them. Nabal not only showed ingratitude by refusing the request, but he sent David's messengers back with insults to David and his followers. This attitude infuriated David. Impulsively, he decided to launch a revenge attack on Nabal and to wipe out all that belonged to him. Not long before, David had condemned Saul for his hatred; now he was in the same boat.

One of the servants told Abigail, Nabal's wife, how her husband had treated David's messengers. Abigail realized that such a blatant insult would not be ignored. She and her servants immediately prepared a lot of bread, wine, raisins, meat, grain, and figs, loaded these on donkeys, and set off to meet David before he could start his revenge. She met him halfway, bowed before him, and begged his forgiveness to prevent bloodshed. She offered the gifts she had brought. Diplomatically, she expressed hope in David's coming kingdom and prayed that God would protect him from danger and from wrongdoing so that he would rule with a clear conscience. She ended her plea with the request that he would remember her.

God used Abigail to open David's eyes to what he had been contemplating. He thanked God and Abigail for stopping him in time. He accepted her gift and turned back. When Abigail told Nabal the next morning what had happened, it was such a shock to him that he suffered a stroke. He died ten days later. David saw it as God's answer to the injustice Nabal had done to him. Some time after this incident, David did remember Abigail. He asked her to become his wife, and she modestly accepted. Wise mediators can calm down hotheaded adversaries. Blessed are the peacemakers (Matt. 5:9).

*A prayer: In my little world, I want to be a peacemaker, not a war-maker.*
*A thought: What techniques can I learn from Abigail?*

# 160. History Repeated
## David spares Saul's life again.

<table>
<tr><td>June 8<br>~ ~ ~<br>1 Sam. 26</td></tr>
</table>

For a second time, the Ziphites betrayed David by informing Saul of his whereabouts. They wanted to finish the job that had been interrupted by the Philistine invasion. They saw it as an unfortunate co-incidence, not as divine intervention. The secular view that excludes the Creator is still with us today.

Saul came again with three thousand soldiers against the six hundred of David. This time the encounter was not in a cave but in the open, not with Saul alone but with Saul in the midst of his army. David's spies led him to the place where Saul's army was camping for the night. God used the fatigue of Saul's men after a long day's trek in the desert to put them into a deep sleep.

David's nephew Abishai volunteered to accompany David for a sneak peek into Saul's camp. As his enemies did not refrain from repeated attacks, David did not refrain from giving them the same message either. He showed them that he was not planning any harm against king or country. By taking something belonging to Saul, he could prove that he could have killed Saul, but had not done so. Abishai wanted to pin Saul to the ground with a spear. David only allowed him to take Saul's spear and water jug with him.

They sneaked out of the camp and stopped at a safe distance to make their point. General Abner awoke with a shock when David called his name from the dark. The refugee roasted the general for not guarding the king properly. Saul also woke up and asked the same pathetic question he had asked with their last encounter: *"Is that your voice, my son David?"* Hypocritically, he called David his "son," knowing well that he had already annulled his daughter's marriage with David.

David asked the same kind of questions he had asked with their previous encounter: What had he done wrong to deserve this treatment? Why did the king waste time pursuing one "partridge" into the desert? Why did Saul force him to flee to other countries with foreign gods? David called on Yahveh to exonerate him and to destroy his enemies. Saul admitted that he was wrong and asked David to come back to his service. Who would trust such a fraud? Saul repeated his conviction that David would reach high peaks of success.

David ignored Saul's invitation and let a soldier come and fetch Saul's spear and jug. Saul's false promises disgusted and exasperated David. He knew he could not trust the king. He decided to flee his country.

*A prayer: Lord, let the repeated attacks of Satan not break my spirit.*
*A thought: Do I get weary of fighting off repeated attacks?*

# 161. Conflicts of Trust
## David's despair makes him reckless.

The Ziphites' repetitive betrayal, Saul's relentless persecution, and Samuel's lamentable death made David feel like an outcast without friends. He had been exasperated by eight years of fleeing. Without consulting God, he decided to move with his small army to Philistine territory in the hope of getting Saul off his back. He did not know that by a sudden turn of events, he would become king of Judah within two years.

June 9<br>
~~~<br>
1 Sam. 27,<br>
28:1-2, 29:1-11
</div>

David was making a dangerous move from trust-in-God to trust-in-self, exposing himself and his people to the whims of their sworn enemies. In his despair he became reckless, engaging in treacherous war games. After a year of daredevil acts Yahveh shocked him back to reality and to obedience.

This time, king Achish of Gath received David with more respect. Since David's first visit eight years ago, his reputation as Saul's slippery adversary had spread even to Philistine country. Achish embraced the old saying that an enemy of his enemy was his friend. David's six hundred brave men were a force King Achish could use to his advantage. He granted David's request to stay in the small town of Ziklag. From there, David made regular raids on southern tribes who belonged neither to Israel nor to Philistia. David now did what Joshua should have done four centuries earlier, namely, to wipe out those tribes completely. By leaving no survivors, nobody could tell Achish what David was doing. He shared the loot with Achish, pretending that he had raided Israel. He was playing with fire and enjoying it. Eventually, he would burn his fingers.

When the Israelites and Philistines prepared for war again, Achish commandeered David and his army to join forces with him against Israel. That put David in a tight spot. A refusal would show disloyalty to his host. If he fought for them, he would betray his country and never be forgiven. Still trusting his own wit, he decided to go along with Achish, either hoping the other Philistine kings would send him home or planning to switch sides and fight for Israel once the battle had started. In His mercy, God pulled him out of the mess by using the distrust of the other Philistine kings.

As soon as David and his men were out of sight, they probably released their pent up tension by laughing and joking about this close call. They did not know that what awaited them in Ziklag would be no laughing matter. The formidable raiders of the south would soon be weeping like children.

*A prayer: God, withhold me from testing You by reckless behavior.*
*A thought: Where have I made major decisions without consulting God?*

# 162. From Grief to Joy
## Tribulations drives David back to God.

June 10

~~~

1 Sam. 30
</div>

While David and his men prospered in Philistine territory, they did not seek God's guidance. Now that their town had been ravaged and their families captured, some thought of turning against David. In his grief and fear, David set the example. He found his strength in God and shifted attention from the past to the future. Now God's guidance was again sought as before. God assured them through Abiathar, the priest, that they would be victorious against the Amalekites.

Their concern for their families dulled their fatigue, so they pressed on right away. At a certain point, two hundred men could not keep up the pace. David left them with the supplies, thus allowing the weary ones to recover and freeing the other four hundred men to move faster.

A sick, starving slave, left behind by the raiders, was revived by David's men. He knew where the raiders were heading and gave David that information in trade for his life. With a surprise night attack, David overwhelmed the raiders and took all the loot they had acquired.

Some of David's men did not want to share with those who stayed with the supplies. David made it clear that God had given them the victory so the loot actually belonged to God. David celebrated the victory by being generous—not only toward those who guarded the supplies, but also toward the towns where they had received hospitality in the past. Unknowingly, David was creating goodwill where he would shortly be crowned as king.

This incident near the end of David's fugitive era demonstrated the queer mix of supporters he had gathered around himself in those difficult years. Some were valiant warriors and some frail followers, some cold-blooded killers and some emotional fathers. David kept this diverse group of fugitives together by good leadership that was built on faith in God. In spite of their diversity, their unity made them a formidable force. We also learn about the non-perishable food they used: Grain and dried fruits did not spoil on their journeys.

David's good and bad survival strategies show us how to survive in a hostile environment. It is wise to make friends (his followers), but unwise to side with the enemy (Philistines). Our trust must be focused on God and not on our wit. We must foster goodwill (as David did to Saul) and avoid personal revenge (as David planned against Nabal). By rendering services (as they did to the farmers) and being generous, we may win vital support.

A prayer: God, I want to stay true to You and turn problems into challenges.
A thought: Is my prayer life determined by my needs only?

163. Deliberate Disobedience
Saul turns to the occult for guidance.

Because of Saul's unfaithfulness, God's Spirit had left him, and an evil spirit plagued him. He had been pursuing David relentlessly, and he had massacred the priests of God. The Philistines were mustering their forces against him. From the heights of Gilboa, he could see the enormous army of his enemy in the plain of Jezreel. He felt the need to be directed by God but got no answer.

> June 11
> ~~~
> 1 Sam. 28:3-25

He was in such dire need for some kind of supernatural support that he decided to consult a witch—a direct and deliberate transgression of the Law. Now we learn that the same man who had killed the priests also had killed or expelled the witches. Was that an effort to compensate for his sin against the priests? However, one of the witches had escaped his witch-hunting. She lived at En Dor near Gilboa. God had kept her alive for His own purpose.

To avoid recognition, Saul and two of his men disguised themselves and under cover of darkness visited this woman. Fearing it was a trap, she at first refused to cooperate, but when Saul vowed that no harm would come to her, she complied. He asked her to call up Samuel.

When the woman saw the form of an old man appearing, she was terrified, probably because she never had made visual contact with a spirit before and because God revealed to her that her customer was no other than Saul himself, the witch-hunter.

Then the Bible describes a conversation between Samuel and Saul that was apparently not through the woman. Saul could hear Samuel's voice: "*Samuel said to Saul ...*" As Moses and Elijah appeared to Jesus, God here allowed Samuel to appear to Saul to give him God's final judgment. The next day Israel would lose the battle, and Saul and his sons would die.

Hearing the well-known voice and the judgment it contained completely drained Saul. Powerless and forsaken, his pathetic figure fell facedown on the ground as if the Philistines had slain him already.

Eventually the woman convinced Saul to eat. To show her respect and to safeguard herself against prosecution, she treated them to the best she had. She slaughtered a calf and baked fresh bread to strengthen them for the fight to death. In spite of the pending judgment, Saul picked himself up, went back to his army, and prepared for the last battle of his life.

He knew he could not run away from God. However, he did not repent either. He had landed himself in this situation by a series of bad decisions.

A prayer: Lord, I want to stay in touch with You.
A thought: Have I exposed myself to Satan by playing with the occult?

164. How The Mighty Have Fallen
Saul and three of his sons die in the battle of Gilboa.

<table>
<tr><td>June 12
~ ~ ~
1 Sam. 31,
2 Sam. 1</td></tr>
</table>

When Saul and his two men returned from En Dor, they reached their camp on Gilboa shortly before daybreak. Within hours they had to face the battle with exhausted bodies worn down by a long walk, a sleepless night, and by a debilitating message of doom. Going into battle in that physical, emotional, and spiritual condition was a recipe for failure.

To fulfill His judgment on Saul, God instigated courage into the Philistines and fear into the Israelites. Saul's army fell back, and soon they were fleeing as fast as possible. The bravest, like Saul and his sons, fought while retreating, trying to stem the tide. The enemy swarmed to these pockets of resistance, and soon they were overwhelmed by sheer numbers.

Instead of engaging Saul, a fierce fighter, in man-to-man combat, the Philistine archers assaulted him from a safe distance. He could not shield off so many arrows and was eventually fatally wounded. He commanded his armor bearer, possibly Doeg, to kill him in order to rob the enemy of that satisfaction. Fear of reprisal made him refuse. Saul then committed suicide with his own sword and his armor bearer followed suit. The enemy left their bodies there to proceed with their victorious pursuit. Yahveh's judgment had been executed.

The next day the Philistines returned to the corpses, strewn over a large area, to rob them of valuables. Saul's body was decapitated and his head exhibited in their cities and temples as a victory sign. In gratitude for what Saul had done for them years before (1 Sam. 11), the men of Jabesh Gilead came by night and took the bodies of Saul and his sons from the wall of Beth-Shan, cremated them, and buried the remains. David appreciated that.

While Saul's army was fleeing, David's army was victorious against the Amalekites. A few days after they had returned to Ziklag (in the south), they got the shocking news about Israel's defeat (in the north). Apart from the fact that the messenger was an Amalekite, he made the mistake of claiming that he himself had killed Saul. His lie led to his execution.

While mourning the death of Saul and Jonathan, David wrote the Song of the Bow to commemorate this sad event. As is proper at funerals, he only praised the virtues of the dead, while keeping silent about their vices. David's striking empathy with Jonathan—in his last anxious fighting moments—is captured in the phrase, "I am in agony for you, my brother, Jonathan ..."

A prayer: Father, help me to live and to die in faith and dignity.
A thought: In what state of mind do I want to meet my Maker?

165. Recognition Resumed
David is anointed as king of Judah.

David's triumph over Goliath had brought him instant fame. For a year or two his fame had increased as commander of the most successful regiment in Saul's army. When Saul had fallen out of grace, he eyed David with envy. At first, Saul had tried to get rid of him

> June 13
> ~ ~ ~
> 2 Sam. 2, 3:1-5

secretly, but later he persecuted David openly for about ten years. During those years, nobody dared to support David openly, although many towns and farmers in Judah did so secretly.

After Saul's death, David returned from his self-imposed exile. He moved with his followers to Hebron, and there the tribe of Judah anointed David as their king. Yahveh was fulfilling the prophecy made by Samuel. David sent men to Jabesh in Gilead to thank them for giving Saul an honorable burial. By this, he tried to win the support of other tribes as well.

Although the house of Saul had suffered a severe blow, it was not yet overthrown. Saul's general, Abner, who had survived the defeat at Gilboa, made one of Saul's sons, Ishbosheth, king over the other tribes of Israel. Because the Philistines had temporarily occupied some cities of Israel, including Saul's old capital, Gibeah, Ishbosheth made his headquarters east of Jordan.

Two kings in one country inevitably led to civil war. The two generals, Abner and Joab, first tried to limit bloodshed by having teams from both sides compete in combat. When the twelve pairs killed each other simultaneously, the battle started. David's men got the upper hand, and set Abner and his army on the run. Joab's swift-footed brother, Asahel, pursued Abner. He ignored Abner's warning to follow someone else. Asahel paid with his life for the mistake of overestimating himself and underestimating the enemy. This event brought bad blood between the two generals and would later have tragic consequences for both Abner and Joab.

At the end of the day, with twenty needless deaths on Joab's side and 360 on Abner's side, the two generals agreed to call the battle off and to return home. Without going into details, the Bible tells us that these kinds of clashes between Israel and Judah recurred over seven years. Gradually David's army became stronger, while Ishbosheth's became weaker. David did not force Israel to accept him as king, but when they attacked him, he defended himself well.

In that time, David took four more wives and had a child with each of his six wives. His weakness for women would eventually lead to his fall.

A prayer: God, I don't want to harm people to reach my goals.
A thought: How do I treat my competitors and opponents?

166. Power Games
Israel's king and general are murdered.

June 14
~ ~ ~
2 Sam. 3:6 - 5:5

The political history of the world is a record of power struggles. If the biblical record about power games three thousand years ago makes you raise your eyebrows, just look at today's newspaper and ask yourself if we are doing any better. Most "stabbing" today is subtler, but it can be just as devastating.

Abner was the real power behind the puppet-king, Ishbosheth. When the king accused Abner of an affair with Saul's concubine, Rizpah, Abner was offended and told the king that he was going to give the kingdom of Israel to David. He started to prepare the tribes under his command for the transfer of power and sent David word about it. David used royal language of the time when he replied that his wife Michal had to be returned to him before Abner could "see his face." He let Abner know who's in control. Abner immediately complied to secure David's goodwill.

In Joab's absence, Abner visited David in Hebron to make arrangements to unite Israel and Judah. Abner undoubtedly expected to become David's chief general as reward for bringing Israel over to David. They feasted to celebrate the deal, and then Abner departed with David's blessing.

When Joab returned and learned what had transpired, he was furious. He accused David of being blind to the real objectives of Abner. Without David's knowledge, Joab sent a messenger to call Abner back to Hebron. Joab met him in the city gate, called him aside for a private talk, and then suddenly stabbed him to death. David was stunned by the news. He declared his innocence regarding this murder and arranged a state funeral for Abner. David wept at the burial and publicly praised Abner while he cursed Joab. David made it absolutely clear to the whole nation that he had no part in Abner's death.

Without Abner, Ishbosheth had no real power. Two of his commanders decided that they would take Abner's place and give Israel to David by giving him the head of their king. Of course, they too expected high positions in David's army for the favor. They were grossly mistaken. For David, there was a vast difference between killing someone in battle and killing someone in bed. He had the two murderers executed immediately.

With the king and general of Israel removed, the elders of Israel decided to join forces with David. For the third time he was anointed king, now in reality and over the entire nation. Yahveh's plan had become reality.

A prayer: I want to make progress with a clean conscience.
A thought: What I do to others will be done to me.

167. Diverse Perspectives
on the same history

As the wise and patient teacher, God knows the importance of repetition. He lets us study the same truth from different angles so that we will not be led astray by one-sided viewpoints. His Son's incarnation was recorded by four gospel writers, records that are not contradictory,

June 15

~~~

1 Chron. 1-10

</div>

but complementary. In the same way, the kingdoms of Israel are portrayed from different angles in the books of Samuel, Kings, and Chronicles, as well as in the poetic and prophetic books of the Bible.

The Chronicles were completed after the exile. They give genealogies till about 400 B.C. The genealogies reminded Israel of its roots. All twelve tribes were uprooted by the exiles. In their confusion and dispersion, their tribal heritage could easily get diluted by foreign influences. The Chronicles connected the lines running from them back to Abraham and to Adam. They had to regain perspective and rediscover their special place in history. The Chronicles showed them that no person is insignificant or forgotten in God's family tree.

Chronicles focus on the Davidic lineage only and refer to Israel only when their path crossed with that of Judah. The Chronicles highlight the positive contributions of the Judean kings. Special reference is made of their religious reforms and their enhancement of the temple worship. More attention is given to David's preparations for temple building and Solomon's execution of those plans than to their political achievements.

The Chronicles' purpose apparently was to give the nation of Israel, devastated after the exile, a new understanding of their history from a faith perspective. Instead of the factual, political approach of the books of Samuel and Kings, Chronicles looks at the same events from a priestly viewpoint of service to God. Yahveh's book describes His kingdom, not man's.

Reevaluating the past from the faith perspective is important for every generation. We should not fraudulently rewrite history by omitting and highlighting what suits us, but rather look at the lessons of history in such a way as to get a better understanding of where we have come from, who we are, and where we should go. Then the good and the bad of the past were not in vain, but teach lessons that make us wiser for future enterprises.

Maybe God is telling us to revisit our national and personal past and to discover His fingerprints, His interventions, and His purposes. Yahveh yearns for our trusting and loving cooperation with His plan for humanity.

A prayer: Help me to build a better future on the good of the past.
A thought: Do I stay in touch with my roots and my destiny?

168. Devoted Friends
David's mighty men

June 16
~~~
2 Sam. 23:8-39
1 Chron. 11:6-47

In 1 Chronicles 11 David's renowned warriors are named at the beginning of his reign, while 2 Samuel 23 lists them at the end of his reign. Both views are valid: God used these men to make David king and to support him during his reign. Chronicles add men who joined the ranks of the heroes at a later stage. We too can be more than conquerors through Christ (Rom. 8:37).

Joab was David's general. The other mighty men are listed in three categories. Each of the First Three (Adino, Eleazar, and Shammah) earned their position by single-handedly conquering hundreds of enemy soldiers. To accomplish that, they needed more than enormous strength, dexterity, stamina, and bravery—they enjoyed the grace of God, as Samson did when he eliminated a thousand men with the jawbone of a donkey.

We get an idea about the intensity and length of these battles when we read that Eleazar kept on fighting, in spite of his exhaustion, until his hand froze to the handle of his sword. When the fight was over, he could not open his hand to put his sword away. It is a moving picture of how we should cling to our sword, the Word of God (Eph. 6). We must become one with it.

During a Philistine invasion, David and his men took refuge in a mountain stronghold in the Judean desert, several miles east of Bethlehem. An enemy garrison was stationed at Bethlehem. In the hot, dry weather David casually said that it would be nice to have a drink from the cistern at Bethlehem's gate. The Three winked at each other, and without David's knowledge later sneaked away, crossed enemy lines at Bethlehem, drew water, and brought it to their leader as a surprise gift. Realizing that they had attained that water by risking their own lives, he could not drink it. To him the water was equal to their blood, and blood had to be sacrificed to God. That's how much they loved David, and how much he loved them.

Of the Second Three, only Abishai and Benaiah are mentioned with the mighty deeds they accomplished. Abishai also stood his ground against several hundred. He was always ready to wipe out those that tried to harm or insult David (1 Sam. 26:8; 2 Sam. 16:9). Benaiah triumphed over the champions of Moab and Egypt. He killed a lion in a pit on a snowy day. David made him commander over his guard. About the other mighty men, we are told that they came from all over Israel. It was important for military chain of command.

A prayer: I want to stand my ground against the enemies of God.
A thought: Do I get weary of fighting off the devil?

169. Massive Support
All the tribes show military allegiance.

Toward the end of David's fugitive era, some of the best warriors in Israel noticed Saul's decline and decided to join David. Some came from Benjamin (Saul's tribe), some from Judah (David's tribe), and some came from Manasseh and Gad, east of Jordan. Amasai voiced their support for David: *"We are yours, O David; we are on your side, O Son of Jesse! Peace, peace to you, and peace to your helpers! For your God helps you."* We can support Jesus likewise.

| June 17 |
| ~ ~ ~ |
| 2 Sam. 5 |
| 1 Chron. 11, 12, 14 |

These words were fulfilled after David's reign of 7½ years in Hebron. When Ishbosheth's kingdom collapsed, the nation knew it was time to make David king over all Israel. The elders came to him in Hebron, pledged their support, made a covenant with him, and anointed him as king over the entire nation. David's coronation was accompanied by a display of massive military power. God inspired each tribe, even the Levites, to send a regiment of their elite corps with armor and provisions to take part in the inauguration ceremonies and feasting, which lasted for three days at Hebron. Although fourteen tribes are mentioned, the two half-tribes of Ephraim and Manasseh should count for one because they were descendants of Joseph, the eleventh son of Jacob.

David grabbed the opportunity, using this high-spirited army of about 340,000 to start his kingdom with two resounding victories. First, they captured Jerusalem from the Jebusites, something Israel had not done in the previous four centuries. Second, they dealt the marauding Philistines two heavy blows. While David and his men fought on the ground, God let them hear the footsteps of the angels above the treetops. David honored God for His protection by destroying the idols left behind by the enemy.

David followed up on these successes by fortifying Jerusalem as the new capital of Israel and by beating the Philistines into increasing submission in the first years of his reign. The first international recognition of David's power came from his northern neighbor, King Hiram of Tyre.

This human support for David was only confirmation of the most important support—the blessing of Yahveh for a man after His own heart, the shepherd boy of Bethlehem He had called to shepherd His people Israel. David was a very human person who made mistakes, but God loved him for his unwavering, wholehearted trust in God. His psalms show us how he anchored himself to the LORD, Yahveh, in good and bad times (Ps. 23).

A prayer: Jesus, I want to stand with You through thick and thin..
A thought: I must be alert to snatch victories for Christ.

170. Worship Attitudes Tested
Bold reverence contrasted with bold arrogance.

June 18
~ ~ ~
2 Sam. 6
1 Chron. 13, 15

When David had made Jerusalem the City of David, God spurred him on to go a step further: to make Jerusalem the City of God (Ps. 87:3). Up to this point, the political and religious leadership in Israel had not been centralized in one city. The judges and kings had been living where they wanted. The Tabernacle had been at Shiloh and later at Nob and Gibeon, while the ark had been at Kirjath Jearim since Eli's death. Now Jerusalem became the permanent religious and political capital of Israel.

Although the ark had been in obscurity for about a century, it had not diminished in significance in God's sight. By a shocking event, He reminded Israel of the holiness of the ark and sent them back to His Word.

David organized a massive military march to accompany the ark to Jerusalem. Maybe he was more concerned about the honor the ark would bring to him and the city than he was about God's honor. Instead of consulting the priests about the proper way to move the ark, he followed the example of the Philistines by conveying the ark on a cart, as though it were common goods.

Uzzah had become so familiarized with the ark in his father's house that he did not refrain from grabbing it when the oxen stumbled. Maybe there was some showoff in his behavior too: showing to the crowds his importance as guardian of the ark. He paid with his life for his arrogant boldness.

David's frolicsome attitude now changed to anger and fear—anger toward himself for the mistakes made and fear toward God for punishing Uzzah so severely. David did not want such a dangerous object near him, so he passed the ark off on the nearest house, that of Obed-Edom. Strangely, this man did not complain that he was saddled with the danger. He received the ark with bold reverence. For him the ark was an honor and a blessing.

After three months David had done his homework better. He had studied God's Word and discovered the proper way to move the ark. He also took notice of the blessings Obed-Edom had received. David decided to proceed with his plans, and Yahveh blessed them. The Levites carried the ark. David, dressed in the simple clothes of a priest, took part in the joyful procession with bold reverence, singing, and dancing. His wife Michal stayed uninvolved at a distance and later scorned David with bold arrogance for his childlike spontaneity, which she labeled as childish impulsiveness.

A prayer: Lord, purify my attitude so my worship will be a blessing.
A thought: How can my worship get spoiled by wrong attitudes?

171. The Beginning of Zionism
Moving toward one religious center

When David put the ark in Jerusalem, the Tabernacle with its contents remained at Gibeon, six miles north of Jerusalem. David organized the priests and Levites to serve at both places. He saw this arrangement as a transitional phase until the temple would be built. In this early stage of the reunited kingdom, he probably did not want to affront the

| June 19 |
| ~~~ |
| 1 Chron. 16 |
| 2 Chron. 1:3-4 |

northern tribes by moving the place of worship to the south. Meanwhile they could get used to the idea that the ark was in Jerusalem and that a temple would be built there.

Since this time, the name Zion was used as a synonym for Jerusalem. Of the 152 times the word is used in the Old Testament (KJV), 54% occur in the Psalms and Isaiah. Psalm 48 is the renowned song about Zion. Although the word refers to the city of Jerusalem from its small beginnings to its later expansions, it also refers to the temple mount, the focal point of Jerusalem in biblical times. Zionism in the Bible was inextricably connected to the worship of Yahveh as explained in Mosaic Law. The prophets continually warned against secular Zionism, a shell without living faith inside.

The important move to make Jerusalem the religious center of Israel was not without hazards and delays. First they handled the ark contrary to God's commands—with disastrous effects. Then David had to hear that he would not be allowed to build a temple but that his son would complete that task. Zeal alone is not enough for worshiping the true God. The worshipers have to do it God's way. He is not a passive receiver of man-made worship; He is in control of God-given worship, the only worship acceptable to Him.

David was actively involved in the celebrations, and he enjoyed it tremendously. Michal watched the procession uninvolved from a distance with sour feelings. For those outside Christianity, the gospel of Jesus Christ doesn't make sense. For those on the inside who are experiencing salvation in Christ, the gospel shows the wisdom, power and love of God (1 Cor. 1:18-24, 2:14). The sharpest criticism of the church usually comes from the uninvolved. They may be members of the church or sworn enemies. Those who roll up their sleeves and get involved enjoy God, His Word, His people, and His gifts.

For David the ultimate purpose of Israel's worship was that all the nations should know and honor the LORD, Yahveh (1 Chron. 16:8, 24, 28, 31). Isaiah later also said that Israel should be a light to the Gentiles (Is. 49:6).

A prayer: Lord, I want to be involved in Your kingdom.
A thought: Do I make wise farsighted moves to promote God's kingdom?

172. Building a House
God's covenant with David

<table>
<tr><td>

June 20

~ ~ ~

2 Sam. 7

1 Chron. 17

</td></tr>
</table>

Soon after David had brought the ark of the covenant into Jerusalem, he started to feel guilty that he was living in a beautiful house made from the best Lebanon wood while the ark was sitting in a tent.

He got a bright idea: Why not replace the Tabernacle, made of fabric, with a more permanent structure made of stone, wood, and gold? After all, the reason for the tent-like sanctuary was to fold it up and carry it from place to place during Israel's sojourn in the wilderness. Yes, a permanent structure would now better symbolize their permanent stay in their permanent inheritance.

He discussed his idea with Nathan the prophet who thought it was a great idea. He encouraged David to proceed with it. That night God spoke to Nathan and sent him back to David the next day with a message that was both a deep disappointment and an exciting encouragement for David.

Knowing that David's idea came up from a devoted heart, God found it somewhat amusing. God asked: "Since Israel had settled in Canaan, did I ever tell any of the judges to build Me a house?" Then God gave David some more perspective over history. During the time of the judges, Israel was repeatedly oppressed by their enemies. God had called David, the shepherd, to shepherd His people Israel and to start a new era in which they would no longer be oppressed by their enemies. In this new dispensation David would not build a house for God, but God would build a "house" for David.

The house God was going to build for David would not be a house of bricks and timber, but a family tree, the lineage of the Messiah. The Son of David who would rule forever did not refer to inherited kingship that proceeded from father to son, but it referred to the eternal rule by one Son, the Son of God, who would become a human being, the Son of David. He would build a spiritual temple consisting of believers (1 Cor. 3:16, 1 Pet. 2:5).

On top of this awesome long-term prophecy, God also sent David an encouraging short-term prophecy: When his life was over, one of his own sons would be allowed to build a physical temple for God in Jerusalem. God had *commanded* Moses to make the Tabernacle; He *allowed* David's son to build a temple for Him. In spite of David's disappointment that he himself could not build this temple, he praised God in humble gratitude for His promises about the future. For David, Yahveh's honor, not David's glory, was predominant.

A prayer: O God, great is Your faithfulness.
A thought: Do I see my contributions in humble perspective?

173. Peace Through War
Keeping aggressors at bay

In the message that God sent to David through Nathan, God said that the "sons of wickedness" would not oppress Israel any longer because God would subdue all Israel's enemies (1 Chron. 17:9-10). That implied that David had some unfinished business to attend to. The aggressive neighbors of Israel had to be subdued so that Israel could

| June 21 |
| ~ ~ ~ |
| 2 Sam. 8, 10 |
| 1 Chron. 18-20 |

have peace. These wars would occupy David and the nation so much that they could not give their full attention to the building of the temple.

Looking at the disastrous effects of war, how can good come from something so horrific? Yet there always have been greedy aggressors wanting to take by force what belongs to others. Consequently, stalwart defenders of justice have to mobilize to protect the rights of the afflicted. Something good can come from battling the enemies of society—enemies like criminals, drug lords, murderers, abusers, tyrants, and terrorists. If we don't fight them, evil will take over like weeds in a garden.

When Israel conquered the Promised Land, they executed God's wrath on nations with evil practices. After that, Israel suffered attacks by their neighbors. God now used David to break the power of those nasty neighbors for good.

He started with the Philistines on the west and proceeded on the east with Edom, Moab, Ammon, and Syria (in order from south to north). The main results of these victories were breaking the military power of those nations, taking their treasures, receiving their taxes, and using their workforce. In this way David's kingdom received a powerful boost toward prosperity. David's mighty men, under Joab and Abishai, played a major part in these wars and victories, which took several years to complete.

Israel's history is an object lesson to the church (1 Cor. 10:11). David's wars and victories tell us something about ours. Our battles can be physical (like illness or disability), emotional (like depression or anxiety), spiritual (like sin or persecution), material (like poverty or debt), social (like gossip or loneliness), and ecological (like pollution or natural disasters). We have to fight each battle with appropriate weapons—a Bible text will not help for a hungry stomach (James 2:15-16); neither will drugs help for an empty spirit. We have to address the problem with faith in God. We must be bold but not arrogant, strong but not cruel, modest but not fainthearted, compassionate but not pampering, and open to suggestions but not gullible to deceit.

A prayer: Lord, I want to be part of Your wars and victories.
A thought: Do I try to avoid spiritual warfare?

174. By My God
I can leap over a wall.

June 22
~ ~ ~
2 Sam. 22

The author of the Samuel books did not always place events in chronological order (2 Sam. 23, 24). Most likely, David's song of victory was not written near the end of his life. His affirmation of his innocence (verses 20-25) can be interpreted in various ways. First, it may point to the Messiah, the only one who is really blameless before God. Second, it may show that God's forgiveness does wipe out all sin. Third, it may place this song before David's sins of adultery and murder.

His triumphant boldness suggests that he was on an emotional and spiritual peak when he wrote this song that became Psalm 18.

David's success in breaking the military power of Israel's aggressors and harnessing their economical power for Israel's prosperity inspired David to give all the honor to God. He looked back on his life, applying this song to all his struggles, even to the days he had been fleeing from Saul.

He painted his own predicament and Yahveh's merciful intervention in poetic metaphors. He saw himself as drowning in a stormy sea, covered by waves and strangled by seaweed. In his agony he called to God for help. God came down in a terrible thunderstorm. The lightning bolts were His flying arrows, and the roaring thunder was His mighty voice. He grabbed David and pulled him out of his sea of troubles.

David saw the reason for God's intervention as God's love for him and his love for God. David's righteousness was not based on his own merit. He was made right with God by God's grace. God gave David faith, and God used that faith to forgive David and to declare him righteous, just as He had done for Abram (Gen. 15:6). That is how God's righteousness-by-grace works.

Then David described how Yahveh enabled him to win battles for God. God gave him the know-how, the speed, and the power. With God on his side, he could defeat armies and jump over the walls of fortified cities. Paul echoed these words when He said that he could do all things through Christ who strengthens him (Phil. 4:13). David crushed his enemies underfoot like dust and mud. He did not return until victory was complete.

We can apply these metaphors to spiritual warfare. We have to fight against the forces of evil with complete trust in God and with all our might—without breaking the law.

Then we can say with Paul, *"I have fought the good fight, I have finished the race, I have kept the faith"* (2 Tim. 4:7).

A prayer: By my God I can leap over a wall.
*A thought: Am I fighting the **good** fight?*

175. Loyalty Generates Charity
David cares for Jonathan's son.

Time was flying. Mephibosheth was five years old when his father Jonathan died. As they fled from the invading Philistines, Mephibosheth was injured in a fall and became paraplegic (4:4). When David became king over all Israel seven years later (5:5), this boy was twelve years old. After eight years of war had elapsed, he already had a child of his own, and David was in his mid-forties. As peace and rest gradually settled over Israel, David pondered on the past. He recalled his friendship and covenant with Jonathan and wondered what had happened to Jonathan's children. The desire arose in David to show his goodwill toward Jonathan's offspring.

> June 23
> ~ ~ ~
> 2 Sam. 9

David made enquiries and learned about the fate of Mephibosheth, who was cared for by a generous rich man east of Jordan. David sent for him. Not knowing what to expect, the lame Mephibosheth prostrated himself before the king and hoped for mercy. David picked him up physically and emotionally. The king ordered that all Saul's properties be transferred to Mephibosheth and that Ziba had to work that land for the benefit of Mephibosheth's family. Then king David invited Mephibosheth to be his permanent guest. It must have given David tremendous joy to extend these graces to his friend's son.

This episode shows us another side of David's character. The man who relentlessly had subdued the enemies of God's people now showed tender care for the disabled. When David was about to conquer Jerusalem, the Jebusites said that the lame and the blind would drive him off. David's response: He hated the Jebusites, who were "the lame and the blind" in his sight. His charity toward Mephibosheth showed he was not against disabled people but that he had turned the Jebusites' phrase onto themselves (5:6-8).

David was a type of Christ pointing to the Messiah by his good deeds and words. Though Christ was not bound by a covenant like David, He also sought after a human race exiled from Paradise—poor and lame, powerless to recover from their moral misery. Without any merit on their side, Christ bestowed mercy on them, on those who humbled themselves and accepted His grace. They were made children of God the Father and may sit at His table together with His Son who had reconciled them with the Father.

As Christians we are named after Christ and have to follow His example, reaching out to the less fortunate, not in a condescending way, but as brothers and sisters who also were disabled once.

A prayer: Lord, I want to be generous toward the afflicted as You are.
A thought: Do I search for opportunities to extend a helping hand?

176. The Process of Sin
David and Bathsheba

June 24
~ ~ ~
2 Sam. 11

Power corrupts. When David reached his peak, royal lifestyle fostered self-indulgence. He did not accompany his army to the battlefield anymore. He was willing to misuse his power for sexual adventure and for covering up his sin. However, David did not plan the whole sordid process beforehand. Satan got him to take the first step and urged him to improvise as he waded deeper into the marsh.

The palace overlooked the David City, located on the southeastern slope of Mount Moriah. Enjoying the cool breeze one evening on the flat roof of his palace, David laid his eyes on an enticing scene. A pretty woman was taking a ritual bath by pouring water over herself to cleanse herself of the "impurity" of her monthly period, seven days after her period had ended (Lev. 15). She would be on the peak of her fertility for the next few days.

Bathsheba bathed in clear view of the palace at the time of day when the king strolled on the roof. She readily complied with David's wishes when he invited her to the palace. She was probably as guilty as David in this whole affair. She showed her femininity, and David watched with lust. Then he took the initiative. He enquired, and she waited. He made contact, and she responded with charm. He touched her gently, and she allowed him. A kiss became a passionate embrace, and then all resistance crumbled. Either one of them could have stopped the process before it got too far.

Her pregnancy was a threat to their secret. Now sins multiplied in an effort to cover up the first one. David tried to cheat Uriah to believe that the child was his, but Uriah's high standards sank that effort. Then David sent a sealed command with Uriah to Joab to ensure Uriah's death. As one of David's mighty men (23:39), Uriah had been risking his life for David repeatedly. David rewarded him by stealing his wife and planning his death.

David's plan forced Joab and Uriah's comrades to become accomplices. Because Joab had murdered Abner, he realized David's plan would make David guilty of the same crime. Then the pot could not blame the kettle anymore, so he willingly obliged and faultlessly staged Uriah's death in battle.

Protecting his public image was so important to David that he silenced his conscience and became blind to his sin. He was relieved when he heard of Uriah's death, thinking his smartness got him off the hook. He forgot that God was watching and would not let him get away with such an injustice.

A prayer: Holy Spirit, help me prevent temptation from becoming sin.
A thought: Let him who thinks he stands take heed lest he fall. (1 Cor. 10:12)

177. Boundless Grace
Repentance and forgiveness break through.

The days rolled by, weeks became months, and months a year. Bathsheba's child had been born, but David had not yet come to repentance. He had lost his fellowship with God. With an empty heart, he recited old psalms. He had no inspiration to write a new one. His harp hung silent and his soul was starving, but he remained blind to his own condition and to what had caused it.

> June 25
> ~ ~ ~
> 2 Sam. 12

Yahveh reached out to David. He sent the prophet Nathan to him with a simple yet revealing message. The same friend who had told David of God's everlasting covenant with him now had to announce God's judgment.

It is easier to recognize sin in someone else than in ourselves; therefore, God let Nathan tell the story about the rich and poor men. Taking it for an injustice committed in his kingdom, David projected his guilt onto the culprit and sentenced him to death without thinking twice. Nathan's words hit David like a hammer: *"You are the man!"* David was the rich man who had taken the poor man's only lamb by taking what was dearest to Uriah: his wife and his life.

In a moment, God opened David's eyes to what he had done. An overwhelming sense of guilt engulfed him. He could hear God sobbing when Nathan said, *"Why have you despised the commandment of the LORD ...?"* Apart from the wrongs David did to others, he had caused pain to the One he loved most, Yahveh. He choked up under the immense remorse and muttered, "I have sinned against Yahveh!" In his repentance and pleas for forgiveness, expressed in Psalm 51, one thing haunted him: He had offended God Himself.

In God's sovereign mercy, He took the innocent child to Himself and let David live to face the results of his deeds. God forgave him, but God did not relieve him of the consequences that He had announced by the prophet.

Ten centuries later another Son of David would die so sinners could be saved. Out of Adam's miserable fall, God shaped His glorious salvation. From David's infamous relationship with Bathsheba, Solomon ("Peace") was born to affirm that peace between David and God had been restored and to point to the Prince of Peace (Isaiah 9:6), who would reconcile humanity with their Creator. In His grace, God often turns calamity into triumph.

After this sad, shocking interruption David and Joab conquered Rabbah on the banks of the Jabbok River where Jacob had struggled with God. It would have reminded David of his own wrestling with God in repentance.

A prayer: O God, have mercy on me, a sinner.
A thought: Do I try to paint over sins with excuses?

178. A Broken and Contrite Heart
is not despised by God.

June 26
~ ~ ~
Ps. 51

When David became aware of his sin and repented with sincerity, God immediately announced His forgiveness through the prophet Nathan. However, it would take some time before David would be able to accept that forgiveness. He had to go through an emotional and spiritual process before he got inner assurance that his sins had been forgiven.

This process is normal, but if we stretch it out too long it may become an effort to pay for our sins by self-punishment. Beating ourselves up cannot wipe out our sin or guilt feelings.

That is not what David did in Psalm 51. He did not minimize his sins or pain but allowed himself to go through a grieving process. He allowed himself to experience the dark depth of guilt created by his sinful **being** (verse 5) and by his sinful **deeds** (verse 14). During that week of fasting and pleading for the baby's recovery, he also battled with his own sin that had caused the baby's illness. He had wronged people; he had offended God.

David fled to God, who alone could cleanse him from the **guilt** of sin and give him victory over the **power** of sin. His plea for forgiveness (verses 1-5, 7, 9, 14a, 17) was accompanied by heartfelt sorrow and was mingled with prayers for spiritual recovery (6, 8, 10-13, 14b-15). He wanted to return to that wonderful closeness with God that he had experienced before.

David did not try to make himself look a little better by giving good reasons for his behavior or by putting the blame on others. He accepted full responsibility. Neither could he offer anything to make amends. Not even the sacrifices prescribed in the Law could eliminate the stains of his sins. He threw himself onto God's mercy (verse 1), which cannot be earned, only accepted with deep humility and gratitude (verse 17).

Writing down his remorse, repentance, and struggle helped David get clarity about God's precious forgiveness. This psalm also shows us the true nature of sin and the path of true repentance. Sin destroys our most valuable relationships: with God, with others, and with ourselves. Forgiveness has to start with God and then proceed to others and self. Yes, eventually we have to stop self-blame and replace it with jubilation over God's forgiveness.

Israel also prayed this repenting psalm during their exile, and therefore they added the last two verses about the joy that they would experience when God would restore the walls and sacrifices of Jerusalem.

A prayer: O God, I praise You for Your tender mercy and loving kindness.
A thought: Do I use defenses when I ask forgiveness from God or people?

179. Family Discord
in David's household

David's sin caused trouble in his household (12:11). His bad example was soon followed by his oldest son. Amnon's sexual drive got fixated on his half-sister, Tamar. She and Absalom were born from David's wife Maacah, daughter of Talmai, king of Geshur (3:3). Amnon decided to follow the advice of a friend and seduce Tamar. David's visit to the "sick" Amnon showed that in spite of his royal duties, David had still time for his children. He granted the seemingly innocent request of Amnon that Tamar should prepare something for him to eat.

> June 27
>
> ~ ~ ~
>
> 2 Sam. 13-14

Everything was kosher until Amnon sent all except Tamar out of the room. When Amnon revealed his real motives, Tamar showed her noble character by pleading with him neither to disgrace her nor to drag his own name through the mud. Although the Law forbade it (Deut. 27:22), she was even willing to become his wife if he would follow the honorable road by asking their father's permission. Her refusal changed the planned seduction into an impulsive rape. Instead of joy, Amnon reaped self-hate, which he projected onto the devastated Tamar. She could not hide her shame and pain. Soon everybody in the royal family knew what had happened.

David was angry but did nothing to help Tamar or to discipline Amnon. Absalom decided to avenge the shame of his sister. To avoid any suspicion, he waited two years before he invited all the king's sons to a shearing feast several miles north of Jerusalem. When everybody was merry and off guard, Absalom gave the signal to his servants to kill Amnon.

While the others fled in panic to Jerusalem, Absalom and his men fled to his grandfather at Geshur, a small kingdom northeast of the Sea of Galilee (15:8). In his youth David also had to flee abroad, but not because he had committed a crime. After three years David let Absalom return to Jerusalem, thanks to the intervention of Joab. After another two years David agreed to see Absalom. Apart from Absalom's self-imposed exile and two years of house arrest in Jerusalem, David did nothing to punish him.

Absalom did not live up to his name, meaning *father's peace*. Shortly after David had pardoned him for avenging his sister's rape by murder, Absalom started to organize a revolt against his own father. Apparently both his values and his emotions were rather shallow. He used his father's killing of Uriah as an excuse to kill anyone who stood in his way.

A prayer: Holy Spirit, help me overcome temptation in view of the consequences.
A thought: Can anticipation of consequences help me make good decisions?

180. Fugitive Again
David flees from his rebelling son.

<table>
<tr><td>

June 28

~~~

2 Sam. 15-16

</td><td>

Being the most assertive of all David's sons, Absalom decided that he would be his father's successor and that he would not wait for his father's natural death. He wanted to accelerate the process. In a rather transparent way, he began to win the favor of ordinary citizens. In the four years

</td></tr>
</table>

Absalom had been doing this, David's advisors would have informed him about it. Maybe David thought it was a good thing that the royal family stayed in touch with the man in the street.

When Absalom sensed that he had gained widespread popularity, he set the wheels in motion for his decisive move. Like his father, he started his claim to the throne in Hebron, nineteen miles south of Jerusalem. When his intentions became public, Jerusalem was shocked into commotion. The loyal decided to stand with King David, while the opportunists thought the time of the aging king was over and that it was safer to side with Absalom.

David knew they had to move fast to prevent an easy victory by the rebels, especially when he learned that his highly respected advisor, Ahithophel, had walked over to Absalom. David decided to flee to the region east of the Jordan in the hope of saving Jerusalem from destruction. He took his entire household except ten concubines with him. His guard and his Philistine friends who had stood with him since the days he took refuge in Gath stayed loyal to him. While they crossed the Mount of Olives in grieving spirit, some pledged their loyalty to David, while Shimei cursed him as a villain and a murderer.

In spite of his distress about his son's revolt, David was planning with a clear mind and with a trusting heart to outsmart the rebels. He sent the priests and the ark back to Jerusalem so that they could keep him informed about Absalom's plans. He persuaded Hushai, his trustworthy advisor, to stay in the city and try to undermine the good advice of Ahithophel.

It was a terrible day for David and his loved ones. The day before, they were still enjoying their privileges in Zion, the city of the LORD (Joel 3:21); now they were fleeing on foot for their lives. When they arrived at the edge of the mountains near the Jordan River, Absalom arrived with his chariots in Jerusalem, which he took without any resistance.

You may have had this experience somewhere in your life: the moment all your certainties collapse and you realize that only God can save you now. Then do what David did: Cling to God in spite of your past mistakes.

A prayer: Lord, You are my only comfort in life and in death.
A thought: In a crisis, do I blame God or do I trust God?

181. Man Proposes, God Disposes
God defeats Absalom's plans.

The wind was taken out of Absalom's sails when he arrived in Jerusalem—no battle, no surrender. Uncertain what to do next, he asked Ahithophel for advice. He suggested that Absalom first go to bed with his father's concubines to portray himself as his father's successor and to make the breach between him and his father final.

June 29
~~~
2 Sam. 16:15 -
17:29

Next, Ahithophel would immediately go with twelve thousand men and surprise David and his people while they were still tired, weak, and disorganized. Ahithophel would kill only David, and then all Israel would accept that David's kingdom was something of the past.

But God had other plans. He heard David's prayer (15:31) and used Hushai to nullify Ahithophel's advice. Hushai impressed Absalom with his father's experience as warrior and strategist, as well as the motivation and skills of David's mighty men who had stood their ground against hundreds in the past. The only way to overcome warriors like that was to outnumber them with a superior army. They needed time to call up all Israel. Actually, Hushai was buying more time for David to escape and redeploy.

Amazing everyone, Absalom accepted Hushai's advice. Absalom still must have highly respected his father's war reputation. Ahithophel realized that Absalom would now lose the battle, and that he, Ahithophel, would be executed for treason. He gave orders to his family and hung himself.

Ahimaaz and Jonathan, sons of priests Zadok and Abiathar respectively, were sent off to warn David about Ahithophel's plan—just in case Absalom changed his mind. Someone spotted them and informed Absalom. God used a woman to hide them and to send their pursuers in the wrong direction. When David got the news, he decided to cross the Jordan that same night.

When they reached Mahanaim the next day, their friends welcomed them with food and shelter. To feed so many people every day required excellent organization. God had provided for the helpers so that they could provide for the needy. David had come full circle: As a young man he had been a fugitive who had been dependant on the goodwill of others. After about thirty years of plenty, the king was back where he had started.

God brings us into situations where we realize we cannot survive without God's mercy. Paul learned this lesson too: *"I have learned both to be full and to be hungry ... I can do all things through Christ who strengthens me."* (Phil. 4:12-13).

A prayer: Thank You, Lord, for providing in good and bad times.
A thought: Do I see God's grace in both success and hardship?

182. The War of Contrasts
The emotional king and the pragmatic general

> June 30
> ~~~
> 2 Sam. 18-19

These chapters are woven with contrasts. The armies of father and son prepared for battle. While the son's main aim is to kill his father, the father pleads that his son's life be spared. Eventually, the father mourns the death of his son instead of celebrating the crushing of the revolt.

Trusting in God, David divided his men into three regiments to break up Absalom's army. He chose a hilly forested terrain that would further disperse the enemy and make ambushes possible. The forest became a mighty ally. Absalom's beautiful hair became his deathtrap. The small army of shrewd veterans defeated the large inexperienced army.

Due to David's emotional involvement with his son, he lost perspective of the long-term political significance of the battle for his kingdom. Joab was more pragmatic and did not take the wish of the king seriously that his son be spared, because that son also happened to be the chief commander of the rebels. So when Joab heard that his fierce adversary was hanging by his hair in a tree, pathetically kicking and yelling and swearing, Joab callously put three spears through his chest. With Absalom dead, the battle was over.

The good news about David's victory was bad news about his son. His personal loss overshadowed the gain of his country. Though one has empathy with David grieving his son's dishonorable death, Joab's realistic point about the negative effect on the troops is understandable. Joab swayed David to make his personal loss secondary to the good of his country.

The return of David to Jerusalem was just as confusing as his flight from it. The people who had used the king's embarrassment to further their own cause now had to beg for mercy. The people who tried to get rid of David now argued about the question who of them loved him the most. David pardoned Amasa, Absalom's general, but Joab murdered him nonetheless. David offered his hospitality to the aged Barzillai, but he preferred to die in his hometown.

The period of conflicts and contrasts had come to an end. David was restored as king over all Israel. The messianic lineage was saved after another satanic endeavor to sink it.

In times of internal or external conflicts and confusion, we have to hang on to God's steady hand. He will lead us through the dark valley: *"Yea, though I walk through the valley of the shadow of death, I will fear no evil; for You are with me; Your rod and Your staff, they comfort me."* (Ps. 23:4).

A prayer: Lord, in Your hands I am safe.
A thought: Is God's Word my compass in fine and bad weather?

183. Haunted by Problems
Bad choices lead to bad consequences.

David's sin regarding Bathsheba and Uriah had a ripple effect—from family to state affairs. David was angry at Joab for killing Absalom and tried to replace Joab with Amasa as his chief general. To replace the loyal victorious general with the defeated rebelling general was a bad move. Totally ignoring Joab, David

July 1
~ ~ ~
2 Sam. 20, 21, 24

asked Amasa and Abishai to deal with the rebellion of Sheba. By killing Amasa and quenching the rebellion swiftly, Joab reestablished himself as general and let David know that he could not rule without him.

After three years of drought, David enquired of God what the reason was. God told him that Saul's injustice towards the Gibeonites had not been punished. When Israel had conquered the Promised Land four centuries earlier, they had sworn to the Gibeonites that they would not kill them (Josh. 9). Saul broke that oath when he tried to wipe them out.

Instead of enquiring of God how to rectify the injustice, David asked the pagan Gibeonites how they wanted justice to be done. When they demanded the death of seven of Saul's sons, David granted their request, which was a violation of the Law (Deut. 24:16). By this he also broke his oath to Saul (1 Sam. 24:21-22). While the bodies hung in wind and weather for six months, another violation of the Law (Deut. 21:23), Rizpah showed her motherly love by scaring off scavenging birds and animals. Eventually David secured a proper burial for the remains of these men and for those of Saul and Jonathan.

God allowed Satan to lure David into an illegal census (Ex. 30:11-16). In spite of Joab's warning, David went ahead with it. When David realized his mistake, he had to choose between three forms of punishment. He chose to surrender himself into God's hands rather than into men's hands. It was also the shortest punishment. Seventy-thousand of his people died of the plague.

God stopped the angel of death at the threshing floor of Araunah, just outside Jerusalem. David purchased the site and the oxen from the owner to sacrifice to Yahveh. By this transaction this piece of real estate, the present temple mount in Jerusalem (2 Chron. 3:1), became the property of Israel—not by capture but by purchase. Jerusalem has been captured many times since then, but this property has never been sold to anyone. Israel still holds the deed of sale recorded in the Bible. In spite of the mistakes David made, Yahveh steered history in the direction that He wanted it to go.

A prayer: Father, I need Your guidance to make good decisions.
A thought: Have I made major decisions without prayer and consultation?

184. Weaker, Yet Stronger
The forte of the aged

July 2

~ ~ ~

2 Sam. 21, 24
1 Chron. 20-29

As was the case with the judges, the Bible reports little about the regular work of the kings. Moses had instituted a judiciary system from grassroots level up to the high priest (96), but the king later became the supreme court. Some compared David's wisdom as judge to that of an angel (2 Sam. 14:20). For the people of his time, David's virtues overshadowed his vices by far.

The king was also the supreme commander of the armed forces. While still strong, kings took part in combat. Though David might have fenced regularly with his mighty men to keep fit, his strength was decreasing. Once he almost got killed by a Philistine giant. Abishai came to his rescue. His spirit was willing, but his body was weak. He was only a shadow of the young man who had killed Goliath. His mighty men relieved him of any further close combat—*"lest you quench the lamp of Israel."* They retired him from active duty with the most honorable medal: "the lamp of Israel."

When the aging process slowly but surely drains one's physical abilities, it is a good time to focus more on one's spiritual activities. Paul knew from personal experience what he was talking about when he wrote, *"Therefore we do not lose heart. Even though our outward man is perishing, yet the inward man is being renewed day by day"* (2 Cor. 4:16).

David concluded his career by preparing Solomon to succeed him and build the temple. David pressed it on his son's heart that God would bless him if he stayed true to God by obeying His Word. David made it known to all his state officials and army officers that Solomon was his successor.

David had all the plans for the temple drawn and all the building material collected and prepared: more than enough gold, silver, bronze, iron, wood, and stone. He said to the great assembly of officials, *"I have set my affection on the house of my God"* (1 Chron. 29:3). O, that all God's children would love His house as much as David did! He was not only focused on the physical building but also on the worship that would take place in that building. Therefore, he organized the Levites and priests so that they could prepare themselves for their crucial task once the temple would be erected (1 Chron. 22-26). These rules were followed for centuries. He also organized the army, the community leaders, and the state departments into efficient teams (1 Chron. 27). It highlights yet another side of this gifted leader, strategist, believer, poet, singer, judge, survivor, and king.

A prayer: Father, please empower me spiritually as I grow weaker physically.
A thought: I want to stay active in God's kingdom till the end.

185. The Final Victory
David crowns Solomon as his successor.

When David was seventy years old, his health was failing fast. He was bedridden and was nursed by the beautiful Abishag. His son Adonijah, the late Absalom's brother, saw his father's frailty as a chance to grab the throne for himself. He got some important leaders on his side: Joab the general, Abiathar the priest, and leaders from Judah. He invited them to a coronation party near Jerusalem.

> July 3
>
> ~ ~ ~
>
> 1 Kings 1-2

Nathan the prophet heard about it, and he informed David through Bathsheba. After a while, Nathan joined Bathsheba and confirmed what she had said. In spite of his weakness, David ordered quick and decisive moves. Zadok the priest, Nathan the prophet, and Benaiah, the captain of the guard, had to assemble the people of Jerusalem at the Gihon fountain, take Solomon on the king's mule to them, and anoint him as king. This plan was executed swiftly and effectively. The whole Jerusalem was excited about the move and cheered, "Long live king Solomon!"

It took the wind from the sails of the conspirators and they dispersed quickly. Solomon assured Adonijah no harm would come to him as long as he behaved himself. Victorious kings usually took the wives and concubines of conquered kings to confirm their dominance, so when Adonijah asked that Abishag become his wife, Solomon saw that as another arrogant effort of Adonijah to seize the throne. He sentenced him to death for treason.

Because Abiathar the priest had assisted David over many years, Solomon did not have him executed for siding with the conspiracy, but discharged him as priest. As requested by David, Solomon had Joab executed for murdering Abner and Amasa. Solomon limited Shimei's freedom for cursing his father, David, but when Shimei broke the rules, he brought the death penalty onto himself. Solomon appointed Zadok as high priest and Benaiah as general. Now he could start his kingdom with a clean slate.

During all his life, David had to fight adversaries. As shepherd he fought against lions and bears. Then he faced Goliath and Saul. As king he subdued the enemies of his country to secure peace for his people. He prevailed against four rebels: Abner, Absalom, Sheba, and Adonijah. It is not surprising that in his psalms he cried out to Yahveh for protection from enemies. Eventually, he died in peace and contentment. He could say with Paul, *"I have fought the good fight, I have finished the race, I have kept the faith!"* (2 Tim. 4:7).

A prayer: Lord, empower me so I will not grow weary in my battles.
A thought: Do I take fast, decisive steps when I realize Satan's plans?

186. The Right Prayer
God inspires Solomon to want what God wanted.

<table>
<tr><td>

July 4

~ ~ ~

1 Kings 3:1-15
2 Chron. 1:1-12
</td><td>
Solomon had started off with a rough ride. After completing some unfinished business of his father, he married an Egyptian princess to secure his southern border. He sought God at the "high places," which were usually defiled by immoral pagan practices. God
</td></tr>
</table>

intervened and led him in the right direction.

When Solomon came to the Tabernacle at Gibeon near Bethel where his forefather had the famous dream of "Jacob's Ladder," Solomon, too, had a dream that changed his life. The LORD, Yahveh, appeared to him in a dream and asked him what he wanted most. Dreams often reflect the needs and fears of the dreamer. God blessed Solomon for desiring wisdom so much that it was reflected in his dreams. *"If any of you lacks wisdom, let him ask of God, who gives to all liberally and without reproach, and it will be given to him"* (James 1:5).

We have here a striking illustration of an important biblical principle. The only prayer that is completely in line with God's will is the prayer that God puts into one's heart by His Spirit (Rom. 8:26-27). Such a God-inspired prayer will be answered by God. That is why the prayer for salvation is always answered by God (John 6:37), because it is inspired by God (John 6:44) and therefore completely in line with His will (John 3:16, 2 Pet. 3:9).

Prayer is not a tool with which we can persuade God to grant our wishes. Prayer is quality time with our Father, a togetherness where we show Him that we love and trust Him so much that we want what He wants (Luke 22:42).

Solomon went back to Jerusalem to pray and offer where he should have started: at the ark of the covenant, the mercy seat of God, where his father David had experienced quality time with God many times. Solomon discovered that we don't have to go far to meet God. He is omnipresent; He is always near (Ps. 139, Rom. 10).

We don't have to invent new ways to communicate with Him either. Rather try the proven ways that have stood the test of time for many generations. Solomon did not meet God at the new popular "high places," but at the age-old Tabernacle and the ark of the covenant. There God had met the childless Hannah when she poured her heart out before God, and there He met little Samuel who said, *"Speak, for Your servant hears."* Solomon grew up with these stories for his father knew Samuel well. Solomon just had to rediscover the truth of these stories for himself.

A prayer: Lord, put the right prayer in my heart at the right time.
A thought: Do I allow God's Spirit to pray through me?

187. Honoring God
The starting point of true wisdom

Solomon became famous for his wisdom more than anything else. His temple, his palace, his riches, his wives, his chariots, his politics, his trade, and his organization were remarkable, but his greatest forte was his wisdom. He knew his wisdom was a gift from God; therefore, he believed that true wisdom could only be received from the one true God:

July 5
~ ~ ~
1 Kings 5 - 7
2 Chron. 2 - 4

"The fear of the LORD is the beginning of wisdom, and the knowledge of the Holy One is understanding" (Prov. 9:10).

This link between wisdom and worship inspired the authors of the Kings and the Chronicles to devote several chapters to the building and inauguration of Solomon's temple, which was erected on the threshing floor that David bought from Araunah. On today's Temple Mount, that spot is just north of the Dome of the Rock.

Although the basic plan had already been drawn by his father David, Solomon put his own touch to the decoration of the temple. The building had the same three parts as the Tabernacle—the court, the holy, and the most holy sections—but now it was built with stone and wood, and the dimensions were double that of the Tabernacle. The main building (the holy and most holy parts) was gold-plated on the inside, and on the outside it was surrounded by rooms on the south, north, and west sides. The east facing entrance was flanked by two colossal bronze pillars with decorated heads.

The furnishings in the temple were almost the same as in the Tabernacle. In the Most Holy were the ark and two huge golden cherubim. In the Holy were the incense-altar, the tables with bread, and the lamp-stands. In the court were the altar for burnt offerings and a large bronze container with water.

David and Solomon merged the old and the new in the temple. The worship of Yahveh, as described by Moses, proceeded unchanged. This strong bond between the old and the new enabled the nation to identify with the new sanctuary and to give it their full support.

By combining faith and wisdom, old and new, the wisest man left an important message to the world: Those who try to be smart and cool without God are unwise, and those who don't incorporate the good of the past into new developments will impoverish themselves. Wise people acknowledge the almighty and all-knowing Creator and Sustainer of the universe when they deal with important realities of the past, present, or future.

A prayer: Lord, without You we can do nothing. (John 15:5)
A thought: Are secular views and values encroaching on my life?

188. God Honors Man
with His presence in true worship

July 6
~ ~ ~
1 Kings 8, 9:1-9
2 Chron. 5-7

Eleven years after king David's death, his dream about a temple came true. Solomon was relieved and delighted that he could successfully complete this major task his father had placed on his shoulders. Looking at the magnificent building, he must have thought: "I wish Dad were here to see this."

When the ark was placed in the Most Holy by the Levites, God honored this small human effort on this small planet by making His presence visible to the people. The CLOUD that guarded Israel during their wandering in the wilderness appeared, came down, and filled the temple. When God honored their worship like that with His presence, everybody knew that their sanctuary was accepted and blessed by the Most High. That inspired them to worship with even more devotion and jubilance.

In his speech, Solomon acknowledged the influence of his father and the grace of God in finishing the temple. In his prayer, he praised the greatness of Yahveh: as the heavens could not contain God, how much less this temple built by man. Nevertheless, Solomon beseeched Yahveh to graciously hear the prayers of those in need who would pray in or toward this temple in Jerusalem. God answered his prayer with FIRE from heaven. It devoured the burnt offering. Solomon then blessed the people and urged them to stay true to Yahveh.

Additional space in the temple court was sanctified for sacrifices because Solomon offered so many animals that the altar could not handle all of them. Most of these offerings were of the shared type: The blood was sprinkled against the altar, the fat was burnt on the altar, and the cooked meat was eaten by the people. God's children were feasting with their heavenly Father.

God further honored Solomon's dedication by appearing to him in a dream again. God reaffirmed His earlier promise that He would bless Solomon and his descendants if they would walk in the ways of Yahveh.

God did not order them to build a temple to His honor, but He accepted their desire to do so. He honored their effort by clear signs of His presence. Likewise, God honors all genuine efforts to worship Him, no matter how diverse those efforts may be in different cultures. However, Solomon and his people stuck to the God-given form of worship that pointed to Christ. When He came, the symbols pointing to Him fell away and contact with the Father through His mediating Son was established (John 14:6).

A prayer: Thank You, Father, for accepting our humble worship.
A thought: When I honor God's Word, He will honor mine.

189. Practical Wisdom

Solomon pours his wisdom into songs and proverbs.

Solomon's wisdom was not abstract. He loved practical wisdom that could help ordinary folks do right and avoid the wrong. The case of the two mothers and the baby became the classic example of Solomon's practical wisdom. Like the parables of Jesus, his wisdom could be taught to children and shared with friends.

> July 7
> ~ ~ ~
> Proverbs 3

To help the memory, Solomon poured his wisdom into songs and proverbs. Some of these were preserved for us in the Psalms (72, 127), Proverbs, Ecclesiastes, and the Song of Solomon. Today we take a quick look at Proverbs 1-29, which is attributed to Solomon (except for 22:17 through 24:34).

He covered a wide variety of subjects, but these can be grouped into a few main categories. The focus of the first nine chapters of Proverbs is on the excellence of wisdom itself. Fathers are encouraged to teach wisdom to their children, and children are admonished not to despise the wisdom that is handed down from one generation to the next. They should use it as a tool to make the right choices. It is repeated several times that wisdom protects against sexual temptations. From the priest's perspective, immorality is impurity, for the prophet it is sin, and for the wise it is folly. All three perspectives are valid. Although Proverbs do not refer much to religion and worship, God is portrayed as a Person who is the source of true wisdom.

In poetic metaphors, wisdom is personified as God's assistant when He created the universe (Prov. 8). Christ is also described as the Word and Wisdom of God, by whom all things were made (John 1:1, 1 Cor. 1:30).

As Solomon observed life, he formulated truth about man's thoughts, feelings, willpower, values, hopes, actions, relationships, possessions, goals, pleasures, attitudes, and much more. An interesting way to study Proverbs is to sort the individual proverbs into categories—for example, this one is about marriage and that one is about career, etc. Eventually, one has all the proverbs about a specific subject together. Pages 352 to 358 cover some of these themes. (See also the Index of Proverbs in the Appendix).

We cannot save ourselves with wisdom. We are saved by God's wisdom and love. After that happens, we can start to practice God-given wisdom and "work out" (apply) our salvation to everyday living (Phil. 2:12-13). Jesus promised wisdom to His followers, *"For I will give you words and wisdom that none of your adversaries will be able to resist or contradict"* (Luke 21:15 NIV).

A prayer: Lord, open my eyes to see the wisdom of Your Word.
A thought: What is the difference between knowledge and wisdom?

190. Wise Management
Shared responsibility

July 8
~ ~ ~
1 Kings 4
9:15 - 10:29
2 Chron. 8-9

Wise leaders don't try to do everything and to reach everywhere. They create a system of shared responsibilities from the highest to the lowest level. Good two-way communication between and on all levels ensures that problems are identified and addressed as they arise and that opportunities are noticed and utilized as they occur.

King David had started with this policy on a small scale, and king Solomon developed it to an extensive enterprise. He applied it to the temple and those who served there, to his army and horses, to his laborers and building projects, to his trade and mining, to his fiscal and foreign policies, and to his servants and household. He delegated power and responsibilities to the leaders of these fields, and they gave orders to sub-leaders, who organized the citizens to do their share for king and country.

Of course, workers and overseers had to report back to the leaders who informed Solomon on what was going on. In this way he could hold his hand on the pulse of every department. Although this method is well known to us, such an extensive, well-organized administration was a major achievement three thousand years ago.

However, this concept was not completely new. Five centuries before Solomon, Moses' father-in-law had advised him to delegate responsibilities to leaders under him to prevent burnout for himself (Ex. 18). This system had been preserved by the elders of Israel. Solomon both expanded and centralized this custom, like the spokes of a wheel. Jesus followed the same principle when He called the twelve disciples. He trained them, empowered them, and sent them out to preach the gospel and to train others to proceed with kingdom work till He comes again. In his missionary work, the apostle Paul appointed elders and deacons in every church he planted. He compared the mutual cooperation of church members with the interdependent organs of the body (1 Cor. 12).

Shared responsibilities are still of vital importance for the church. Every member should be involved in some way, whether leading or following. However, to be a blessing, the church needs more than good organization. A church may be well organized, but still spiritually dead. Every member must seek a daily contact with, and anointing by, the Holy Spirit. The sap of the vine must flow through the branches to produce fruit (John 15).

A prayer: Lord, show me my place in Your organization.
A thought: Where will I best fit in with my talents and temperament?

191. The Wisdom of Trust
Unless the LORD builds and guards ...

This psalm reflects Solomon's belief system for most of his reign. In addition to the glorious temple, palace, city wall, and towers he erected in Jerusalem, he rebuilt many cities into fortresses (1 Kings 9:15-19; Eccl. 2:4-9). When he inspected the work in progress, he thought to himself: "Unless Yahveh builds the house and unless Yahveh guards the city, all our building and guarding are in vain."

> July 9
> ~ ~ ~
> Psalm 127

In Psalm 127 this thought is developed further to include all work and family life. People focused on material things only strain themselves by hard work from dawn to midnight, cutting down on sleeping and eating, often with little to show for their efforts. However, those who trust in God and adjust their values and lifestyle accordingly do a good day's work, have a good night's sleep, and are blessed by God because He loves them.

When Solomon was a baby, God ordered the prophet Nathan to call him Jedidiah (*"beloved* of Yahveh", 2 Sam. 12:25). Solomon uses the same word in Hebrew when he says, "He gives His *beloved* sleep" (Ps. 127:2). He meant, "I sleep restfully because God loves me." God had indeed given everything to Solomon in his sleep because at the start of Solomon's reign God had appeared to him in a dream and promised him success because he had chosen wisdom.

Jesus said that the kingdom of God is like a man who has seeded his fields "and should sleep by night and rise by day, and the seed should sprout and grow, he himself does not know how" (Mark 4:27). Because Jesus was the beloved Son of God, He could sleep on a boat that was caught up in a raging storm. The apostle Paul echoed this truth when he said that "all things work together for the good of those who love God" (Rom. 8:28), and "I can do all things through Christ who strengthens me" (Phil. 4:13).

Solomon applied this truth that God provides for those who trust Him to family life as well. Children are gifts from God; therefore, He will guard and nourish them when parents trust Him. Because of their inquisitive, risk-taking behavior, children can hurt themselves many times a day if it were not for God's protection. Solomon compared children to arrows in the quiver of an archer. They enable the parents to hit the target of a meaningful life.

In this well-known psalm, the wisest man urges us to put our full trust in the one true God, Yahveh, who alone can bless our building, guarding, working, and parenting. Without God, our best efforts are fruitless.

A prayer: Lord, with You I can jump over a wall. (Ps. 18:29).
A thought: Do I only know Psalm 127, or do I live it daily?

192. The Search for Meaning
Solomon shares his unsuccessful search with us.

<table>
<tr><td>July 10
~~~
Eccl. 1-10</td><td>God gave Solomon *revealed* wisdom through His Word and Spirit and *acquired* wisdom by studying His creation. The two kinds of wisdom can be in harmony if we keep them in the right order. We must also remember that our insights into both are incomplete. Where the two seem contradictory, we should ascribe that to the gaps in our knowledge and understanding.</td></tr>
</table>

So Solomon (1:12, 16) set off to increase his understanding of the Creator and His creation in order to discover the meaning of life. His search on the *intellectual* level disappointed him, for all his arduous study delivered little knowledge (1:16-18). His *material* riches and pleasures did not satisfy him either. His houses, vineyards, gardens, parks, dams, channels, herds, flocks, silver, and gold did not still the hunger of his soul (2:4-11). Even when he shifted his focus from things to people, singers, and women (2:7-8), these *social* pursuits did not fill the inner void either. He tried wine and mirth (2:1-3), but pleasure induced by *chemicals* missed the mark as well.

His unsuccessful search pushed him into deep depression (2:17-20). He then made many cynical conclusions (chapters 3-10). He cried out 28 times that life is meaningless and 10 times that our best efforts are like chasing the wind.

He despaired about the *endless cycles* in nature we are subjected to (1:3-10). He observed the *ups and downs* in history and that conflicting opposites come and go, like war and peace, grief and joy, birth and death (3:1-8). He hated the *injustices* of society (3:16) such as the oppression of the poor (4:1-3), the persecution of the just (8:14), and the lack of recognition for the wisdom of the poor (9:15). He lamented the *hardships* of life, and he could not see the benefit of all our hard labor. His joy was often spoiled by the *shortness of life* and the fact that someone else would reap the fruits of his labor. All end in death.

Although he repeatedly concluded that we cannot understand God or His works, he could not get away from God either. He referred to God 36 times in this short book. When he eventually made peace with God, he discovered the meaning of life. He tells about that in the last two chapters.

Solomon was honest about his fruitless search for meaning and about the effect it had on him emotionally and intellectually. God made his road map part of the Bible so that we can see what is in vain and what is not.

A prayer: Show me Your ways, O Lord, teach me Your paths. (Ps. 25:4)
A thought: Am I repeating Solomon's fruitless search?

193. From Searcher to Teacher
Peace with God, self, others, and nature

In chapter 11, the trend of Ecclesiastes changes from cynical to constructive. Solomon did not tell us how he found peace, only that he found it and how it changed his outlook and conduct. Instead of banging his head stubbornly against closed doors, he entered the open door to God and found what he was looking for.

July 11

~~~

Eccl. 11-12

</div>

The teacher admonishes his readers, *"Remember now your Creator in the days of your youth."* The Apostle's Creed starts with the same truth: "I believe in God the Father, the Almighty, *Creator* of heaven and earth." The wisest person inspired the church of all ages to acknowledge God as Creator and to accept the fact that He created the universe.

Any theory of evolution that does not acknowledge God as Creator opposes God and His Word. And if God, the supreme intelligence and power, created the universe (which is so vast that we know only a little about a small part of it), then it is obvious that He is also sustaining His creation. The massive heavenly spheres keep gliding in the orbits God set up for them. In spite of the process of aging and dying in all life forms on earth, God replenishes life continuously.

If one makes peace with God and His creation early in one's life, valuable years are not wasted in fruitless searches. Then you have a compass to plan your voyage with. Remember your Creator in the days of your youth.

Peace with God led Solomon to peace with himself. The fact that his life would gradually decline and end in death did not bother him any more. On the contrary, he wrote one of the most beautiful poems on old age (12:1-7) and rejoiced in the fact that his death would not be a sad ending, but a joyful beginning. He would be going home when his spirit returned to God, who had given it. Jesus confirmed this truth when He said that He is preparing a place for us in the Father's house (John 14:1-3).

Having made peace with God and with himself, Solomon could also make peace with others and with nature. He said we have to cast our bread on the water for later that bread will return to us in another form. The fish and waterfowl we have fed may feed us in future. If we help people in need, we will receive help when we are in need. The teacher taught reverence for life and respect for all peoples and creatures. Look after this planet, and it will look after you. His grabbing, self-serving approach to life changed to an attitude of generous giving. Part of his giving was to share his search with us.

A prayer: Our Father, in Your light we see light. (Ps. 36:9).
A thought: Do I have this peace, and do I share it with others?

194. Foolish "Wisdom"
Solomon exchanges wisdom for wit.

<table>
<tr><td>July 12
~ ~ ~
1 Kings 4, 9-11
2 Chron. 8-9</td></tr>
</table>

David created peace for Israel by subduing their enemies, making them pay taxes and render services. Solomon secured his inherited peace by establishing treaties with other countries, treating them like equals. Marrying their princesses was part of the process to maintain good relationships with his neighbors. To deter military ambitions by these political in-laws, Solomon stationed thousands of horses, chariots, and charioteers at strategic fortresses.

This political wisdom was religious folly. The Law of Moses strictly forbade Israelites to marry foreigners (Deut. 7:3-4) and kings to acquire many wives and horses (Deut. 17:16-17). Solomon was gradually trading divine wisdom for human smartness. He was transgressing his golden rule for true wisdom: The fear of the LORD is the beginning of wisdom.

Maybe Solomon's riches and successes went to his head. He began to see himself as smart, instead of realizing that he had to receive his wisdom every day from God. Solomon's lavish lifestyle was sustained from afar: gold mines at Ophir; trading ships with exotic animals and merchandise from Africa, Europe, and the Orient; and so much silver that it lost its value. The Queen of Sheba marveled at Solomon's knowledge, palace, food, servants, and temple. Centuries later Jesus still referred to Solomon's luxurious garments (Matt. 6:29).

When Solomon was old, his foreign wives pressured him to make dangerous compromises, demanding shrines where they could worship their own gods. To keep the "in-laws" happy, Solomon granted these wishes. Next they invited the king to make official visits to these shrines. His people-pleasing diplomacy made him bow before idols. Replacing God's wisdom with man's wisdom made a fool of the wisest man.

Yahveh announced His judgment on Solomon. For the sake of His promise to David, God decided to postpone His judgment till after Solomon's death. By this delay, Solomon got the opportunity to repent. Apparently he was so caught up in his own schemes that he did not turn around. It brought a tragic close to the life of a great person. The Chronicles omit the low points in the lives of David and Solomon. Because this book was written about five hundred years later, after the exile, its aim was to rebuild the self-respect of a devastated nation. Without denying the sins of their leaders, it focused more on their achievements. We, too, should make a fair appraisal of others and ourselves.

A prayer: Lord, help me discern between divine and human wisdom.
A thought: Do I sometimes think I know better than God?

195. The Divided Kingdom
God's discipline is merciful.

Solomon had been warned, but he did not change his ways. At the end of his reign, God raised up adversaries to his kingdom. While Hadad waited in Egypt and Rezon in Syria to take revenge on Solomon, God prepared Jeroboam through the prophet Ahijah to reign over ten tribes of Israel.

July 13
~ ~ ~
1 Kings 11-12
2 Chron. 10-12

After reigning forty years Solomon died, and his son Rehoboam, who succeeded him, got the chance to make a wise decision. Instead of winning the goodwill of the overtaxed nation by easing their burden, he rubbed salt in their wounds by threatening to increase their taxes. When he realized his mistake, it was already too late. Once a kingdom has been ripped apart, reunification is not easy. The ten northern tribes seceded, crowned Jeroboam as their king, and called themselves Israel. The southern kingdom of Rehoboam was called Judah and included Benjamin and later Levi.

Hurt in his pride, the arrogant Rehoboam called up his army to subjugate the north by force. They were stopped by the prophet Shemaiah, who told them that the split of the kingdom had come from the LORD. They felt so vulnerable that they strengthened all their cities with walls, garrisons, weapons, and food. To teach them to seek refuge in God and not in military power, God send the Egyptians and their allies against them. When they repented and returned to God, He saved them from destruction but subjected them to Egypt so they could learn that it is easier to serve God than to serve foreign nations.

When people stray from God, they can quickly lose their privileges. The freedom David had bought for Israel by war and blood slipped through their fingers, and they had to serve the Egyptians again—that nation from which Moses had led them to freedom five centuries before. The 500 golden shields Solomon had made—the luster of every royal parade—were taken by the Egyptians. Rehoboam replaced them with bronze ones. And yet, they were lucky that they still could have bronze shields in their own country—they and their families could have been taken back to Egypt as slaves.

Yahveh is merciful in His discipline. He lets us taste the consequences of our unfaithfulness, but He also eases the pain when He notices real repentance. In spite of the abundant proof at our disposal, we repeatedly trade God's gold for Satan's bronze pennies. Satan pays with short pleasure and long misery.

A prayer: Lord, I want Your riches, not Satan's trash.
A thought: Do I guard my precious spiritual inheritance diligently?

196. Evil Spreads Fast
Evil kings attract evil priests and evil prophets.

<table>
<tr><td>
July 14
~ ~ ~
1 Kings
12:25-14:20
</td></tr>
</table>

The book of Chronicles does not describe the history of the northern kingdom. It names some of those kings only when their paths crossed with kings of Judah. All the kings of the north practiced idolatry, while six kings of the south started significant reforms.

Jeroboam realized that if the ten northern tribes would regularly return to the temple of Jerusalem, they would soon return to the king of Jerusalem. To lure them away from Jerusalem, he erected golden calves at Bethel (his southern border) and Dan (his northern border).

He also encouraged the people to worship idols on the "high places." In view of the well-known history of the golden calf at Mount Sinai, one would expect that Israel would have rejected Jeroboam's golden calves, but sadly they accepted these abominations uncritically. They were not even alarmed when Jeroboam turned his back on the priests and Levites and appointed his own priests. For their own safety, the Levites moved to Judah, where they had a positive influence.

Yahveh sent an unnamed prophet from Judah to prophesy against the idolatry of Jeroboam. The king's withered arm and cracked altar showed that Yahveh had indeed sent this prophet. He predicted that a future king named Josiah would burn human remains on Jeroboam's altar to desecrate it for good. It happened almost three centuries later (2 Kings 23:16).

As he was ordered by God, the prophet returned on another route to Judah, without eating or drinking. Tragically, he allowed a false prophet to seduce him into disobedience and he paid with his life for his sin. The unnatural behavior of the donkey and the lion showed God's control over His creation. The same was demonstrated in the illness and death of Jeroboam's child. By giving Jeroboam ten tribes, God had put great success at his disposal, but by turning his back on God, Jeroboam staged his own demise.

This tragic history shows that when one person sins, many others may suffer because of it. Jeroboam led the nation into idolatry, gathered false prophets and priests around him, and cheated the Levites out of their inheritance; his false prophet robbed a godly man of his life. Jesus pronounced severe sentences on those who lead others into sin (Matt. 18:6, 23:13) and great rewards for those who give a helping hand to others (Matt. 25:34-40, Dan. 12:3).

A prayer: Father, help me to help others, not harm them.
A thought: Today I want to have a positive influence on others.

197. Faithfulness Rewarded
In spite of weakness, Judah keeps the faith and prevails.

In the first eighty years of the divided kingdom, Israel went from bad to worse spiritually while Judah made steady progress in many ways. In Judah, the Davidic dynasty continued from father to son.

> July 15
> ~ ~ ~
> 1 Kings 15:1-24
> 2 Chron. 13-16

In spite of Rehoboam's arrogant attitude in the beginning of his reign, he learned to humble himself before God when the Egyptian army besieged Jerusalem. He lost much of his gold, glamour, and pride, but he, his people, and his cities were spared. The prophet Shemaiah played a significant role in the attitude change of the king and the kingdom. Rehoboam's trust in God was tainted by his neglect to destroy the pagan high places.

His son Abijah succeeded him. The book of Kings paints Abijah as unfaithful to God, but the Chronicles report about one positive episode in Abijah's life. While the armies of Israel and Judah faced each other, Abijah criticized Israel for their idolatry and reminded them that the worship of Yahveh, as instituted by Moses, was still proceeding at Jerusalem. Because they professed their allegiance to Him, Yahveh gave the victory to Judah in spite of the fact that they were far outnumbered by Israel.

Abijah's son Asa succeeded him. He stayed true to God and destroyed the idols and the immorality associated with them. He even deposed his grandmother as "queen mother" and crushed the idol she had made for the goddess of fertility in Jerusalem. During ten years of peace, he improved the fortification of Judean cities. When an Ethiopian king marched against Judah with an army of one million men, Asa met him with his smaller army, trusted in Yahveh, and defeated the enemy completely. Massive spoils were taken.

The prophet Azariah assured Asa that if he stayed loyal to God, God would bless him, but if he abandoned God, God would abandon him. Encouraged by this prophecy, Asa organized a great feast in Jerusalem in the fifteenth year of his reign. Some of the northern tribes joined them. With loud shouts they vowed to serve Yahveh faithfully.

Unfortunately, Asa gradually drifted away from God. When Israel began to build a fortress five miles north of Jerusalem, Asa did not seek God's protection as before, but hired the services of the heathen king of Damascus to help him. When the prophet Hanani admonished the king for that, Asa jailed him. Asa's foot disease drove him to physicians, but not to God.

A prayer: Lord, help me not to drift away from You.
A thought: Is God the spare wheel or the steering wheel of my life?

198. A Picture of Grace
God searches for people who trust Him.

July 16
~ ~ ~
2 Chron. 16:9

Hanani's message to Asa became one of the well-known verses about God's willingness to help those who trust Him: "The eyes of the Lord scan the whole earth to show Himself powerful to those who trust Him wholeheartedly." Because Asa had not done that in the latter part of his life, the prophet announced God's discipline for him. Instead of thanking God and Hanani for opening his eyes, Asa imprisoned God's prophet. Later the same would happen to Jeremiah, John the Baptist, Jesus, and the apostles for bringing God's message.

Jesus reiterated Hanani's message to the Samaritan woman: The Father seeks true worshipers who worship Him in Spirit and in truth (John 4:23). In His Word, God portrays Himself as eager to help those who trust and obey Him. This message has been stressed repeatedly in the whole history of Israel as we have followed it from Abraham to the time of the kings. When Israel stayed loyal to God, they prospered; when they drifted away, they suffered.

But is life that simple? Hanani and Jeremiah stayed loyal to God, and yet they suffered. The rule for Israel—does it not work for individuals? We have two aspects of reality here that seem contradictory, but which are actually complementary. God's definition of *prosper* differs from ours. His servants prospered spiritually even when they suffered abuse.

What looked like Jesus' darkest hour was actually His greatest triumph—when He paid the sin debt of believers on the cross. While Paul was imprisoned, he wrote letters of vital importance to the church of his time as well as to the church of all ages. The list goes on and on: Noah in the flood, Abraham offering Isaac, Joseph in prison, Moses leading the moaning Israelites, David writing beautiful psalms as a fugitive. All of God's children can testify of spiritual blessings during testing times.

The heart of the matter is to trust God wholeheartedly in good and bad times. David said that we must delight ourselves in the LORD, and He will fulfill the desires of our hearts (Ps. 37:4). When we are delighted in God, our desires are aligned with His desires, we want what He wants, and then our prayers are answered.

That's why Jesus taught us to pray: *"Your will be done on earth as it is in heaven"* (Matt. 6:10). The angels want what God wants. They know that His will is the best for everybody and everything. God's eyes scan the whole earth for those who believe in Him like that.

A prayer: Father, I believe in You. Help me with my unbelief.
A thought: Do I try to persuade God that my will is better than His?

199. Spiritual Warfare

Jehoshaphat prevails by God's grace.

So far every king of Judah had come a little closer to God than his predecessor had been. The trend continued with Jehoshaphat. Regarding his faith, the chronicler compared him to David and added that God blessed him for that. He was enriched by enormous gifts from Judah, Philistia, and Arabia, and he enjoyed peace with his neighbors—even with Israel.

> July 17
> ~~~
> 1 Kings 22:41-50
> 2 Chron. 17-20

Jehoshaphat reached out to the people by sending teams of Levites and priests to teach them God's Word. He appointed and trained judges to maintain justice in all cities according to God's Word. The king visited the cities, encouraging the people to serve Yahveh only. He delighted himself in the ways of the LORD, the God of the Bible (2 Chron. 17:6).

The fact that he put his trust in God did not withhold Jehoshaphat from investing in the defense of the country. He fortified cities and stacked them with provisions so that they could survive enemy onslaughts. He could muster an army of more than a million soldiers. His generals were "mighty men of valor," devoted to God, king, and country. God used Judah's military and spiritual preparedness to put fear and respect into surrounding nations.

The miraculous defeat of three approaching armies from the southeast was a classic example of how the yearning of God and man met. Jehoshaphat called the nation to a prayer meeting where the king cried to Yahveh for deliverance. Jahaziel, a Levite from the sons of Asaph, prophesied that Yahveh would give them the victory without engaging in battle themselves.

While they praised the LORD with songs and instruments, they went out to meet the enemy. When they came to the ridge of the escarpment, they saw the valley was strewn with dead soldiers. The three armies had fought amongst themselves and had destroyed each other. Judah praised Yahveh from the heart for the deliverance and called the place "Valley of Praise." It took them three days to transport all the spoils to Jerusalem.

Sadly, Jehoshaphat made some grave errors. To secure peace between Judah and Israel, he had his son marry a daughter of Ahab, the ungodly king of the north. God scolded him by the prophet Hanani for joining Ahab in war against Syria. When he tried to become a trade partner with Ahab's son Ahaziah, their ships were destroyed in a storm. Jehoshaphat learned that one cannot befriend both God and the wicked (James 4:4).

A prayer: Lord, show me how to strengthen myself in You.
A thought: Do I try to please both God and the world?

200. Light in Darkness
A great prophet emerges in troubled times.

July 18
~~
1 Kings 15:25 -
17:7

The bad times in Israel contrasted sharply with Judah's good times. The memory of Jeroboam's sins was kept alive by the often repeated phrase about his successors: They "walked in the sins of Jeroboam with which he had made Israel sin." In the 22 years he reigned, the idolatry he introduced became entrenched, and Israel never shook it off before their exile.

A bloody history followed. His son Nadab reigned for only two years before he and all the male descendants of Jeroboam were killed by Baasha, who then ruled Israel for twenty-four years. The prophet Jehu, son of Hanani, announced God's wrath on Baasha because he continued in idolatry. Baasha's son Elah reigned for two years before he was killed during a drinking party by Zimri, who then also wiped out all Baasha's male offspring, family, and friends. After only seven days in power, Zimri committed suicide when the army, led by Omri, besieged him. For four years, half of Israel supported Omri and half supported Tibni. When Tibni died, Omri became the undisputed ruler. He built a new capital named Samaria, where he prospered.

He was succeeded by his son Ahab who became the most notorious king of the northern kingdom. He married the Sidonian princess Jezebel and together they introduced the Baal and Asherah idolatry to Israel. These idols were respectively the god of rain and the goddess of fertility.

Suddenly God's mighty prophet appeared as a light in darkness. To expose the impotence of these dead idols, God inspired Elijah to pray for a severe drought (James 5:17-18). Assured that God would hear his prayer, Elijah announced the drought to King Ahab without further explanation. The test was obvious: See if your gods of rain and fertility can help you!

Elijah was sustained by God in a secret place while the waiting game became increasingly serious day by day. *"But those who wait on the LORD shall renew their strength; they shall mount up with wings like eagles"* (Isaiah 40:31). God used ravens, greedy scavengers, to bring bread and meat mornings and evenings to His faithful servant. Elijah gratefully received the morsels God provided by these "unclean" birds. Centuries later Peter had to learn this lesson too: *"Do not call anything impure that God has made clean"* (Acts 10:15, NIV). Elijah patiently stayed put until God directed him to a new spot where even more fantastic miracles would happen.

A prayer: Father, You are in control.
A thought: Do I bring light into darkness?

201. Awesome "Small" Miracles
The flour and oil keep flowing.

Ahab's spies searched for Elijah everywhere, even in neighbor countries (1 Kings 18:10). The king's herds and flocks were in jeopardy, and he wanted Elijah to call off the stifling drought. Ironically, God hid His prophet near Sidon, the territory of Jezebel, the place Israel's Baal and Asherah idolatry came from.

<table>
<tr><td>July 19
~ ~ ~
1 Kings 17:8-16</td></tr>
</table>

God prepared Elijah and the widow of Zarephath for their encounter. As the prophet approached the town, the widow was gathering sticks to cook her last meal. For a while they watched each other from the corner of the eye. Elijah tested the waters by asking her for a drink. Centuries later Jesus would have a similar encounter with a Samaritan woman.

When the widow walked off to fetch the water, Elijah asked for a piece of bread too. Then the silent woman turned around and opened her burdened heart to the man of God. She and her son were on the brink of starvation—and the stranger wanted to share in their meager meal! Then came God's revelation to Elijah: God would provide for the widow so that she could provide for His prophet. Every day there would flow enough flour and oil from the empty jars to provide for their needs.

A cupful of flour and a spoonful of oil do not look like much of a miracle. Yet, in the long run it was far more impressive and mysterious than a wagonload of flour and oil donated by a rich person. The latter could easily be ascribed to natural causes. But two empty jars that pour out the necessities of life day by day for years—that blows the mind away!

Though this pagan widow might have had doubts, she gave the promise a try. She was surprised: Today there was enough for all three of them. Oh well, maybe there was more in the jars than she had thought. The next day would be the real test, for now she knew the jars were empty. Her hands began to shake and her heart raced when the jars delivered the needed amount the next day. And so it continued until she became used to it.

We should not overlook small miracles. Actually they are fantastic: the right word at the right time; the right person at the right place; the right plan at the right moment; our health, food, shelter, clothes and safety; the wonder of sight and hearing—so that we can see and hear our loved ones and the beauty of creation. There are so many miracles we have become so used to that we no longer praise God for them—until we suddenly lose one of them.

A prayer: Thank You, Father, for all the fantastic small miracles in my life.
A thought: Do I savor my daily spiritual bread as coming from God's jar?

202. Crisis-corrected Faith
Death brings new life.

July 20
~ ~ ~
1 Kings 17:17-24

It is amazing how people can get used to the wonders of everyday living. Awakening every morning in health and happiness is taken for granted until disease strikes. When the widow got used to the miracle of the generous jars, God staged a crisis to prune her faith and to stimulate growth.

She felt safe with God's prophet and provision. Then her son fell ill and got sicker by the day until he died. Anger and bewilderment are mixed into the first phase of grief. She projected her anger on Elijah and accused him of bringing her sins before God, who then turned on her in wrath. When calamity strikes, we start to search for the cause and a culprit to blame. So this woman added two and two, coming up with a totally wrong answer.

When something bad happens to them, most people say, "What have I done to deserve this?" It is based on the premise that good behavior is always rewarded and bad behavior always punished. If so, then all of us must receive both rewards and punishment since all of us are imperfect.

Furthermore, rewards and punishments are not restricted to the physical and material levels only but may also be felt on the emotional and spiritual levels. God's children may be spiritually blessed while suffering (198). God may use a crisis to correct our faith, to get us out of stagnant self-satisfaction, and to stimulate growth in the right direction. That was His goal with this widow.

Elijah carried the boy to the upper room where he lived. Then he also cried out to God with why questions. But he did not stop there. He prayed that something would happen that had never happened before: that the boy's life would return to him. Then Elijah stretched himself out on the boy. It might have been to symbolize his identification with the child, or, as some think, to give the kiss of life. After he had repeated his prayer and ritual three times, the boy's life returned to his body. It demonstrated the power of prayer and that the spirit lives on when the body dies.

In her jubilant joy, the widow received new insight into the character of God and of His prophet. Though she had hated them for a moment, she would now love and adore them forever. The miracle of her revived child corrected and revived her faith. Her question marks had turned into exclamation marks.

She could rejoice in the wonder of the generous jars again. She had a new sensitivity and appreciation for God's daily "small" miracles.

A prayer: Father, let me discover the blessing of my crisis.
A thought: When I have a crisis, do I blame or do I pray and act?

203. Stepping Forward
Risking one's neck for God

For three and a half years Baal and Asherah could not produce rain or grain. The suffering nation was now more inclined to listen to the true God. Elijah came out of hiding to make arrangements for the spectacular display of Baal's impotence and God's omnipotence. The prophet

> July 21
> ~ ~ ~
> 1 Kings 18:1-20

did not go to Ahab's fortress where he could easily be arrested and killed. He sent Obadiah, an official of the king, to call the king to a secret meeting place. All he had to say was, "Elijah!" and point the way.

Obadiah's reaction shows the humor of the situation. Knowing how Elijah could disappear without a trace, Obadiah was extremely worried that while he was fetching the king, Elijah would evaporate again and expose Obadiah to the whims of the disgruntled king. He reminded Elijah of his credentials: When Jezebel tried to wipe out God's prophets, he had risked his life by hiding and feeding a hundred of them in caves. "Please, don't do this to me," he pleaded.

Elijah assured Obadiah that he would not let him down. This was an appointment he would not miss. When the king arrived in a cloud of dust with his chariot and horses, the first thing he could snarl at the simply clothed prophet was, "Is that you ... you troublemaker!" Calmly, but firmly, Elijah corrected the arrogant king: It was the king and his family who were responsible for all Israel's troubles because of their idolatry.

Elijah, taking control of the situation, did not allow the king to respond. He laid out the conditions for the termination of the drought. God had the initiative, for only He could end the drought. The king had to summon the nation to Mount Carmel and see to it that the priests of Baal and Asherah were there too—all of them. The rest of the plan Elijah kept to himself, but Ahab could sense that there would be some kind of showdown.

Above everything, Ahab wanted the drought to end so that he and his country would not be completely ruined economically. Although Jezebel was fanatic about her gods, Ahab didn't care which one was the true God, as long as the drought could be broken. So he called the nation up to the spot that Elijah had indicated. He had no idea how brilliantly the power of God would shine at a meeting led by a true man of God.

Elijah and Obadiah risked their lives when they stepped forward to serve God's kingdom. In many places believers still do that—not only in Muslim countries, but also in secular western countries. Pray for them.

A prayer: God, please create the opportunity for people to meet You.
A thought: Do I risk my life or popularity to serve God?

204. The Choice
How long will you falter between two opinions?

<table>
<tr><td>

July 22

~~~

1 Kings 18:20-46

</td><td>

God is in control of His universe, but He wants people to honor Him voluntarily. He had brought the drought, and He was going to end it in such a way that the people could choose their own destiny without interference by the royal family. God's prophet presided over the meeting he had asked for.

</td></tr>
</table>

Elijah didn't waste words. He came to the point right away and reproached Israel for their double-mindedness. They had to choose: If Yahveh is God, serve Him; if Baal is, then serve him. To help them make the choice, he challenged the Baal priests to a test of truth, a test they could not refuse without losing face. The Baal priests would erect for their god an altar, complete with wood and sacrifice, but without putting fire to it. Elijah would do the same for Yahveh. The sacrifice that would be ignited by fire from heaven would show who the true God was, Yahveh or Baal.

For the Israelites who knew their history, there shouldn't have been any doubt about the outcome of this experiment. Yahveh had brought them out of Egypt after He had defeated all the Egyptian gods with ten plagues and into the Promised Land by defeating all the idols of the peoples in Canaan. In the time of the judges and the first kings, the LORD had saved His people repeatedly from oppression when they had returned to Him.

Obviously, the dramatic rituals of the Baal priests could achieve nothing. They were praying to a dead image, the product of human imagination. Who did they try to fool? The crowd had all day to come to grips with reality. They may have felt lingering uncertainty, though, about Elijah's ability to call fire from heaven. They knew of such occasions in their history, but will it really happen today? What if Elijah fails ..?

To ensure that there was no hidden flame in his altar to do the trick, Elijah had it soaked with water from the brook. When Elijah cried out to Yahveh to prove Himself to His people, Yahveh answered in a spectacular way. Fire roared down from heaven and devoured Elijah's offering—including the altar. It proved there was only one true God, Yahveh, and He should be worshiped in the temple in Jerusalem. That's why God removed this altar completely.

The shaken people shouted with awe: "Yahveh is God! Yahveh is God!" Elijah seized the moment and got rid of all the Baal and Asherah priests. Then God added to the test of fire the test of rain. Soon it poured down.

A prayer: Father, we have abundant proofs in the past and the present.
A thought: How could Israel proceed with idolatry after this incident?

205. From Peak to Valley

The jubilant Elijah receives a death threat.

Elijah was overjoyed when Yahveh had been glorified while Baal and Asherah had been ravished. Even before there was a cloud in sight, Elijah urged King Ahab to have supper served—the rain was imminent. The clouds appeared after seven prayers, and Elijah, elated in his victory, girded up his clothes and ran in front of the king's entourage to show them the

> July 23
> ~ ~ ~
> 1 Kings 18:41 -
> 19:8

way in the dark, rainy night. He safely escorted them down from Mount Carmel to the Valley of Jezreel on the north side of the mountain.

Maybe Elijah was still celebrating with friends that night when he was called to the front door. A messenger of Jezebel bluntly informed him that the queen had sentenced him to death. Elijah and his friends were shocked back to reality. Jezebel was still in power, and the nation did not have the guts to stand up to her and end her tyranny.

Disillusioned and robbed of his victory, Elijah grabbed his backpack and fled to Judah. In the past he had trusted God for his safety; now he depended on his own wit. Israel and Judah had sealed their peace with a royal marriage, so Elijah would not be safe in Judah either. He fled into the Negev desert south of Judah. He covered the hundred miles from Jezreel to Beersheba on foot. He did not dare get food anywhere, lest his whereabouts become known. Exhausted and devastated, he took shelter beneath a broom bush to shade off the scorching desert sun.

He was drained in body and spirit. In his exasperation, he whispered, "O God ... I've had enough ... I can't take it any more ... let me die ... I'm no better than my fathers ... "

In His infinite mercy, God did not blame Elijah for his depression. He knew how several factors had converged to bring about this low point in his prophet's life: disappointment, rejection, fear, exhaustion, sleep-deprivation, hunger, and thirst. God let Elijah first have some rest and sleep. Then He supplied food and drink. The yearning of God and man met in a desert.

When Elijah was physically restored, his emotional and spiritual levels had recovered to such an extent that he proceeded with his journey to Mount Horeb in the Sinai desert where he had an appointment with God. This "vacation" in new surroundings was part of God's treatment for Elijah's condition.

This is an old proven recipe for treating emotional shock and depression: physical restoration followed by emotional and spiritual recovery.

A prayer: Father, I commit myself into Your care today, every day.
A thought: Do I drive myself until my tank is empty?

206. The Whispering Voice
God is not in the wind, earthquake, or fire.

<table>
<tr><td>
July 24
~~~
1 Kings 19:8-18
</td></tr>
</table>

It took Elijah forty days from the Negev to Mount Horeb, a journey that could be done in a week. We can assume that God provided food and water to Elijah on the way as He had done before. Most likely it was not Elijah's physical weakness that delayed his progress, but rather his struggle with himself. He must have asked himself a thousand times how he suddenly could slide down from the spiritual heights on Carmel to the emotional depths in the Negev.

The more he searched for real reasons, the more he got entangled in his own web of self-pity and the defenses around it. Eventually, he convinced himself of the worst case scenario: Israel had completely abandoned the worship of Yahveh, all God's prophets were killed, he was the only one left who served God, and now Jezebel would not rest till he too was dead.

At last, with great anticipation, he reached the mountain where God had spoken "face to face" with Moses about seven centuries before. This time it was quiet at Mount Horeb—no fire and smoke on the mountain, no thundering voice from heaven. He rested in a cave and listened to the awesome silence. Then the LORD spoke to his heart: *"What are you doing here, Elijah?"* Elijah responded with the excuse he had put together on the way, as if he wanted to say, "Can't You see, God, how terrible my situation is? Can You blame me?"

God told him to get out of the hole where he was hiding and stand in the open before God. Elijah cringed when a tornado-like wind roared over the mountain, sweeping small rocks along, crushing them against larger ones. Maybe he wanted to crawl back into the cave, but when an earthquake shook the mountain, he realized it was safer outside. Then a scorching fire swept by. However, Elijah did not sense God's closeness in these mighty powers of nature. Elijah was listening; God did not have to yell at him.

In a soft, whispering voice, God asked Elijah again why he was there. The prophet gave the same self-pitying response. God assured him that he was not alone: There were 7000 believers (symbolizing completeness) who had stayed true to Yahveh, and there were leaders who would execute God's will when Elijah was gone. God's plan for the world was not dependent on Elijah alone.

God sent Elijah back—out of his comfort zone into the danger zone to complete his mission. On his "vacation," Elijah regained perspective. At God's time—not on his time—the prophet would be taken up into glory.

A prayer: Father, empower me to fulfill the task You have given me.
A thought: Am I running away from my God-given duty?

207. Follow Me

Leaving all for the sake of God and His kingdom

On the long road back, Elijah had enough time to digest the message God had given him on Mount Horeb. God's wrath, symbolized by the wind, earthquake, and fire, would be executed on those who persistently ignored God. However, prophets had to speak of more than God's wrath; they also had to bring God's Word—Yahveh's loving, whispering voice—to His people.

> July 25
> ~~~
> 1 Kings 19:19-21

Two of his assignments, appointing two kings, Elijah left to his successor. Appointing his successor was of primary importance to this prophet who sensed that he was near the end of his ministry. As God had given him the name and address, he went straight to that person, who happened to be an industrious farmer. While Elisha was plowing, Elijah threw his mantle over him without a word and walked on. God revealed the meaning of this gesture to Elisha; he recognized God's calling in his heart.

When he asked Elijah's permission to say goodbye to his parents, Elijah let him know that he was not called by Elijah but by God. Jesus also rebuked someone who came to Him with the same request (Luke 9:61-62). Maybe Jesus referred to Elisha's calling when He used a metaphor from the farm: "No one who plows and looks back is fit for God's kingdom." Elisha immediately demonstrated his total devotion to God's calling by slaughtering two oxen, preparing a feast for the workers, and following Elijah, apparently without good-byes to his parents.

When Jesus called four industrious fishermen, they left everything and followed Him. The same happened to a successful tax collector and probably to the rest of the disciples. Jesus made them fishers of men and sent them out to proclaim His Word.

He urged them to carry the cross of discipleship every day. If they loved anybody or anything above Him, they were not worthy to be His disciples. He promised them that those who left family for the sake of His kingdom would receive many "family" in their place (Matt. 10:37-39, 19:29).

Although God stresses in His Word that we have to love and honor our parents (Mark 7:10-13), He also expects us to put His calling to kingdom work above family ties. Most children leave their parents anyway to start their own families and careers. If we do that for this short life, how much more should we be willing to do it for God's kingdom, our future eternal home? Like Elisha, we may gain friends and miracles to compensate for our losses.

A prayer: Father, help me keep my priorities right.
A thought: Am I willing to sacrifice my "oxen" and follow God's calling?

208. Messages of Grace

God gives Ahab two victories to change his heart.

July 26

~~~

1 Kings 20:1-30

This chapter does not mention Elijah, but the fruits of his labor are quite evident. In the recent past, the prophets of God were either killed or hidden; now they were openly testifying, even to the king. Carmel and Horeb had made a difference! Elijah had come back to do what he should have done in the first place: follow up on the Carmel victory by training prophets to bring God's Word to the people. In this way, Baal worship could be replaced by Yahveh worship.

Israel and Syria had been taking and retaking land repeatedly from each other. In Ahab's time, Syria invaded Israel several times with its stronger army and Israel succumbed to their demands. Ahab admitted to Ben-Hadad, king of Syria, that all he owned actually belonged to Syria, but when Ben-Hadad demanded that Ahab surrender to him all his valuables, including his prettiest wives, Ahab refused, backed by the elders of Israel. When Ben-Hadad tried to intimidate Ahab with his great army, Ahab shut him up with a proverb that meant: Don't count your chickens before they are hatched.

God sent one of His prophets to Ahab to assure him that God would give him victory against Syria so that *"you shall know that I am the LORD."* The political balance of power was not God's first priority, but Ahab's faith in God. How easily God can turn the tables! The Syrians were so over-confident that they had a booze party at noon. Ahab attacked as directed by the prophet, and the strong army fled in drunken panic. Ben-Hadad escaped.

A prophet warned Ahab that the Syrians would try to regain control by the next spring. Ahab had to prepare. He did not follow this advice; the next year he faced the Syrians with a pathetic little army. However, God again assured him of victory so that *"you shall know that I am the LORD."*

The misconception of the Syrians—that Yahveh only reigns in the mountains and not in the plains—was refuted by Israel's God-given victory on the plains. Many of the enemy were killed when they fled into one of their fortresses and a wall tumbled in on them.

In addition to Carmel, Ahab had thus received another two calls to surrender himself in faith to Yahveh. Alas, he did not. He could not stand up to Jezebel, as will become clearer in the next chapter.

Pleasing people has shut the gates of heaven for many. Jesus reiterated that we must put Him, God incarnate, above anybody else (Luke 14:26).

A prayer: Father, thank You for Your amazing grace.
A thought: How much do others shape my choices and lifestyle?

209. You Shall Not Covet
Ahab destroys himself with greed and lust.

In these passages we get a glimpse of Ahab's character. He was not a man of principle but was swayed in different directions by different people. Impressed by Jezebel's idolatry, he let her kill God's prophets; impressed by Elijah's victory, he let him kill Jezebel's priests. Ahab was submissive toward Ben-Hadad at first

July 27
~ ~ ~
1 Kings 20:31 -
21:29

but turned against him when he was backed by the elders and a prophet. He ravished the Syrian army, but when he captured their king, he treated him as a brother. He was governed by his appetites and not by his conscience. When he did not get his way, he reacted with childish moodiness.

Ahab made a seemingly fair offer to Naboth for his vineyard, which was next to the palace. However, the Law stipulated that the land belonged to God; therefore, only the harvests of a specific piece of land could be sold for a specified number of years (Lev. 25:23-28). It was Ahab, not Naboth, who acted illegally. Ahab knew Naboth was right, but he was still upset.

When Jezebel heard why Ahab was unhappy, she devised a plot to have Naboth killed by the leaders of his community on completely false accusations and without a trial. The fact that not one of the leaders protested against this injustice showed how much they feared the intimidating queen. Callously they executed her wishes, and gloatingly she informed Ahab that he could now claim the late Naboth's land as a gift from her.

God sent Elijah to meet the king on the confiscated land and to announce God's judgment on him. Ahab had thrown away three opportunities to get reconciled with God and had now committed a grave sin on top of that. His time of grace was definitely over, we would think. And yet, when he showed repentance, God still took away some of the pain. The prophecy about the extermination of his offspring would be postponed till after his death.

Looking at the sexual immorality of the Baal and Asherah idolatry, as well as Jezebel's effort to seduce Jehu later (2 Kings 9:30), we can assume that Ahab's weakness toward Jezebel was seated in the way she satisfied Ahab's lust. As Delilah had conquered Samson with sex, so Jezebel maintained a hold on Ahab.

His second weakness was his greed for possessions, and that made him an accomplice to murder and robbery. His days were numbered. Elijah's words would be fulfilled when both Ahab and Jezebel met with violent deaths. Those who reject God's mercy will face His holiness.

A prayer: Lord, I want to stand firmly on Your principles.
A thought: Do I stay on course or do I drift along?

210. God's Timetable
Ample time for repentance

July 28
~~~
1 Kings 22:1-40

</div>

Ahab probably humbled himself before God in an effort to escape punishment, not to change his heart and lifestyle. Nevertheless, God granted him time to get his heart and life in order. Eventually, his time was up, and the day of reckoning arrived. God staged Ahab's demise in such a way that this evil king had the opportunity to make peace with God till his very last breath.

The political marriage between Princess Athaliah of Israel and Prince Jehoram of Judah sealed a peace treaty between the two kingdoms that were headed by Ahab and Jehoshaphat respectively. When Jehoshaphat paid Ahab a royal visit, Ahab persuaded him to go into battle with him against the Syrians and reconquer Ramoth in Gilead. In spite of Ahab's idolatrous record, Jehoshaphat requested that they first seek God's guidance in the matter.

It did not take Ahab long to gather four hundred prophets who eagerly supported the idea of taking Ramoth back from Syria. It turned out that these "prophets" were not Yahveh's prophets who were trained by Elijah. Therefore, Jehoshaphat asked specifically for a prophet of the LORD. Ahab knew of only two. As Elijah had already announced the total destruction of Ahab and his family in the most gruesome terms, he would never ask him for an opinion. The other one, Micaiah, was not a supporter of Ahab either. But when Jehoshaphat insisted, Ahab sent a messenger to fetch Micaiah.

In spite of the pressure on him to support the other prophets, Micaiah reluctantly brought the sad message from God that Ahab would be killed and Israel would be scattered. With a parable he explained that God had allowed a lying spirit to enter the other prophets.

Micaiah was jailed for his truthfulness. Ahab marched against Ramoth in spite of the warning. He tried to outwit the prophecy, but a God-directed arrow wounded him seriously. Because of the fierce battle he could not retreat for medical attention. He was slowly bleeding to death in his chariot while the "soft small voice" kept whispering in his ear to take God's hand of grace.

Ahab's body received a royal funeral, but when his blood was washed from his chariot at the pool of Samaria, it mingled with dogs and harlots. Apparently, Ahab did not surrender himself to Yahveh; therefore, God's judgment came down on him.

*A prayer: Lord, help me accept the many mercies You extend to me.*
*A thought: Why does God invest so much grace in people like Ahab?* (2 Pet. 3:9)

# 211. Fire from Heaven
## The ironic humor of God's judgment

Ahab was succeeded by his son Ahaziah, who persisted in his father's idolatry. God's wrath was first shown in the wrecking of the ships he and the king of Judah had built (2 Chron. 20:35-37) and secondly in his injury and in his dealings with Elijah.

> July 29
> ~ ~ ~
> 2 Kings 1

Ahaziah was injured by a fall and sent messengers to consult Baal-Zebub, *lord of flies*, a Philistine idol, about his chances for recovery. On God's command, Elijah intercepted them with a question and a prophecy: "Why do you consult the 'lord of flies,' the lifeless idol of your enemies, and ignore the living God, the Lord of the universe? The true God says: 'You have insulted Me and therefore you will die of your injury!'"

The messengers turned back and delivered Elijah's prophecy to Ahaziah. From their description of the prophet, the king knew it was Elijah and sent 50 men with their officer to bring Elijah to him. Maybe he wanted to use the prophet to change God's mind. The posse found Elijah on a hilltop and commanded the *ish* (man) of God to *come down* to them. Instead, Elijah asked the *"eesh"* (fire) of God to *come down* on them. It also happened to a second group of 51 men who were even more demanding.

Like their king, these men were Israelites who willfully chose false gods and spurned Yahveh, the true God who had brought Israel out of the slavery of Egypt to the freedom of the Promised Land. When they meant to harm His prophet, God's fire devoured them. Again Elijah saw the difference between the judgment of God on the unfaithful, and the mercy of God for the faithful, as it was shown to him on Mount Horeb.

The third group of soldiers humbled themselves before God and His prophet, and their lives were spared. Elijah went with them and repeated God's message to the king. Ahaziah could not force God to change His mind. Had he humbled himself in true repentance, his life might have ended differently. It shows how enslaving sin is: Ahaziah could not break with idolatry.

When the disciples of Jesus wanted to use this piece of history to take revenge on some hostile Samaritans, Jesus rebuked them for their wrong attitude (Luke 9:51-56). Elijah had not called fire from heaven for personal revenge, but to execute God's wrath on Israelites who had deliberately rejected God. In Elijah's case, God's fire did not come down on Gentile idol worshipers, but on God's own people who preferred idols above their heavenly Father.

*A prayer: Father, You are my God.*
*A thought: To whom do I turn in a crisis?*

# 212. Chariot of Fire
### Elijah is taken up into heaven.

July 30

~ ~ ~

2 Kings 2:1-15

Some of Elijah's assignments, like the anointing of two kings, were left to his successor. God's time for Elijah's departure had come, and God revealed it to those near to Him. Elijah thought he could secretly slip away, but God wanted his prophets to be involved in this unique event. Elisha and some other prophets knew what was going to happen, and they whispered about it.

The prophetic interactions were repeated several times, affirming the certainty of what was to happen. Elisha was determined not to let Elijah out of sight for a minute. He knew that when Elijah was taken to heaven, he (Elisha) would be empowered to proceed with God's work on earth.

When Elijah parted the water of the Jordan with his cloak and they walked through on the riverbed, the anticipation of these two men must have peaked in various ways. Elijah was excited to go to heaven, yet he might have been sad to leave his friend behind in the mess. Elisha, on the other hand, was excited for his friend's sake, yet he felt uncertain and inadequate to proceed with his work. Elijah urged Elisha to ask for something special at this crucial moment. Elisha felt so much weaker than his teacher that he thought he needed twice the grace that Elijah had received.

Suddenly the great moment was upon them. For the fifth time in Elijah's life, there was fire from heaven. This time it was not to consume, but to save. Elijah was swept up with a whirlwind to God. Their mutual yearning was satisfied. While Elijah departed, his cloak fell on Elisha, as did his ministry. Suddenly the breathtaking moment was over. Only the forlorn figure of a man with a cloak in his hand remained in the dusty wind. When the reality of his loss struck him, Elisha tore his garment to show his grief.

As Elisha returned in a somber mood, he did not feel as if a double portion of Elijah's spirit was upon him. Then he faced his first problem: crossing the Jordan on his way back. He asked for a sign that the God of Elijah was also his God. As he took the leap of faith, the water parted as before, and then he knew that his prayer for a double portion of grace had been granted. Elisha would indeed work more miracles than his teacher.

On Pentecost the Holy Spirit descended on believers with the signs of wind, fire, and special gifts. Jesus said their works would exceed His own (John 14:12). We too will see God's power when we take the step of faith.

*A prayer: Father, help me to see death as a homecoming.*
*A thought: Do I fret over losses, or do I proceed in faith with my task?*

# 213. Authentication of a Prophet
## The signs verify Elisha's calling.

The student prophets had been waiting on the west bank of the Jordan on Elisha's return. They saw that he was alone, that he was wearing Elijah's cloak, and that he did the same miracle Elijah had done. That convinced them that God had taken Elijah to Himself and that He had appointed Elisha as Elijah's successor. They bowed in respect and in willingness to serve.

> July 31
> ~ ~ ~
> 2 Kings 2:15-25

Elisha's calling was also evident in his insight into Elijah's destiny. The student prophets thought that Elijah's body might have been dropped somewhere by the wind, so they wanted Elisha's permission to organize a search party. At first Elisha refused, but later allowed them to go so that it could be established with certainty that Elijah had indeed been taken up in his body. The searchers returned empty-handed after three days, confirming what Elisha had told them before they embarked on the search.

Elisha's authority was demonstrated to the people of Jericho by the healing of their fountain. When they complained about the bad taste and effects of the water, Elisha asked for a new bowl filled with salt. He poured the salt into the fountain, and immediately the water was sweet and fruitful. It was a God-given miracle, and the salt had only symbolical meaning. Likewise, God's children must be the salt of the earth, and they must eliminate evil at its source.

The enemies of God got a very gruesome affirmation that Elisha was Elijah's successor. Children of the Baal worshipers had heard of Elijah's ascent to heaven and mocked Elisha, shouting: "Go up, baldhead! Go up, follow your master!" Elisha put a curse on them and they were mauled by bears. The religious leaders of Jerusalem mocked Jesus on Calvary in a similar way, daring Him to show His power. Some of them were crushed by the Romans in A.D. 70, and some were saved on Pentecost by the forgiving prayer of Jesus on the cross.

The authenticity of God's Word and God's prophets has been shown through the ages to believers, to people in need, and to God's enemies. God's ongoing revelation, salvation, and condemnation have not happened secretly in a remote corner of the earth. On the contrary, all three started in Israel, the crossroads between Asia, Europe, and Africa.

From there God's Word has been dispersed over the whole planet. Parts of the Bible have already been translated into 2700 languages and dialects and brought to those people. God has revealed His will to mankind.

*A prayer: Father, please confirm Your Word through Your signs.*
*A thought: Does my light shine forth to friend and foe?*

# 214. Facts and Truth
## Understanding history from God's viewpoint

<table>
<tr><td>

August 1

~ ~ ~

2 Kings 3

</td><td>

Some interpret this chapter as a series of mistakes. They think that the kings landed their armies in trouble by taking the wrong road; that Elisha illicitly advised the destruction of Moab; that Israel was too harsh on the enemy and drove them to a desperate deed; and that the wrath of God came on Israel, maybe as disease, forcing them to withdraw and thus forfeit a complete victory.

</td></tr>
</table>

The Bible is divine revelation, not political commentary. God's book is for His children's edification (1 Cor. 10:11). From God's perspective, it is feasible that He led the kings via the desert to make them dependent on Him so that He could provide in a miraculous way and show them who the true God is.

Elisha rebuked Jehoram for his idolatry and praised Jehoshaphat for his faith. He then prepared the scene for the wonderful provision of water without rain. The crimson reflection of the morning sun on the water lured the enemy into a trap and secured victory for the forces of Judah, Israel, and Edom. The whole situation showed that God was in control, not the kings.

Elisha's advice of destruction was not against the law because Moses talked about the Promised Land (Deut. 20:19-20), and Elisha about Moab. It would have been stupid for Israel to destroy the fruit trees of the land that they were about to inhabit themselves. But destroying the trees, fields, and fountains of Moab would keep Moab busy for many years so that they would not have time or energy to harass Judah and Israel soon again.

If the whole campaign had been orchestrated by God, then He would not punish Israel for being too hard on Moab. Surely Israel could not be held responsible for the child sacrifice performed by the Moabite king. Child sacrifice was a regular part of Moab's religion. It was not vile to them, but to Judah and Israel. Killing enemy soldiers in combat was inevitable then as it still is now, but killing a child as a burnt offering was unthinkable for the Israelites. Had God not stopped Abraham from such a deed? When they saw what the Moabite king was doing, they were so abhorred by this gruesome act that they turned around and went home. And yet, Judah would later defile themselves with the same abomination by sacrificing children to idols (Jer. 19:4-6).

Facts can be spun to paint various scenarios, depending on what one wants to prove. We have to understand the facts in the light of God's truth, that is, within the context of God's entire revelation.

*A prayer: Father, help me understand history from Your perspective.*
*A thought: God's truth helps us discern facts from fiction.*

# 215. What Do You Have?
## God can do miracles with the little we have.

When one of the student prophets died, his widow and kids were in trouble because of debt. The children could be forced into slave labor. Believers are not exempt from hard times that may result from their own mistakes or from circumstances beyond their control. In spite of our best efforts to provide for our loved ones, things may go wrong and leave our families in dire straights.

> August 2
> ~ ~ ~
> 2 Kings 4:1-7

This widow took her problem to Elisha and hoped that God would reveal to him a solution to her plight. Like a wise counselor, Elisha first searched for positive factors in the situation that may be used to solve the problem. "What do you have?" he asked. God revealed to Elisha that He would use the little jar of oil this widow had left to provide miraculously for her needs.

Faith starts with positive thinking about available resources—however insignificant they may seem. Put them into God's almighty hands, like the boy who entrusted his lunch box to Jesus to feed the five thousand, and you too may be amazed how much God can do with a little.

Elisha challenged the widow to take a ridiculous step in faith. She had to borrow huge earthen jars, as many as she could get, lock herself up with her sons, and fill the big jars from the small one. She passed the test of faith and followed Elisha's instructions. It was not a public event—only she and her sons saw how the miracle happened. They would have to testify about it to others, and the listeners would then be challenged to take a step of faith too: to believe on account of the testimony of the widow and her sons.

Jesus sometimes took people aside before healing them so they could testify about the mercy they had received. His greatest sign, His resurrection, was not shown to the world, but only to his followers. People can only be saved if they accept the Word of God as brought by Christians (Rom. 10:17).

When the widow had filled the last big jar, the oil stopped flowing from the small one. The widow received according to her faith. If she had borrowed another jar, it would have been filled too. How much God will do through His children is often limited by the boundaries of their faith. This woman sold the oil, paid her debt, and lived from the rest. Her overflowing joy was perhaps only occasionally plagued by regret that she had not borrowed more big jars so that the miracle could have lasted a little longer.

*A prayer: Thank You, Father, for the flowing oil of every day.*
*A thought: Do I limit God's provisions with my small expectations?*

# 216. Friends in Need
### Are friends indeed

August 3
~~~
2 Kings 4:8-37

This episode gives us insight into the logistics of Elisha's ministry. He moved around in the country to reach as many people as possible. When he visited Galilee, he often stopped at a farm near Shunem where he enjoyed the hospitality of the farmer and his wife.

After this had happened several times, the couple decided to build on their house a small upper room for Elisha's use when he visited that area.

The prophet sincerely appreciated their gesture of friendly support and expressed his wish to do something for them in return. Cordially, the woman let him know that they were happy and satisfied with what they had. They did not want to be rewarded for their hospitality. Elisha's assistant, Gehazi, suggested that something be done about the couple's childlessness. Elisha took the matter to God and received a favorable answer.

When he told the woman of the gift she was going to receive, it excited and agonized her. "Please, don't lie to your servant!" she whispered. Her fate was painful enough; she did not want to be hurt by false hopes anymore. In her heart she wished Elisha's prophecy were true, but she feared at the same time that her hopes might be dashed again!

Within a year, the miracle did happen and her hopes did become a fantastic reality. For several years the prophet and his hosts enjoyed their privileges and their friendship in mutual gratitude. Then disaster struck! The boy suddenly got a severe headache and died shortly afterward. The woman put him in Elisha's room and set off by donkey as fast as she could to find the prophet, who was probably at Carmel, about fifteen miles away.

Elisha was shocked by the news and tried to fix the problem in a hurry. He told Gehazi to go at top speed to the boy and to lay Elisha's staff on him. He hoped that God would use this simple instrument to bring the boy back to life. The plan did not work. God wanted to work through a living person, not through a dead instrument. The woman suspected that and persuaded Elisha to attend to the boy personally. When he did that with trusting perseverance, God answered their prayers.

After this crisis in which these friends in need showed themselves to be friends in deed, their friendship became closer than ever. After all, the prophet had not disappointed the trust of the Shunammite woman. Compare this episode to a similar situation experienced by Elijah (1 Kings 17).

A prayer: Lord, I want to be Your living instrument.
A thought: Do I put my trust in things, in people, or in God?

217. Death in the Pot
Poison can enter unnoticed.

Instead of focusing on the political headlines of the day, God's Word attends to the spiritual truth of the day that had meaning for God's people of all times. While the rich and powerful were impressing their guests with gorgeous meals on glittering tables, hungry prophets searched for

> August 4
> ~ ~ ~
> 2 Kings 4:38-41

food in the wild to cook a humble stew in a severe famine. Unknowingly, they poisoned the meal. With the first bite, one of them realized the danger, and he sounded the alarm: "There is death in the pot!"

This cry became proverbial for any situation that looks good from the outside, but which harbors dangerous hidden flaws. A new law or policy, a proposal or a contract, a treaty or agreement, a speech or even a sermon may be dished up attractively, but it may contain catches that may be misused later by those who search for loopholes. Human rights documents, meant to protect the rights and privileges of all, have been misused to rob some of their rights and privileges. At the moment, Christian values and practices are threatened in this way, and Christians should cry out relentlessly to God and to government: "Death in the pot!"

Elisha cured the poisoned stew miraculously with ordinary flour. God calls us to cure "stews" that have become "poisonous" to society. Members of policy-making bodies of church and state, local, and national government should continuously review old laws whose flaws have become evident.

When it becomes clear that a constitution can be interpreted contrary to the views and values of the majority in a nation, then the lawmakers should rectify those weaknesses in the constitution so that the courts cannot interpret the constitution contrary to the views and values of the majority. The rights and privileges of minority groups can be protected without robbing the majority of their rights and privileges.

Many government decisions are not based on what is right or wrong in the long term, morally or scientifically, but what will secure their own political survival in the medium term. Therefore, Christians must stand together and send a strong message to governments that they will vote them out of office if they do not protect the rights and privileges of Christians. Then they must follow through on that. They must vote for the party that will best protect their Christian values. In countries where Christians are in the minority, they have to fight for minority rights.

A prayer: Lord, with You we can take the poison out of society.
A thought: Am I vigilant against the poisons Satan tries to sneak in?

218. Fighting World Hunger
Enough food, uneven distribution

August 5

~ ~ ~

2 Kings 4:42-44

There can be death in the pot, not because of poison but because of inadequate food. While millions struggle daily against overweight, other millions struggle in skeleton bodies against gnawing hunger. Sometimes famine is due to natural causes, sometimes to human mistakes such as overpopulation and unwise farming practices. Often the causes of such disasters are complex, many lines intersecting at one point.

While the student prophets tried to make ends meet during the drought, Elisha got some barley rolls as a gift from someone who managed to bring in a small harvest. Elisha decided to share it with a hundred students and their families. Like the disciples of Jesus, someone voiced what all were thinking: Twenty rolls wouldn't go around. Elisha urged them to just start serving and to leave the rest to God. As people kept on taking from the basket, there still remained a few rolls in the basket. The widow's oil was flowing again.

We can learn a lot from this incident to battle world hunger today. First, some people were willing to share. The farmer shared a portion of his crop with Elisha, and he shared the small gift with many others. In spite of the growing problem of overpopulation, there is still enough food in the world to feed everyone every day. The problem is that there is too much food in some places and too little elsewhere.

The "have's" want to share with the "have-not's," but the cost of moving the surplus foods to the underprivileged is too expensive for individuals to undertake. The richer countries have to budget for this charity, but often they have more urgent matters to attend to, like launching expensive rockets and buying destructive weapons. They may one day hear the most awful words: "I was hungry and you did not give Me food."

Second, when we start to disperse our gifts, they will increase as we proceed. Neither Elisha nor Jesus first multiplied the bread and then dispersed it; the bread was multiplied in the act of giving. We have to start with the little we have, like the widow with the one small jar of oil, and just keep on pouring until the oil stops. We don't have to buy a lot of bread to feed the multitude—we have to share what God is giving us as we go.

Helping poor countries, with means and knowledge, to employ better farming methods can be part of a giving attitude. Handouts can make people dependent; teaching them sustainable development is a long-term solution.

A prayer: Father, please show us ways to bring bread to the hungry.
A thought: My country can distribute more food, medicine, and know-how.

219. A Hero with Leprosy
Salvation demonstrated

People who suffered from leprosy or skin diseases were pushed out of society to prevent the illness from spreading (Lev. 13-14). So when Naaman, the valiant Syrian general, noticed the first signs of the disease on himself, he knew that his time of fame was coming to a sudden end.

> August 6
> ~~~
> 2 Kings 5:1-19

This battle he could not win. At first, he tried to hide his problem; then his family started to whisper about it, and eventually the news hit the streets of Damascus: "General Naaman has leprosy!"

The sad story of a young Israelite slave girl who was torn from her family by this general suddenly brought hopeful light into Naaman's dark days. She brought the good news that her master might be healed by the prophet of the God of Israel. The doomed man grasped at this straw and asked his king to arrange a meeting between the prophet and him.

The king used official channels and contacted the king of Israel. He assumed that the king of Israel would order the prophet to heal the general. The kings in the story are not identified. The king of Israel freaked out when he got the letter from the king of Syria, thinking that Syria was just looking for a good reason to attack Israel again. God revealed to Elisha what was going on, and he sent a message to his king: "Send the general to me, and then he will know who the true God is and who is His prophet."

Naaman stopped with his impressive horses and carriages at Elisha's modest dwelling and sent a soldier to tell the prophet to start his magic ritual. Now Elisha sent his assistant to tell the important visitor to wash himself seven times in the Jordan River. Naaman felt insulted by Elisha's attitude, so he drove off in fury. He despised the humbling healing method too.

On the way, when Naaman had calmed down, his advisors persuaded him to give the prophet's easy advice a try. Why not? There was nothing to lose except his pride. When he got off his high horse and submerged himself in God's humble remedy, he was changed in body, soul, and spirit. Jubilantly, he drove back to Elisha to thank and reward him. Because God had healed Naaman, Elisha refused any payment.

Well, if the God of Israel healed him, the general thought, then he was going to serve only this God in future. Although his knowledge about this God was still poor, his attitude was right. Jesus referred to this incident when He preached in Nazareth (Luke 4:27).

A prayer: Jesus, I bow humbly at Your feet and accept Your salvation.
A thought: Am I waiting in vain for smart solutions?

220. Easy Money
at a high price

August 7
~ ~ ~
2 Kings 5:20-27

With coveting eyes, Gehazi watched the bags of money and cases of clothing Naaman offered to Elisha as payment for his services. Gehazi's greedy heart twitched when his master declined the gifts. To let such an opportunity pass by unutilized was just inconceivable for this earthly-minded assistant. Quickly, he concocted a plan to get something for himself out of this enticing situation.

He followed Naaman's procession at a distance and caught up with them at a safe place. He lied to the general about fictitious needy visitors who had arrived at Elisha's home and said that his master would now accept a modest gift on their behalf. He got even more than he had asked for, and two of Naaman's men helped him carry the gift to a safe place. Then Gehazi returned to Elisha as if nothing had happened. He should have known better.

When Elisha asked him where he had been, he told another lie to cover up the first one. Elisha informed him that in his spirit he had seen what Gehazi had done. He rebuked his assistant for putting his own interest before the kingdom of God and announced the consequences of his choice: The leprosy that was taken from Naaman would cling to Gehazi and his descendants.

In our materialistic society this seems like a harsh punishment for a minor crime, but this kind of self-enrichment is the soil from which large-scale fraud sprouts. The greed of countries, companies, and individuals spawns the scandals that erode public trust in the main systems of society, leading to downturns in the economy and other fields. Often ordinary people have to pay the high price of greed and fraud in the form of decreased income, increased insurance and taxes, or even in the form of blood on the battlefield.

We read about Gehazi in subsequent chapters without reference to his leprosy. Either he repented and was forgiven and healed, or the book of Kings may not always describe events in precise chronological order. Those "later" Gehazi-episodes might have occurred before his leprosy.

The Bible tells us of God's mercy for repentant sinners; therefore, I prefer the first option. If Gehazi was forgiven and healed, the "leprosy" that would cling to him and to his descendants "forever" might have been this story about his fraud and punishment. All the good that people have done through their lives is often overshadowed by one wrong choice and its sad consequences. Don't allow greed to nullify your good work.

A prayer: Lord, help me not to damage Your Name and my reputation.
A thought: Has self-interest made me violate the Great Commandment?

221. The Floating Ax
Good provision on a good mission

We have noticed that Elisha moved around in Israel to reach as many people as possible. Prophet schools existed at various places, and Elisha attended to their needs as well. The number of students increased after the victory over Baal at Mount Carmel. At one of these schools

> August 8
> ~ ~ ~
> 2 Kings 6:1-7

they discussed the problem of inadequate living quarters with Elisha and suggested that all of them go down to the Jordan and that each one bring back some timber. This wood could then be used to expand the buildings. Elisha supported the idea and accompanied them.

While they were cutting down trees, one guy had bad luck on this good mission. The iron ax head flew off the handle and landed in deep, muddy water. Being poor, he had borrowed the ax and could not replace it. He shared his trouble with Elisha. When Elisha threw a piece of wood on the spot where the ax had sunk, the iron came up and floated on the surface, and the man could reach out and recover it. The merciful power of God turned the bad experience into a good one. The good mission ended well that day.

A lot of instruction is imbedded in these few verses about the floating ax. First, the increased number of students who prepared themselves to preach God's Word to a straying nation is a call to young people today to seek God's guidance about going into the same ministry. Second, sharing the physical burdens of communal living urges us to share household chores instead of shifting them onto one person. Third, the importance of a leader to coordinate efforts is shown by Elisha's willingness to go with the students to ensure good teamwork and a positive outcome.

Fourth, the borrowed ax reminds us of the privileges God has put into our custody for a specific time, place, and purpose, such as family, friends, work, income, health, talents, and opportunities. Fifth, when something bad suddenly spoils our good efforts, we have to share it with God and with fellow believers in the hope that God will turn things around. Sixth, like this student, we have to reach out to regain what was lost. Lost axes don't jump into our laps. When God brings them to the surface, we have to do our share to regain them.

What is your lost ax? Is it a neglected friendship, an unused opportunity, a neglected talent, or a lost person? The shepherd must seek the lost sheep and rejoice when it is found. There is rejoicing in heaven when one lost sinner has been saved (Luke 15:4-7).

A prayer: Thank You, Father, for teaching me the basics of Christian teamwork.
A thought: Has God brought some of my lost opportunities to the surface again?

222. God's Army
Elisha is protected by chariots of fire.

<table>
<tr><td>

August 9

~ ~ ~

2 Kings 6:8-23

</td><td>

Elisha was a busy prophet. On top of his ministry to the people and to the prophets, he still found time to minister to the king and his army. God revealed to Elisha the plans and the movements of the Syrian forces. Thus he could help the king of Israel avoid ambushes and score

</td></tr>
</table>

victories.

The king of Syria was perplexed by these events and suspected that one of his closest advisors was a double agent who informed Israel of their top secret operations. His advisors then told the king about their suspicion that it was the prophet Elisha whose God revealed to him all the secrets of Syria. Knowing Elisha's powers by what he did for Naaman, the Syrian general, the king agreed to test their theory. If they capture or kill the prophet, he could not help the king of Israel any more. Strangely, they did not consider the possibility that God might reveal this plan to Elisha as well.

The Syrian army marched during the night and encircled the town of Dothan where Elisha was. When his young assistant, probably not Gehazi, panicked about the siege, Elisha remarked that God's army was stronger than the Syrian army. His prayer that his assistant might behold God's invisible army was granted. In amazement and awe the man looked at the fiery horses and chariots all around the town. A second prayer of Elisha was answered when the Syrians were struck with a strange blindness of eye and mind. The Syrian army was then led by Elisha to Samaria, about ten miles from Dothan.

When the Syrians were surrounded by the Israelite army in Samaria, the sight of the Syrians was restored on Elisha's prayer. Because they were God's captives, the army of Israel was not permitted to slay them. Instead, they were ordered by God to give them food and water and let them return to their own land to tell the embarrassing story to their king and to their people. The good treatment they had received in spite of their bad intentions shamed them so much that for a long time they refrained from attacking Israel again.

God gives us in this passage a glimpse of how He protects His children by His invisible forces. No matter how desperate the situation looks, we have to keep our eyes fixed on Jesus, the author and finisher of our faith (Hebrews 12:1-2). When someone focused on God and not on the problem, Jesus called it "great faith" (Matthew 8:10, 15:28), and when someone focused on the problem only, He called it "little faith" (Matthew 14:28-31).

A prayer: Father, let my faith see Your continuous, invisible protection.
A thought: Do I panic easily when things go wrong?

223. Wonderful Provision
in a dismal situation

Man's material greed often overrides his spiritual views. In spite of the healing of their general by a prophet in Israel, and in spite of the embarrassing encounter their army had had with that prophet, the Syrian king and his advisors talked themselves into another war with their benevolent neighbor.

August 10
~ ~ ~
2 Kings 6:24 -
7:20

Their siege of Samaria eventually caused a severe famine in the city. Why the rest of Israel did not come to their rescue is not clear. The dismal situation in Samaria is vividly illustrated by two pieces of information. People paid exorbitant prices for disgusting "food" like donkey heads and dove droppings. Those who could not afford such luxuries began to kill and eat their own children. When the king heard about it, he tore his clothes. Then people saw that he was wearing mourning clothes beneath his royal robes. He thought he could appease God with secret repentance.

Powerless to help his people, he looked for someone to blame. He assumed that God had brought this calamity on them; therefore, he decided to avenge himself on God's prophet. When he came to Elisha's house with a few men to kill the prophet, Elisha greeted him with a promise from God, a promise so fantastic that it was incredible to the officer at the king's side. Because the man doubted God's ability to provide in a miraculous way, a curse was put on him: He would see God's provision, but he would not taste of it.

God made the Syrians hear the noise of an approaching army. They were so terrified that they fled on foot, leaving their whole camp with tents, food, and animals behind. The deserted camp was discovered by three leprous men. First they grabbed as much as they could for themselves, but later realized that they should tell it to the dying city. Their sharing of the good news became a maxim for sharing the good news of the gospel. Though the king feared it might be a trap, he had the situation investigated. When it became evident that the enemy had indeed fled, the whole city came out to help themselves to the abundant provisions. The unbelieving officer was trampled to death in the city gate, and food became as cheap as Elisha had predicted.

In the most desperate situation, God's provision may be just next door, and it could be ours if we trust Him with all our hearts. He can turn the tables in a moment, either for us or against us, depending on our relationship with Him. But when He provides, we have to share.

A prayer: Father, help me to trust You completely in all circumstances.
A thought: Do I keep God's good news to myself?

224. History and Reality
The past walks into the present.

<table>
<tr><td>
August 11
~ ~ ~
2 Kings 8:1-8
</td></tr>
</table>

At the start of a seven-year drought, Elisha advised his friends in Shunem to take refuge in another country until the drought was broken. They followed his advice and moved to Philistia. The earth and everything on it belongs to the LORD (Ps. 24:1); therefore, He can provide for His children anywhere.

Abram had moved to Canaan and to Egypt, Jacob to Haran and to Egypt, Moses to Midian, Naomi to Moab, David to Philistia, and Elijah to Phoenicia. Staying in a foreign country is never easy, but sometimes it can't be avoided. However, in every immigrant lives the hope to return to the old country again, even if it is only for a while. And so it happened that the woman of Shunem returned with her family to her land after the drought had ended.

We don't know if they had sold their rights to their land when they had left, or if someone had taken it without permission, but apparently they could not gain access to their land when they returned. Years ago the woman's husband was already old (2 Kings 4:14), so now she was probably a widow. She took her problem to the king and asked for mercy.

At that very moment Gehazi, apparently cured from his leprosy and narrating all Elisha's miracles to the king, was telling the story of how Elisha brought the son of this woman back to life. When Gehazi saw her, he shouted with excitement, "Here she is! This is the woman I'm telling you about!" Then the king got excited too and asked the woman to tell the story herself. History comes to life when someone who lived through that history can give firsthand information about it. Then history becomes real.

This episode poignantly illustrates the tension that often exists between past and present, between what WAS and what IS. In the past, this woman and her husband had the joy of a happy family and a successful farm; now she was a poor, homeless widow. Then Elisha brought their son miraculously back to life and restored their joy; now she begged for mercy from a king who served idols. In the past, Gehazi saw the miracles happen through the hand of Elisha; now he lived with the scars of leprosy and by fading memories.

The king restored the woman's right to her land. At least that piece of history could be restored. When she walked into the king's presence that day, the reality of the past changed the reality of the present. History helps us to heed the lessons of the past and to correct injustices where we can.

A prayer: Father, help me to build the future on the good of the past.
A thought: How do I link the reality of the past to the reality of the present?

225. The Wages of Sin
God's judgment executed on scoffers

The second part of 1 Kings and the first part of 2 Kings focus on the prophets Elijah and Elisha, not on the kings. As the history of the kings is resumed, the judgments announced by the prophets are executed on those who taunted God continuously in spite of His calls to repentance. This history can be

> August 12
> ~ ~ ~
> 2 Kings 8-10
> 2 Chron. 21-22

described in the words of the apostle Paul: *"For the wages of sin is death, but the gift of God is eternal life in Christ Jesus our Lord"* (Rom. 6:23).

Through Elisha, God appointed Hazael as king of Syria, confirming God's rule over all the earth. God would use Hazael to judge His mockers.

For several years the kings of Israel and Judah had the same name, Joram (short for Jehoram), underlining the close ties between the two kingdoms after the marriage of Joram of Judah and Athaliah of Israel. She lured her husband into the idolatry of her parents, Ahab and Jezebel. It started thirteen years of religious and political decline in Judah. Joram of Judah tried to secure his reign by murdering his brothers, but he lost ground when various subjugated nations rebelled, took his wives, and murdered his children, except for Ahaziah. Before Elijah was taken up, he told Joram in a letter that he would die of a painful digestive disease, which occurred. *"To no one's sorrow"* Joram passed away.

When Ahaziah succeeded Joram of Judah, he followed in his footsteps. He joined forces with his uncle, Joram of Israel, against Hazael, king of Syria. Like his father, Ahab, Joram was wounded at Ramoth in Gilead. He retreated to Jezreel to recover. While Ahaziah of Judah paid him a visit, Jehu was anointed king over Israel by a prophet sent by Elisha. Jehu drove in haste to Jezreel, killed Joram, and fatally wounded Ahaziah near Samaria.

Jehu returned to Jezreel and brought judgment on Jezebel. Her corpse was devoured by dogs, as Elijah had predicted. With shrewd manipulation Jehu had the sons of Ahab, the relatives of Ahaziah, and the Baal worshipers killed. Ahab's family was wiped out completely (1 Kings 21:21-23).

Although Jehu did all this killing in the name of God, he was actually acting out his own bloodthirsty drives. He did not serve Yahveh, but the golden calves of Jeroboam instead. He would be judged accordingly.

God patiently extends His mercy toward sinners, but if they persistently reject it, they have to face God's wrath. The New Testament says, *"Whoever rejects the Son will not see life, for God's wrath remains on him"* (John 3:36, NIV).

A prayer: Father, I accept Your love, expressed in Jesus, Your Son.
A thought: What can I do for those who reject or ignore God's grace in Christ?

226. The Day of the LORD
Joel calls Judah to repentance.

August 13
~ ~ ~
Joel 1 - 3

When we see the prophets against their historic background, their messages become more meaningful. Some scholars date the prophecy of Joel in the time of Judah's first major apostasy, while others think it was written after the exile. The same arguments are used to support both theories, namely: Joel refers to the temple and to the wall of Jerusalem but not to a king or to Assyria and Babylonia.

By means of the prophetic word and a natural disaster, God made a strong appeal to the nation to return to Him. Joel used a vivid description of a devastating drought and locust plague to highlight the desperate situation of people, livestock, and plant life. He compared it to an invasion of a fierce and merciless army. This comparison may be a symbol of future destruction of the land by real armies. In view of the end-time "day of the LORD" announced by Joel, these plagues may also point to end-time disasters.

If the people would repent and return to God, they would experience times of plenty. The locusts would be driven into the sea, and timely rains would refresh the land. On top of material prosperity, God would send them wonderful spiritual blessings. He would pour out His Spirit on all people and let them "prophesy"; that is, they would bring God's message to the world. These words were fulfilled at Pentecost, and the apostle Peter referred to Joel to explain to the people of Jerusalem what was going on (Acts 2).

Joel also pointed to the cosmic disturbances in the end time. Thick smoke clouds will darken the sun and make the moon appear red. Then all nations will be summoned to judgment day. The only ray of hope will be that those who call on the name of the LORD, Yahveh, will be saved. The apostle Paul cited this promise in Romans 10:13 when he explained salvation to the Romans.

Although we know nothing about Joel, God used him to give us soul-searching prophecies on both God's wrath and God's love. He told us how to be saved and how to be fruitful in God's service. By calling to God and standing with Him, we not only escape His wrath, but He also fills us with His Spirit, enabling us to do His will and His work wholeheartedly.

Joel had a powerful message for the people of his own time and for believers of centuries to come. Under the leadership of the high priest Jehoiada and his protégé Jehoash, there did occur a turning back to God in Judah. And the prophecy is still being fulfilled in Christianity.

A prayer: Father, I would rather have Your blessing than Your wrath.
A thought: Have I taken what God offers through Joel?

227. The Boy-King
He and the temple protect each other.

When Ahaziah was killed by Jehu, his mother Athaliah grabbed the throne of Judah. She tried to kill all royal heirs, including her own grandchildren. Jehosheba, the sister of the late king and wife of the high priest, hid her brother's baby, Joash, in a room of the temple for six years. We can only imagine how this limited space, secrecy, and isolation restricted the normal play of this preschool boy.

August 14

~ ~ ~

2 Kings 11-12
2 Chron. 22:10-
24:27

When Joash was seven years old, the high priest, Jehoiada, staged the crowning of the legitimate king with the help of the Levites. Athaliah was killed and her Baal temple and idols completely destroyed. Her husband had died "to no one's sorrow"; her own death caused jubilation.

Joash was already married, probably in his early twenties, when he gave the first command to the priests to use the temple tax to repair the temple. It was about 145 years after Solomon had finished the temple, and the gradual damage caused by wind and weather became evident and disturbing. The temple had protected Joash as a stowaway boy-king; now it was his turn to protect the temple, the only house he had known for his first seven years.

However, when he was already thirty years old, not much had been done yet to restore the temple. So Joash commanded the high priest to put a chest at the temple entrance so that the public could contribute voluntarily to the repair of their sanctuary. It worked. Soon enough money came in to start the work. The treasurers and the workers used the money so efficiently that they did not have to prove their accountability. All could see it.

Sadly, the man who grew up in the temple and who restored the temple eventually forgot the temple. As long as Jehoiada lived, Joash followed the right path, but when his mentor died, he was lured into idolatry by the leaders of Judah. Maybe this man who missed out on a normal childhood wanted to taste pleasure when Jehoiada and all his rules fell away.

God sent prophets to bring him back, but he would not listen. He even ordered the execution of Jehoiada's (grand)son Zechariah, a sin referred to by Jesus (Luke 11:51). This sin is omitted by the book of Kings but exposed by the Chronicles.

God used the Syrians to punish Joash. Were they the "locusts" Joel spoke of? They ravished the cities and the people. Joash was wounded and then murdered by two of his guards.

A prayer: Father, open my eyes to the tricks of the devil.
A thought: Which childhood values have I abandoned to my peril?

228. Mercy for the Undeserving
A straying nation gets a golden opportunity.

<table>
<tr><td>

August 15
~~~
2 Kings 13,
14:23-29

</td><td>

We have been following the history of the divided kingdom for 130 years until about 800 B.C. In spite of the ongoing idolatry in Israel (the northern kingdom), God had compassion on them and blessed them with about fifty good years. In this time God sent His prophets to them to call them back.

</td></tr>
</table>

Jehu's son, Jehoahaz, was defeated and humiliated by the Syrians. He had only a few chariots and horses left, and he was heavily taxed by the oppressor. Although he did not turn away from idolatry completely, he cried out to the LORD for help. Even with this weak sign of repentance, God had compassion on His people for the misery they had brought onto themselves. He decided to give them a break from oppression, minister to them through the prophets, and hope for a general turning back to God.

The anonymous "deliverer" could have been Jeroboam II, but it may also point to God Himself as the real Deliverer for sinners. In the fullness of time (Gal. 4:4) God would send His Son as the one and only Savior for mankind. Those who believe in Him will escape God's judgment (John 3:18).

Jehoahaz was succeeded by his son Jehoash in 798 B.C. Like many before him, he tried to serve both idols and Yahveh. When Elisha was severely ill, Jehoash visited him and honored him with the same words with which Elisha had described Elijah: "chariot and horsemen of Israel." Elisha let him perform two symbolic actions with bow and arrow and prophesied that he would have victories over the Syrians, which did happen.

After Elisha's death God did one more miracle through his bones. When a funeral procession was attacked by raiders, the mourners dumped the corpse hastily into Elisha's tomb. When the body came into contact with Elisha's remains, God revived the person. Likewise, God has used many believers after their death to give life to sinners by means of their recorded words.

Jehoahaz was succeeded by his son, Jeroboam II, who reigned forty-one years. He recaptured the land of Israel that had been taken by the Syrians. In spite of his idolatry, God used him to secure some breathing space for Israel and to give them the chance to repent. His son, Zechariah, was the fourth and last descendant of Jehu on the throne of Israel (2 Kings 10:30). Unfortunately, they did not listen to God's prophets and did not turn away from idolatry. Their golden opportunity slipped through their fingers.

*A prayer: Father, You give us ample time to be reconciled with You.*
*A thought: How do I use my God-given opportunities?*

# 229. Doomed Prosperity
## Amos rebukes Israel for injustice and idolatry.

Amos was a sheep and fruit farmer. He sold his products on major markets, bringing this farmer of Tekoa, near Bethlehem, in contact with the lifestyle and idolatry of the northern kingdom. God burdened his heart with a message to a sinful nation.

> August 16
> ~ ~ ~
> Amos 1-9

The breathing space God had given to Israel under Jeroboam II stimulated the economy, and many got rich. Unfortunately they greedily built their fortune on corruption and injustice, which robbed the poor of their land and forced them into slave labor.

They also proceeded hypocritically with the false religion that had been introduced by Jeroboam I about 160 years before. They tried to serve God by means of the golden calves, blending Mosaic Law with pagan practices. The remnant of 7000 who stayed true to Yahveh—as God had told Elijah (1 Kings 19:18)—were not part of this potpourri-religion practiced by Israel.

With poetic metaphors from urban and rural life, with ringing refrains and striking visions, with persuasive reasoning and lively dialogues, and with scary warnings and soothing promises, Amos' message confronted the false security of wayward nations. By addressing Israel, Judah, and several of their neighbors, he showed that God is Ruler of all the earth.

God told Israel through his prophet unambiguously that they would go into exile far beyond Damascus if they did not repent and change their ways. The rich who gorged themselves with food and wine on ivory-decorated sofas probably laughed at the babbling farmer-preacher from the south who had the audacity to prescribe to the elite of the north.

The false priest of Bethel tried to scare Amos away as if Amos were a scoundrel. This gave Amos opportunity to tell us something about himself. He was not a professional prophet, but an ordinary citizen, a fig farmer, who felt compelled to testify for God: *"A lion has roared! Who will not fear? The Lord God has spoken! Who can but prophesy?"*

Moses had longed for the day when God would put His Spirit on all the people so that they would prophesy (Num. 11:29). Amos was an early example of the prophetic office of Christian believers who would be filled by the Holy Spirit to speak to all nations about the good news of salvation in Christ (Acts 1:8). Yes, after Amos had chastised Israel and had announced their exile, he also brought God's good news of restoration to the doomed nation.

*A prayer: Cure us of false worship and unjust practices.*
*A thought: Do I testify as an ordinary believer to church and world?*

# 230. Ministering to the Enemy
## Jonah does not like his assignment.

Jonah also ministered to the northern kingdom during the reign of Jeroboam II (2 Kings 14:25), a time when the rising kingdom of Assyria was becoming a problem for Israel. In fact, thirty years or so down the road Assyria would send most people of Israel into exile. When God asked Jonah to go and preach in Nineveh, the capital of Assyria, he tried to run away from this assignment by fleeing to Spain. In the world concept of the day, Tarshish was the remotest place Jonah could think of.

Jonah did not mind pouring fire and brimstone sermons onto Nineveh. That he would like to do. The possibility he dreaded was that the Assyrians might repent, be forgiven, and so escape the wrath of God (4:2). So he silently packed his bags and secretly sneaked away by sailboat to Tarshish.

He knew God's judgment and love, but he did not know God's fatherly discipline well enough. The Father would not relent on His child's upbringing. He stopped Jonah with a storm at sea. Jonah tried to escape into sleep, and then into death, but to no avail. For His purpose, God prepared a fish that scooped Jonah from a drowning death into a stinking belly with enough air to sustain the bewildered prophet. What a moment of truth!

While the pagan sailors prayed to their idols on the ship, Jonah did not pray, but slept—like the disciples in Gethsemane. Now that he sat with seaweed around his head inside a sea monster, his prayer life came back to life. And he glorified God with a prayer of sincere gratitude, repentance, and submission. At last, Jonah was willing and ready to go to Nineveh.

What he had feared happened. When the people of Nineveh heard his message, they repented and were saved from imminent disaster. Any Christian preacher would be overjoyed by such a response by the audience, but Jonah sulked. First Jonah had acted like the "lost son" (running off to a far country), then like his brother (grumbling about repenting sinners).

Again Yahveh worked on Jonah's education. He showed Jonah how many innocent children and livestock would have died if Jonah's wish had been fulfilled. Jonah grew enough to leave a record of Yahveh's yearning.

Without knowing it, Jonah also left an awesome prophecy about Christ. The only sign Jesus gave to the Pharisees was the "sign of Jonah." As Jonah had been in the fish for three days, so Jesus would be in the tomb for three days before He would emerge from death as the conqueror of death.

*A prayer: Thank You, Father, for the lessons of Jonah and Jesus.*
*A thought: Have I tried to run away from God-given assignments?*

# 231. Meddling with Trouble
## Like parasites, arrogance destroys its host.

While Israel was enjoying their last chance, King Amaziah of Judah was looking for trouble and got it. To begin with, he served God, but he allowed idolatry to continue at the "high places." His partial loyalty to Yahveh would cost him dearly later. The example of his late father Joash, who served God in his youth and strayed from God later in his life, might have influenced Amaziah in the same direction.

> August 18
> ~ ~ ~
> 2 Kings 14:1-22
> 2 Chron. 25

His second mistake was to hire a hundred thousand soldiers from Israel for his planned invasion of Edom. A prophet warned him that he would not be successful if he included these idol worshipers in his army. When he sent them home—with pay but without loot—they ravished Judean cities to make up for their perceived losses. That soured relationships between Judah and Israel.

Amaziah conquered Edom and butchered its people by sword or by pushing them over a cliff. Then he foolishly took some of their idols to Jerusalem and sacrificed to them. Maybe he thought that pleasing the gods of Edom would secure peaceful subordination of Edom. God saw no logic in that—why worship the dead idols that could not protect their own people? Instead of listening to God's prophet, he threatened him into silence.

Proud about his victory over Edom, Amaziah then decided to punish Israel for the looting done by their returning mercenaries. By means of a fable about an arrogant thistle, the king of Israel advised Amaziah not to meddle with trouble and to reconsider his war plans against Israel.

Again Amaziah refused to listen to good advice; headstrong, he proceeded and paid a heavy price. He was defeated and captured, and Jerusalem was looted and its wall destroyed. Apparently Amaziah's son, Uzziah, ruled while Amaziah was held captive.

Outraged by Amaziah's bad decisions, some people of Judah plotted his death. He fled to Lachish, was pursued there and killed—an unnecessary sad end to a king to whom God still had been talking through His prophets. By not consulting God, he had made bad decisions with bad consequences. And by shutting up God's prophets, he hastened his own downfall.

Jesus underlined it to His followers that without Him they can do nothing. The branch can only bear fruit when it stays connected to the vine. Severed from the vine, the branch withers and dies (John 15:1-8).

*A prayer: Father, I want to stay in contact with You.*
*A thought: Have I failed because I left God out of my planning?*

# 232. Love for God and Nature
## does not cancel out God-given boundaries.

August 19

~ ~ ~

2 Kings 15:1-7
2 Chron. 26

Uzziah (also called Azariah) was sixteen years old when he began reigning in place of his captive father. He had splendid testimonials for the best part of his life. He started off with love for God and for the soil. He enjoyed the instruction of a prophet, and he had many livestock and large fields and orchards. He came to know the Creator through His Word and through creation.

Yahveh liked that and blessed him exceedingly. Uzziah subdued several other nations and received tribute from them. He used his wealth to fortify his strongholds. His large army was well equipped with offensive and defensive weaponry. He had "canons" made for his towers. These devices could hurl heavy stones at approaching enemies. He reigned for fifty-two years.

Unfortunately, his success went to his head. Arrogantly he assumed the role of high priest and tried to bring the incense offering into the Holy Place himself. The Bible states that his pride made him do this foolish thing. The history of the nation was told from generation to generation, so Uzziah had to be acquainted with the sin of Saul, Israel's first king, who had been heavily punished for playing priest (1 Sam. 13).

The high priest, accompanied by eighty other priests, admonished the king not to step over God's rules for the sanctuary. While Uzziah was raging at them, leprosy broke out on his forehead. He was hurried out of the temple and was isolated from people in a separate house for the rest of his life. His successful life had taken a sudden downturn. If he had not made this mistake, he could have been one of the most honored kings of Judah.

It is often said that power corrupts. Success may have the same effect if we do not stay humbly at the foot of the cross. When the big ego syndrome emerges, people start to step over boundaries and to walk over other people. They start to prescribe to all in a condescending way, instead of realizing their own limitations. Senior citizens have to be on their guard against this attitude too. Although their years of experience may have blessed them with knowledge and wisdom in a certain area, they have to remember that their knowledge covers only a small part of the total reality.

We have to keep on honoring God for the good in our lives while we modestly recognize the many shortcomings we still have to work on. A little bit of humor toward both aspects makes it easier to avoid the pride trap.

*A prayer: God, keep me humble in spite of success.*
*A thought: Where did I step over boundaries because of pride?*

# 233. God Is On His Throne
## Isaiah's calling as prophet

In the year king Uzziah of Judah died (± 740 B.C.), Isaiah was called as prophet of the Lord. He would fulfill this ministry for about fifty years, covering the reign of three Judean kings.

> August 20
> ~ ~ ~
> Isaiah 6

In a vision, Isaiah saw God sitting on His throne. It affirmed that God is in control in spite of what earthly leaders may say or do. The train of God's robe filled the temple, and Isaiah was struck by an awesome sense of God's holy presence on earth. Seraphim angels flew around in the temple and shouted in deafening voices to one another: *"Holy, holy, holy is the LORD of hosts; the whole earth is full of His glory!"* In awe, Isaiah humbled himself, fearing that he would die because he had seen God.

In bold stupidity, we sometimes ask God cocky questions about what happens to us. However, people who really became aware of God's presence prostrated themselves before God, or hid their faces, in overwhelming reverence, like Abraham (Gen. 17:3), Moses (Ex. 3:6), Elijah (1 Kings 19:11-13), David (2 Sam. 12:16), Paul (Acts 9:4-6), and John (Rev.1:17).

The one thing Isaiah felt most guilty about was his "unclean lips," that is: his verbal sins. One of the seraphim took with tongs a live coal from the incense altar, touched Isaiah's lips with the coal, and proclaimed that his sins were taken away. When God asked who He could send to his people, Isaiah immediately volunteered and eagerly said, *"Here am I; send me!"*

When Isaiah heard what he had to say to the people, it must have been a shocking disappointment to him. He had to tell them that they hear but they don't understand, they see but they don't perceive. Instead of rectifying this inability, Isaiah had to speak to them in such a way that their hearts would become even more dulled, their ears more blocked, and their eyes more shut so that they would not be healed. Isaiah's message would not have positive results. Israel would turn their backs on Yahveh's yearning.

Jesus referred to this passage when He said that He spoke in parables so that people could not understand Him (Matt. 13:10-17).

In shocked amazement Isaiah asked how long this fruitless preaching would have to go on. God said that Isaiah (and others) had to proceed until the people were carried off into exile. However, God promised to keep the stump of the tree alive, that is, the remnant who would remain loyal to Him, the symbolic "seven thousand" He told Elijah about long ago.

*A prayer: Here am I, Lord, send me!*
*A thought: Am I willing to be cleansed to be a useful instrument?*

# 234. Unassuming Leadership
### Heaven and earth defines 'colorful' differently.

August 21
~~~
2 Kings 15:32-38
2 Chron. 27

The book of Kings and the book of Chronicles each have only one short paragraph on King Jotham of Judah. From these passages the world would not conclude that he was a colorful celebrity. However, with close scrutiny it becomes clear that Jotham received heavenly colors: *"So Jotham became mighty, because he prepared his ways before the LORD his God"* or as the NIV puts it: *"he walked steadfastly before the LORD his God."*

For king Jotham, there was only one true God, namely the LORD (Yahveh), the God of Israel. "Before the LORD" means in His sight, conscious of His watching eyes. Jotham maintained a close relationship with God, and that determined what he did and how he did it. He "prepared his ways": He planned his actions in such a way that they were in line with God's will. Therefore he "walked steadfastly"; he did not stumble, but proceeded firmly toward his goals, undistracted by the devil's bait.

His trust in God did not make him passive. He did not wait for the golden apple to fall into his lap, but he pursued his goals while trusting God. He had extensive building projects: at the temple, at the wall of Jerusalem, at Judean towns, and in wooded areas. In addition to his defensive strategy, he also acted offensively when needed. He conquered the Ammonites and made them pay large tribute which enabled him to expand his operations.

As had happened with "good" kings before him, his good example was not followed by all, either by the general population or by his son Ahaz, who later succeeded him. It was as if Judah, like Israel, was sinking into a quagmire of idolatry, and they would not take the rescue ropes that God hurled to them.

As we have seen with the judges, the flamboyant but erring leaders like Samson usually got more attention than the "ordinary" leaders who did a great job without fanfare. God had His book written that way, not because He is focused on negative news, but because He wanted to show us the consequences of both negative and positive behavior.

Although good behavior is not always highlighted, we have to open our eyes for it. It is there. Beauty is in the eye of the beholder. Jesus said good eyes illuminate the whole body (Luke 11:34).

We must practice our eyes to see the colors of heaven in ordinary lives. The unassuming faithful are colorful flowers in God's garden.

A prayer: Lord, I want to prepare my ways before Your eyes.
A thought: Is my aim on applause and fame, or on doing God's will?

235. Immanuel
A divine promise to a wicked king

King Ahaz decided to be his dad's opposite, and he succeeded in more than one way. He not only took idolatry to new depths, but also went out of his way to damage and to desecrate the temple of God. Instead of his father's strong military position, he suffered severe attacks from surrounding nations, and he paid through his neck in an effort to save himself.

August 22
~ ~ ~
2 Kings 16
2 Chron. 28
Isaiah 7

Ahaz went out of his way to insult Yahveh. He served Baal, burnt incense to idols at high places, brought some of his children as burnt offerings to idols, replaced the bronze altar in the temple with a replica of a pagan altar in Damascus, closed the Holy and Most Holy parts of the temple, removed the king's pavilion from the temple, and broke down the staircase between the palace and the temple. On top of all these offenses, he sacrificed the regular Mosaic offerings in the temple court on his Damascus altar and dedicated these to his pagan gods. He deliberately looked for trouble—and got it!

"The LORD brought Judah low because of Ahaz." God punished him for his impudence by means of the kings of Syria, Israel, Philistia, Edom, and Assyria. They took many of his fortified cities and took many of his people captive. He paid the king of Assyria a lot of money but got little in return.

And yet, in spite of his vile apostasy, Yahveh reached out to him and tried to make him change his mind. When Israel killed 120,000 soldiers of Judah and took 200,000 women and children captive as slaves, God persuaded Israel by the prophet Oded to send these captives home.

God also sent the prophet Isaiah to Ahaz to assure him that his enemies would not conquer Jerusalem. He challenged Ahaz to ask for a sign, and when Ahaz refused, God Himself gave him a sign: *"Behold, the virgin shall conceive and bear a Son, and shall call His name Immanuel"* (Isaiah 7:14). For Ahaz, this meant that before the child could understand, the kings of Syria and of Israel would be defeated by the superpowers of the day, Assyria and Egypt.

For the far-off future it meant that God would come to the world as a human being so that "Immanuel" (God with us) would be a wonderful reality. Some say that the God of the Old Testament is a God of wrath. When we see how Yahveh pleaded with them for centuries and reached out to the most wicked, like Ahab of Israel and Ahaz of Judah, then there can be no doubt that God's wrath only came into effect after His love had been rejected repeatedly.

A prayer: Praise God, there is still time for sinners to be saved.
A thought: How can we reach out to hardened hearts?

236. Spurned Love
Hosea scolds unfaithful Israel.

<table>
<tr><td>
August 23
~ ~ ~
Hosea 1, 3, 14
</td></tr>
</table>

Hosea was ordered by God to marry a prostitute who would bear children conceived in adultery. This strange command could be reality, allegory, or vision. Each of these views is both supported and opposed by strong arguments. For this author, the vision option seems the most plausible because it eliminates the moral and practical problems faced by the other two approaches.

However, there is no difference of opinion regarding the fact that Hosea's marriage, real or imaginary, symbolized Israel's infidelity toward God, who yearned for the love of His unfaithful "wife." Their sins not only resembled adultery, but sexual immorality was one of their many sins. It was associated with the idolatry of the surrounding nations (4:10-14).

Hosea's successive messages rolled onto Israel like breakers onto a beach. Each wave contained a charge about sins, about judgment because of sins, and about promises of future recovery by God's grace.

Israel, and sometimes Judah with them, was accused of idolatry, human sacrifices, rejection of God's law, a lack of knowledge, inebriety, prostitution, fraud, theft, perjury, murder, and relying on Assyria and Egypt instead of on God. These sins penetrated all layers of society, from prince to pauper.

Hosea underlined the cause-effect relationship between sin and judgment. They had sown wind and reaped whirlwind; they had sown wickedness and reaped evil. By the names Hosea had to give to his children in the vision, God warned Israel that there could come a time when He would not have mercy on them any more and would not regard them as His people any longer.

Animals would die in drought, women would be barren, the nation would be ripped apart like prey mauled by predators, swords would flash in their cities, women and children would be smashed to death, and survivors would go into exile. Proceeding with unfaithfulness would end in grim consequences.

In these dark paintings about sin and judgment, there are a few bright rays of hope. After they had been sitting in a foreign land for a long time, without king, priest or sacrifice, God would show mercy and make them His people again. It would be like being raised from the dead on the third day (6:2, 13:14). Hosea concluded his book by calling Israel to repentance and painting for them the glorious picture of healing, using beautiful metaphors from nature: flourishing lilies, vines, cedars, and olive trees.

A prayer: God, I don't want to hurt Your love; I want to stay true to You.
A thought: Do I see the warning signs for my nation?

237. False Religion
Isaiah (1-12) rebukes Judah and Israel.

The first 39 chapters of the book of Isaiah deal mainly with Judah and Israel (1-12), other nations (13-23), the world (24-27), and Judah's and Israel's relationship with Egypt and Assyria (28-35). There are also historic passages (chapters 6-7, 36-39).

August 24
~~
Isaiah 1:1-3
1:12-20, 5:20-22
8:23-9:6, 11:1-12

In the first twelve chapters, Isaiah addresses the sins and the false religion of Judah and Israel. Most likely it is a compilation of messages that are not ordered chronologically, so sometimes the message seems to be delivered before, and sometimes after, the fall of Samaria. Although Isaiah worked in Jerusalem, God's message was for all people. From God's perspective, Judah and Israel were His people, one nation. God's prophets were not limited by the border between the two.

Isaiah chastised Judah and Israel for their unfaithfulness. He compared them to a child who rebels against a parent (1:2), to an adulterous wife (1:21), and to a vine that bears sour grapes (5:2). He rebuked their formalistic religion, which observed rituals but allowed crimes too (1:15). He reprimanded them for their greed (5:8), luxury (2:7; 3:16-24), and snobbery (2:11,17), for corruption of justice (1:23; 3:9,14; 10:1-2), for reversal of values (5:20), and for inebriety (5:11, 22), idolatry (2:8), and sorcery (8:19).

In His mercy, God told His people clearly through the prophet what the punishment would be if they persevered in their sins and what the reward would be if they repented and changed their ways. Punishment would mainly come by the sword of their enemies (1:7, 3:25, 5:26-30), but eventually those enemies would take them into exile if they didn't listen (5:13).

Amid all these taunting sins and impending judgments rise the promises of Yahveh's forgiveness and love like islands in the ocean. These promises are so immensely wonderful that they cover much more than a specific nation, situation, and era. They span all humanity of all ages. To every sinner comes the invitation, *"Come now, and let us reason together," says the LORD, "though your sins are like scarlet, they shall be as white as snow; though they are red like crimson, they shall be as wool."*

To all people come the promises of the Messiah (2:1-5; 4:2-6; 7:14; 9:5-6; 11:1-8) who would restore Israel and the world to what God had intended them to be: a community who lives in harmony with God, self, others, and creation. Whoever believes in Christ will be saved (John 3:16, 6:37).

A prayer: Lord, help us to heed Your Word through Isaiah.
A thought: Does my life show the choice I have made?

238. Message to the Nations
Isaiah (13-23) addresses neighbor countries.

August 25
~~~
Isaiah 13:9-13
19:18-25
22:12-14
</div>

If one does not know the reason for these prophecies to the nations, these eleven chapters can be tedious reading. From Abram's calling in Genesis 12, the focus of the Bible is on God's chosen people and on the Savior that would be born from them. However, God promised that in Abram all nations would be blessed (Gen. 12:3).

Throughout the Bible, God's plan of salvation is focused on the whole world: *"For God so loved the **world** that He gave His only begotten Son..."* (John 3:16). Israel is presented as a "light to the nations" in the second part of Isaiah (chapters 55 and 60). Jesus commanded His followers to disciple all nations (Matt. 28:19).

Although a lot of judgment is proclaimed on ten nations, as well as on Jerusalem and on a person called Shebna, there also are some promises of blessing in these chapters. Ethiopia (18:7), Egypt, Assyria, and Israel (19:18-25), as well as Tyre (23:17), could look forward to wonderful blessings.

However, as maker and ruler of the universe, God had an ax to grind with these nations. The two superpowers, Assyria (10:5-19, 14:24-27) and Babylon (chapters 13, 14 and 21), which God would use to discipline His people, especially receive much attention. God's main charge against them was the arrogant and cruel way in which they would exercise judgment on Israel and Judah. They did not realize that they were only an ax in God's hand; they thought they were the person using the ax (10:12-16). They would get the same treatment and would be utterly destroyed.

Tyre is roasted for its arrogance regarding its extensive trade links and economic power. Because it helped to bring kings into power, its traders were treated like princes. When God would destroy all this haughtiness, their trading partners would be amazed (23:5-9). Like Judah, they would be restored after seventy years (23:17). But for those in Judah who said, *"Let us eat and drink, for tomorrow we die,"* there would be no forgiveness (22:13-14).

Most prophecies had a message for their own time as well as for the future. We can hear the rumbling of end-time thunder in some of Isaiah's messages to the nations. "The day of the LORD," about which Joel also had spoken, would affect the stars, son, and moon (13:9-10).

Some doom-prophecies about Egypt also look like end-time disasters (19:5-9), while some promised blessings pointed to the eternal peace of the Messiah's reign (11:6-8).

A prayer: The earth is the LORD's, and all its fullness. (Ps. 24:1)
A thought: Is my vision for God's kingdom narrow or wide?

239. The Two Paths
Isaiah (24-35) shows the two alternatives.

Prophecies are not logical three-point sermons. Prophets underlined truth by wrapping it in word pictures, stacking one metaphor on the other, either to paint vivid scenes of sin and judgment or to describe the alternative of good deeds and blessings.

> August 26
> ~ ~ ~
> Isaiah 25:6-8
> 28:7-13, 29:13-16
> 35:1-10

Although not all of the picturesque details may have deeper meaning, it is clear that some important prophecies were sometimes uttered in these word pictures. We can recognize them thanks to later developments described in the New Testament.

In this part of his book, Isaiah describes the inebriety and animosity of the false prophets and priests (28:7-13). With slurred speech they accused Isaiah of stammering about the commandments of God. They said that his teaching was for babies and toddlers.

Isaiah replied that God would destroy the wisdom of the wise (29:14), a prophecy that was centuries later quoted by Paul to contrast the wisdom of the gospel with that of philosophy (1 Cor. 1:18-25).

Another common sin which Isaiah exposed was to honor God with their lips while their hearts were far from Him and to serve God with man-made rules while neglecting God-given commands (29:13). Jesus cited these verses to the Pharisees when they condemned the disciples for omitting man-made rituals, while the Pharisees violated God-given commandments (Mark 7:6-7).

Again the judgment for sin had an end-time ring. The earth would be destroyed by drought, floods, and earthquakes (24:1, 4, 18-20), stars would fall like leaves from a tree, and the heavens would be rolled up like a scroll (34:4). Jesus used the same language about the end time (Mark 13:8, 24-25).

Isaiah also proclaimed the alternatives to sin and judgment, namely righteousness and blessings. They had to destroy their idols (27:9), trust in God and not in Egypt (30:1-7, 15), increase their knowledge of God (30:20-22), and be filled with God's Spirit and do what is right (32:15-17).

Some of the promised blessings were fulfilled by Jesus: People were raised from the dead (26:19), while the deaf received their hearing and the blind their sight (29:18, 35:5).

Spiritual or material blessings are promised in almost every chapter in this section of Isaiah's book. However, these could only be received in humble obedience and trusting love. They had to put themselves like clay in the hands of the heavenly Potter (29:16).

A prayer: Lord, make me and form me just as You will.
A thought: Who or what is the "Egypt" I put my trust in?

240. Bethlehem-Ephrathah
Micah announces where Christ would be born.

<table>
<tr><td>

August 27
~ ~ ~
Micah 1-7

</td></tr>
</table>

The "minor" prophets got this name not because their influence was small, but because their writings were brief. All their writings together made up one scroll of equal size as that of Isaiah or Jeremiah or Ezekiel. One of the minor prophets, Micah, recorded important viewpoints about the Messiah and about the essence of the Law.

Isaiah and Micah worked in Judah at the same time. They addressed the descendants of Jacob, which included both Judah and Israel. Micah exposed a variety of sins like idolatry, prostitution, injustice, greed, cheating, domestic violence, and false prophecy.

Just as the prophets were not vague in their identification of sin, so they were not vague in their announcement of judgment. Micah described both the pain of the guilty and the causes of that pain. They would cringe in agony and cry for help in vain when they saw the destruction of crops by drought, the destruction of cities by war, and the devastation of the nation by exile.

Asked what they should do to please God, Micah replied that God did not want big sacrifices and expensive offerings. *"He has shown you, o man, what is good. And what does the LORD require of you but to do justly, to love mercy, and to walk humbly with your God?"* It is one of those golden verses that summarize the whole Bible in a nutshell, like Samuel's word about obedience (1 Sam. 15:22) and Jesus' words about God's love for the world (John 3:16), about the Great Commandment (Matt. 22:37-40), and about His purpose to seek and to save the lost (Luke 19:10).

Micah matched his preaching about sin and judgment with rich promises about God's mercy: *"Do not My words do good to him who walks uprightly?"* (2:7). He brought God's promise to His people about their restoration (2:12-13) and about their forgiveness (7:18-20) after their purification in Babylon (4:10). Their dispersal among the nations would bring blessings to those nations (5:6). These nations would come up to Jerusalem to receive true knowledge of God and to be part of the reign of peace of the Messiah (4:1-4).

The Messiah would be born at Bethlehem-Ephrathah, the city of King David, close to Jerusalem. Micah was the only prophet who predicted the exact location of the Savior's birth. The Jews were acquainted with this fact; they immediately directed the wise men to this blessed little town (Matt. 2).

A prayer: Father, thank You for the great work of the Minor Prophets.
A thought: I will do my humble part in spite of important contemporaries.

241. Decline and Fall of Israel
Israel's addiction to idolatry leads to exile.

Four of the last five kings of Israel grabbed the throne by killing their predecessors. They did nothing of importance except to follow in the footsteps of Jeroboam "who had made Israel sin."

August 28
~ ~ ~
2 Kings 15:10-31
2 Kings 17

Some of them tried to buy some extra time for Israel by paying off the king of Assyria. However, once Assyria conquered Damascus and took the Syrians into exile (2 Kings 16:9), as Amos had predicted (Amos 1:5), there was not a buffer left between Israel and the northern superpower.

In spite of Hosea's and Isaiah's warning not to put their trust in Assyria or Egypt, Israel's last king, Hoshea, foolishly stopped paying tribute to Assyria while he negotiated with Egypt for help. The king of Assyria punished Hoshea for his rebellion by capturing Gilead and Galilee and by taking many people into exile. Then the Assyrians besieged Samaria for three years. Eventually they took the city in 722 BC with disastrous consequences for the inhabitants. Of those who survived, many went into exile. Most of them never returned.

The warnings of God by Amos and Hosea were ignored by Israel to their own peril. Although Isaiah and Micah mainly prophesied in Judah, they too had uttered stern warnings toward Israel to return to the LORD.

The second book of Kings devotes a whole chapter to the reasons why this tragedy came over Israel. Some of the sins committed by Israel were already mentioned in the narrative, but some additional ones are now added to show how far Israel had strayed from the commands of the LORD. On top of idolatry, they also got involved in astrology, divination, and sorcery.

It is stressed that God continuously reached out to them through named and unnamed prophets—for 210 years! After they had consistently rejected Yahveh's yearning love, He eventually removed them from the Promised Land. It is a solemn object lesson about eternal hell for those who keep on rejecting and ignoring the love of God as revealed in His Son.

Hosea said that on judgment day Israel would pray that they could be covered by mountains and hills (10:8). On His way to Calvary, when He was rejected by the people of Jerusalem, Jesus quoted those words to the wailing women along the way (Luke 23:30).

The Father and the Son paid a high price for our salvation. Those who reject it have no hope whatsoever (John 3:36). Yet, in His patience, God still invites sinners to find rest in Him (Matt. 11:28-30).

A prayer: Father, I choose reconciliation with You.
A thought: Do I take God's will as revealed in Scripture really seriously?

242. Reform in Judah
Hezekiah leads his people back to God.

<table>
<tr><td>August 29
~ ~ ~
2 Kings 18:1-6
2 Chron. 29</td></tr>
</table>

People dated events in those days with reference to the year a king was crowned. Overlapping occurred as one king's last year was also his successor's first year, and the son sometimes started to reign while his ailing father was still alive. When a very young king reigned with the help of a regent, those early years were sometimes included and sometimes excluded from his reign. That's why the start of Hezekiah's reign is put either shortly before or after the fall of Samaria.

The fact is that Hezekiah came into power in Judah when the northern kingdom ceased to exist. God used this godly king to heed what happened to Israel and to lead Judah back to God. Hezekiah's father, Ahaz, had made Judah a vassal state of Assyria in order to protect it against Israel and Syria. Therefore, Assyria did not attack Judah when it conquered Israel in 722 BC.

To restore true worship, Hezekiah had to remove the bad and rebuild the good. With the help of the Levites, he destroyed the idols, including the bronze snake Moses had made (Num. 21), and broke down the high places where idolatry had been practiced. He restored the temple of Yahveh by removing from it the idols and Damascus-altar of Ahaz, by opening the doors to the Holy and Most Holy, by having the temple sanctified by the priests, and by resuming the temple activities ordered by God through Moses.

This basic reform was celebrated by the leaders in Jerusalem. They brought many sacrifices while the Levites sang the songs and played the instruments that dated back to the time of King David. It must have stirred up deep feelings of repentance, gratitude, and praise.

At first, there was a lack of enthusiasm among the priests. Maybe they were ashamed (2 Chron. 30:15) because of their participation in the idolatry of Ahaz (2 Kings 16:11, 16). However, they eventually caught up with the Levites, sanctified themselves, and performed their duties according to God's Law (2 Chron. 30:24). Better late than never.

This initial cleanup by the political and religious leaders formed the basis for the subsequent two-week festival in which the whole nation would participate. Although this reform started at the top, it would eventually reach the grassroots where revival was really needed. In spite of many shortcomings, this turning back to Yahveh pleased Him.

God-fearing leaders can have a tremendous positive influence on the moral and spiritual direction of a nation.

A prayer: O God, give us leaders like Hezekiah!
A thought: Am I doubtful or enthusiastic about reform and revival?

243. A Feast to Remember
Passover and two weeks of Unleavened Bread

To involve the whole nation in the reform, Hezekiah called them up to take part in a Passover in Jerusalem. Practical reasons prohibited the preparation of the Passover in the first month, so they organized it in the second month, as was allowed by the Law (Num. 9:11). This gave the priests time to prepare themselves

August 30
~ ~ ~
2 Chron. 30-31

for their duties, and the king had time to invite remnants of the northern kingdom to join Judah in the celebration of the Passover, which apparently had not been observed for a long time. Although some snubbed and mocked the messengers, many did respond and attended this feast. It was the greatest Passover since the time of King Solomon.

There were some shortcomings though. The people from the north did not purify themselves properly for the occasion due to a lack of knowledge. Hezekiah prayed that God would accept their imperfect worship, and graciously, He did. At least they had taken an important step in the right direction. God looks into the heart. When the spirit of the Law is fulfilled, He honors our efforts even when we fall short on the letter of the Law.

The Passover was followed by the weeklong feast of Unleavened Bread. The Passover lamb reminded them of salvation—the angel of death passed over the Hebrew firstborn the night when Israel was freed from slavery in Egypt. The unleavened bread pointed to sanctification—out of gratitude Israel had to eliminate sin from their lives (like leaven from bread). Both symbols were fulfilled in Christ, who died in our place (like the lamb) and who was without sin (like bread without leaven).

During that week, sacrificial meals took place in which the sacrificed animal was eaten by the family and the priests while the blood was sprinkled against the altar and the fat was burnt on the altar. Thanks to the abundance of animals donated by the king and the leaders, the assembly extended the feast of Unleavened Bread for another week. Hezekiah answered Yahveh's yearning.

However, it was not a feast of eating only. The priests and Levites led the assembly in worship by music and song and by teaching *the good knowledge of the* LORD." It resulted in a thorough cleanup of idols, not only in Jerusalem but also in the whole country. The nation resumed their offerings and tithes to Yahveh so that the priests and Levites had more than enough to live from and could devote their attention to spiritual matters.

A prayer: Praise God from whom all blessings flow!
A thought: Do I put my heart into my worship?

244. The Ways of a Bully
How to handle intimidation

August 31

~ ~ ~

2 Kings 18-19
2 Chron. 32:1-23
Isaiah 36-37

In Scripture, the most profound facts are sometimes stated in one short sentence, like God's love (John 3:16), Christ's birth (Luke 2:7), and the church's task (Acts 1:8). Many details of the rule of the judges and the kings are omitted. Of Hezekiah is said that he served God and prospered (2 Chron. 31:21). This went on for many years. Then Satan disrupted the good with the bad.

Hezekiah became proud (2 Chron. 32:25) and mistook God's blessing for his own success. He stopped paying tribute to Assyria. That brought the armies of the superpower back to that region.

Sennacherib, the Assyrian king, acted like all bullies do. He tried to bulldoze his way, first by intimidation and then by physical force. Hezekiah reacted correctly by safeguarding Jerusalem's fortification and water supply. Then he made the mistake of negotiating with the bully, hoping to satisfy him by paying ransom money. That is always seen by bullies as a sign of weakness, and they will come back for more.

Part of Sennacherib's intimidation was to first conquer the weaker cities, thereby cutting off support for and stirring up fear in the stronger cities. Then he sent an impressive contingent to Jerusalem and tried to scare them into compliance with threats and demands, hoping they would cave in and save him the trouble of a long siege.

When Sennacherib (the bully) did that to Jerusalem (the victim), Hezekiah took his problem to Isaiah (the comforter) and to God (the Savior). With the help of a comforter and a savior, the power of bullies can be broken.

Through Isaiah, God encouraged Hezekiah to stand his ground and to ignore the threats and demands of Sennacherib. Hezekiah followed the best path by keeping his silence and teaching his people to do the same. They did not provoke the fury of the bully. Puzzled by Hezekiah's silence, Sennacherib sent him a letter with the same message in writing. Hezekiah responded in the same way. God assured Hezekiah that He would handle the bully because God was the One who had been offended by the bully's remarks.

Suddenly the situation was reversed. Thousands of the Assyrian soldiers died mysteriously, the mighty king packed up and went home ashamed, and later he was assassinated by his own sons. The bully was silenced for good.

A prayer: God, please come to the aid of all victims of bullying.
A thought: Have I used bully tactics to get my way?

245. The Blessing of Healing
Hezekiah turns to God and is healed.

To lose something valuable and then recover it increases our appreciation of that thing. When a lost sheep, coin, and son are found, there is joy. Likewise, there is joy in heaven for every lost sinner who is reconciled with God (Luke 15). Hezekiah lost his health and almost his life, only to recover it with immense gratitude and joy.

> September 1
>
> ~ ~ ~
>
> 2 Kings 20:1-11
> 2 Chron. 32:24-26
> Isaiah 38

His beloved pastor, Isaiah, brought the bad news that he would not recover from an infection. Hezekiah turned to God with a weeping heart and pleaded for mercy on account of his righteous living. God sent Isaiah immediately back to the king to tell him that his trusting prayer and humbling tears, not his good works, had made a difference. Within three days he would be able to worship in the temple again. Fifteen years would be added to his life.

The fact that the prophet had brought him two opposite messages within half an hour made Hezekiah ask for a sign to confirm that the second message was true. And in His infinite mercy, God agreed. He made the shadow go back ten degrees on the sundial. It baffles our imagination why and how God did this astounding miracle to give assurance to one small man. From the viewpoint of the Almighty, it was a tiny favor for an important person—His child.

God blessed the medicine to achieve Hezekiah's healing. The hot paste of figs stopped the inflammation caused by the abscess. The king recovered swiftly and could worship God in the temple on the third day. Hezekiah expressed his agony during his illness and his gratitude after his healing in a poetic prayer that was saved for us by Isaiah.

We can learn a lot about sickness and healing from this episode, which is recorded three times in Scripture. Note that it was a conscientious believer who was afflicted, just as in the case of Job. God had a purpose with the affliction. He knew exactly how Hezekiah would react and what He would do in view of Hezekiah's reaction. God was not changing His mind; He was changing Hezekiah's heart. God was drawing His child closer to Himself.

Note how God used means to reach His goal: the sickness, the prophet, the prayer, the remedy, and even the shadow on the sundial. The end result was the glorification of God by a devoted believer. When Hezekiah climbed the stairs from the palace to the temple again, he thanked Yahveh for his restored health.

A prayer: Please, God, heal me in body, soul, and spirit.
A thought: Have I discovered God's blessing in my sickness and healing?

246. A Dangerous "High"
makes Hezekiah vulnerable.

September 2
~~~
2 Kings 20:12-19
2 Chron. 32:24-31
Isaiah 39

Satan knows when to strike. He is an expert in selecting the right psychological moment. When we are at a low or high point emotionally, we are off balance and may easily step into his trap. After his miraculous recovery and the extension of his life, Hezekiah was overjoyed and excited. In this high he was inclined to be too generous and overly optimistic.

He was elated when Babylon, the new rising power, extended a hand of friendship to him. With such an ally, Judah had a better chance to survive the onslaught of Assyria. He felt that an enemy of his enemy was his friend.

He received the Babylonian delegation with a hearty welcome and showered them with hospitality. In his excitement, he overstepped the boundaries of common sense and of state security. He not only showed them the interesting sites in and around Jerusalem, but also his fortifications and treasures, obviously with a good measure of personal pride.

As soon as the visitors had left, the prophet Isaiah requested an audience with the king. He rebuked the king for his unwise sharing of top-secret information with representatives of a foreign power, and he announced God's judgment on Hezekiah's pride. He warned that the king's "friends" would later return as enemies who would rob him of all those treasures. Hezekiah realized his mistake and submitted to God's higher wisdom and power.

In spite of Hezekiah's error of judgment, he is still hailed as the best king Judah had had since King David. Although the Bible does not hesitate to expose the sins and blunders of kings and other leaders, it is also fair in its appraisal of the entire life of these people.

We dare not rest on our laurels, especially with regard to spiritual warfare. Till the very end of our lives, we have to brace ourselves against the relentless attacks of the evil one. When we are emotionally low or high, we have to be even more alert for the tricks and traps of Satan.

When we are emotionally high, we are inclined to show, give, say, or promise too much—generosity that may cost us dearly.

At a low point we may drift in the opposite direction: Doing too little positive or saying too much negative, and both of these may also hurt others or ourselves. The Bible urges us to stay positive in all circumstances but to practice generosity wisely.

*A prayer: Lord, please help me to avoid the traps of Satan.*
*A thought: Where have I goofed at a low or high point?*

# 247. Tarnished Rulers
## Manasseh and Amon taint Judah's history.

Manasseh was born after Hezekiah's life had been extended for fifteen years for Manasseh was only twelve years old when he succeeded his father as king. Why did this boy decided to go in exactly the opposite religious direction as his dad? The Bible does not explain this sad phenomenon, and it does not blame Hezekiah either for his son's apostasy. The responsibility for this choice is laid squarely on Manasseh himself, and he had to bear the consequences.

> September 3
> ~ ~ ~
> 2 Kings 21
> 2 Chron. 33

Manasseh not only rebuilt the pagan "high places" over the whole country, but he also brought idolatry back into the temple, like his Grandpa Ahaz had done. Amongst other idols, Manasseh worshiped the stars and practiced fortune telling and sorcery. This could have been done to please the Assyrian king to whom he paid tribute. Manasseh even sacrificed his own son to his false gods. He was also terribly cruel toward any form of dissent and executed many of his opponents. He stained Jerusalem with innocent blood.

God punished him by having his Assyrian boss capture him, take him in chains to Babylon, and let him waste away in a dark dungeon. There this evil king came to himself, like the prodigal son (Luke 15:17). God's Spirit convicted him of sin, righteousness, and judgment (John 16:8). He confessed his sins and pleaded for God's mercy. God did not say: "Sorry, man, you don't qualify for mercy; you have gone way too far in your wickedness." It is good news for those who think that they have sinned away all their chances.

In His unfathomable loving kindness, Yahveh accepted Manasseh's repentance, knowing that it was a genuine change of heart worked by His Spirit. God also convinced the king of Assyria to send Manasseh back to Jerusalem so that he could put things right where he had messed up. He destroyed his idols and served Yahveh. The people, however, did not turn around completely. They tried to serve the true God at the "high places."

It is better to rehabilitate where people know about your problem. When you start over where people don't know you, you may always live in fear that someday they may find out and reject you. Unfortunately, not all wrong deeds and their consequences can be reversed. Some people will never trust you.

Manasseh's son, Amon, did not heed his father's mistakes. When he became king he followed his dad's bad example, not his good example. After two years Amon was murdered. His God-fearing son, Josiah, succeeded him.

*A prayer: O God, please change or replace all wicked leaders.*
*A thought: Have I lost hope for some sinners?*

# 248. Destruction of an Oppressor
## Nahum announces Nineveh's fall.

<table><tr><td>September 4<br>~ ~ ~<br>Nahum 1-3</td></tr></table>

The historic events referred to by the prophet Nahum place him in the time of King Josiah. Though Nahum mentioned Israel's sin and punishment, his focus was on Assyria's fall. The main players in this drama would be God, Israel, Nineveh and its enemies.

Nahum started with a few simple facts about God's power, mercy, and judgment. His power is revealed in the forces of His creation: winds, clouds, rivers, oceans, mountains, and woods. He is merciful and patient, but He is also strict and holy. He disciplines with rewards and punishment. Like a good parent, He practices tough love.

God's chosen people experienced this fatherly love when they strayed and ignored God's warnings. However, when they would have learnt their lesson and returned to Him, He would return them to their country (1:12-13; 2:2). Like Isaiah (52:7), Nahum awaited the messenger who would bring the good news to Israel that their punishment was over (1:15). Paul applied this picture to those who bring the good news of the gospel (Rom. 10:12-15).

Nineveh's repentance in Jonah's time, 130 years before Nahum, had not lasted. Now the city would be razed to the ground for their cruel and arrogant ways. They are compared to lions ripping their prey to pieces (2:12). When they conquered Egypt, they smashed babies to death on street corners (3:10). They also lured nations into idolatry, sorcery, and immorality (3:4).

They would taste God's judgment in 612 BC. Their enemy's attack, as well as their own defense, is painted in brief but lively word pictures (2:3-6; 3:2-3). One can see the splashes of colorful uniforms and the flashes of swords, spears, and shields. One can hear the rumble of chariots, the shouts of soldiers, and the clashes of weapons and armor. One can observe the futile efforts of the Ninevites to stop the tide (2:1, 5; 3:14).

Then the prophet describes the plundering of the city and the flight of its inhabitants. It would be like water flowing from a broken dam (2:8-10) and like locusts flying away from a stone wall when the sun rises (3:17). The once mighty city would never be rebuilt, and it would take ages before its ruins would be uncovered by archaeologists.

This "minor" prophet of God once again underlined the great truth that the one true God, Yahveh, is the Creator, Sustainer, and Ruler of the world and that He determines the rise and fall of nations and their leaders.

*A prayer: God, use nations and their leaders to serve Your kingdom.*
*A thought: The best policy is to take my stand on God's side.*

# 249. Why Do the Wicked Prosper?
## Habakkuk finds peace in God's answer.

The circumstances described by Habakkuk suit the early part of Josiah's reign, shortly after the wicked Manasseh and before the reforms of Josiah.

September 5

~ ~ ~

Hab. 1-3

Habakkuk cried out to God about the sins of the nation, dismayed about God's apparent indifference to the wickedness of mankind. His dismay about the prosperity of the wicked resembles that of Asaph in Psalm 73.

God answered him that He would indeed punish Judah for their sins if they did not repent. God would use a new world power, the Chaldeans of Babylon, to come down on them like an eagle on its prey. This answer awakened a new question in the prophet: Seeing that the Chaldeans were guilty of the same sins as Judah, how can the holy God use such a wicked instrument to punish His own people? Habakkuk did not hesitate to bring his haunting questions to God, and God did not hesitate to reveal the answers to His prophet.

God told Habakkuk that He would bring judgment on Babylon too for the atrocities they would commit in their lust for power. Though it might seem as if God's judgment lingered, it would come at the appointed time. God's children had to wait patiently for that. The wicked would be arrogant in their sins, but *"the just shall live by faith."* This short statement became crucial in New Testament theology. What Christ earned by His life, death, resurrection, and ascension can only be accepted in faith. It is the key to both justification (Rom. 1:16-17; Gal. 3:11) and sanctification (Heb. 10:36-38).

God affirmed His judgment on Babylon with five woes that pointed to their greed, destructiveness, killing, inebriety, and idolatry. When Habakkuk had seen the end of the wicked he could rejoice with Asaph (Ps. 73:16-18). Habakkuk responded with his own psalm about the sovereign power of Yahveh that had been demonstrated in the history of His people. Among others, he referred to the splitting of the sea, rock, and river.

In ecstasy, the prophet ended his book with the famous testimony about his trust in Yahveh in spite of adverse circumstances: *"Though the fig tree may not blossom, nor fruit be on the vines; though the labor of the olive may fail, and the fields yield no food; though the flock may be cut off from the fold, and there be no herds in the stalls—yet I will rejoice in the LORD, I will joy in the God of my salvation."*

Habakkuk's believed that God would eventually restore His people. Israel's unfaithfulness would be wiped out by Yahveh's love.

*A prayer: Father, I find rest in Your omniscience and omnipotence.*
*A thought: Do I discuss my questions and problems with my heavenly Father?*

# 250. Planting the Seed
## Zephaniah's ministry precedes Josiah's reform.

September 6

~~~

Zephaniah 1-4

</div>

King Josiah and the prophet Zephaniah were contemporaries, and both were descendants of the great reformer King Hezekiah. The young king Josiah would also become an important reformer after he had reigned for eighteen years, but in his early years there was still a lot of idolatry left that had been introduced by his predecessors Manasseh and Amon. Zephaniah prophesied against those idols and practices that angered God. The seeds that this minor prophet had planted later sprouted and delivered the great harvest of Josiah's reform.

Zephaniah addressed the sins of Judah and surrounding nations like the Philistines to the west, the Moabites and Ammonites to the east, the Ethiopians to the south, and the Assyrians to the north. He named some of their idolatrous practices, but he focused the spotlight on the attitude of arrogance, which propelled their deeds. Therefore he called them to humble repentance and to make humility part of their lifestyle (2:3; 3:12).

Jerusalem is reprimanded for its obstinate rebellion against God. Its inhabitants deliberately disobeyed God, and they refused to be corrected. They did not trust God, and they did not serve Him. The leaders would be held accountable for leading the people astray. When God's wrath had come on the northern kingdom in the form of the exile, Jerusalem did not take this lesson to heart. After Hezekiah's reform, they easily went along with the idolatry of his successors in spite of what happened to their northern neighbors.

Therefore, Zephaniah directed their attention to the imminent "day of the LORD," a reality of which several other prophets before him had spoken. He saw that day as a time of intense fear, of raging war, of plundered properties, of security collapse, of dark storms, of devastating fire, and of futile cries for help. The rich would find neither refuge in money nor in powerful fortresses. Zephaniah called on them to repent and to change their lives before it was too late. Under King Josiah's leadership, there did occur a drastic reform.

Zephaniah also spoke of Israel's restoration and even of the salvation of the nations (3:9-20). God would gather His people from amongst the nations where they were scattered and bring them back to their land.

God would also touch the lips of the nations so that they could worship Him wholeheartedly and serve Him with their gifts. It became a reality in the Christian church.

A prayer: God, I plant the seeds of Your Word and leave the harvest to You.
A thought: I will proceed with God's work in spite of hardened hearts.

251. The Last Reform
Josiah leads a penetrating reform in Judah.

Josiah was only eight years old when he became king of Judah. He avoided the wicked ways of his dad (Amon) and grandpa (Manasseh) and decided to follow in the footsteps of his great-grandfather, Hezekiah. He started with the restoration of the temple because the temple had suffered several onslaughts since the last restoration under Joash almost 200 years before. Some kings, especially Ahaz and Manasseh, had done much damage to the temple by bringing idolatry into God's sanctuary.

September 7
~ ~ ~
2 Kings 22-23
2 Chron. 34-35

While the restoration of the temple was in progress, a priest discovered a scroll of the Law in one of the temple's side-rooms. When it was read to the king, he was deeply touched by it and humbled himself before God. Josiah called the leaders of Judah and the people of Jerusalem to the temple, had the scroll read to them, and led them in a renewal of the covenant with God. That implied that they had to discard the wrong and do what was right.

Josiah not only destroyed idols; he desecrated all pagan altars by burning human remains on them, ensuring that they would not be used for sacrifices again. Two special types of idolatry that had survived previous reforms were also destroyed by Josiah, namely the idol-temples that Solomon had built for his foreign wives outside Jerusalem and the golden calf altars erected at Bethel by Jeroboam I shortly after the split of the kingdom of Solomon. Thus a prophecy of 300 years before was fulfilled (1 Kings 13:2).

To get true worship going again, Josiah first organized the priests and Levites according to the rules instituted by Moses, David, and Solomon. When the priests and Levites were ready, a great Passover was held. The yearning of God and man met once more. Because of the thorough preparations and correct procedures, this Passover was regarded as even greater than Hezekiah's Passover (2 Chron. 30:15-20).

When Pharaoh Necho passed through Israel with his army on his way to Assyria, Josiah unwisely attacked this formidable force at Megiddo. The Pharaoh warned him not to get involved because the Pharaoh was not marching against Judah. Josiah ignored the good advice, proceeded with his attack, and was fatally wounded. The untimely death of this devoted young king was deeply mourned by the people, including the prophet Jeremiah. Josiah could have consolidated his reform if he had not been distracted by unwise politics.

A prayer: Father, let me stay on course in spite of disrupting storms.
A thought: Do I consistently fight the bad and promote the good?

252. To Destroy and to Build
Jeremiah addresses Judah's unfaithfulness.

September 8
~ ~ ~
Jeremiah 1-6

Instead of building on the reforms of King Josiah, three of his sons (Jehoahaz, Jehoiakim, and Zedekiah) and one grandson (Jehoiachin) returned to the evil ways of Manasseh and Amon. They ignored the stern warnings of God through the prophets.

Jeremiah was called to be God's prophet in the 13th year of King Josiah. Jeremiah felt inadequate for the task because he was young and not eloquent, but as in Moses' case, God did not accept that as an excuse. God would be with Jeremiah and would give him the words to say. Jeremiah had to break down the bad and build up the good.

Jeremiah's first two visions confirmed his task. The blossoming almond branch, the first fruit tree to wake up after winter, confirmed that God was alert to fulfill His Word. The boiling pot in the north, tilting to the south, confirmed that God would bring judgment on Judah by armies of the north.

The first six chapters of the book of Jeremiah contain prophecies probably delivered in Josiah's time before the reforms. They point to idolatry and other sins introduced by Manasseh and Amon and still prevalent at that time.

God reminded Israel of their liberation from Egypt and their inheritance of the Promised Land (2:4-7). Instead of showing their gratitude by doing His will, they exchanged Him for other gods, something that is unknown even among the pagan nations (2:10-11).

Jeremiah used metaphors to illustrate how illogical their conduct was: They exchanged a flowing fountain for a dry, cracked cistern (2:13); a bride will not forget her wedding dress, but Judah forgot God (2:32); the sea stays within its boundaries, but Judah did not stay within God's will (5:22-23).

They put their trust in Assyria and Egypt instead of in God (2:18). As mares in heat eagerly succumb to stallions, so Judah lecherously ran after idol worship (2:24). Judah was scolded for following Israel's example of playing the harlot with false gods and hurting Yahveh, her real "husband."

Because Judah had seen the judgment that had come on Israel but still proceeded with idolatry, Judah would receive even harder punishment than Israel had (3:8-10). Like the criminal mind, Judah was clever to think out wicked things but dull in planning good things (4:22). Today there are still people, like terrorists, who are set on harming others instead of helping them. Yahveh is in control and eventually He will judge them.

A prayer: Father, help me to be eager and clever in doing good.
A thought: Which are my most exciting activities?

253. False Security
The temple would not protect them.

The pro-Assyria Jehoahaz reigned for only three months before Pharaoh Necho took him captive to Egypt and replaced him with his brother, Jehoiakim, who was pro-Egypt and who reigned for eleven years. The second part of Jeremiah's ministry took place during his reign. Jehoahaz died in Egypt.

> September 9
> ~ ~ ~
> Jer. 7-15

When Jeremiah repeatedly warned the people of Jerusalem that they would be overrun by a strong northern power (1:14, 4:6, 5:15, 6:1, 22), they shrugged it off, thinking that God would never allow His temple to be destroyed and therefore Jerusalem was safe. Jeremiah pointed out to them that they were guilty of theft, murder, adultery, perjury, idolatry, and injustice (7:9, 5:28), and yet they came to the temple as if nothing had happened. Thus they turned the temple into a robber's den, an accusation repeated by Jesus to the Pharisees (Mark 11:17). How could they think that the temple would save them (7:4-6) when the whole family eagerly served the "queen of heaven" (7:18) and when parents sacrificed their children to idols in Murder Valley? (7:31-32)

They were hiding in false security, reassuring one another of peace while there would be no peace (6:14, 8:11). They could not expect blessing when they cheated, lied, and bribed so much that no one could be trusted (9:4-9).

Jeremiah gives a convincing description of the worthlessness of idols and the power and love of God as Creator of the earth. For Jeremiah, it was inconceivable how people could leave the true God and serve idols (10:1-16).

As Jeremiah pleaded with the people to stop their sinful practices and to do God's will, he met with opposition and rejection. Chapters 11 to 13 show the first signs of persecution. God encouraged Jeremiah to stay on course and to ignore the threats. God would protect him. The people's pride would be ruined like a sash that has been buried in the ground (13:1-11).

In chapters 14 and 15 Jeremiah proceeded with his work and announced drought, war, famine, and pestilence on those who ignored God's warnings. However, he began to suffer increasingly under rejection and loneliness. He complained to God that all people cursed him and that he could not rely on God anymore (15:10, 18).

Yahveh called His wavering prophet to repentance (15:19). He had to take his stand with God, and then God would use and protect him. He should take his cue from God, not from the straying, criticizing nation.

A prayer: All-seeing One, protect me from secret sins and from false worship.
A thought: Do I allow criticism to break my spirit?

254. The Clay and the Potter
The Creator is in control of His creation.

September 10
~ ~ ~
Jer. 16-20

To show that God had withdrawn Himself from Judah's joys and sorrows, God prohibited Jeremiah from marrying, sympathizing with the bereaved, or rejoicing with the merry (16:1-13). And yet the soft music of future reconciliation could occasionally be heard (16:14-21). But Judah would first be purged while working as slaves for a foreign nation (17:1-5).

Then Jeremiah started to address the individual in a very personal way: *"The heart is deceitful above all things, and desperately wicked; who can know it?"* The answer was that God could change a person's heart from trusting in things and in people to a heart trusting in God alone.

This shaping of the heart by God is compared to the shaping of pottery by the potter (18:1-11). If the potter's first effort is not successful, he does not discard the clay but tries again to shape the clay into a useful vessel.

Likewise, the heavenly Potter yearns to reshape individuals, families, and nations into better vessels for carrying His grace to others (2 Cor. 4:7). As the failed vessel has to be broken down in order to reshape it into a new form, so we have to be broken to be healed. Judah's exile would serve that purpose too.

Jeremiah had to perform another object lesson with a clay jar (19:1-11). He had to smash it into pieces outside the city at Tophet where children had been sacrificed. This jar was not in the making, but it had been baked hard already. When it was shattered, it could not be repaired. Although archaeologists put together pieces of dug out pots, they are only for display, not for use. Just as we do not patch up a broken glass or cup, so people in those days did not mend broken jars. This act of Jeremiah symbolized the complete destruction of the city and the nation. They would not be restored, but their children would.

His message elicited angry resistance. The hostile talk against Jeremiah (18:18) now became physical abuse (20:2). The governor of the temple, Pashhur, had Jeremiah beaten and then restrained in wooden blocks.

When Jeremiah was released the next day, he first prophesied to Pashhur his destiny, and then the injured and insulted prophet cried out to God about his fate. When he tried to keep silent, God's Word became like a fire in his heart (20:9). When he spoke up, he was treated like scum.

Jeremiah praised God for His mercy in all of this, but he cursed the day of his birth (20:13-14). He was at a very low point, like Elijah (1 Kings 19).

A prayer: Father, please empower Your children to keep faith.
A thought: How do I handle fierce opposition and rejection?

255. Burning the Bible
Jehoiakim tries to silence God's voice.

The book bearing Jeremiah's name was written by Baruch. Some parts of the book were dictated by Jeremiah, and other parts were written by Baruch about Jeremiah and about events of that time. This book contains more biographical information about the prophet than any other prophetical book.

<table><tr><td>September 11
~~~
Jer. 22, 26, 36</td></tr></table>

Storytellers often go back and forth in history as they recall relevant episodes that are connected to the present story; therefore, events in the book of Jeremiah are not presented in strict chronological sequence. Because the prophecies and events were written on a scroll, they could not be reshuffled.

Chapters 22, 26 and 36 tell about episodes in the time of Jehoiakim. God ordered Jeremiah to repudiate the king for the luxurious improvements on his palace in a time when many people struggled to make ends meet (chapter 22). To make things worse, the king did not pay the workers regularly, he did not care for the poor and the orphaned, he took part in extortion and murder, and he did not uphold justice in courts.

When Jeremiah told the people, on God's order, that the temple and the city would be destroyed if they did not repent (chapter 26), the false priests and prophets grabbed Jeremiah and were ready to kill him right away. God used the king's officials to save Jeremiah's life. They reminded the mob that Micah had said the same in Hezekiah's time and he was not killed for it.

After Jeremiah had prophesied for 23 years (25:3), God told him to put his prophecies in writing and to read it to the people—maybe they would repent if they heard all the prophecies together (chapter 36). Jeremiah asked Baruch to do the writing while he dictated. When they were done, Baruch read the scroll to the people in the temple on a day of fasting. When the king's officials heard about it, they wanted to hear the scroll too. They advised Baruch and Jeremiah to hide from the kings guards.

It was winter and king Jehoiakim was sitting in his sunroom with a pot of fire at his feet. As soon as a few columns of the scroll had been read to him, he cut that part off with a knife and burnt it on the fire. So he eventually burnt the whole scroll. The king performed this defiant act in spite of his officials' plea not to. He sent guards to arrest Jeremiah and Baruch, but God had hidden them.

God told Jeremiah to rewrite the scroll and to expand it. Yahveh has protected His Word against many onslaughts through the ages.

A prayer: Please God, save us from arrogance.
A thought: Do I read and heed God's Word daily?

256. Seventy Years of Servitude
Build houses, plant gardens, take wives.

September 12
~ ~ ~
Jer. 24:3-10
25:11-12
29:1-10

Jehoiachin surrendered to the king of Babylon and lived. Zedekiah would not and suffered a terrible fate. Both were fulfilled prophecies of Jeremiah. Chapters 22, 24, 25, and 29 of the book Jeremiah contain information related to Jehoiachin, son of Jehoiakim, and those who went into exile with him.

Jehoiachin was eighteen years old when he became king for only three months. In his short reign he followed his father's evil ways and was repudiated by Jeremiah (22:24-30). When Jerusalem was besieged by Nebuchadnezzar in 597 B.C., Jehoiachin surrendered and he and many others were taken prisoner to Babylon, but Jerusalem was spared. The prophet Ezekiel was among this second group of captives who were deported to Babylon.

With the vision of the two baskets of figs, God showed Jeremiah that those in exile were like good figs, and God would provide for them and would eventually bring them back. Those who stayed in Jerusalem were like bad figs that God would discard because they put their trust in Egypt and not in God. They and the surrounding nations would drink the cup of war presented by Babylon for seventy years (25:15-29).

God told Jeremiah to write a letter to the deportees in Babylon and to admonish them not to listen to the false prophets who kindled false hope about a swift return to Israel. They had to prepare themselves for a long stay—till seventy years had expired. Jeremiah encouraged them to build houses, plant gardens, marry, and have children. For their own good, they had to work and pray for the prosperity of the place where they lived because the well-being of their environment would be to their own benefit.

Unfortunately, this piece of practical logic is not understood by those who try to fight for a good cause with bad weapons. Terrorists destroy the lives, happiness, goodwill, and infrastructure that are needed for the development of the very people they claim to fight for. Violent demonstrations may shatter the human rights and environment they try to defend.

Good goals may be destroyed by bad methods in the home too. In an effort to get attention or recognition, people may hurt their loved ones and hate themselves for doing so. By perfectionism, some parents try to push their children up, but by harming the children's self-esteem they push them down. Preserving a positive atmosphere serves the best interest of all.

A prayer: God, help us to use positive means to achieve positive goals.
A thought: I will work and pray for the betterment of my environment.

257. In the Pit
Jeremiah is jailed for his prophecies.

Instead of a detailed analysis of the prophetical books, this study only shows the general trend of a prophet's work so that it may be understood within the historical context.

The book Jeremiah reports on many episodes that took place during the reign of Zedekiah, the last king of Judah (ch. 21-39). Jeremiah warned the king (ch. 21) as well as the false prophets and priests (ch. 23) to stop their wicked ways and to return to Yahveh, the one true God. When Jeremiah carried a yoke on his shoulders to symbolize that Judah would carry the yoke of Babylon, Hananiah broke the yoke and falsely prophesied that God would break Babylon's yoke within two years. God told Jeremiah to reiterate that the exile would last seventy years and that Hananiah would die for his lies. It happened that year (ch. 27-28).

> September 13
> ~ ~ ~
> Jer. 27, 28
> 37:11 - 38:13

Chapters 30 to 34 are known as the "book of comfort" in Jeremiah's prophecies. Here God promised the restoration of Israel (Lesson 273).

Judah's treacherous dealing with Hebrew slaves (ch. 34) and the obedience of the Rechabites to their ancestor (ch. 35) gave reason for the repudiation of Judah's disobedience to God.

When the Chaldean siege of Jerusalem was interrupted by the approaching Egyptian army, Jeremiah wanted to visit his hometown. He was arrested at the Benjamin gate by Hananiah's grandson, accused of treason, and imprisoned in a dungeon.

After "many days" the king called him to ask for God's guidance. Jeremiah repeated that Jerusalem would be destroyed unless they surrendered. On the prophet's urgent plea, the king did not return him to the dungeon but fed and guarded him in the court of the prison.

Jeremiah persisted with the message that surrender to the Chaldeans of Babylon would save both the people and the city. Some leaders asked the king to sentence Jeremiah to death for treason. They put him into a muddy pit near the prison and hoped he would die. A black servant of the king pleaded with the king for Jeremiah's life, and was allowed to pull him out. God promised to save this man's life because of his mercy (39:15-18).

Once more God emphasized that the city and the people would be spared if the king surrendered to Babylon. How different Judah's history could have been if they had heeded God's advice through Jeremiah. Till the very end, Yahveh promised mercy if they repented.

A prayer: Father, make people aware of Your merciful promises.
A thought: How can I help pull others out of the pit of despair?

258. Decline and Fall of Judah
The last four kings all miss the mark.

<table>
<tr><td>
September 14

~~~

2 Kings 23:31-25:30
2 Chron. 36
Jer. 39, 52
</td></tr>
</table>

The last years of Judah were messy and confusing. Both Jehoahaz and Jehoiachin reigned for only three months before they were taken captive, the first to Egypt where he died, the latter to Babylon where he was eventually released after 37 years in prison. Jehoiakim and Zedekiah both reigned for 11 years. It was a time of sad decline, a slow slide to destruction.

Jehoiakim (609 B.C.) had to pay tribute to Egypt, so he overtaxed Judah. In 605 B.C. Judah became a vassal state of Babylon and then had to pay tribute to them. At this time some of the brightest young men of Judah, including Daniel and his friends (Dan. 1:1-7), were taken to Babylon. Only Daniel tells of this first exile. Apparently Nebuchadnezzar took Jehoiakim captive but released him, maybe on promises of loyalty. When Jehoiakim broke his promises, Babylon sent raiders of other vassal states against him. Apparently, Jehoiakim was killed in one of these raids.

Three months after he was crowned, Jehoiakim's son, Jehoiachin, with many others of Judah, was taken prisoner to Babylon. The prophet Ezekiel was among the captives of this second exile. Jehoiachin was replaced by another son of Josiah called Zedekiah, who could not decide between two strongly opposed sections in Jerusalem: the pro-Babylon people and the pro-Egypt people. Because Egypt was already defeated by Babylon, the prophet Jeremiah urged the king to stay loyal to Babylon. For this, Jeremiah was rejected and persecuted by the opposition.

Eventually Zedekiah went along with the pro-Egypt group, rebelled against Babylon, and brought about the inevitable destruction of Jerusalem by the Babylonians in 586 B.C. The temple, the city wall, and all the best homes were destroyed and burnt. Most people of Judah, except for the poorest, were taken into exile in Babylon. The unthinkable had happened: The temple of God was no more. Zedekiah's sons were killed in his presence, and then his eyes were gouged out. The lineage of David was almost extinct except for Jehoiachin.

Although God had said that Jehoiachin would have no children (Jer. 22:30), he apparently had a change of heart in prison, was forgiven, had children, and is named as one of the ancestors of Joseph, the legal father of Jesus (Matt. 1:12). God's promise to David was not broken (1 Chron. 17:11-14).

A prayer: O God, please keep the remnant alive.
A thought: Brinkmanship can make fools of the obstinate.

259. Squandered Opportunities
They spoil their chances with wrong choices.

After the fall of Jerusalem, the Chaldeans gave Jeremiah complete freedom, knowing what his advice to Judah had been during the siege. They appointed Gedaliah as governor, and he made Mizpah his head-quarters. Many refugees returned from their hiding places and settled in Mizpah.

September 15
~ ~ ~
Jer. 40-45

Gedaliah followed a policy of tolerance toward the remaining warlords. Although he was forewarned about a conspiracy against him, he proceeded with his goodwill approach. One of the warlords, Ishmael, killed Gedaliah as well as many others to establish control over the people. Fearing revenge by Babylon, the other warlords joined forces against Ishmael, freed the hostages, and moved in the direction of Egypt.

At Bethlehem they sought God's will through Jeremiah. After ten days God gave His answer to Jeremiah: The people had to stay in Judah. If they would disobey and go down to Egypt, they would die of the sword, famine, or pestilence. After Jeremiah had spelled it out to them, they decided to ignore Jeremiah and to proceed to Egypt. They took Jeremiah along.

In Egypt they resumed their worship of the "queen of heaven," ignoring God's Word by Jeremiah that the same fate awaited them that had come on the people in Jerusalem who had practiced this idolatry. Except for a small remnant, all would die in Egypt for this hardheaded rebellion against God.

These people got the opportunity to stay on in their homeland while many of their fellow citizens went into exile. Nebuchadnezzar gave them the vineyards and orchards of the deportees. That summer they had a bumper crop (40:12). However, they blew their golden opportunities by wrong decisions. They could not say that they did not know God's will for them.

Jeremiah's credibility had been established by what had happened to Jerusalem. In no uncertain terms he showed them the way several times, but they thought they knew better than God. Likewise, God's great plan of salvation in Christ is regarded as foolishness by the world (1 Cor. 1:18).

This sad history was taken up in God's Word to help us to make better choices in difficult circumstances. God's guidance did not change. His message through the prophets was consistent and was repeated many times: Serve God and receive His blessings, or stray from Him and suffer His wrath. Likewise, He urged them to depend on Him, not on the powers of the world.

A prayer: God, help us to see Your will clearly and to obey faithfully.
A thought: Where have I blown golden opportunities by wrong choices?

260. The Gloating Will Be Judged
Obadiah scolds Edom for their conceit.

<table><tr><td>September 16
~ ~ ~
Obadiah 1</td></tr></table>

Although there were other times when Edom took advantage of Judah's distress (2 Kings 8:21-22, 16:6), Obadiah's description of the situation (verses 11-16) best matches the time of Jerusalem's destruction in 586 B.C.

The charges God laid against Edom were two-fold. Firstly, they felt exceedingly proud and secure in their impenetrable mountain fortress, today's Petra. It could only be entered by a narrow gorge that was easy to defend. Although they thought they were as safe as an eagle in its nest on a high cliff, God said that He would throw them down. They would be infiltrated by their allies, people they lived in peace with. While they would feast together, the "friends" would turn to enemies and destroy them.

Secondly, God scolded them through Obadiah for gloating over Judah's destruction by the Chaldeans and even taking part in the raid. They caught fugitives from Judah and handed them over to the enemy. It is repeated seven times that "in the day of calamity" they turned against their "brothers" (their ancestors, Esau and Jacob, were brothers). They celebrated this brother betrayal with a drunken party on the temple mount.

Their punishment would suit their crime. They would be driven from their stronghold and cease to exist as a nation. They were later driven out by the forces of Nabataea and lived in the Negev, called Idumaea by the Romans. After a general circumcision, the Edomites were eventually taken up into Judah. God's discipline is merciful.

Like other prophets, Obadiah saw "the day of the LORD" that would come over Edom in a more universal sense too. The final day of the LORD in the end time will involve all nations. All will eventually be accountable before the supreme Judge of heaven and earth.

However, there is good news too. On Mount Zion there would come deliverance for all as well (verse 17). This prophecy was fulfilled when the incarnated Son of God was crucified on Mount Zion as the substitute for sinners, paying the price for sin so that sinners could be saved—including Judah, Edom, and the rest of the world.

That is the message of Obadiah and of the whole Bible: The beauty of God's creation was marred by the ugliness of sin, but in His mercy God used this blot to restore His creation through the beauty of salvation. Then the "Kingdom shall be the LORD's" (verse 21, Phil. 2:5-11; Col. 1:13-20).

A prayer: Thank You, Father, for Your merciful discipline.
A thought: Do I pray for the salvation of my enemies?

261. The Battle for Values
Daniel stands with God in a foreign culture.

While the aging Jeremiah ministered under Judah's last three kings, a few bright Jewish teenagers were trained for public service in Babylon. Daniel and three of his friends were among these displaced youngsters. A destiny-determining question hovered over them: To what extent would they become part of the foreign culture, and to what extent would they remain faithful to their old values?

> September 17
> ~ ~ ~
> Daniel 1

King Nebuchadnezzar did not leave the outcome to chance. He set a process in motion to brainwash these young captives as soon as possible so that they could replace their old Jewish education with a new Babylonian one. Within three years they had to think, look, and live like Chaldeans. They had to start with the easy external transformation of customs regarding eating, clothing, and behaving. Then the internal transformation of views and values would be achieved through a new language, religion, and philosophy.

These young men immediately saw through the plan, and by trusting in God, they sought a way out of the dilemma. Open rebellion would lead to prison or death, robbing them of the opportunity to introduce the true God to their conquerors. By staying submissive and cooperative, they suggested a way to serve the king even better.

A short experiment would convince their supervisors. Instead of gorging themselves on the king's unhealthy diet, which had been dedicated to Babylon's idols before consumption, they requested a simple vegetarian diet. Daniel did not abstain from meat and wine permanently—chapter 10:3 proves that—but he abstained in certain circumstances for good reasons.

God brought Daniel into the favor of his supervisor. Because he liked Daniel, he decided to do the experiment Daniel asked for. After all, ten days would not make much of a difference in a three-year course. After ten days Daniel and his friends looked much better than the other guys who had gone through ten hangovers. The supervisor decided to prolong the experiment.

After three years Daniel and his friends were physically and mentally far superior to the other students. They even surpassed the wise men of the king. What the king did not know yet was that they looked like Chaldeans, but in their hearts they were true to Yahveh, and He would bring them safely through all the tough tests ahead of them.

And they would survive the king by many years.

A prayer: Help me to discern between cultural and moral values.
A thought: Have I compromised regarding my moral values?

262. Empires Come and Go
God reveals His control in a dream.

<table>
<tr><td>

September 18

~ ~ ~

Daniel 2

</td><td>

The king of the mighty Babylonia thought he could transform the world and its people to his taste. However, the episodes recorded in the book of Daniel show that superpowers could only do what God allowed them to do. Time and again they had to change their plans to fit in with God's plans.

</td></tr>
</table>

Like an ordinary human being, the mighty king also had to sleep. He had a dream that puzzled and perplexed him severely. Realizing that his wise men could easily fabricate a meaning for the dream, the king challenged them to prove that the gods really spoke to them. They had to reveal the content of the dream and then give its meaning. If they failed, they would be executed.

The wise men's frantic complaints were ignored, and orders were given for their execution. When Daniel and his friends heard of the crisis, Daniel negotiated for a short delay of the execution so that he could seek the counsel of his God. Daniel and his friends prayed, and God answered them.

Daniel spoke to the king and emphasized that not he, but God, had to be thanked for the unveiling of the king's dream and its meaning. When he spoke to the Babylonian kings, Daniel referred to the "God of heaven," but in his prayers he did use the name Yahveh. Daniel said that the king had dreamt of a huge statue. Its head was made of gold, its arms and chest of silver, its belly and hips of bronze, its legs of iron, and its feet of iron and clay. Without human help, a rock came down and crushed the statue to dust. The wind scattered the dust, but the rock filled the earth.

Knowing that he was right on, Daniel proceeded to explain the meaning of the dream. The five parts of the statue, made of different metals, resembled five consecutive world empires. The current Babylonian empire was the head of gold. Each of its successors would be weaker than the preceding one. They would all be crushed by and replaced with a God-given kingdom that would last forever. The history of several centuries was squeezed into a simple image.

This dream is a permanent reminder that earthly empires with their leaders come and go and that their limited time is a divine gift that can be well used or abused. Eventually the kingdom of God will replace them all.

God's kingdom centers on Christ, the rejected stone that became the cornerstone, the stone of stumbling, and the rock of offense (1 Pet. 2:4-9).

A prayer: Thank You, Father, that I am part of Your kingdom.
A thought: Through Christ we are more than conquerors. (Rom. 8:37).

263. True and False Worship
The powerful testimony of young believers

The mighty king of the great Babylonian empire did not take to heart the humbling message of his dream. To be only the golden head of an image with feet of clay was not good enough for Nebuchadnezzar. Therefore he had a statue made, ninety feet high, all covered in gold. It probably was

September 19
~~~
Daniel 3

an image of one of his gods, but the magnificence of the statue was more to the king's own honor. He summoned all the officials of his kingdom to the dedication of this colossal idol. When the orchestra started to play, all had to bow down to pay homage to the idol and to the king. Those who would dare to refuse would be burnt to death.

For some unknown reason, Daniel was not present at this charade. His three friends, Hananiah, Mishael, and Azariah, did not bow down to the idol, and their jealous colleagues immediately reported their dissent. The haughty king was furious but decided to give them a second chance. They told the king that they would not bow to the idol and were ready to face the punishment. They testified that their God could save them from the fire, but if He wanted them to die for His name's sake, then they were willing to do that. They put their lives on the line for their God.

In his rage, the king had the furnace heated to its maximum. It probably had one opening on top and one on the side for feeding the fire. The heat of the furnace was so intense that the soldiers who pushed the condemned men from a stand into the top opening were fatally burnt themselves. The king's angry pride changed to amazement and fear when he saw through the side door how not three, but four, men walked around in the fire, and the fourth looked like a divine being!

When his officials assured him that his eyes were not deceiving him, the king called the three men out. Casually they stepped out by the side door of the furnace and faced the king. There was no sign of fire on them: no ash, no singe, and no smell. Their Savior, the Son of God, had protected them completely from the hell of the king. And so He will protect anyone who trusts, loves, and obeys Him. He also takes us safely through the fire of our tribulations of this life.

Then the king changed his tune and ordered that all should revere the God of these young men. He promoted them for their integrity to rather face death than to be unfaithful to their God. In the end time, believers will be ordered to worship the image of the Anti-Christ (Rev. 13:14-15). Will we go with the flow, or will we stand up for the true God as Daniel's friends did?

*A prayer: Lord, make me faithful unto death.*
*A thought: How do I handle the pressure that people put on my faith?*

# 264. Pride Spawns Humiliation
## A haughty king is cut down to size.

September 20
~ ~ ~
Daniel 4

Those who exalt themselves will be humbled, and those who humble themselves will be exalted—so said the humble carpenter of Nazareth. The great king who conquered and exiled God's people thought that his gods had to be greater than Judah's God.

With three lessons, God gave him insight into his misunderstanding. First, he had the dream of the image with golden head and clay feet that was destroyed by God's rock. Second, the king's colossal idol was obliterated by the God who worked the miracle of the fiery furnace. Third, he was warned in a dream about his pride, and when he did not listen, he was disciplined harshly.

Nebuchadnezzar dreamt about a huge tree with widespread branches, delicious fruit, and shady protection for birds and animals. A divine being ordered the tree to be cut down, leaving only a chained stump that would live like an animal from dew and grass for seven periods (months or years).

This time the king told his dream to his wise men, but they could not figure it out. Again, Daniel was called in to show his superior God-given wisdom. When God revealed the meaning of the dream to Daniel, he felt sorry for the king and was speechless for a while. The king urged him to go ahead and reveal the meaning of the dream. Daniel told the king that the tree in the dream symbolized the king himself, who would be struck with a disorder that would cut him down, rob him of his sanity, and make him behave like an animal. The purpose of this ordeal would be to show the king that his greatness did not come from his own ingenuity and power but from God's grace.

Big egos are not easily cured. One year later the lesson was forgotten. The king viewed the beautiful city he had built and bragged about his own achievements. A voice from heaven announced that the stern warning of the dream would now become a gruesome reality. The glorious king turned into a savage brute with the looks and behavior of a wild beast. It showed to king Neb and to all who glorify themselves that if we don't give the honor to God, He may degrade us to something inhuman—the lot of many successful people. Like the king, we all forget this lesson on humility all too often.

Eventually, the king's sanity was restored, and he recognized the omnipotence of the God of heaven. The king even wrote a letter to all his provinces, told them about his humbling and illuminating experience, and urged them to honor the God from whom all blessings flow.

*A prayer: Help me not to think too much or too little of myself.*
*A thought: Where have I over- or underestimated myself?*

# 265. Feast of the Doomed
## Mene, mene, tekel, upharsin!

The former achievements of the elderly are easily forgotten. At the age of eighty, Daniel was a forgotten old man in Babylon. Nebuchadnezzar was followed in quick succession (562-539 B.C.) by less successful rulers. Nabonidus, the last one, fought the Persians on the front line, while he left the defense of Babel in the hands of his impetuous son, Belshazzar.

September 21
~~~
Daniel 5

As the Babylonian army gradually retreated, the front line came close to the capital. In these dark circumstances, Belshazzar treated the royal family and officials to a wild party to lift up their spirit.

In their drunken bravado, they had the holy Hebrew vessels brought and frivolously drank from them. Amid the noisy, drunken laughter, a huge hand appeared and started writing on the wall. As the heads turned in that direction, the noise died down, and a sobering fear got hold of their souls. With a choking voice, the shaking Belshazzar called for the wise men to decipher the writing on the wall.

Although the writing was in Aramaic, the official language, the wise men could not make sense of it: "number, number, weigh, broken." Then the old queen mother remembered that in the time of Nebuchadnezzar there was that brilliant man who could unravel the greatest mysteries. "What's his name again ... oh yes, now I remember, Daniel! Fetch him—he will tell you!"

The grey-headed, dignified old prophet looked at the writing and slowly nodded as the meaning was revealed to him. First, he reminded the royal guests of the humiliating experience the proud Nebuchadnezzar had and that the present rulers had repeated the same folly. Then Daniel read the words on the wall and gave their somber meaning: "Mene, mene, tekel, upharsin. The days of your kingdom are numbered; yes, they are numbered. You have been weighed and found wanting. Your kingdom will be broken up and given to the Medes and the Persians." That same night the city fell into the hands of the enemy, and the feasting doomed were killed. God proved that He was in control.

Those who try to escape their problems by means of alcohol or other drugs should take note of Belshazzar's story. However, there are many other escape mechanisms people resort to every day without success because these defenses do not solve problems realistically—they only use denial, excuses, blame, dependence, and daydreaming to sidestep the real problem.

A prayer: God, give me the courage to face reality and to deal with it wisely.
A thought: Which problems do I try to handle with escape mechanisms?

266. The Lion's Den
Daniel is saved from envy, pride, and fear.

September 22

~ ~ ~

Daniel 6

When Cyrus conquered Babylon in 539 B.C., he apparently appointed Darius the Mede as king (or governor) in Babel for a short period while Cyrus was completing his conquest. Darius took note of Daniel's record and planned to promote this experienced senior to chief of staff. Daniel's envious competitors conspired to secure his downfall. They influenced the king to issue an apparently innocent decree that they later could use to sink Daniel and to destroy freedom of religion.

This loathsome strategy is still around in our time. Constitutions that were meant to protect freedom of religion and freedom of speech are now employed to silence and even to persecute Christians when they defend their values. God will judge these persecutors as He judged Daniel's enemies.

Darius was flattered by the request of his officials. Not sensing their real motives, he proudly signed the decree, stating that for one month all requests and prayers should be directed to him only. Daniel knew what the vicious purpose of the decree was and that it put him before a serious choice: Either he allowed fear to destroy his prayer life, or he proceeded as usual with the risk of severe punishment. He decided to put God's kingdom first.

Daniel did not taunt his enemies by praying in public. He went into his private upper room and prayed in the direction of Jerusalem, as his custom had been. Apparently his prayers were answered: Within three years Cyrus allowed the Jews in exile to return to Judah.

While Daniel was interceding for his people, his enemies sneaked up the stairs and trapped him in the act of asking from God while in that month he should have asked only from the king.

Darius was utterly dismayed when he realized that he had been used to stage the execution of a dear friend. He tried to get out of the trap, but the conspirators held him to his decree. Unwillingly, he had to allow the dirty process to continue. All he could do was to wish that Daniel's God would protect him. The old prophet was lowered into the den of lions, and the opening was sealed to prevent any secret intervention by the king.

After a long, sleepless, distressful night, Darius rushed to the lions' den and called anxiously to Daniel. Minutes later, two grateful friends embraced each other while praising God and laughing in relief. Then Darius issued two new decrees—to punish the wicked and to honor Daniel and his God.

A prayer: God, I will look at You, not at the enemies or at the lions.
A thought: Do I take a clear stand against misleading or misusing legislation?

267. Secrets Revealed and Sealed
Daniel's visions show God is in control.

Although some aspects of his visions were explained
to him, Daniel remained extremely puzzled and perplexed
about the full meaning of what he had seen. He was told to
seal some of the visions, for their true meaning would be
revealed in the end time. We look at the revealed secrets
and leave the others in peace.

> September 23
> ~ ~ ~
> Daniel 7 - 12

The information contained in Nebuchadnezzar's first dream (the giant
statue) is repeated in the visions with new data added as well. The four animals
(ch. 7) represented four superpowers: Babylon, Medo-Persia, Greece, and Rome.
The four horns of the last animal, like the statue's feet of clay and iron, pointed
to the weaker kingdoms that would arise from the fallen Roman Empire.

One of them, the "little horn" (Syria), would bring cessation of sacrifices in
Jerusalem for several years due to the desecration of the second temple by
Antiochus Epiphanes. He became a type of the Antichrist because of his
blasphemous words and deeds (7:8, 24-25; 8:9-14; 11:31-37). The Anti-Christ is
further described in Matt. 24:15, 2 Thess. 2:4, 1 John 4:3, Rev. 13:1-8. The Roman
general Titus also desecrated the temple before he destroyed it in A.D. 70.

The ram with the two horns (ch. 8) refers to the Medo-Persian Empire,
which would be conquered by the he-goat, Greece. The goat's big horn,
Alexander the Great, would soon be replaced by four other horns/kingdoms.

Daniel's prayer of confession and intercession for his people (ch. 9) is
followed by more visions, including the "seventy weeks" and the Messiah's life
and death. The angels affirmed God's love for Daniel repeatedly and gave a
glimpse of spiritual warfare (ch. 10). Then the futile conflicts between the
Ptolemaic and Syrian empires are described to Daniel (ch. 11).

The message in these visions is that God controls the rise and fall of
nations. Eventually, His eternal kingdom will replace all earthly powers (7:14,
27). God's Messiah will make this kingdom a reality by reconciling people to
God: *"Messiah shall be cut off, but not for Himself."* (9:26). Because He leads many
to righteousness, He will shine like the stars forever (12:3).

Chapter 12 concludes with the physical resurrection of both the saved and
the doomed. Those who had led people to Christ will be richly rewarded. In the
end time, knowledge will increase tremendously. However, the wicked will
rush forth in ignorance, but God will protect and enlighten His children.
Yahveh, the One who lives forever, will fulfill His prophecies to His people.

A prayer: Father, in Your hands I am safe.
A thought: Do I surrender myself completely into God's hands every day?

268. Glory Amid Tragedy
Ezekiel sees God's glory and Judah's disgrace.

September 24

~ ~ ~

Ezek. 1-7

We now go back to the year 593 B.C. to follow the ministry of the prophet Ezekiel during the exile. Five years after he had arrived in Babylon with the second group of captives, Ezekiel had an awe-inspiring vision of the LORD (1:3). Four cherubs (10:15) supported God's chariot-like throne. Each cherub had four faces: that of a lion, a bull, a man, and an eagle (compare Rev. 4:7). The chariot had wheels full of eyes, and when it moved it made a roaring sound. The brilliant Person on the throne was beyond description.

Yahveh then appointed Ezekiel as prophet and warned him that the people were hardheaded and would not listen. Nevertheless, Ezekiel had to be more obstinate than his audience and had to proceed in spite of resistance. To show that God's Word had become part of himself, God gave Ezekiel a scroll to eat (see Rev. 10:8-9). God appointed him as watchman to warn people about coming doom. If he did not warn them, they would die for their sins, but God would hold Ezekiel responsible for their demise (33:1-11).

Because the people did not listen to *words*, God told Ezekiel to bring God's message by *deeds* so the people could see them. God muted him and told him to draw a picture of a besieged Jerusalem on a clay tablet, to put a separation between himself and the tablet, and to lie beside the tablet 390 days on his left side (for Israel's sins) and 40 days on his right side (for Judah's sins). During that time, he had to use small amounts of impure food and water.

This demanding object lesson symbolized the siege of Jerusalem and the famine its inhabitants would suffer. As they had defiled themselves with idolatry and immorality, so they would be defiled with impure foods in the foreign countries to which God would scatter them. Although Ezekiel could not speak, he could write and thus conveyed his message.

Ezekiel had to shave off his hair and beard and divide the hair into three parts. At the end of the siege, he had to burn one-third of the hair on the drawing of Jerusalem; one-third he had to chop up with a sword; and one-third he had to scatter in the wind. Likewise, a part of Israel would die of hunger in Jerusalem; a part would be killed outside the city; and another part would be scattered amongst the nations.

God's anger about Judah's unfaithfulness is described in chapters 6 and 7. God's Word through Ezekiel was for those in Judah and for those in exile.

A prayer: Jesus, You bridged the gap between God's holiness and our sinfulness.
A thought: Do I observe God's mercy in unexpected places?

269. The Saddest Moment
God's glory leaves the temple.

Ezekiel's visions were very powerful. God spoke to him directly in the first person, using very strong language. God addressed him as "son of man" 93 times to make him realize how small he was in the presence of the Almighty. To accentuate the serious and inescapable consequences of their sins, Yahveh used the phrase 67 times: They/you *"will know that I am the LORD."*

September 25

~ ~ ~

Ezek. 8 - 14

While Ezekiel met with elders in exile, he was taken by the Spirit to Jerusalem where he again saw the vision of the cherubs and God's glory. God showed him the open and secret idolatry taking place in Jerusalem. The leaders and the people reasoned that since God had left them, He would not notice what they were doing (8:12). They ignored the words of the prophets, thinking that prophecies were only meant for the far off future (12:22-25).

The vision in Jerusalem continued with the marking of the few who were still concerned about the nation's apostasy and the slaying of all who did not care. Fiery coals from beneath God's throne were thrown over Jerusalem to symbolize how God's wrath would come on the city.

When a teenager has been violating the feelings of his parents deliberately and repeatedly, they may eventually break off contact with that child. It is a very sad moment. It happened between God and His children.

God promised Abram that he and his descendants would be a blessing to the nations. Now the glory of God departed from the temple and the city and rested on the Mount of Olives. This surely was the saddest moment in the history of Israel. It looked as if Yahveh's yearning was brought to naught. Yes, God did leave His obstinate children, but He waited nearby, yearning for their repentance. He promised a future revival (11:17-21).

After the vision, Ezekiel again had to perform an action-prophecy. It portrayed the futile attempt of King Zedekiah to flee from Jerusalem (see also 17:16-20). It showed the inevitable fall of the city.

The false prophets and female magicians who promised good times for the straying nation would be harshly punished for they encouraged people in the wrong direction (ch. 13).

It is a serious warning to all leaders, including teachers and television staff, not to lead the public astray by inaccurate and misleading information. Jesus identified the devil as the father of lies (John 8:44).

A prayer: Help us rectify the wrong before it is too late.
A thought: Do I fool myself with misleading proverbs?

270. Specified Sins
God describes the problem and the solution.

September 26
~ ~ ~
Ezek. 14-24

Ezekiel was esteemed by the Jews in exile. On various occasions, the elders consulted him about the concerns of the captives. Many still hoped that Babylon would soon be overthrown so they could go home. Therefore Jeremiah (in Jerusalem) and Ezekiel (in Babylon) emphasized that the exile would not be over soon and that they had to plan for a long stay.

On two occasions God refused to grant consultation to the elders because even in exile they had not discarded all their idols and sins (ch. 14, 20, 33:31). God was so determined to punish His people for their sins that He said not even Noah, Daniel, or Job, if they were among them, would be able to rescue anyone except themselves. It is repeated several times to stress the point.

To show that He was not unfair (14:23, 18:25), God gave a specified list of sins to the Jews through Ezekiel. First, their obsession to serve other gods deeply offended Yahveh because He saw it as adultery toward Him, their real "husband." God had laid this charge through several prophets. God compared His people to abandoned babies whom He had rescued and brought up but who surrendered themselves to unbridled harlotry when they matured (ch. 16 and 23).

Judah would be punished more severely because she saw what happened to Israel, and yet she did not change her ways but became even worse.

When categorized, their sins invaded all levels of society: religious mixing, social injustice, dishonest business, sexual immorality, and bloody revenge (18:5-9, 22:6-12, 23-29). Sexual sins included severe forms of incest. Violation of the Sabbath is stressed because that was usually where the straying started.

With a proverb they complained that they were punished for the sins of their ancestors. God emphasized that every person would be accountable for his/her own sins (18:20). God said that He enjoys the forgiveness of the penitent, not the punishment of the impenitent: *"Do I have any pleasure at all that the wicked should die?"* says the Lord God, *"and not that he should turn from his ways and live?"* (18:23, John 3:16-17, 2 Pet. 3:9).

God promised that a small remnant of faithful believers would come back to the Promised Land. They would understand God's dealings with His people and serve Him sincerely. The true Israel would be saved and again inhabit the mountains of Israel (20:40-44, Rom. 11:22-26).

A prayer: Lead us not into temptation but deliver us from evil.
A thought: Is my lifestyle determined by both God's love and God's holiness?

271. Death and Life
Grieving about losses, rejoicing about gains

There is a continuous cycle between life and death. Decaying leaves sustain new growth. Grazed plants are fertilized by grazing animals. In the food chain, some die so that others may live. Many life-forms procreate before they die, and so secure the future of the species. From the ashes of one civilization a new one usually rises.

> September 27
> ~ ~ ~
> Ezek. 24, 34-37

The most painful action-prophecy Ezekiel had to perform involved the death of his beloved wife. He called her "the delight of my eyes." What made his loss even more painful was God's command not to mourn her with the usual external customs of his culture but to suffer his grief in silence.

When the captives would hear about the destruction of Jerusalem and the temple, the delight of their eyes, they had to do the same: suffer in silence on the inside. Hosea had to suffer the pain of an unfaithful wife to realize how God felt about Israel's unfaithfulness. Ezekiel had to feel the pain of God's loss, His chosen people, by experiencing the loss of his beloved wife.

This tragic point in Ezekiel's ministry signaled the end of his doom-messages and the starting point of good-news messages. In his prophecies too, death was followed by new life. After he had addressed the nations (ch. 25-32), God commanded him to speak about the restoration of Israel. A powerful and hopeful call to repentance (33:11) and a stern warning about self-profiting leaders were followed by a wonderful promise about the Messiah who would be the Good Shepherd to His people (ch. 34).

God's new-life messages through Ezekiel culminated in the prophecies on the prosperity of the mountains of Israel (ch. 36) and the vision of the dry bones that were brought back to life by the Almighty (ch. 37). Although Israel's future looked as bleak as those dry, scattered bones, Yahveh would do the impossible. He would bring Israel back to life.

God reminded His people that they could not take any credit for this restoration—they had nothing but shame on their side. Yahveh would restore them for His own name's sake: *"I do not do this for your sake, O house of Israel, but for My holy name's sake, which you have profaned among the nations ... and the nations shall know that I am the LORD"* (36:22-23).

By God's mercy alone, He would replace the grief of loss and death by the joy of renewal and revival (36:26-28). From the seeds that fell into the soil, a life-sustaining crop would sprout (John 12:24). God's yearning love would prevail.

A prayer: Thank You, Father, for Your prevailing love.
A thought: Will losses stop me, or will I proceed with God-given life?

272. World, Church, and God
Ezekiel sees the effects of the bad and the good.

<table><tr><td>September 28
~ ~ ~
Ezek. 38-48</td></tr></table>

In general, Bible students explain Ezekiel 38-39 either literally or symbolically. Both camps think they have good reasons for their viewpoints. When both sides listen with open minds to each other, they may realize that these viewpoints are not excluding each other but complementing each other. In line with the goal of this study, we will rather look for the main message embedded in the details of chapters 38-48.

Under the leadership of Gog, many nations attack Israel who are prosperous back in their land. This war should not be confused with Armageddon. One can just look at the hundreds of UN resolutions against Israel, in addition to several wars and intifadas, to see how real this animosity is. However, this big show of power comes to nothing because God intervenes with natural disasters. Before the hordes can be buried, birds of prey have a feast. It takes a long time to get rid of the aftereffects of war. This scenario may happen literally in the future, but in a symbolic way it has already started—the deaths, the weapons, Israel's miraculous survival, and the "vultures" that feed on this situation.

In contrast to the fatal actions of Israel's enemies stands the constructive influence of God through believers, both Jewish and Christian. In a vision, Ezekiel saw a new temple to which the glory of God had returned (43:1-5). God had entered through the east gate; therefore, it was closed afterward. Because God entered the temple, a blessing flows from it: a river that grows stronger the farther it goes, with lush, healing, fruitful trees on it banks. The river brings life to the Dead Sea and transforms it into a fishing paradise.

This may literally come true, but symbolically it is already happening. Each believer is a temple of God (1 Cor. 3:16). Jesus and His Father stay in us through the Holy Spirit (John 14:23). Therefore, streams of living water can flow from us to others (John 7:37-39). We do have a healing influence on our environment. Millions of Christian missions and charities all over the world, from the smallest villages to the largest cities, testify to the healing stream that is flowing from the "temple" of God.

However, the most profound, life-giving river flowing from God's temple is the saving message of the gospel, transforming people who have been "dead" in their sins into God's children, who rejoice in eternal life (Eph. 2:4-10). This spiritual resurrection (John 5:24-25) occurs when we are reconciled to God through Christ (2 Cor. 5:18, Col. 1:13-14). God's yearning love is touching the world.

A prayer: Help us replace harmful behavior with a healing influence.
A thought: Do I always have a healing influence on others?

273. The New Covenant
Jeremiah's view on Israel's restoration

While Ezekiel's vision of Israel's comeback centered on the revived dry bones and the healing river, Jeremiah's view was focused on a new attitude and a new relationship. This passage is the pinnacle of Jeremiah's "book of comfort" (30-33) and is quoted in full in the New Testament (Heb. 8:7-12).

> September 29
> ~ ~ ~
> Jer. 31:31-34

With tender, comforting words Yahveh assured Israel and Judah, through Jeremiah, that after their purging exile He would bring some of them back to the Promised Land. Their healing and prosperity are portrayed with various metaphors: singing and dancing people, happy brides and grooms, flocks of sheep and herds of cattle, flourishing fields and gardens, a buzzing economy, and a hot real estate market.

Above all, they would seek and find the LORD and serve Him in the way He wanted to be served. This would be possible through a new covenant. Because of their sinful nature, Israel could not keep God's law voluntarily. The **new covenant** would include a **change of heart** through the Holy Spirit so that they would have the desire and the ability from the inside to do God's will. When they lived in this new relationship with God, He would forgive their sin and never think of it again. The yearning of God and man would be satisfied.

The new covenant announced by Jeremiah became a reality with the death, resurrection, and ascension of Christ, followed by the outpouring of the Holy Spirit. At the Last Supper, the night before His crucifixion, Jesus said of the wine, *"For this is My blood of the new covenant which is shed for many for the remission of sins"* (Matt. 26:28). Those who have accepted Jesus as their personal Savior (Jews and Gentiles) share in this new covenant.

However, for those who think that Israel was replaced by the church, God has big news: As long as day and night exist, as long as the sun and stars are there, so long will His covenant with Israel last (31:35-36, 33:17-21). Jesus said to the Samaritan woman that salvation is of the Jews (John 4:22) because the Messiah was born from them and God has given His Word to them. The Word was later dispersed by Churches and Bible societies.

Paul explained that Israel's rejection of Christ is temporary and it gives the opportunity to the Gentiles to accept Jesus as Savior (Rom. 11). Like wild olive branches, they are grafted onto the stem of the olive tree (Israel), but God can graft the old branches back when He wants to.

A prayer: Father, fill me with Your Spirit, so I will want what You want.
A thought: Is God's will for me an external law or an internal desire?

274. The Deliverer
Isaiah sees the redemption of Israel and the world.

September 30
~~~
Is. 40:1-5, 25-31
53:3-9, 55:3-11

Isaiah 40-66 is a box filled with magnificent jewels. Some of the most comforting passages in Scripture are found on those pages. God showed Isaiah the universal meaning of Israel's redemption, thus the promises speak to the heart of every person.

More than a century before the exile, Isaiah told the people that there would come a day when the good news would reach them: *"Speak comfort to Jerusalem, and cry out to her, that her warfare is ended, that her iniquity is pardoned"* (40:2). God called king Cyrus of Persia (45:1-7) to facilitate the return of God's people to their land, *"Thus says the LORD to His anointed, to Cyrus ... For Jacob My servant's sake, and Israel My elect, I have called you by your name; I have named you, though you have not known Me."*

A wider application is suggested with the promise of the Messiah's herald: *"The voice of one crying in the wilderness: 'Prepare the way of the LORD!' "* (40:3, Matt. 3:3). The attention then shifts to the Messiah Himself: *"Say to the cities of Judah, 'Behold your God!'... He will feed His flock like a shepherd; He will gather the lambs with His arm, and carry them in His bosom"* (40:9, 11; Luke 18:16). The messianic theme is resumed repeatedly: *"Behold! My Servant whom I uphold, My Elect One in whom My soul delights! ... A bruised reed He will not break, And smoking flax He will not quench"* (42:1-3, compare 61:1-2, Matt. 12:17-21).

The suffering by which the Messiah would accomplish salvation is described in detail: *"He was wounded for our transgressions, He was bruised for our iniquities; the chastisement for our peace was upon Him, and by His stripes we are healed"* (53:5). On account of His atonement, the good news of salvation can be offered to all: *"Seek the LORD while He may be found, call upon Him while He is near ... For as the rain comes down ... So shall My Word be that goes forth from My mouth; it shall not return to Me void"* (55: 6, 10, 11).

Because of the reconciliation accomplished by the Messiah, promises of blessing are poured on those who accept Him. The weary and worried (40:28-31, 41:10, 43:1-2), the lonely and elderly (49:15-16, 46:4), all share in the blessings of God's people. However, to warn us about the alternative of not accepting God's grace, Isaiah ended his book with a picture of hell—where the fire never stops and where the worms never die, a reality affirmed by the mediating Messiah Himself (66:24, Mark 9:48). The only way we can get rid of our sins and the punishment attached to them, is to hand them over to Jesus.

*A prayer: Lord, You have prepared a feast; I don't want to miss it.*
*A thought: Have I returned to God, or do I remain in the far off land?*

# 275. The Great Moment
## Going home!

Time is important to the eternal One. When God's time had come He convinced a pagan king to let His people go home. The king even paid for the rebuilding of their temple. Likewise, in the fullness of time, God would send His Son as Savior to the world (Gal. 4:6) and convince a pagan king to have a census so that His Son could be born in Bethlehem as predicted by God's prophet (Micah 5:2, Matt. 2:1-6, Luke 2:1-4).

> October 1
> ~ ~ ~
> Ezra 1-4

Like many nations today, the Jews had doubled twice in seventy years: Ten had become twenty, and twenty had become forty (thousand). The seventy years predicted by Jeremiah (25:11, 29:10) stretched either from 606-536 B.C. (from first exile to first return) or from 586-516 B.C. (from destruction of the first temple to the dedication of the second temple).

It must have looked like a second Exodus when more than forty thousand people packed up and returned on foot and by carts to their homeland with thousands of livestock among them. In addition to the problems on the way, the situation in and around Jerusalem was precarious. The city was in ruins. The wall, temple, and homes were demolished. There was no protection against suspicious and hostile neighbors. They had to start with food production from scratch. In the beginning it was like a huge refugee camp. Most of them settled in other towns of Judah. Jerusalem remained uninhabited (Ezra 2:70, Neh. 7:4).

First, they restored the altar of the temple. They started off with the feasts of autumn: trumpets, atonement, and Tabernacles. These feasts demanded self-search, repentance, and thanksgiving—all very suitable to their position. Then they laid the temple's foundation, which consisted of large stones, not of concrete as today. The old people wept when they compared the modesty of their present effort with the grandeur of Solomon's temple. The young people, who had never seen the old temple, rejoiced when they looked forward to the completion of the new one. Jesus and Paul encouraged us to look forward and not backward (Luke 9:62, Phil. 3:13).

When their northern neighbors, the Samaritans, who were of mixed descent and religion (2 Kings 17:24-41), offered their help to rebuild the temple, their offer was declined. The Jews used as excuse the command of Cyrus that they should rebuild the temple. The Samaritans felt snubbed and retaliated by dragging the name of the Jews through the mud at the palace. It brought the work to a standstill for about sixteen years. The great moment had turned sour.

*A prayer: Help us to see the great moments of small beginnings.*
*A thought: I will not lose my vision because of temporary problems.*

# 276. Build the Temple!
## Haggai spurs the people on to resume building.

<table>
<tr><td>October 2<br>~ ~ ~<br>Haggai 1-2</td><td>In 520 B.C., sixteen years after they had returned from exile, the people were so engaged with their own daily business and agriculture that the original reason for their return to Jerusalem was completely out of their minds. God used the prophet Haggai to open their eyes and to wake up their consciences.</td></tr>
</table>

Haggai used two convincing arguments. First, he pointed to the contrast between their wood-paneled houses (in cities around Jerusalem) and the ruined state of God's house. Second, he drew their attention to the recent disappointing yields of their crops. They reasoned that they could not build the temple because of their poor crops. Haggai told them that actually it was exactly the opposite: Because of their neglect of God's house, God did not bless their efforts in making a living.

The leaders and the people responded positively and resumed the work on the temple. A month later Haggai noticed a spirit of despondency among the workers. God gave him a powerful message of encouragement to the leaders and to the people. Although the second temple looked much less glorious than the first one, God Himself would honor it with His unique presence. The real glory of any temple is not related to its physical qualities but to the spiritual meeting between God and people that takes place there. *"The Desire of All Nations,"* the incarnated Son of God, would come to this humble temple and *"and I will fill this temple with glory."* By His atoning death, the Messiah would reconcile God and man and thus *"in this place I will give peace."*

Three months later God sent Haggai to the people with two messages. It was winter and in that region it was time for seeding. God said that He would bless their crops that coming year because they had been faithful.

He also had a special message for their leader, Zerubbabel. Seventy- seven years before, God had said through Jeremiah that He would pull king Jehoiachin like a signet ring from His finger and cast him into exile (Jer. 22:24). Now God bends down in mercy to the grandson of that king and tells him that He will make him His signet ring again.

God had not asked anyone to build the first temple (1 Chron. 17:6), but He ordered the people of Israel to build the second temple. Through Haggai God showed us to put God's kingdom first continuously so that our own little "kingdoms" will not stand in the way of God's eternal kingdom.

*A prayer: Lord, I want to be involved in the building of Your kingdom.*
*A thought: How much time have I given to God's kingdom lately?*

# 277. Cleansed and Empowered
## Zechariah sees God's provisions for our deepest needs.

As a contemporary of Haggai, Zechariah too encouraged the people to proceed faithfully with the rebuilding of the second temple. Unlike God's direct approach through Haggai, He spoke by visions to Zechariah in his early ministry (ch. 1-8).

> October 3
> ~ ~ ~
> Zech. 1-8

The vision of the horsemen showed that the restfulness of the nations while God's people still suffered was not acceptable to God. The vision of the horns and craftsmen showed that the nations who had harmed Israel would be punished for their excessive violence. The vision of the man with the measuring line predicted that a time would come that Jerusalem would be so large that it would not be enclosed by a wall. God would then be their protective wall. The Jews who were still living abroad were called to come to this new city.

The vision of the high priest with filthy clothes, accused by Satan as being unfit for his duties, accentuates the sinfulness of Israel. God Himself would cleanse them and enable them to serve Him. This cleansing would be made possible by the Messiah, called Branch (see Isaiah 11:1). He would bring peace in and among people who would then enjoy their vines and trees. When Jesus had paid the sin-debt of believers, Satan could not accuse them anymore.

The vision of the lampstand that was connected to the olive trees showed that Zerubbabel had to rely on God's Spirit, not on human power, to finish the rebuilding of the temple. It also points to the Messiah who would be anointed by the Spirit in a unique way and to His followers, who would enjoy the continuous flow of power ("oil") from the Spirit after Pentecost.

The visions of the scroll, basket, and chariots portrayed how evil would be eradicated by God. It would be accomplished by the Messiah (Branch) who would be both king and priest. He is portrayed here by the priest Joshua, the Hebrew name of Jesus. Kings who had tried to be king-priests, as Saul and Uzziah did (1 Sam. 13, 2 Chron. 26), were severely punished.

Zechariah admonished the people to turn away from external formalism and to serve God and fellow human beings from the heart. That would become evident in their relationship with God and with others.

Zechariah visualized a new Jerusalem where justice, peace, prosperity, and true worship would be practiced. God would bring His people from afar back to the Promised Land. That would entice other nations to seek contact with Yahveh, the God of Israel, in order to experience true spiritual peace.

*A prayer: Thank You, God, for the continuous "oil" of Your Spirit.*
*A thought: True joy comes from the right relationship with God and people.*

# 278. Humiliation and Glorification
## Zechariah sees the Messiah's first and second coming.

October 4
~ ~ ~
Zech. 9-14

The prophecies in the second part of Zechariah's book differ in content and style from those in the first part because he received them in a different situation when he was already a senior citizen. His prophetic view had a "telescopic" effect on nearby and far-off events, making them look closer to each other than they were. Zechariah intertwined events of his own time with that of the Messiah's first and second coming.

Zechariah's message included judgment and mercy for both Israel and the nations. Some nations would support the "bad shepherd," the Antichrist (11:15-17), for the final onslaught of Jerusalem (14:1-2) called Armageddon (Rev. 16:16). However, some nations would become part of God's people (9:7) and take part in the feast of thanksgiving called Tabernacles (14:16-19).

Judgment is preached on Israel's sins (10:2-3, 13:2-6), but the forgiveness and restoration of Israel are promised because of the atonement the Messiah would accomplish (10:6-12, 13:9). They would return to their country (10:9). Eventually they would realize that Jesus is the Messiah and feel deep remorse because they had rejected Him (12:10-14). Then the fountain of living water will be opened for the Jews to wash away their sins (13:1).

References to the Messiah as "Branch" in the first part of the book are backed up by several prophecies in the second part that were literally fulfilled in Christ. Zechariah portrayed Christ's first coming in humility by describing His entry into Jerusalem on a donkey (9:9). Christ would bring peace with God (9:10). By His blood covenant He would set captives free (9:11).

He would be rejected as the Good Shepherd (11:8, John 10). He would be betrayed for thirty silver pieces (11:12). This money would be thrown back into the temple to buy the potter's field (11:13). Christ as the Shepherd would be struck and His flock would be scattered (13:7). His hands, feet, and side would be pierced (12:10). He will return in glory on the Mount of Olives (14:4) for the final victory over evil.

The prophecies about Christ's first coming in humility were literally fulfilled (see also Ps. 22 and Is. 53). We can therefore be completely sure that the prophecies about His second coming in glory will be fulfilled too.

Zechariah also got a glimpse of the new earth where peace will reign (9:10) in continuous light (14:7) and where everything and everybody will be dedicated to God (14:20-21). Every knee will bow before Christ (Phil. 2:9-11).

*A prayer: God, You gave us Your schedule ahead of time.*
*A thought: God has kept His promises in the past. He will do so in future too.*

# 279. Arrival After Detours
## Israel and Ezra make some baffling diversions.

Ezra came to Jerusalem with a group of exiles about 80 years after those who had returned with Zerubbabel. When Ezra told the history of the first group, it struck him that they had received the same kind of animosity from the Samaritans which Ezra and Nehemiah experienced many years later.

October 5
~ ~ ~
Ezra 4-6

Ezra used a recent piece of history (known to his readers) that occurred during the reign of king Artaxerxes (in the 5$^{th}$ century B.C.), to illustrate what had happened earlier during the reigns of Cyrus, Cambyses, and Darius I (in the 6$^{th}$ century B.C.). After this diversion (4:7-24), Ezra continued with the original history (5:1) to show how the temple was eventually completed.

After the rebuilding of the temple had been interrupted for about sixteen years (536-520 B.C.), God used the prophets Haggai and Zechariah to inspire the leaders and the people to resume the real mission they had come for. Again their adversaries tried to stop the work, but this time they did not succeed.

The leaders of the exiles gave a concise and accurate historical background of the destruction and rebuilding of the temple to the governor of that region. He conveyed this information to King Darius I and asked him to verify it with facts from the king's archive. By this process the exiles were vindicated. They could proceed with the work on the temple without further interference.

All these letters to and from Persia show how God controlled the situation to suit His own purpose. First, He allowed the work on the temple to be delayed. Then at the right moment He restarted the work so that the temple would be finished seventy years after it had been destroyed. Someone said: "God often shows up on the last minute, but He is never late."

After four years the temple was finished and dedicated to the service of Yahveh, the God of Israel. A sin offering of twelve goats was brought for the twelve tribes of Israel. The temple was for all Israel, not only for the tribes of Judah, Benjamin, and Levi, who rebuilt it.

The priests and the people prepared themselves appropriately for the feasts of Passover and Unleavened Bread. They celebrated these feasts with genuine joy and thanksgiving—praising Yahveh for His mercy to purify them of idolatry, to forgive their sins, to bring them back to the Promised Land, and to enable them to celebrate Passover in the second temple.

The promises given through God's prophets came true.

*A prayer: God, You sustain us through difficult times.*
*A thought: God's detours are shortcuts to His goals.*

# 280. The Danger of Contamination
## Ezra and Nehemiah fight against fatal infiltration.

October 6

~ ~ ~

Ezra 7-10
Neh. 13:23-28

In the 20th century the world has been shocked by horrific forms of "ethnic cleansing," massacres on innocent people for one reason only: They belonged to a specific ethnic group. Consequently, any discrimination based on ethnicity is now strongly condemned.

However, there also exists ambiguity with regard to culture. Immigrants are allowed to keep up their culture of origin, but they are also encouraged to assimilate the culture of their host country. Today's global transport and communication stimulate cultural interaction and blending. Emphasis on cultural purity is regarded with suspicion because it can easily escalate to intolerance toward other cultures.

Ezra and Nehemiah's opposition to intermarriage with other nations was based on religious reasons. Mixed marriages were forbidden by the Torah because this kind of social blending could lead to mixing of religion—which happened many times in the history of Israel. Even the wise king Solomon was not immune to this influence. His foreign wives seduced him into idolatry in his old age. The mixed religion of the mixed race, the Samaritans, was another example of the contamination of religion by intermarriage. To secure the survival of God's Word and the messianic lineage, Ezra and Nehemiah insisted that this command of God had to be strictly adhered to.

Realizing that the repatriation of foreign wives and children would cause much emotional pain and social hardships, Ezra turned to God in prayer. While he was praying, God worked a miracle in the hearts of the guilty to volunteer to put the matter in order. Thus the contamination was eliminated by the people themselves and not by force from the authorities.

We have to discern between snobbish isolation and spiritual protection. We should not isolate ourselves from others in a better-than-you attitude but rather reach out and render help where it is needed. Yet, we should guard against contamination by worldly influences. Music and other forms of entertainment are routes by which evil ideas may enter our minds.

People working with addicts must ensure that they do not become addicted themselves. When Jesus reached out to sinners, they did not pull Him down into sin, but He pulled them out of sin.

We must keep our faith pure without bigotry toward those who believe differently. We must "speak the truth in love" (Eph. 4:15).

*A prayer: Holy Spirit, please keep me pure and humble.*
*A thought: Is my thinking contaminated by worldly ideas?*

# 281. Divine Love
## Malachi calls for the right response.

Looking at the sins of deed, neglect, and attitude addressed by Malachi, his ministry probably took place before the great revival in the time of Nehemiah. The second temple had been functioning for about 65 years already, but the spiritual level of priests and people was low

> October 7
> ~ ~ ~
> Mal. 1:1 - 2:9

and lax. God called Malachi to dispute the popular lies and cynicism in society with a question-and-answer approach.

The short book of Malachi starts and ends with God's love. The people's response was, "Really? How does He love us?" God answered through Malachi that He had loved Jacob and hated Esau even before they were born. It means that God's love is not dependant on human merit but on God's grace. His love enables people to respond with love toward God. Jesus conveyed the same truth to His disciples: *"You did not choose Me, but I chose you and appointed you that you should go and bear fruit"* (John 15:16).

Then God confronted the priests with a question. If God was their Father, Owner, and King, why were they dishonoring Him by accepting blemished offerings from the people and defiling God's altar with these? God challenged them to bring such a pathetic gift to the governor. In contrast with the lax attitude of the priests, God drew their attention to the Gentiles who had come to know the God of Israel and who served Him according to His will.

The priests could just as well lock up the temple because what was happening there was not pleasing to God. He was deeply disappointed in the quality of worship taking place in the second temple. He was so disgusted with them that He wanted to cast them out—like the animal dung.

The priests not only did wrong themselves, but they also led the people in the wrong direction. They violated God's covenant with the tribe of Levi. This tribe had been appointed at Mount Sinai to be the spiritual teachers of the nation. The task of the priests and other Levites was to teach God's will to the people. The priest should be *"a messenger of the LORD of hosts."*

It is also a warning to Christian preachers, teachers, and witnesses. Our lives, attitudes, and words should honor God, not disgrace Him. The big divide runs right through the church and right through our hearts. Our old sinful nature cannot please God (Rom. 8:8), and by the power of God's indwelling Spirit we have to overcome it. At the same time we have to strengthen our reborn spirit by God's Spirit so we can delight in God's will.

*A prayer: By Your Spirit we can do Your will—loving You and loving others.*
*A thought: Is my worship guided by love and respect for God?*

# 282. The Poor Response
## Malachi assesses their love for others and for God.

October 8
~~~
Mal. 2:10 - 4:6

After he had finished with the priests, Malachi turned to the nation. They too had violated the two greatest commandments: love for God (Deut. 6:5) and for each other (Lev. 19:18). Malachi started with the latter, especially the love between husband and wife.

Firstly, he warned them about the spiritual danger lurking in marrying foreign women who worshiped foreign gods. It always led to cultural and religious blending, which eventually eroded the faith of Israel. Malachi pleaded for a no-tolerance policy towards this phenomenon.

Secondly, he scolded them for a permissive approach toward divorce. They moaned and groaned at God's altar because of unanswered prayers, but they forgot that they angered God by violating their marriage vows with divorce. By mouth of Malachi, God let them know that He regarded marriage as a holy covenant and that those who broke it actually committed violence because they violated a God-given institution.

Their question on how they had offended God was further answered by pointing to their cynical remark that it made no difference whether they served God or not. In their view, the wicked often flourished while the righteous often suffered.

God answered with a prophecy about the coming Messiah and His herald: *"Behold I send My messenger, and he will prepare the way before Me. And the Lord, whom you seek, will suddenly come to His temple."* He would refine and purify the Levites and the nation like silver. Then they would see the difference between those who serve God and those who do not.

When they asked how they should return to God, God pointed to their tithes and offerings. These were barometers of their faith. God challenged them to try Him on this. He would bless them abundantly if they gave generously to God's work on earth.

When the "day of the LORD" eventually arrives, the wicked will be devoured by fire, but the children of God will jump with joy. The Sun of Righteousness will rise over them and cure them of all sickness and sin.

Before the "day of the LORD," God will send an Elijah-figure to bring unity between fathers and children, the old and the new, the Law and the Gospel. Then Israel will fully understand how God's revelation in the Old Testament fits in with His revelation in the New Testament.

A prayer: Fill us with gratitude and love so that we will give with joy.
A thought: What does the barometer of relationships tell me about myself?

283. Restoring the Infrastructure
Nehemiah restores the wall and economy of Jerusalem.

When Nehemiah, the wine-master of the Persian palace, learned from his brother that the walls and gates of Jerusalem were still in ruins ninety years after the return of the first group of exiles, he was shocked. He prayed and fasted and hoped that God would open an opportunity to restore the city so that it could be repopulated and become a living city again.

October 9

~ ~ ~

Neh. 1-7, 11:1

The king learned about his passion and authorized and equipped him to fulfill his dream. He arrived in Jerusalem with a royal guard, presented his documents to the leaders, and assessed the work to be done.

The second temple was completed in 516 B.C., and Ezra had ministered in and around Jerusalem since 458 B.C., but the city wall and many houses remained in ruins till Nehemiah's arrival in 445 B.C. He convinced the people of their God-given obligation to bring the city back to life again. Various family groups started to work on various parts of the city wall—even those with no building experience got their hands dirty.

Their adversaries immediately started to discourage them with insults, ridicules, accusations, threats, and conspiracies. Nehemiah did not allow any one of these to succeed. As a man of prayer, he took these problems to God and returned to the workers with renewed vigor. He complemented his prayers with commonsense measures to prevent any intervention by their enemies. He fortified the weakest spots in the wall first; he posted guards day and night; he let the builders work with their weapons close at hand. In only 52 days the wall was restored to a point where it offered real protection again.

However, a city does not consist of bricks, stones, and mortar only. The people of the city had to be restored as well. Nehemiah addressed the poverty problem by convincing the rich to adopt a more lenient policy toward the poor, as commanded by God through Moses. That gave a boost to the economy and won the support of the poor to make Jerusalem livable again. By casting lots, some people were chosen to take up residence in Jerusalem.

Nehemiah had reached his first goal to restore the city physically, socially, and economically. In spite of the rebuilt temple and resumed sacrifices, there was still something important missing—a spirit of true devotion to God, who gave them back their life after they had almost been obliterated. The second part of Nehemiah's book deals with this spiritual revival.

A prayer: Father, please set the stage for a revival in our country.
A thought: What infrastructure is needed to sustain a living church?

284. Spiritual Renewal
God uses Ezra to revive the restored city.

October 10

~ ~ ~

Neh. 8 - 13

It all began with the reading of God's Word. This was initiated by the people, not by the priests. It could have resulted from Malachi's ministry. The priests and Levites recognized the opportunity and responded with a system that brought the Hebrew Torah to life for the Aramaic speaking audience. They not only translated the Torah as it was being read by Ezra, but they also explained it to the people.

The result was overwhelming. The congregation burst into tears of guilt when they realized how far they had fallen short of God's commands. Ezra and Nehemiah realized that this remorse was actually a good sign, the starting point of a genuine return and devotion to God. They encouraged the people not to mourn but to rejoice in the fact that God's Spirit was working in them. So the people feasted and provided for the poor so that they too could share in the praising of God from whom all blessings flow.

When the Feast of Tabernacles ended the people met in repentance. The Levites recited to them a summary of Israel's history. They underlined Israel's propensity to sin from the time of the patriarchs to their own time, and they highlighted God's patience with them and His mercy to forgive when they had repented. The people identified themselves with the recital and expressed their sorrow for sins of past and present. God's Word reached its goal. Therefore, the recital ended by renewing the Sinai covenant with God. They pledged to do their duty in obeying the Law and providing for the priests and Levites to keep up the continuous worship of Yahveh.

After this spiritual revival, Nehemiah knew the time was ripe to celebrate the restoration of Jerusalem. The physical wall and temple of Jerusalem were worthy symbols of the people's spiritual protection by the God who had carried them through many misfortunes that they had brought onto themselves.

At this point Nehemiah returned to Persia to report to the king. When he returned to Jerusalem, probably a few years later, he had to put a few things in order again. It shows that revival is not self-sustaining; it has to be empowered continuously by God Himself. In A.D. 70 the city and the temple were destroyed and the Jews scattered again. Nineteen centuries later the state of Israel was reborn and the Jews returned to rebuild once more. Unfortunately, this material restoration of Israel has not yet been transformed into a spiritual revival.

Yahveh is still yearning for the salvation of Israel.

A prayer: How great is Your faithfulness. Your mercies endure forever.
A thought: How can I keep up continuous spiritual renewal?

285. The Good, Bad, and Ugly
When the bad seems to overcome the good

What happened to the Jews who decided to stay in foreign countries? The book Esther gives us a peek into their circumstances. Like the Jews in Judah, they had to cope with adversaries too. Although God is not mentioned by name in Esther, the story is told in such a way that one realizes that the Jews were persecuted mainly for their faith and that only their faith in God could save them.

October 11
~ ~ ~
Esther 1 - 4

King Ahasuerus (also known as Xerxes) of Persia celebrated his success and glory for six months with his officials, probably one group after the other. At the end of these state banquets, the drunken king ordered his beautiful queen, Vashti, to show her beauty to his guests. When the good queen refused to obey the bad king, he deposed her right away.

The king was then advised to have a beauty contest and to choose a new queen from the prettiest girls in his empire. In this way a good and beautiful orphaned Jewish girl named Esther became queen of Persia. However, her fortune was short-lived, as a man with an ugly attitude, Haman, got it into his wicked head to annihilate the Jews with the bad king's permission.

The reason for Haman's hatred was that the good Mordecai, Esther's cousin who brought her up, did not show Haman due respect. However, this same Mordecai who was number one on Haman's hit list also had won the king's favor by alerting the king to a conspiracy to kill the king.

Here we sense a strong presence of the intervening Almighty. Haman thought he could have his way with the Jews, but he did not know the God of the Jews. Though unnamed and unseen, He was controlling the situation.

Mordecai put on sackcloth and loudly bewailed the threat against the Jews on the town square at the palace gate. Esther heard about Mordecai's behavior and the reason for it. She negotiated with him through a palace servant. She told him that she could not plead with the king because no one could go to the king uninvited. Mordecai then reminded her that she was a Jew too, and she would not escape death. He persuaded her with these famous words, *"Who knows whether you have come to the kingdom for such a time as this."*

Esther decided to place her life on the line for her people and for Mordecai. She asked him to fast with her and with other Jews for three days, and then she would present herself to the king, come what may. Fasting and praying were connected in Jewish thinking. They probably did both.

A prayer: God, You are not neutral in the battle between good and evil.
A thought: I am at this place at this moment for a divine purpose.

286. The Big Surprise
Evil is exposed and destroyed.

October 12
~ ~ ~
Esther 5 - 10

In the first part of the book Esther, the survival of the good people hangs as it were on a spider's thread. The bad guys had everything in their favor, except for the One who is not mentioned in the book. It was as if Esther and Mordecai were going through the lion's den and the fiery furnace, as Daniel and his friends had.

When Esther showed up uninvited at the king's throne room, his officials froze in uncertain anticipation of what would happen next. Then the king smiled and called his lovely bride to him. He urged her to ask anything from him, but she modestly only invited him to a dinner, requesting that Haman would join them. The king graciously accepted. The first round had been won, but how would she convince the king that one of his chief officials was a callous killer?

At the banquet everything went smoothly, except that Esther felt the time was not yet ripe to expose Haman. Again an unforeseen twist in the story occurred—something that could not be ascribed to Esther's or Mordecai's ingenuity, only to the merciful intervention of the unnamed One.

The king discovered that Mordecai had not been rewarded for his favor to the king. Haman entered and the king asked his advice on how he could show his gratitude to a worthy citizen. Thinking that he was the lucky man, Haman suggested the kind of treatment that his vain ego would enjoy. When he was ordered to bestow that honor on his hated enemy he obeyed grudgingly and then rushed home to seek solace with his shocked advisors.

Haman's first downfall was swiftly followed by the second. At her second banquet for the king and Haman, Esther revealed the evil plot of Haman against her people and herself. Realizing that Haman had tricked him into this vile conspiracy, the king ordered Haman to be hung from the gallows Haman had erected for Mordecai's demise.

The king authorized Esther and Mordecai to use any legal means to prevent the planned massacre of the Jews. The Jews got the right to defend themselves, and thus they were vindicated.

The Purim feast was instituted to celebrate their survival and the saving self-sacrifice of Esther. Though a joyful feast, it is celebrated against the dark backdrop of many efforts in history to wipe Israel out. The Old Testament ends on the hopeful note of a coming Savior who would triumph over sin and evil and thereby save God's people, Jew and Gentile (Mal. 1:11, 4:2).

A prayer: O God, You secure the survival of all Your people.
A thought: Do I stand up for God's plan of salvation?

287. Revelation versus Philosophy
The book Job shows the limitations of human wisdom.

The apostle Paul quotes Isaiah, who said that God would destroy human wisdom (Is. 29:14). Paul then adds that God's plan of salvation is foolish to unconverted people because they lack the insight given by the Holy Spirit (1 Cor. 1:18-25, 2:13-14).

<table>
<tr><td>October 13
~ ~ ~
Job 1-2, 40-42</td></tr>
</table>

The book Job shows the inability of the human mind to comprehend God's ways. Job and his long-winded friends debated at length the question whether personal suffering is linked to personal sin. In the end, this question was irrelevant. Job found peace in God's love, not in human wisdom. God said twice to Job's friends, *"You have not spoken of Me what is right"* (42:7, 8).

These words may also be applicable to chapters 1 and 2 where a fable-like description is given of how God allowed Satan to test Job's faith. The omniscient God knew the state of Job's faith—He surely didn't need an experiment of the devil to determine that. This imaginary contest between God and Satan was also irrelevant because the author didn't bring it back on stage.

These opening chapters of Job are part of the inadequate human effort to explain suffering. No satisfactory answer has yet been found to the question why bad things happen to good people. The fact that it is part of the broken reality after the fall into sin is true in general, but it does not comfort or enlighten any specific sufferer in her/his concrete situation.

Just as the first ten chapters of Ecclesiastes show the cynical conclusions of Solomon in his fruitless search for meaning, so the book of Job is loaded with half-truths coming from people searching for meaning with their limited minds. One should always be cautious in quoting from Job or Ecclesiastes. In these books, God shows us how we should NOT seek Him.

Occasionally God's light broke through the dark clouds over Job's head, *"For I know that my Redeemer lives, and He shall stand at last on earth; after my skin is destroyed, this I know, that in my flesh I shall see God"* (19:25-26). Though Job could not understand his suffering, he kept clinging to God: *"The LORD gave, and the LORD has taken away; blessed be the name of the LORD"* (1:21).

The book of Job ends with the restored relationship between Job and God. Not Job, but God, made that happen. He helped Job to rediscover the Creator in creation. Job's real blessing was not material, but spiritual—his hand in God's hand again. Job fought the good fight and kept the faith.

A prayer: Father, when I suffer I need not fear, for You are with me. (Ps. 23)
A thought: Do I discern between divine revelation and human ideas about God?

288. The Riverside Tree
It is green and fruitful.

<table><tr><td>October 14
~ ~ ~
Psalm 1</td></tr></table>

The book of Psalms starts off with the difference between God's children and the world. In the Psalms the spiritual war between good and evil is played out in songs of praise and lament, in blessings and curses, in triumphs and trials, and in the contrast between believers and unbelievers. The first psalm sets the tone for the big divide.

The psalmist warns against the encroachment of evil on the soul. First one starts to *walk* in the wrong direction, following wrong advice. Then one begins to stop and *stand* at wrong spots, on the way of the wicked. Eventually one begins to *sit* in the wrong company, the circle of the scorners. This downward slide starts passively by listening to wrong council; it ends by actively taking part in ungodly activities.

Those who yearn for God's blessings avoid these slippery slopes by anchoring themselves to the Word of God. Like a rock climber, they hammer their pegs into this rock, hang on to the rope of salvation, and slowly but surely make their way upward. They find delight and fulfillment in reading, studying, and meditating on God's Word. It's far more than a swift, superficial scanning of a few verses to sooth the conscience. It consists of adequate, restful quality time with the one true God, Yahveh, who revealed Himself in the Bible as our Father, Savior, and Comforter.

Avoiding the wrong and doing the right has many rewards. The people who drink from God's Word daily are like trees on riverbanks. They drink from the refreshing stream and feed from the fertile soil. This continuous intake produces a continuous output: green leaves and delicious fruit (see Ezek. 47:12, John 7:38, Rev. 22:2). Each leaf is a little factory that turns sunlight, moisture, and nutrients into food for the tree and for others. God blesses the efforts of the person who daily feeds from His Word.

In contrast to this productivity of the believer who is anchored in God's Word, the unbeliever is like chaff scattered by the wind. Chaff is dead and barren plant material; it will not make roots and produce grain. Eventually it will decompose and disappear: *"For the LORD knows the way of the righteous, but the way of the ungodly shall perish."*

The book of Psalms also addresses the riddle of the wicked's prosperity and the believer's trials, but Psalm 1 puts the record straight for the long term.

A prayer: LORD, I want to be a tree at Your stream.
A thought: Do I drink from this stream as much as I can?

289. False Freedom
Let us throw off the rules!

The rulers of the world and the nations of the earth can't agree on much, but there is one thing on which they are unanimous—their dislike for the laws of God. They think that by joining forces they can outvote God, throw off His chains, follow their own desires, and thus create their own heaven on earth. Ordinary people have more or less the

October 15

~~~

Psalm 2, 110

</div>

same idea, like the prodigal son (Luke 15), to get away from the Father and to have fun on their own—without God's spoilsport restrictions.

The Bible gives us the long and sad story of humanity's persistent effort to live by their own rules on God's planet. Ignoring God's rules led to destruction over and over again for both Jews and Gentiles. Since Israel had been freed from slavery in Egypt, they relapsed into idolatry repeatedly only to taste the bitter fruits time and again, and eventually they lost their country. The great empires of this world came and went, devoured by their own greed.

Yahveh responds to man's love for false freedom with laughter and anger: laughter at the stupidity, anger at the audacity. Yet in His mercy, God's first deed is not judgment but mediation. He anointed His Son as the Messiah, the only one that can bring peace between the holy God and sinful humanity. Christ's first coming was in humility as the eternal High Priest (in the order of Melchizedek) who gave Himself as a sacrifice on the Cross to pay for the sins of all who would accept Him as their Lord and Savior. His Father promised Him many saved sinners—He would give nations for His inheritance and the ends of the earth for His possession.

Christ's second coming will be in glory to gather His own to His eternal kingdom and to judge those who rejected His offer and persisted in rebellion against God. Then all His enemies will be subjected (being His footstool) and shattered to pieces (like pottery).

In view of the accomplished salvation and the coming judgment, His enemies are warned to rethink their position. It does not make sense to be on the Messiah's wrong side—rather make peace with Him while there is still time: *"Kiss the Son, lest He be angry, and you perish in the way."* This warning comes especially to the rulers and judges, that is, the governments and the judiciary. Don't put up man-made rules above God-given commandments.

Unfortunately, that is what more and more governments and courts do: propagate laws that directly oppose God's Word. In North America they also violate the rule of democracy, namely that the majority makes the rules.

A prayer: O God, open the eyes of leaders to the quicksand they are facing.
A thought: I take my stand with Christ, come what may.

290. Glorifying the Creator
When I consider the work of Your fingers ...

<table>
<tr><td>

October 16

~ ~ ~

Psalm 8
19:1-6

</td></tr>
</table>

As a shepherd-boy, David kept watch over his flock at night—just as the shepherds of Bethlehem did when Jesus was born ten centuries later. When he looked up to the glittering firmament, he marveled at the wisdom, power, and greatness of the One who had made it all. He saw the stars as part of the creation of the almighty and eternal God and not as "gods," as the pagans did.

David probably wrote Psalm 8 and 19 later in his life. He watched the same stars from the flat roof of his palace in Jerusalem, only a few miles from Bethlehem. The stars looked the same, but he was not the same. He knew that within a few decades he would be gone, but God and the stars would still be there as they had been for many ages before him. He realized how great God and His creation were: *"The heavens declare the glory of God"* (19:1), *"LORD, our Lord, how excellent is Your name in all the earth"* (8:1).

The greatness of God and His works made David aware of how small he was: *"When I consider Your heavens, the work of Your fingers, the moon and the stars which You have ordained, what is man that You are mindful of him, and the son of man that You visit him?"* He was amazed that such a mighty Creator could have any interest in such a small creature as himself. Then it struck him how often God used small things like the voices of children to glorify Himself. Jesus referred to these words when children sang praises to Him in the temple (Matt. 21:16).

The second thing that surprised David was that God appointed such small creatures to rule over God's creation. In spite of man's insignificance, God appointed him a glorious place just below the angels. The fact that this privilege is totally undeserved is part of David's thoughts. That such a small creature can be honored so highly is not based on merit but on pure grace.

David not only marveled at man's position of power but also at his capability to gather knowledge. As the days, years, and centuries rolled by, man could discover more and more of the knowledge embedded in God's creation (19:2-4). God had put that knowledge into His creation and has been watching with a smile how man discovers these treasures one by one. It must have delighted God tremendously when man first discovered how to write, to make a wheel, to sail around the earth, and to turn sand into a microchip.

However, man could not plan and execute his own salvation from sin. Man's reconciliation with God was given and revealed by God Himself.

A prayer: LORD, our Lord, how excellent is Your name in all the earth!
A thought: I am humbled that God expects so much of me.

291. If The Foundations Are Destroyed
What can the righteous do?

When an animal's life is endangered, it resorts to either flight or fight. David showed us that human beings have a third option: to trust God and to receive help from Him.

> October 17
> ~ ~ ~
> Ps. 11
> 55:5-10

In his lifetime, David had to outmaneuver foes like Saul, Abner, Absalom, Sheba, and Adonijah. When David cried out in his psalms for God's help against enemies, he was thinking of his personal enemies inside Israel, not of the international enemies outside Israel. Paul also found that the worst persecution came from his own people (2 Cor. 11:22-33). These people waited in the "dark" to ambush believers; they had the arrow ready on the bowstring. They concealed their intentions and struck unexpectedly.

Sometimes David resisted the advice from friends to flee to a safe place: *"In the LORD I put my trust; how can you say to my soul, 'Flee as a bird to your mountain'?"* Nehemiah also took up this position when people advised him to take shelter in the temple (Neh. 6:10-12). These friends focused on the danger, not on God. They saw only the ambushes, the weapons in the dark, and they sighed helplessly, *"If the foundations are destroyed, what can the righteous do?"*

For David, this fatalistic question became a war cry: Indeed, when the foundations of the nation are threatened, what should the believer do? He and she should take refuge in God, make themselves strong in Him, and launch a counterstrike from the position of faith. He emphasized that Yahveh is in control, that He sees everything, and that He will protect the believer.

However, David also knew those days when he felt so overwhelmed by acute or chronic adversity that he wished he had the wings of a dove to fly away to the far off desert and to hide there in a safe place until the storm had passed (Ps. 55:6-8). From the days he had fled from Saul, David knew that sometimes fleeing was better than fighting. He fled from Absalom too and redeployed in a forested and hilly region where his small army had a better chance.

One can flee and try to avoid confrontation to a certain point, but there comes a time when one has to take one's stand and face the enemy for the better or the worse. Joab and Abishai entered the battle with that attitude and prevailed (1 Chron. 19:10-14). Jesus said that when we confess Him before men, then He will also confess us before His Father in heaven (Matt. 10:32).

Many foundations are threatened today. What should believers do? Be part of the silent majority or stand up for what is right?

A prayer: Father, make me brave and wise to stand up for You.
A thought: Am I a hidden enemy, a hidden refugee, or a soldier in God's army?

292. Are Atheists Fools?
The fool says, "There is no God."

<table>
<tr><td>

October 18

~ ~ ~

Ps. 14, 53
Romans 3

</td><td>

David did not waste words on atheists. In his mind, they are fools. God was so real to David all his life that to deny that divine presence would just be utterly foolish to him. God's existence was evident to David in the sun, moon, and stars (the macro-cosmos) and also in the way God provided in all his needs as a tiny human being (the micro-cosmos).

</td></tr>
</table>

It is meaningful that this psalm is not only repeated in the book of psalms, but that both Jesus and Paul referred to it. Jesus said to the rich young ruler, *"No one is good—except God alone"* (Mark 10:18, NIV), the central thought of this psalm. Paul quoted Psalm 14 and other passages to show that all people, Jews and Gentiles, are lost sinners who can only be saved by accepting in faith the salvation earned for them by Christ (Romans 3).

David depicts Yahveh in a humanlike way—bending over to see more closely if He could find one person on earth who is completely blameless. However, through all the ages He could not find one. It is stressed: not even one. Yes, not even Enoch, Noah, Abraham, Moses, David, the prophets, or the apostles qualified. Therefore, God sent His Son to walk this earth as a human being to fulfill for us what we could not do, that is: to live a perfect life for God. Of Him, the Father testified in a loud voice more than once, *"This is My beloved Son in whom I am well pleased!"* (Matt. 3:17, 17:5).

Thanks to the salvation God offers as a gift through His Son, there now are righteous people (verse 5)—those who were made right with God by grace. Through the gratitude worked in them by the Holy Spirit they no longer indulge in the works of the flesh (verse 4-6: sins against God and neighbor), but delight in studying and obeying God's Word. Because they are on God's side, He is on their side (James 4:8).

David's prayer that salvation might come out of Zion was fulfilled in Christ. He spoke wonderful words in and around Jerusalem. He worked miracles there and cleansed the temple. He paid the sin-debt of sinners on Calvary just outside Jerusalem. There He rose from the dead, appeared to His followers, and ascended into heaven. And in Jerusalem His Spirit was poured out on His followers, thus creating the early Christian church.

The psalm that starts negatively with the words and deeds of unbelievers ends with the righteousness and the joy of believers.

A prayer: Thank You, Jesus, for opening the way to the Father.
A thought: I will delight myself in this restored relationship.

293. True Worshipers
Their attitudes, words and deeds please God.

While Psalm 14 describes the lifestyle of the ungodly, Psalm 15 focuses on the conduct of the righteous. The question on who is qualified to enter the sanctuary probably referred (in David's time) to either the Tabernacle in Gibeon or the tent for the ark in Jerusalem. However, this psalm is primarily about not the *where* but the *how* of true worship.

October 19

~ ~ ~

Ps. 15, 24:3-6
Luke 18:9-14

When the Samaritan woman was concerned about the right place for worship, Jesus told her that it was not important where one worships but how: *"Yet a time is coming and has now come when the true worshipers will worship the Father in spirit and truth, for they are the kind of worshipers the Father seeks"* (John 4:23, NIV).

In this psalm, the *how* of worship is not determined by external things like sacrifices or posturing, things on which the Pharisee focused (Luke 18), but on internal values and attitudes that determine external choices and behaviors. Verse 2 traces the life of the true worshiper back from "walk" and "work" to "words" and "heart." The heart determines the quality of one's life (Mark 7:20-23, Luke 6:45). These attitudes and deeds are characterized by not harming anyone but doing good things to others in word and deed.

David specified three good deeds: no interest on loans (to the poor), no bribes to undermine justice, no broken oaths and promises—keeping your word even when it hurts you. Such a person practices charity and integrity. The LORD loves such worshipers; they are welcome in His presence.

Does this Old Testament perspective on good works disagree with the New Testament view of salvation through grace alone? In all Paul's letters, he shows his readers the practical implications for their lives when they have been saved by grace alone. James 2:17 states clearly that faith without works is dead. Loving deeds show that our faith is genuine (1 John 3:14-18). Paul concludes his great chapter on love (1 Cor. 13) with these words, *"And now abide faith, hope, love, these three; but the greatest of these is love."* Love and faith are two sides of the same coin. God yearns for quality time with us.

If you wait till you're perfect, you will never come to God. It's not a matter of perfection but of true intention. The prodigal son returned just as he was and was forgiven (Luke 15). If you want to come clean with God, you're welcome. But if you willfully proceed with the wrong and try to worship God at the same time, He will not accept you (Jer. 7:9-11).

A prayer: O Lord, cleanse me and change me.
A thought: I cannot serve both God and Satan.

294. Our Glorious Inheritance
Resurrection and eternal glory foretold.

<table>
<tr><td>
October 20
~ ~ ~
Psalm 16
Acts 2:25-33
</td></tr>
</table>

In a limited sense, Psalm 16 is true of David and of true believers, but in absolute sense, this psalm is true of Christ. The former is dependent on the latter: Because of Christ's victory, we can be victorious.

As Jesus committed Himself to His Father, so believers should commit themselves to God, their **refuge** against evil and danger. The Father was the **highest good** for Jesus, and Christians should follow in His footsteps, not only in theory but also in practice. In spite of the imperfection of the "**saints**," they are precious to Christ, who bought them with His own blood. Because we are precious to Christ, we should treat each other with respect and courtesy and not with contempt and animosity.

Christ knew that He was the way, the truth, and the life, and that no one could come to the Father except through Him (John 14:6). He knew that those who rejected the only way of salvation would remain under God's wrath (John 3:18, 36). *"Their sorrows shall be multiplied who hasten after another god."* The names of and offerings to idols have to be avoided because there is only one Name by which we are saved (Acts 4:9-12), and only His blood is sufficient to pay for our sins (Heb. 9:12, 1 John 1:7).

The LORD is the inheritance of Jesus and of believers, an inheritance that surpasses all other blessings. In Psalm 2 the Father promised to give nations as inheritance to His Son—millions of saved sinners who will praise God forever. We too must put our priorities in order and appreciate our true inheritance, our salvation. God's daily guidance and counsel is part of that.

God's salvation includes spirit and body. The Father did not allow His Son's body to experience decay (Acts 2:25-33, 13:33-37) but resurrected His body into a new kind of body. So He will resurrect our bodies from the dead to be equal to Christ's body (Phil. 3:20-21, John 5:28-29). That will be followed by the joy of eternal life: *"You will show me the path of life; in Your presence is fullness of joy; at Your right hand are pleasures forevermore."*

Indeed, the measuring lines have fallen for us in beautiful places, and our inheritance surpasses anything that we could have imagined: *"Eye has not seen, nor ear heard, nor entered into the heart of man the things which God has prepared for those who love Him"* (1 Cor. 2:9). It is not only something for the far off future; we can begin to experience the joy of salvation already in this life. Real joy starts with real gratitude for real blessings.

A prayer: Fill me with the joy of salvation.
A thought: Do I realize from what and to what I have been saved?

295. Nature and Scripture
God's general and special revelation

When we look at a painting, listen to music, read a book, or stare at a construction, we get an idea about the mind of the person who created the product. When we observe the colors of a sunset, the vastness of an ocean, the splendor of a mountain, the odors, sounds and atmosphere of a rain forest, the diverse beauty of fauna and flora, and the uniqueness of individuals, we get an idea of the power, intellect, and caring love of the One who made and sustains it all.

> October 21
> ~ ~ ~
> Psalm 19

Paul said that certain attributes of God could be seen in His creation from the beginning; therefore no one can excuse him- or herself that they did not have enough knowledge of God to do His will (Rom. 1:19-20). In Psalm 19, David also points to this knowledge of God's general revelation, a knowledge that is passed on from one generation to the next.

However, specific knowledge about man's sinfulness and about God's plan of salvation cannot be learned from nature but only from Scripture. The Bible is God's special revelation. In His Word, God spelled out His will, as well as the consequences of obedience or disobedience to His will. In David's time, God's written Word was not yet completed, but the part David did have impressed him so much that he praised it in poetry and music.

He stacked the synonyms, adjectives, and benefits of Yahveh's Word one upon the other. For David, the Word is perfect in what it is and does—it is the Word of God, and it converts the soul. It is sure and trustworthy, giving wisdom to all, even to those of limited understanding. The Word is always right and true; it works, and therefore practicing it will make people happy and joyful. The Word is radiantly pure like springwater—it cleanses the eyes and mind to see properly. The Word instigates in us holy respect for God and keeps us on the right path. It gives us a healthy sense of right and wrong.

Because of its wholesome effect, God's written and incarnated Word is more precious than gold and more delicious than honey. It shows us the right way and warns us against the wrong way. If we follow its directions, we will be richly rewarded. When David thought about the alternative, he became extremely worried about his sins. He pleaded for God's forgiveness for his unknown sins and for God's protection against deliberate sins. Then his inner attitudes and thoughts, as well as his expressed words and deeds, would be acceptable to God, who knows the heart and sees the act.

A prayer: O God, purify my heart, mouth, and actions to Your glory.
A thought: I will feed my soul regularly from nature and Scripture.

296. The Crucifixion Foretold
They pierced My hands and My feet.

October 22

~~~

Psalm 22:1-20

While David tried to describe in poetical terms the severity of his own tribulation, the Holy Spirit inspired him to give, perhaps unknowingly, a vivid description of the suffering and death of the Messiah, the Son of David, ten centuries later.

Glimpses of the Messiah have already surfaced in several psalms. He is the Son of God (Ps. 2:7, Matt. 3:17), He is ruler of all (Ps. 2:8-9, Ps. 110:1-2, Heb. 2:8, Phil. 2:9-11), He is praised by children (Ps. 8:2, Matt. 21:15-16), and He is risen from the dead (Ps. 16:10, Matt. 28:7). Psalm 22 depicts the details of the crucifixion and its fruits precisely. One can't deny the similarity.

Maybe Christ recited the whole psalm by Himself during the hours of darkness, saying only the opening verse aloud, *"My God, My God, why have You forsaken Me?"* Because He took our sins onto Himself, He suffered hell in our place on the cross, that is: He was completely forsaken by God so that we could be reconciled with God and never forsaken by Him. Jesus cried out at night in Gethsemane and by day on Calvary and was not saved because He was saving us. He was the lamb that died in Isaac's place (Gen. 22).

The lamentations in Psalm 22 are alternated with passages of faith and comfort. Verses 3-5 praise God as the Holy One who repeatedly saved Israel when they cried out to Him. This is followed by three verses describing another scene on Calvary: Jesus crushed like a worm by the scorn of the leaders who question His relationship with His Father. Then again follows two verses of comfort about the fact that God knew and cared for Jesus.

The focus shifts to another scene on Calvary: Jesus is deserted by all while his enemies, like fierce bulls and hungry lions, surround Him, ready to destroy Him. His physical suffering is described by seven references to death by crucifixion: His **power** is drained out of Him like water; His **joints** felt dislocated; His **heart** was failing; He suffered terrible **thirst**; He knew His body was **dying** and would be laid in the dust; His hands and feet were **pierced** by pegs that nailed Him to the cross; He suffered excruciating pain in every **bone** of His lacerated body that hung by its own wounds.

The focus shifts again to the social rejection: the staring, gloating crowd and the soldiers who callously divided His garments. The first part of the psalm ends with a prayer of faith to Yahveh, the only One who could put an end to this ordeal. Psalm 31:5 adds the final word: "Into Your hand I commit My spirit."

A prayer: I bow in awe in this scene, foretold so long ago.
A thought: Can the description of Calvary in Psalm 22 be a mere coincidence?

297. World Evangelism
All the nations shall worship God.

We may become so intrigued by the thirteen points of correspondence between Psalm 22 and the crucifixion of Christ that we overlook the fourteenth one, the outcome of this cosmic event. In verse 21, halfway in a cry for help, the tone suddenly changes to thanksgiving: *"Save me from the lion's mouth ... **You have answered me!"***

> October 23
> ~ ~ ~
> Psalm 22:21-31

On Calvary too, apparent defeat suddenly turned into clear victory. Before Jesus committed His spirit to His Father, He cried out with a loud voice, *"It is finished!"* (Luke 23:46, John 19:30). The phrase He used literally meant "the goal has been reached" or "the debt has been paid." His victory would become clear when He rose from the tomb as the conqueror of death.

The first people to whom this victory was proclaimed was Israel (22-24). The women and disciples who saw the risen Christ first were Jews. Most members of the early church were Jews. In his prophetic vision, David foresaw a great assembly praising God for His salvation and reaching out to the poor with their charity (Ps. 22:25-26, Acts 2:41-47). He saw all congregations together on Sundays, feeding people spiritually, emotionally, and physically.

The early church was amazed when the first Gentiles accepted Christ as their Savior and received the Holy Spirit as the Jews did (Acts 10-11). If they had remembered Psalm 22, they would have realized that Yahveh had foretold that centuries ago through David: *"All ends of the earth shall remember and turn to the LORD, and all the families of the nations shall worship before You. For the kingdom is the LORD's, and He rules over the nations"* (verse 27).

Long after David, the prophets would announce both God's judgment and salvation to the nations and confirm that the earth is the LORD's and everything in it (Ps. 24:1). Isaiah (49:6) said that the Messiah would be "a light to the Gentiles" and He would bring salvation "to the end of the earth." Jesus sent His apostles to "make disciples of all the nations" (Matt. 28:19) and to be witnesses for Him "to the end of the earth" (Acts 1:8). Before His return "the gospel must first be preached to all the nations" (Mark 13:10).

World evangelism is important because all "who go down to the dust," shall realize who Christ really is and will have to bow before Him (Ps. 22:29, Phil. 2:9-10). To ensure it will happen in joy, Christians have to tell the gospel to their children (Deut. 6:7) so that God's salvation shall roll forth from one generation to the next—to those who still have to be born (Ps. 22:30-31).

A prayer: LORD, *let Your kingdom come in and through me.*
A thought: I want to take part in the expansion of God's kingdom.

298. The LORD is my Shepherd
He makes me lie down in green pastures.

<table>
<tr><td>
October 24
~ ~ ~
Psalm 23
</td></tr>
</table>

Psalm 23 is renowned for its simplicity of words and depth of meaning. It should be read with John 10:1-18. The metaphor of sheep and shepherd comes from a farm setting, unfamiliar to city dwellers, but it is easy to visualize. It is an endearing assurance of Yahveh's loving care for those who trust Him.

David remembered how much he cared for his flock when he was a shepherd. The sheep had nothing to fear when they followed him. He brought them to green pastures and to refreshing water. Sheep's main business is to graze. So when they stopped grazing in a green field and lay down to doze off while ruminating, he knew for sure they were satisfied.

David realized that the LORD did the same for him: *"He makes me lie down in green pastures; He leads me beside the still waters."* It is a picture of safe, calm gratification and fulfillment. We too have to re-chew God's messages. God gives us spiritual nourishment to restore our souls and to empower us to walk on the "path of righteousness," doing God's will to God's glory.

This path reminded David of the dangers on the narrow way. Just as he sometimes had to lead his flock through deep gorges in the Judean wilderness where deadly predators might be lurking, so God's path sometimes takes us through difficult situations. But we need not fear—God will protect us just as the shepherd watches over his flock. God's rod and staff, His Word and Spirit, comfort us with the assurance of His mighty presence.

The idyllic scene of sheep and pasture now shifts to the royal scene of king and feast. David had been anointed by Samuel to be king of Israel by God's command. God had prepared a lavish banquet for David in spite of the plans of his enemies like Saul. His cup overflowed; he was showered with blessings. God's goodness and mercy were with him all his life and enabled him to be good and merciful toward others.

God's love for him and his love for God would inspire him to visit the "house" of God often and to feel at home there. God's house is like the sheep's pen (John 10). He was speaking of the tent in Jerusalem where the ark stood and of the temple he was planning. Because of the angel of death David had seen north of Jerusalem, he avoided the Tabernacle in Gibeon (1 Chron. 21:28-30). Eventually the angel of death took him to the eternal home of God the Father's house with many mansions, where all fear is shut out (John 14:1-3).

A prayer: LORD, You are my Shepherd; I will lack nothing.
A thought: I trust my Shepherd for food and safety.

299. The King of Glory
Open the gates and He will enter.

Psalm 24 starts off with the fact that the earth belongs to Yahveh. He is Lord of His creation. And yet, He does not force Himself onto humans but waits for them to invite Him in. Likewise, He expects of us to show the same courtesy when we enter His house and that we observe the rules for entering His sanctuary.

October 25
~ ~ ~
Psalm 24

He welcomes those who have received righteousness from Him through His salvation (verse 5). They know they are saved by God's grace, not by their own merit. They avoid false gods and false oaths. Their hearts (attitudes) and hands (actions) are clean (verse 4). They are the real people of God (verse 6).

How did this reconciliation happen? The King of Glory entered human lives in various ways. He entered the Garden of Eden in the evening breeze. He spoke directly to His servants: to Enoch, Noah, Abraham, Jacob, Moses, Joshua, the prophets, and to some of the kings. The King of Glory entered the world as a Baby in a manger, He entered many lives with His words and miracles, He entered Jerusalem on a donkey, He entered the tomb and overcame death, He entered to His disciples when the doors were locked, and He entered heaven with His own blood to atone for the sins of His children.

Having accomplished salvation in this way, He wants to enter the heart of every human being (John 3:16-17, 2 Pet. 3:9). He stands at the door of the heart and knocks: *"If anyone hears My voice and opens the door, I will come in to him and dine with him, and he with Me"* (Rev. 3:20). Maybe this is the most important gate that has to be opened to Him: *"Lift up your heads, O you gates! Lift up, you everlasting doors! And the King of glory shall come in."*

When the rhetorical question is asked: "Who is this King of glory?" David confirmed three times that this King is Yahveh, the LORD. He is three in one. Jesus said that the Father, the Son, and the Holy Spirit would dwell in believers (John 14:17, 23). Have you let Him in as Savior and as Lord of your life?

This King of Glory has been treated with contempt by individuals and by governments many times. Even in countries where the majority still associate themselves with the Christian faith, human rights and constitutions have been used to shut the King of Glory out from public places. If the King of Glory remains outside our communities and outside our hearts with detrimental effects to groups and individuals, then this King cannot be blamed for our loss. He has been pleading for ages that the gates be opened for Him to enter.

A prayer: LORD, please enter into our hearts, homes, and institutions.
A thought: I welcome the King of Glory with joy.

300. Teach Me Your Paths
Lead me in Your truth.

| October 26 |
| ~~~ |
| Psalm 25 |

This alphabetical psalm consists of three parts: pleas for protection, guidance, and forgiveness (verses 1-7); reminders of God's goodness (verses 8-14); and prayers in severe distress (verses 15-22). However, in all three parts, certain themes surface repeatedly: enemies, sins, and uncertainty.

The distress caused by these earthly problems made David cry out to God: *"To You, O LORD, I lift up my soul. O my God, I trust in You..."* The second sentence explains and accentuates the first one. To lift up my soul to the LORD means to go to Him in trusting prayer. The metaphor suggests that, by faith, David's soul soared up above his troubles like an eagle (Isaiah 40:31).

Because of his vicious enemies, his accusing sins, and his haunting uncertainties, David had an intense need for God's guidance. Psalm 25 has become a suitable and favorite song to sing in church before the reading and expounding of God's Word—teach me Your truth; lead me in Your paths.

Jesus told us where God's truth is to be found: *"Sanctify them by Your truth. Your Word is truth"* (John 17:17). By *Word* Jesus meant the written Word as well as the incarnated Word (John 1:1, 14:6). Jesus is the way, the truth, and the life; nobody comes to the Father except by Him. The Father, the Son, and the Holy Spirit (John 14:17) stand for truth, and the devil for deception (John 8:44).

Because the Bible tells us God's truth and exposes the devil's lies, it shows us the right way to go: *"Your word is a lamp to my feet and a light to my path"* (Ps. 119:105). God's Word is the proven compass for young and old along life's narrow way: *"How can a young man keep his way pure? By living according to Your word"* (Ps. 119:9 NIV).

In Psalm 25, David returns to these truths repeatedly. When sinners humble themselves before God, He teaches them His ways (verses 8-9). So also for the person who fears (respects) the LORD; He will show him which way to go so that his descendants will prosper (verse 12-13). The LORD reveals His secrets to those who respect Him and shows them the deeper meaning of His covenant with them (verse 14).

By holding on to the truth of God's Word, David's uncertainties vanished, his sins were forgiven, and his enemies were vanquished. One can only wonder why Christians so often neglect this proven recipe or wander from this proven path that has stood the test of time.

A prayer: Show me Your path and empower me to follow it.
A thought: How can I better absorb God's truth into my mind and heart?

301. Nonetheless
Persevering faith amid vicious attacks

Psalm 27 is famous for its notwithstanding clause. God's grace and Satan's attacks are lined up against each other like two armies. David saw the danger on the one side, the refuge on the other side, and took his stand in faith on God's side. He was confident of victory notwithstanding the wicked plans of the enemy.

> October 27
> ~ ~ ~
> Psalm 27

The opening lines of this psalm are often used as opening lines for a church service. They express the unwavering trust of the congregation: *"The LORD is my light and my salvation; whom shall I fear? The LORD is the strength of my life; of whom shall I be afraid?"* This profession of faith is also a fitting start for every day: "In spite of all the difficult things I have to tackle today, I will not hesitate in fear of failure; on the contrary, I know I will prevail because the LORD is with me. With Him, I'm on the winning side."

David used a war situation, which he knew well, to depict his predicament (verses 2-3). The charging enemies wished to tear him apart, but they stumbled and fell flat on their faces. Psalm 91:7 became true for him: *"A thousand may fall on your side, and ten thousand at your right hand; but it shall not come near you."* Those who are persecuted and ridiculed for standing up for the principles of God's kingdom should take heart from this psalm.

The focus then shifted to God's sanctuary (verses 4-6). David loved the "house of the LORD," that is, the Tabernacle in Nob (in his youth) and the tent for the ark in Jerusalem (after he became king). He felt at home in God's house. He wanted to enjoy the LORD Himself and to study His Word. David did not ask things from God; he wanted fellowship with God. In God's presence, he felt safe against his spiritual enemies. And when God gave him victory over his enemies, he brought sacrifices of thanksgiving into God's house.

David also knew those times when his faith was weak (verses 7-10). In anguish he prayed that God would neither hide His face nor forsake him. When it felt as if everybody had abandoned him, even his parents, then he had all the more need of God's assuring presence and support.

After David had asked for guidance and protection, he expressed his faith in an uncompleted sentence: "If I had not believed that I would see the goodness of the LORD... (I would have perished)." Therefore, his firm resolution was to wait on the LORD, Yahveh, the only true God. He will not always provide immediately, but He will never forsake His child.

A prayer: LORD, You are my light and my refuge; I will not be afraid.
A thought: In God I trust; with Him I will prevail.

302. Sudden Relief
Tears last night; this morning, laughter!

<table>
<tr><td>October 28
~ ~ ~
Psalms 30, 31</td><td>Because David voiced the suffering and joy of mankind people can easily relate to his psalms. Who does not know the pain of misunderstanding, rejection, animosity, and false accusations? Who has not felt in their body the torture of</td></tr>
</table>

disease and weakness? Who has not struggled with a low mood and an anxious heart? Whose faith has not swung from the depth of despair to the peaks of triumph?

Apparently Psalm 30 was penned after a severe illness. David tells how God healed him (verse 2) after he came very close to death (verses 2-3, 8-10). There came a sudden turn in the course of the illness: "Last night there were tears; this morning there is laughter" (verse 5). God turned the grieving mood of those around him into jubilant dancing and exchanged their sackcloth for feasting garments (verse 11). David confessed that while he was prosperous, he overestimated himself, but after he had gone through the valley of death, he was more modest about his own strength and faith (verse 6-7).

Reading through Psalm 31 makes one soon realize that the sorrows of the Messiah are mixed with ours when we suddenly stumble over the words, *"Into Your hand I commit My spirit; You have redeemed me, O LORD God of truth"* (verse 5). When Christ had redeemed us by His suffering on the cross, He proclaimed that His mission was finished, and then He committed His Spirit to His Father.

Christ took our social, emotional, and physical pain onto Himself (verses 9-13). We can rest assured that just as the times of the Messiah were in God's hand, so too are our times in His hand (verse 15). In caring love, He determines what comes over us, also where, when, and how. Within those parameters there is enough room for personal freedom of choice, but He uses all of that in His great plan for our lives. We can rejoice with David, *"Oh, how great is Your goodness, which You have laid up for those who fear You, which You have prepared for those who trust in You"* (verse 19, compare Eph. 2:10).

Looking at God's goodness that covers His children against adversity as a tent shields against rain, David urged believers to love the LORD—not a vague general idea of God, but the one true God who revealed Himself in the Bible as Yahveh, the LORD. When one studies the gods of other religions, one finds a discouraging absence of two characteristics: personal and compassionate. The LORD excels in both. He is our caring Father, Savior, and Comforter.

A prayer: LORD, I delight in Your personal, loving care.
A thought: How can I live out my gratitude for the mercies of the LORD?

303. Confession and Forgiveness
Sharing of inner pain brings relief.

Long before modern psychology, the Bible advocated speaking out as relief for emotional pain. When Adam and Eve hid in shame after they had fallen into sin, God urged them to come forward and tell Him about it. Their confession of their sin, albeit with some finger pointing, led to redemption by blood and clothing with skins. Many

October 29
~ ~ ~
Psalm 32

others after them had to learn that God heals by opening and disinfecting wounds and not by ignoring or hiding them.

In Psalm 32 David tells how he suffered while he bottled up his feelings: *"When I kept silent, my bones grew old."* He received forgiveness and healing when he confessed his sins to God, *"I have acknowledged my sin to You ... and You forgave the iniquity of my sin."* Against this background, the first two verses make sense. Blessed is the person whose sins are covered by forgiveness AFTER they have been confessed. From his own experience, David knew how his spiritual life deteriorated while he covered up his sin regarding Bathsheba and Uriah. When God used the prophet Nathan to open his eyes, he confessed and received forgiveness and healing (Lessons 176 - 178).

Solomon recorded this life lesson he had learned from his dad: *"He who covers his sins will not prosper, but whoever confesses and forsakes them will have mercy"* (Prov. 28:13). Isaiah (59:1-2) tells us why covering up sin does not pay—it brings about a wall of separation between the believer and God: *"Behold, the LORD's hand is not shortened, that He cannot save; nor His ear heavy, that it cannot hear. But your iniquities have separated you from your God; and your sins have hidden His face from you, so that He will not hear."* Therefore, God called His people to repentance through Isaiah (1:18), *"Come now and let us reason together" says the LORD, "though your sins are like scarlet, they shall be as white as snow; though they are red like crimson, they shall be as wool."*

The apostle John echoed this truth in the New Testament when he said, *"If we confess our sins, He is faithful and just to forgive us our sins and to cleanse us of all unrighteousness"* (1 John 1:9). James applied this principle also to wrong-doing between Christians. He encouraged them to confess those wrongs to each other so that they could be healed (James 5:16).

Jesus included both sins against God and against fellow human beings in the prayer He taught His disciples: *"Forgive us our sins for we also forgive everyone who sins against us"* (Luke 11:4 NIV).

A prayer: LORD, help me to ask and grant forgiveness from the heart.
A thought: Which sins do I try to deny, ignore, or minimize?

304. Taste and See
that the LORD is good.

October 30
~ ~ ~
Psalms 33, 34

In Psalm 33, David calls up the faithful to praise Yahveh joyfully with voice and music for His excellence in creation and in history. By His almighty Word (John 1:1-3), God created stars, earth, and sea: *"For He spoke, and it was done; He commanded, and it stood fast."*

While the plans of nations and their leaders often come to nothing, the counsel of the LORD prevails. Therefore, the nation whose God is the LORD is blessed by His presence, guidance, and provision. He sees what people do, He knows what they think, and He determines what they will accomplish and what they will not succeed with.

Neither the number of soldiers, nor the bravery of heroes, nor the power of horses determines the course of history, but the decision of the Almighty. He is behind the miraculous survival of some, be it in war or natural catastrophe. Therefore, believers trust in this God to shield them in the most difficult circumstances, and they praise Him with joy and thanksgiving.

Psalm 34 proceeds in the same vein. David thanks God for His provision and protection and concludes, *"The angel of the LORD encamps all around those who fear Him, and delivers them."* The prophet Elisha would have the same experience many years later. When the Syrian army surrounded his town to capture Elisha, he assured his fearful servant that *"those who are with us are more than those who are with them"* (2 Kings 6:16). Then God opened the servant's eyes and he saw God's fiery horses and chariots all around them.

From his own experience, David was fully convinced of God's caring love. He urged others to try it out for themselves, *"Oh, taste and see that the LORD is good; blessed is the man who trusts in Him."* As he does in Psalm 23, David emphasized that those who trust in the LORD (as their Shepherd) will lack nothing. David did not overlook the tough times believers have to go through. Many of his psalms tell about his tribulations, the valleys of death, but in those circumstances the LORD did not let him down.

In verses 17 to 20, David refers to the troubles of the righteous, to his broken and contrite heart amid many afflictions. However, the LORD delivers him out of them all. It would also become true of the Messiah. Not one of His bones would be broken (John 19:32-36). Daniel and his friends would experience that during their exile in Babylon too. God did not keep them out of the furnace and lion's den, but He protected them IN those tribulations.

A prayer: LORD, help me to trust You completely in all circumstances.
A thought: Do I accept God for who He is?

305. Delight Yourself in the LORD
and He shall give you the desires of your heart.

David was already old when he wrote this psalm (verse 25). Unlike most of his other psalms, it is not a personal prayer or testimony but a message about the ways of the righteous and the wicked. It reflects the wisdom of a veteran. Asaph addresses the same problem in Psalm 73.

October 31
~~
Psalm 37

Right through the psalm the wicked's mean intentions, vile deeds, and tragic ends are contrasted with the trust, generosity, and victory of the righteous. Yet, in spite of the obvious disadvantages of the wicked's lifestyle, the righteous sometimes envy the wicked for their success. David starts his psalm with this strange incongruity and then presents the evidence to convince the righteous of the futility of envying the wicked.

In David's mind, "wicked" meant people who did not know, trust, and love the LORD. They plot wicked schemes against the righteous and the needy (verses 7, 12, 14, 32), thus showing their true selves in their attitudes and actions. In spite of their temporary prosperity, they are heading for disaster because God is against them (verses 2, 9, 10, 13, 15, 17, 20, 35, 36, 38).

The righteous know, trust, and love the LORD, and it shows in their attitudes, actions, and destiny. Their code of conduct is reflected in verses 3 to 6. They **trust** in the LORD, they are saved by grace through faith (Eph. 2:8). Out of gratitude they **do what is good**; they practice the Great Commandment through the power of the indwelling Holy Spirit. They dwell in the land **faithfully** while they enjoy God's faithfulness.

The righteous study God's Word to improve their understanding of God's will. They see God's will as the best option for them; therefore, they **delight** in God's will. They learn to desire what God desires. Because they have brought their will in line with His will, He gives them the **desires of their hearts**. They **commit** their future to God, trust in Him, and He helps them to **fulfill** their dreams. When they are attacked by the wicked, they **wait** patiently on the LORD; He provides the victory and they are **vindicated**. David does not advocate that the righteous take the law into their own hands.

The rest of the psalm refers to their hope (verse 9), meekness (verse 11), generosity (verse 21, 26), perseverance (23-24), morality (verse 27), wisdom (verse 30), and peacefulness (verse 37). In all circumstances, the LORD provides for those who trust Him (verses 6, 7, 9, 11, 17, 18, 24, 25, 28, 29, 34, 37, 39-40).

A prayer: LORD, I want to delight myself in Your Word and will.
A thought: I will learn verses 3-6 by heart and repeat them often.

306. Rescued from the Pit
His feet on a rock, a song in his mouth

~ ~ ~

Psalm 40

In Psalm 40, David first testifies about his personal salvation; then he prophesies about the Savior, decides how he will respond in gratitude for his salvation, and pleads that God will help him in his present difficulties.

David compares himself to someone who has been thrown into a muddy pit (Gen. 37:24, Jer. 38:6). He can't climb out and nobody answers his desperate cries for help. The mud and mire may symbolize his sins and problems. As his last spark of hope dies and leaves him to rot in dark hopelessness, Yahveh hears him, stoops down, and pulls him out of his misery. Instead of sinking into stinking mud in a dark pit, he now stands on firm rock in bright sunshine. His despair and lament are replaced by joy and praise (verses 4-5). He knows that many will hear of his rescue and come to respect and trust the LORD.

When David thinks about the best way to thank God for His rescue, he uses words that are not only true of himself, but also of the Messiah (verses 6-8). It is true of David that God did not desire animal sacrifices in the first place, but obedience to His commandments (see 1 Sam. 15:22). It is also true of Christ. Because the sacrifices were only symbols pointing to the coming Savior, the sacrifices themselves could not really pay for sin. God accepted them because they resembled the unique efficient sacrifice that His Son would bring.

Only the incarnated Son of God could truly say, *"I delight to do Your will, O my God, and Your law is within my heart."* He first lived a perfect life in our place, and then He paid our sin-debt in full by His suffering and death. His blood was the true sacrifice acceptable to God, and it forever replaced the symbols that foreshadowed this true sacrifice (Heb. 9:12).

Looking at salvation and at the Savior, David's response is to tell others about them (verses 9-10). He does not want to restrain his lips or to shut his heart. He wants to point others to the righteousness that God hands out as a free gift, testifying to His faithfulness and loving-kindness.

However, true believers are hated by the world (see John 15:18-25). After justification comes sanctification, and carrying one's cross (including the cross of persecution) is part of that. Therefore, David pleads for God's protection in his tribulations (verses 11-15). He believes that God will also provide a rescue out of these troubles, as He had saved him out of sin. Believers praise God not only for salvation but also for daily provision on the narrow road (verses 16-17).

A prayer: Thank You, LORD, for pulling me out of the pit.
A thought: In gratitude, I will tell of the salvation God provided.

307. Yearning for God
As deer thirst for water, so I thirst for God.

In Psalms 42 and 43, the sons of Korah (a clan of Levites) voiced their spiritual needs so poignantly that believers can readily relate to that state of mind. Yahveh's yearning for loving contact with believers is here answered by believers who yearn for fellowship with Him too. However, inside them there is an ongoing struggle between faith and doubt, hope and despair.

November 2
~ ~ ~
Psalms 42, 43

The poet's yearning for contact with God is so intense and persistent, he feels like a thirsty deer panting in blistering heat, yearning for a stream of fresh water that is yet not in sight. He fears he will not be relieved soon.

Two things added salt to his thirst: the taunting of the enemy who asks, "So, where is your wonderful God now?" and the memory of those days when he went with a multitude, singing and praising, to the sanctuary. He opens his heart and pours out his sorrows when haunted by these memories.

Then his faith emerges and admonishes him for being so morbid. It encourages him to persevere in his hope in God, for eventually he will be rescued by God and be restored to his former joy. This emerging and sinking faith becomes a refrain that is repeated several times.

On the slopes of Mount Hermon he has seen, after heavy rain, how the water roars down waterfalls and over boulders. It has become a picture to him of how tribulations have engulfed him. When he gets his head above water for a while, he tries to believe that he will see Yahveh's loving-kindness again. However, when he hears the mocking cry of his enemy asking him sarcastically where his God is, he feels as if the enemy is breaking his bones. Once more his faith encourages him to keep on hoping for God's rescue.

The struggle between faith and doubt proceeds in Psalm 43. He pleads that God will vindicate him against his enemies and that God will not abandon him amid the pressure the enemy is putting on him. He longs for God's illuminating guidance, *"O, send out Your light and Your truth! Let them lead me."* Then he will eventually return to God's holy hill and sanctuary. He will worship God there with sacrifices and with songs.

For a third time the refrain is repeated. His faith strengthens him and enables him to proceed in hope. He has progressed from "God" to "O God" and from there to "my God." Apparently he has discovered that he can have contact with God anywhere. In his struggle, his prayers have been heard.

A prayer: Father, make me thirsty for quality time with You.
A thought: How can I improve my personal and communal worship?

308. A Mighty Fortress
that stood the test of time.

Martin Luther's reformation song is based on Psalm 46: "A mighty fortress is our God!" Believers love to sing it when they are in dire straits. Faith is empowered by God's omnipotence in nature and in history. The sons of Korah testify that the LORD has proven Himself as a reliable refuge for those in need.

The poet paints two contrasting pictures in nature to show God's power. On the one side, he observes how God is at work in the mighty forces that make the sea roar, the mountains crumble, and man cringe in fear. On the other side, he notices God's presence in peaceful murmuring streams that provides sustenance to man, beast, and plant. These brooks make people rejoice in gratitude. Although mountains may be removed and may disappear, God will not be removed and He will not disappear. Like the life-giving streams, He calmly provides for His people—as sure as dawn follows the night.

The focus then shifts to the raging nations. Just as the roaring sea pounds the rocks with gigantic breakers, so the nations pound each other with vicious attacks. They think they can move heaven and earth with their clever plans, but they do not consider the Almighty. He speaks, and all their plans melt away. The war ends, and all the weaponry and armor are destroyed. Rusting tanks in the desert and sunken ships in the sea are the only reminders of the big plans of small people.

In view of God's mighty works in nature and in history, mankind should bow in humility and in silence before Him. He alone should be exalted among the nations and in His creation. When man exalts himself, he ignores God's rules for His creation, and by following his own rules he harms himself, others, nature, and God's kingdom.

The opening verses of this psalm become a refrain: *"The LORD of hosts is with us; the God of Jacob is our refuge."* The God who controls nature and history revealed Himself in the Bible as the LORD, Yahveh, the covenant God of Jacob and his descendants called Israel. He is a refuge to those who trust and love Him so much that they accept Him for who He is.

The gods people create in their own minds to serve their own purposes are just as dead and worthless as the idols of old. These false ideas about God cannot help because they are man's creations. The true God is not our creation; He created us, and only He is a mighty fortress and a proven refuge.

A prayer: A mighty fortress is our God, a refuge never failing.
A thought: Are my ideas about God in line with His Word?

309. God and Jerusalem
God gives the city its true meaning.

In this pilgrim song of the sons of Korah, the glory of God and the splendor of Jerusalem are so intertwined that the one can easily be confused with the other. One moment they sing the glory of God, and the next moment they praise the beauty of the city. However, there is a link between the two.

> November 4
> ~ ~ ~
> Psalm 48

Jeremiah warned the people of Jerusalem that if they did not repent, God would not save the city because of the temple (Lesson 253). In Ezekiel's visions, Jerusalem was soon demolished to rubble when the glory of God had left it (Lesson 269). The message of the prophets was clear: With God's presence, the city would flourish; without God, the city would perish.

Consequently, pilgrims saw the restored prosperity of Jerusalem as a visual sign of God's blissful presence. Because Yahveh had returned to Jerusalem, it was again the place of worship for His chosen people. Pilgrims were overjoyed when they got the first view of Zion, the city of God. They praised the God they could not see, as well as the beauty of the city they could observe.

As their eyes glided over the city on a hill, they enjoyed its architectural beauty and its fortified wall and towers. They reminded themselves, however, that Jerusalem's real beauty and strength did not come from building material but from the King of heaven and earth who chose to dwell there. God was their refuge; therefore, His city was their refuge too (verses 1-3).

Many enemies turned away from Jerusalem when they saw its strategic position, its high walls, and its fortified towers. But most of all, they were awestruck by a mysterious awareness of God's presence. They experienced what they had been told: It was the city of the LORD of hosts (verses 4-8).

When they entered the temple, elevated on Mount Zion, pilgrims were filled with sincere gratitude for God's loving-kindness that made it possible for them to enter the courts of the Most High once more. Overwhelmed by the awareness of God's holy presence, their predominant desire was that His Name would be glorified over all the earth (verses 9-11). True worship encourages missions. The righteousness God wants to disperse with His "right hand," His Son, is the reconciliation with God through the atonement of His Son. That is the true purpose and joy of Jerusalem. Those who have tasted the salvation God has prepared for them can praise the glory of God and admire the beauty of the city where it all became a marvelous reality (verses 12-14).

A prayer: Lord, help us to honor the Giver while we enjoy His gifts.
A thought: Idolatry is to honor the gift more than the Giver.

310. True Worship
God tells us how to worship Him.

<table>
<tr><td>

November 5

~~~

Psalm 50

</td><td>

In Psalm 50, Asaph paints a scene in a courthouse. The LORD of the universe is the judge, heaven and earth are called as witnesses, and God's people are the accused. The hearing takes place on Mount Zion where fire and storm surround the

</td></tr>
</table>

Almighty (verses 1-6). It is not the final judgment of the end of time, for God admonishes His people to improve their worship.

Firstly, God addresses the faithful (verses 7-15). He warns them against formalism, a shallow worship that observes the external rituals without real internal devotion. As in Psalm 40, God emphasizes that the attitude of the heart is first priority; after that come the sacrifices. God is Spirit and does not need the flesh and blood of animals. Even if He did, He can take as many as He wants from His own herds because all wild and domesticated animals belong to Him. He wants His people to trust in Him daily and to honor Him for His provisions. This short summary of what God expects of us is similar to those found in Micah 6:6-8 and in Matthew 22:36-40.

Secondly, God confronts the hypocrites (verses 16-23). Although they pretend to serve God by going through the right motions, they have a hidden agenda that is in direct opposition to God's will. He gives them four examples: They are guilty of theft, adultery, deceit, and slander. They either do these sins themselves or give their support to those who do it. They wrongly assume that God does not care about their behavior because He does not punish them immediately. God gives them a stern warning that they will be torn to pieces if they do not change their hearts and their behaviors.

The psalm ends with the affirmation that those who do the right things and who serve God with praises will taste the salvation that God has prepared. Vice versa, those who share in God's salvation will do the right things and will praise God from the heart.

Although the laws God gave to Moses may give the impression that God is legalistic, there is ample proof that the gospel of the New Testament was already given in the Old Testament. The ceremonial law was intended to show in deeds what was going on in the heart of the worshiper. However, when the heart was without love and faith, then the ceremonies became meaningless, empty shells. It is true of formalism and of hypocrisy. Psalm 50 urges us to examine our sincerity and integrity continuously.

A prayer: Holy Spirit, please purify my attitudes and motives.
A thought: I want to be a genuine worshiper, not a pretender.

311. The Pain of Betrayal
when your friend stabs you in the back

Almost all of David's psalms refer to the wicked, those who had shown themselves by attitudes and deeds to be enemies of God. Therefore, David saw them as his enemies too: *"Do I not hate them, O LORD, who hate You? And do I not loathe those who rise up against You? I hate them with perfect hatred; I count them my enemies"* (Ps. 139:21-22).

> November 6
> ~ ~ ~
> Ps. 55, 41, 35

While Solomon had already seen the benefits of doing good to your enemies (Prov. 25:21-22), the Son of David a thousand years later urged His followers to love their enemies and to pray for them (Matt. 5:43-48).

However, what hurt David far more than the expected animosity of his enemies was the unexpected betrayal by trusted friends. All who have suffered such a shock can empathize with David's emotional pain: *"For it is not an enemy who reproaches me; then I could bear it. Nor is it one who hates me who has exalted himself against me; then I could hide from him. But it was you, a man my equal, my companion and my acquaintance."* When he remembers how they worshiped God together with joy, he is absolutely dumbfounded by the person's sudden change of attitude and conduct.

Elsewhere David laments the fact that one who had been a regular guest at his table afterward betrayed him: *"Even my own familiar friend in whom I trusted, who ate my bread, has lifted up his heel against me"* (Ps. 41:9). Jesus said that these words of David were also a prophecy about the Messiah's betrayal by Judas (John 13:18-21). Like David, Jesus was emotionally severely upset when He had to take this insult from one of His disciples.

In another psalm, David complains about former friends with whom he sympathized and for whom he prayed when they were in trouble, but who later turned against him (Ps. 35:12-17). *"They reward me evil for good,"* he concluded, dismayed and puzzled about the behavior of these former friends.

Apart from the betrayal by Judas, Jesus also heard how His leader disciple denied three times that he had any connection with Him. Paul wrote that he had suffered much because of "false brothers" (2 Cor. 11:26), and shortly before he was executed he wrote, *"At my first defense no one stood with me but all forsook me"* (2 Tim. 4:16-17). If your path goes through this dark valley, fall back on the LORD's protection as David, Jesus, and Paul did. This apostle could state with confidence that the Lord stood with him, strengthened him, and used him to further the gospel so that the Gentiles could hear God's good news.

A prayer: Lord, empower me when friends let me down.
A thought: Not people but God will determine my direction.

312. Recorded Tears
God remembers our pain and forgets our forgiven sins.

November 7
~~
Psalm 56
Jer. 31:34

A six-year-old girl huddles in a hidden corner of a burnt down hut in Africa. She sobs softly yearning for her parents, who were killed the day before in tribal war. She does not understand what happened or why. After a while, she starts to rock herself gently while humming the melody she had learned in mission school, "Jesus loves me, this I know, for the Bible tells me so." Fragile and helpless in her desolation, she found comfort in the fact that there was Someone who cared about her tears.

Psalm 56 tells about David's feelings at the beginning of his refugee years. He was a young man about twenty years old. He had suddenly become the hero of the nation when he slew the Philistine giant and became a victorious officer in the choice regiment of the king. Then the king became envious of his popularity and tried to kill him. In his confusion, he fled to his other enemies, the Philistines, who arrested him. In jail he broke down and emptied his heart before the only One who could help him in this real and present danger.

Like the desolate little girl in Africa, he found comfort in the fact that God saw his tears. He made himself strong in the LORD and concluded that God would keep his tears in His bottle and record them in His book. With these poetic metaphors he meant that God was aware of his situation and of his emotional pain and that God would provide the solution. He praised the Person and the Word of Yahveh, trusted in Him, and calmed his fear (verses 4, 10, 11). Christ told us not to fear those who can only kill the body.

One of David's descendants, Hezekiah, wept when the prophet Isaiah announced that he would die. God sent Isaiah back to the king with the joyful message, *"Thus says the LORD, the God of David your father: 'I have heard your prayer, I have seen your tears; surely I will heal you' "* (2 Kings 20:5).

Jesus, the Son of David, wept and prayed at the tomb of His friend Lazarus. His tears were noticed too, and His prayer was answered. Before He called Lazarus out of the tomb, He said, *"Father, I thank You that You have heard Me"* (John 11:35, 41). Although He was forsaken by the Father when He suffered hell in our place, His prayer for His executioners was still answered.

God knows about our tears in this life, and at the right time He does something about them. Furthermore, He promised that in life hereafter, all tears will be wiped from the faces of those who are saved by Jesus (Rev. 21:4). No more suffering, no more distress, no more tears—only eternal jubilation.

A prayer: LORD, You see my tears and hear my prayers.
A thought: In God I trust; I will not fear.

313. Jubilation After Redemption
The darker the night, the sweeter the dawn

In Psalm 57, David reflects on his close encounter with his enemy in a cave at En-Gedi near the Dead Sea (Lesson 158). Apparently Saul and his army came suddenly upon them, forcing them into a risky escape. David and some of his men fled into a cave where they could easily be cornered by their persistent enemy. David describes his peril, his fear, and his prayer for God's miraculous protection.

> November 8
> ~ ~ ~
> Psalms 57
> 108:2-6

David realized what the intentions of his enemies were. They wanted to tear him apart and devour him as if they were ferocious lions. Their "teeth" were spears, arrows, and swords. In his distress, he fled to the Almighty in prayer, as chicks flee to safety under the wings of the mother hen.

The first part of the psalm ends with a refrain that also concludes the second part: God's glory is exalted above heaven and earth. Let there be no doubt that God is in full control of His creation.

Then he gratefully describes his redemption from this perilous situation. His enemies put up a net to catch him like a bird; they dug a pit to catch him like a buck. But suddenly the tables were turned: The hunters became the hunted, and they fell into their own nets and pits.

When the nail-biting threat had passed, David sighed in relief: "I feel safe, O God, I feel safe again!" He responded with song and music; at daybreak he wanted to wake up the dawn with harp and lute. Realizing that the sun shines over all nations, David wanted to make his personal salvation a universal redemption—he wanted to broadcast the good news to all peoples. Real joy over one's own salvation always stimulates evangelization. For God's **mercy and truth** are far greater than one person or one nation. This is a reference to the Messiah of whom John said, *"For the law was given through Moses, but grace and truth came through Jesus Christ"* (John 1:17).

Then the refrain is repeated: God's glory is exalted above heaven and earth. The second half of this psalm itself became a refrain in David's life. He sang it often. The entire second part of this psalm is repeated in Psalm 108:2-6. It is not enough to thank God only once for deliverance. It should become an often repeated melody that we know so well that we can sing it while we enjoy a walk or a drive, or share with others at home or in church: "And His glory is exalted far above the earth and sky!"

A prayer: Our Father, hallowed be Your Name.
A thought: Do I speak the truth in love and mercy? (Eph. 4:15).

314. Finding Rest in God
He is my fortress; I will not be shaken.

<table>
<tr><td>

November 9

~~~

Psalm 62

</td></tr>
</table>

The refrain of a song reinforces the main truth embodied in the song. David used it often to engrave certain beliefs into his soul. Repetition is one of the most powerful tools to sustain memory, to build lasting views, and to develop skills and talents. Practice makes perfect.

In Psalm 62, David again complains about the persistent persecution by his enemies. He pictures his own failing strength as a leaning stone wall that can easily be toppled. His enemies know that and try to push him over with lies, false compliments, and hidden hatred: *"With their mouths they bless, but in their hearts they curse."* (NIV). They practiced dirty politics.

In these circumstances, David flees to God, his fortress on a rock. There he feels safe and finds rest for his soul. He makes this relieving experience the refrain of his song. This is what he needs to remember, and this is what he wants to impress on his audience as well—to find rest in God. When God became a human being in Christ, He invited people to come to Him and to find real rest and piece of mind: *"Come to Me, all you who labor and are heavy laden, and I will give you rest. Take My yoke upon you and learn from Me, for I am gentle and lowly in heart, and you will find rest for your souls"* (Matt. 11:28-29).

After a long search for real happiness and for a meaningful lifestyle, Augustine found this rest David and Jesus had spoken of and concluded that the soul of man is restless until it rests in God.

As king, David then calls on his people to follow his example, to put their trust in God, and to pour out their hearts to Him. David wanted others to share in the wonderful relationship with God that he himself enjoyed. Jesus made it the Great Commission that we should take the good news to others after we have accepted it ourselves (Matt. 28:18-20, John 7:37-38, 2 Cor. 5:18-20).

David then explains the position of those who don't trust and love God. Whether they are from the lowest or the highest levels in society, they are in God's sight only temporary, weightless vapor. Therefore, those who get rich legally or illegally should not trust in their riches but rather in God.

David ends this psalm with two overwhelming truths about God: He is strong and He is merciful. Nothing is impossible for Him, and He likes to help people who trust Him, because that is His nature. He rewards people according to their faith, and even that is a gift from Him (Eph. 2:8).

A prayer: Looking at the alternatives, I'd rather stand with You, O God.
A thought: To rest in God, I must focus on Him and not on the problems.

315. Material and Spiritual Blessings
Let the peoples praise You, O God!

The idea that all nations should praise God becomes progressively stronger in Psalms 65, 66, and 67 so that the latter one is entirely devoted to this matter. Because God cares not only for Israel but also for the whole world, Israel should bring offers of thanksgiving and the world should praise the Creator.

> November 10
> ~~~
> Ps. 65, 66, 67

God's blessings make nature flourish. In Psalm 63, David's flesh cries to God from the Judean wilderness, "a dry land without water." In Psalm 65 he sings about the unbelievable transformation of the same region after good rains. Streams flow again, trees on their banks are green, the soil is soft, farmers can plow, fields are covered with grain, flocks graze in lush pastures, and as far as the eye can see there is abundance and joy.

Since these blessings of the Creator on His creation are enjoyed by all nations, they should praise Him (65:5, 7; 66:1, 4, 7, 8; 67:2-7). Above all material blessings, the nations should praise God that His salvation is also offered to them (67:2). They can share in the benefits of the new heaven and new earth where God will reign in justice (67:4). That was part of God's promise to Abram when God called him to the Promised Land: In his seed all nations would be blessed. Israel had to be a light to the nations.

Unfortunately, Israel strayed many times, and God had to discipline them with hardships to open their eyes and to bring them back. They had to be purified in fire like silver (66:10-12).

David himself felt this discipline in his own life when he went through dire straits. In his calamities, he cried to God for help and made promises and vows. When God heard his prayers and rescued him, he did not forget his vows but brought them to God in deep gratitude: *"I will go into Your house with burnt offerings; I will pay You my vows, which my lips have uttered and my mouth has spoken when I was in trouble"* (66:13-14).

David did not stop with offerings. First of all, God wants our hearts, not our things. Therefore, David honored God also with his testimony in words and deeds. He told people about his redemption, *"Come and hear, all who fear God, and I will declare what He has done for my soul"* (66:16). He also kept his life on the right track, knowing that God would not answer him if he had a wicked hidden agenda (66:18).

David's redemption and gratitude represent the salvation and thanksgiving of all believers. All nations should follow him in this.

A prayer: I thank You, God, for Your blessings in creation and in salvation.
A thought: How can I show my gratitude for God's blessings?

316. God's Record
He carries us through life.

November 11
~ ~ ~
Psalm 68

God has provided in the past; He will do so in the future, as well. That's the message of Psalm 68. It starts off by introducing God's power and mercy (verses 1-6); these are illustrated by the history of Israel (verses 7-19). Finally, the joyful hope is proclaimed that God will keep on providing for both Israel and the nations (verses 20-35).

In the prologue, God's power is hailed by metaphors from nature, and His mercy is sung by examples from family life. Yahveh is like sun and fire to His enemies, but He is a Father to widows and orphans.

When God freed His people from slavery in Egypt, He led them by a column of cloud and fire. In the Sinai desert the earth trembled (when God gave the Ten Commandments), and the heavens dripped food (in the form of manna, quail, and rain). That is why so many people could survive in the desert for so long—by God's mercy and power alone.

The conquest of the Promised Land was just as miraculous. Mighty kings fled from them, driven forth by God-controlled natural forces such as storms and hornets (Josh. 24:12). They were enriched by easy looting. Instead of the impressive Bashan Mountains, Yahveh chose Mount Zion as His dwelling place. He moved with his heavenly hosts from Sinai to Zion. The apostle Paul compares God's moving up to Zion with Christ's ascension to heaven (Eph. 4:8). God has not only received gifts from worshipers, but through His Son and Spirit, He is also dispersing gifts to believers.

God's mercy in the history of Israel makes David burst out in praises toward the God who has carried them through good and bad times. Even when death knocks at the door, they have peace of mind, knowing they are safe in God's fatherly hands. Isaiah also assures us that God is faithful and carries His faithful from birth to old age (Is. 46:3-4).

In view of the mercies God has bestowed on us in the past, we can face the future with confidence. Both Jews and Gentiles can honor God with praises and offerings for His goodness and loving care. David describes in graphic terms the triumph over God's enemies (verses 21-23), the festive parade to the sanctuary (verses 24-27), and the change of heart amongst the Gentiles (verses 28-31).

With a powerful grand finale, the psalm calls up all nations to exalt the God of Israel. God's majesty is visible in the clouds and in the heavens, and His grace is evident in His dealing with those who trust and obey Him.

A prayer: Father, You have carried me through thick and thin.
A thought: When I survey the past, how do I approach the future?

317. Gall and Vinegar
David's personal pain is linked to the Messiah's life.

In Psalm 69, as in the 22nd, we find the Messiah in David's clothing. Though not every word in it can be ascribed to the Messiah literally, the symbolic meaning of the entire psalm points to Him. This psalm is quoted five times in the New Testament.

> November 12
> ~ ~ ~
> Psalm 69

It starts with a cry for salvation. Man has to be saved from the quagmire of sin in which he is sinking (v. 1-3). The Savior took man's sin on Himself and suffered in its place. Thus He was hated without a cause (John 15:25). Though He had stolen nothing, He restored the wrong of others (v. 4). He became sin for us (v. 5) so that we could receive God's righteousness (2 Cor. 5:21). Because of Him, believers will not be ashamed (v. 6). Instead, He was scorned (Rom. 15:3) for our sake and rejected by His own people (v. 7-9, John 1:11, 7:5).

Zeal for God's house devoured Him (John 2:17); therefore, He cleansed the temple and exposed the wrong attitudes of the religious leaders (Matt. 23). This infuriated them so much that they asked the Roman governor to condemn Him to death. The reproaches of those who reproached God fell on Him. Those who sat in the gate, the leaders, spoke against Him (v. 9-12).

Although Christ's agonized prayer in Gethsemane—that the cup of God's wrath over sin be taken from Him—was not answered, and although God did turn His face away from Him on Calvary (Matt. 27:46), Jesus submitted Himself to God's will and the Father gave Him victory over sin and death (v. 13-18). His mother, one disciple, and a few women who watched His hell on the cross could not help or comfort Him (John 19:25-27). His enemies offered Him gall and vinegar to drink (v. 19-21, Matt. 27:34).

The prayer for the punishment of the Messiah's enemies (v. 22-28) was applied to Judas by Peter (Acts 1:20). To some extent it was also true for the Jews who rejected the Messiah. Their eyes were darkened so that they did not recognize Jesus as the Messiah. Their house, the temple, would be destroyed and left desolate for ages, a warning repeated by Jesus (Luke 13:34-35).

The focus is shifted from the plight of the Messiah's enemies to the privileges and jubilation of those who accepted the salvation earned by Messiah (v. 29-36). Because He completed God's plan of salvation, Jesus ascended to heaven where He received the highest honor and power at the right hand of the Father: *"Let Your salvation, O God, set me up on high."* The ceremonial laws and sacrifices of the old era were replaced by the praises of the new (v. 30-31).

A prayer: Thank You, Jesus, for fulfilling these prophecies by Your saving grace.
A thought: Do I recognize the New Testament in the old one, and vice versa?

318. The Senior's Prayer
Pests and petitions, privileges and praises

November 13

~~~

Psalm 71

</div>

The absent heading makes this prayer universal. However, David is the likely author (Ps. 72:20). It seems fitting for the Davidic psalms to conclude with David's old age prayers for himself (Ps. 71) and for his successor (Ps. 72). David represents all senior believers, and Solomon represents the Messiah.

The "enemies" of seniors tend to increase rather than to decrease. Human enemies may become fewer—thanks to death and temperament—but other pests gradually multiply, such as physical decline, social isolation, material insecurity, and personality erosion (in mind, feelings, motivation and self-image). These enemies can be even more relentless than people.

David fled to God with his old age troubles: *"In You, O LORD, I put my trust."* David's trust was not something that he started to learn when old age knocked at his door. He had been using it since childhood (v. 5, 6, and 7). It was a well-known and well-used weapon, like his shepherd's rod, staff, and sling. Because he had been exercising his faith (Eph. 2:8), God had been rewarding him many times with miraculous protections and provisions (v. 7, 19-21).

In spite of his good record of faithful trust and God's excellent record of faithful care, David did not take it for granted that God would continue to bestow blessings on him in old age. David knew that he was undeserving of God's grace: *"My sin is always before me"* (Ps. 51:3). Therefore, he beseeched God not to forsake him in old age, kneeling before God with grey hair, frail body, and troubled spirit (v. 9, 18).

While praying, David was strengthened by God's Word and Spirit. His wavering faith was reassured that God will look after him as He had in the past. He responded by praising God and by testifying to others, especially to the youth (v. 17-18). By telling the new generation how God has provided for them, seniors can help to build up the faith of the youth so that they too may develop a safe "faith home" before the freezing storms of life's winter sweeps down on them. David wants them to share in his privilege (2 Cor. 5:18).

However, even if others are not listening to his old man stories, David enjoys taking up his harp and lute, making music to God, and singing with rasping voice of the great things God has done for him, not because of any merit on his side but just because God is great and good. With God, David prevailed against old age as he had prevailed against Goliath.

A prayer: Merciful Father, have mercy on old and young.
A thought: Do I have this refuge against the winter of life?

319. A Faith Crisis
Human versus divine wisdom

In Psalm 73, Asaph battles with the same problem David wrestles with in Psalm 37—the prosperity of the wicked and the hardships of the just. After a short introduction (v. 1-2), he tells us the nature of his problem (v. 3-14), how he got over it (v. 15-20), and what the benefits of his victory were (v. 21-28).

November 14

~ ~ ~

Psalm 73

Though Asaph had started off with a positive belief system—that God is good for the true Israel, the pure in heart—he almost lost his faith when he made his own observations more important than God's Word. This shift in focus may become a pitfall for any believer.

Asaph didn't like what he saw. It looked as if the wicked did not suffer the same hardships as believers did, like troubles, plagues, ill health, and tragic death (v. 4-5). Instead, the wicked enjoyed good fortune, prosperity, riches, and abundance (v. 3, 7, and 12). This resulted in their big-ego attitudes like boasting, pride and violence (v. 3, 6). While boosting themselves, they made derogatory remarks about heaven and earth, angels and humans (v. 8-9). By their self-confidence, they impressed many who uncritically swallowed what they said (v. 10). Though most of the wicked in Asaph's time were not atheists, they believed that God did not intervene in earthly matters (v. 11).

Asaph's one-sided observations led to the dangerous conclusion that serving God did not make sense. His clean heart and hands brought him nothing but tribulation and chastisement (v. 13-14).

How did Asaph handle his faith crisis? First of all, he wisely decided to shut up and to avoid contaminating other believers with his doubts (v. 15). Secondly, he went back to God's sanctuary and to God's Word and calibrated his personal views with God's objective norm (v. 16-17). He then realized that his own observations were flawed because they were one-sided. When he looked at the whole picture, he got perspective. In this life the wicked's temporary successes often end in disaster, and in life hereafter they will disappear from God's presence like a soon forgotten dream (v. 18-20, 27).

Asaph asked forgiveness for his shortsightedness and rejoiced in God's love, which patiently guarded him while he stumbled (v. 21-23). He came to realize the unfathomable spiritual riches he had in God's presence and that nothing in this life or the next can be compared to closeness to God (v. 25-28). In contrast with the wicked's tragic destiny, he will have eternal glory with God (v. 24).

A prayer: Father, let me see clearly, trust firmly, and live wisely.
A thought: Do I sometimes get confused between human and divine wisdom?

320. Focus Influences Mood
Laments can be exchanged for praises.

<table>
<tr><td>
November 15
~~~
Ps. 74, 75, 76
</td></tr>
</table>

The psalms are not arranged in chronological or logical order. However, sometimes there seems to be a sensible link between consecutive psalms, maybe not intended by man but allowed by God. Psalms 74, 75 and 76 seem to be logically connected though they were probably written in different time frames.

"A song of Asaph" can also mean a song of Asaph's clan. Asaph lived in the time of king David, about 1000 B.C., but his descendants still played a major role in public worship after the exile in the sixth century B.C. (Ezra 2:41, 3:10). They knew the destruction of the temple, which is vividly described in the first eleven verses of Psalm 74. They could have sung this song during their exile in the hope that God would hear their prayers, bring them back to their homeland, and restore the temple.

When they thought about God's miracles of the past, how He freed His people from Egyptian bondage with a mighty hand, they were empowered in their faith (v. 12-17). This turned their wailing (v. 1-11) into intercession (v. 18-23). The hopeless cries of "why?" and "how long?" to a distant God were replaced by passionate pleas to Yahveh, their caring Father, beseeching Him not to let His defenseless "turtledove" (the remnant of Israel and Judah) be harmed.

The next two psalms continue with this process of empowerment by looking back in faith. Psalm 75 fits in well with the righteous rule of King David. It sings about the LORD's love and care for those who trust Him (v. 1-3, 6-7, 9-10) and about His wrath on those who reject Him (v. 4-5, 8, 10).

Psalm 76 describes a God-given victory that fits the defeat of the Assyrian army by the Angel of the LORD in the time of king Hezekiah (v. 1-6, Isaiah 37). Yahveh is hailed as the supreme judge of all nations. Instead of rebelling against Him, they should seek reconciliation with Him. Kings and princes have to bow before the Creator and Sustainer of the universe.

One can imagine a procession of Asaph singers coming down from the Mount of Olives into the Kidron Valley while singing the laments of Psalm 74. As they start to ascend Mount Zion to the temple, their focus shifts from self to God, and their tune changes from melancholy to jubilant praises. Jesus also descended the Mount of Olives while weeping over Jerusalem, but shortly afterward He cleansed the temple from its noisy merchants and demanded that the temple be a house of prayer for all nations (Mark 11:17).

A prayer: Help me change from self-centered lamenting to God-centered praises.
A thought: Do I succeed in changing my mood by changing my focus?

321. The Lessons of History
Past experience can build a better future.

Jesus and Paul warned us not to get stuck in the past and miss the opportunities of the present (Luke 9:62, Phil. 3:13-14). The Bible also instructs us to look back constructively sometimes to strengthen our faith. The Passover (Ex. 12:24-27) and the Lord's Supper (1 Cor. 11:25-26) were instituted as such memorials.

> November 16
> ~~~
> Psalms 77, 78

In miserable circumstances, Asaph and his descendants look back to the great deeds of God in the history of their nation in order to support their wavering faith in the present. Psalm 77 describes how this reminiscence often takes place during sleepless hours at night (v. 1-6). The poet's *"soul refused to be comforted"* and his *"spirit was overwhelmed."* He searches for answers but instead the questions multiply (v. 7-9). Has God's anger over sin locked up His grace and mercies forever?

The poet then starts to fight his doubts with memories of Yahveh's wonderful provisions in the past, especially the liberation from Egypt when He opened the sea so that His people could escape from oppression (v. 16-20). This thought is further pursued in Psalm 78. The poet underlines the importance of telling God's miracles to the next generation, lest people forget (v. 1-11).

Those miracles are then recalled in more detail. In his imagination the poet sees how God *"made the waters stand up like a heap,"* how He led His people by a cloud in daytime and by a fire at night, and how He *"brought streams out of the rock"* (v. 12-16). Yet instead of trusting God, they moaned about food and doubted if God could *"prepare a table in the wilderness."* God shamed their unbelief by giving them *"angels' food"* from heaven and bird meat in abundance. Many died because of greed and gluttony (v. 17-31).

Because of their rebellion and unbelief, God made them wander in the wilderness for forty years so that they could learn to trust God completely. But even when they did repent, they did not do it wholeheartedly. In His mercy, God did not obliterate them for He knew they were only flesh (v. 32-39). The poet finds it hard, though, to understand how Israel could forget the great deeds of God in Egypt so easily (v. 40-51).

Though God cared for Israel in the desert as a shepherd cares for his flock and brought them into the Promised Land, they soon strayed again and served idols. Therefore, God rejected the northern kingdom and chose Judah and the house of David as beneficiaries of His promises.

A prayer: Father, Your past mercies reassure us of Your present care.
A thought: How do I look on the past—with grievance or with gratitude?

322. God Is In Control
What God expects of believers and of rulers

November 17
~ ~ ~
Psalm 81, 82

In Psalms 81 and 82, Asaph changes his style. Instead of depicting man who is crying out to God, as in preceding psalms, God here addresses man—Israel first, and then the rulers and judges (v. 2-4) of nations. In both psalms the emphasis is on listening to God and on obeying His commandments.

Psalm 81 starts with a call to worship God with voice and music (v. 1-5). Then God speaks. He begins with Israel's salvation, their liberation from slavery. God listened when they called to Him in their misery in Egypt, and He led them to freedom; therefore, He demands that they now listen to Him. Four times Yahveh exhorts them to listen to Him (v. 8, 11, and 13). If they would honor Him as their only God, He would provide for them abundantly (v. 10). This appeal and promise were also echoed by Isaiah: *"Incline your ear, and come to Me. Hear and your soul shall live"* (Is. 55:3).

Sadly, they did not listen and obey and had to suffer the consequences. God gave them rope to hang themselves on the gallows of obstinacy. In spite of that, God still pleads with them to turn around and serve Him with the gratitude He deserves. He promises to change their circumstances quickly for the better and to destroy their enemies (v. 11-14). The psalm ends with a curse on those who do not heed God's Word and a blessing on those who do.

Psalm 82 depicts God as standing in the midst of mighty rulers and judges. God rebukes them for judging unjustly and for showing favor to the wicked. He exhorts them to honor His Word by protecting the orphan, the poor, the needy, and the afflicted against the wicked, including wicked rulers and judges. They do not understand God's ways; therefore, they stumble forth in darkness and threaten the fundamental values of society (v. 1-5).

Because of their failure to uphold justice, God will not regard the rulers and judges as "gods," His people who received His Word (John 10:35). They will die just like other human beings (v. 6-7). The psalm ends with the eyes on the end of time when God Himself will judge the earth and rule the nations (v. 8).

Jesus referred to this psalm when the Jews accused Him of making Himself God (John 10:31-38). He said that if God called those people "gods" to whom His word had come, how much more He deserved that description, He who had been sent and sanctified by God. The deeds and words of Jesus showed that He was on a much higher level than the "gods" of the world.

A prayer: O God, help me to listen to You and to trust and obey.
A thought: Do I help the needy, or do I serve the wicked?

323. Thirsting For God
The mysterious joy of true worship

This song of the clan of Korah describes the inner awareness of pilgrims on their way to the autumn Feast of Tabernacles in Jerusalem. Their strong but tender yearning for being with God in the temple has endeared Psalm 84 to Christians as well, poignantly expressing their need for communal worship in church.

November 18
~~~
Psalm 84

The song begins with the longing of pilgrims for the far-off sanctuary with its atmosphere of awe and worship. Their whole being thirsts for contact with the one living God, Yahveh (v. 1-2). In other Korah songs the name Yahveh is barely used, but in this song it appears seven times. The essence of their yearning is for Yahveh, not for a place. In Psalm 42, Korah compared this thirst to that of a deer panting for water in a dry region.

While the pilgrims prepare for their journey to Jerusalem, they envy the priests and the birds who have made the temple their home and who can enjoy God's presence every day (v. 3-4). As sparrows and swallows nest at the temple with their young, so believers should visit God's house so often with their children that those young ones will feel they have grown up in the church.

When the pilgrims embark on their journey to Zion, they have to travel through hot and dry regions. They are refreshed by God-given fountains and rain on the way. Approaching Jerusalem, they are invigorated by anticipation. Shortly they will stand before Yahveh in Zion (v. 5-7).

When they eventually arrive in the holy city, their cups overflow with joy, and they offer prayers of thanksgiving and intercession. God has been their protective shield on the way, and they pray that He will likewise protect their king and country (v. 8-9).

During their stay in Jerusalem, they savor the privilege of being close to God's temple and to God Himself every day. One day in Zion is better to them than the rest of the year at their far-off homes. Being a doorkeeper in God's temple is far more precious than riches gained in dishonesty (v. 10).

When they start their return journey, they put their faith in God's grace and glory to protect them. They know God is good and He will not withhold any good thing from those who trust and obey Him. Although the temple was Yahveh's house, they knew that He protected them everywhere. In the New Testament this truth became prevalent when the Holy Spirit came to dwell in believers, and each one of them became a temple of God (1 Cor. 3:16).

*A prayer: God, awaken in Your children a need for quality time with You.*
*A thought: This psalm has to be experienced, not analyzed.*

# 324. Grace vs. Calamity
## The conflict between faith and observation

November 19
~ ~ ~
Psalm 89

The psalmists described their struggles openly, even when they struggled with God. In Psalm 89, Ethan is confronted by two realities he cannot reconcile: the glorious reality of God's character and promises, and the miserable reality of misfortune and shattered dreams.

The poet starts with the wonderful reality of Yahveh's goodness and power. This is the reality that he believes in and enjoys, the reality he wants to be the only reality. In his introduction (v. 1-4), he tells of his overwhelming desire to *"sing of the mercies of the LORD forever"* and to speak of God's faithfulness from one generation to the next. One example of that is God's covenant with David, the promise to establish his throne forever.

Ethan then describes in more detail how Yahveh's greatness and goodness is displayed in heaven (v. 5-8), in nature (v. 9-13), in a God-serving nation (v. 14-17), and in the Davidic covenant (v. 18-37). The poet's remarks about the blessings for a nation that lives in God's righteousness, justice, mercy, and truth actually provide the answer to his doubting questions at the end of the psalm. Because Israel had not heeded God's Word, they were struck by calamity.

As the psalm goes on to sing about the mercies included in God's covenant with David, the New Testament believer cannot help but sense that these sublime promises are about someone greater than David. Especially verses 26-29 tower above the original words used by Nathan (1 Chron. 17:11-14). Maybe without realizing it himself, Ethan prophesied about the Messiah in whom the Davidic covenant would finally be fulfilled—another answer to Ethan's questions at the end of his song. The Messiah will heal the broken reality.

When the poet looks at the total destruction of Jerusalem and the Davidic dynasty, he is at a loss how to link that to the greatness and goodness of the God he really believes in (v. 38-51). He comes to the horrible conclusion that God has broken His promise to David (v. 39). Many people have experienced this pit of despair where the foundations of their holiest beliefs have been shaken by the tragedies of the broken reality.

Ethan ends his plea by reminding God that the reproach of His people actually leads to the reproach of God Himself. For His own name's sake, God should restore His children. Without finding answers to his echoing questions, the poet rests his case in the hands of the LORD, the God of Israel.

*A prayer: Father, help me to trust You in spite of unanswered questions.*
*A thought: Do I sometimes blame God for the mistakes people made?*

# 325. Two Ways of Counting
## Life is short but it can be meaningful.

Moses paints the shortness and sinfulness of human existence against the backdrop of God's eternal and glorious Being. On Mount Sinai God revealed Himself to Moses as the eternal "I am" (Ex. 3:14). To say God existed "before" or "outside" creation is true but incorrect because it presumes time before time and space outside space—both absurd ideas. As Creator, God transcends time and space.

November 20
~~~
Psalm 90

The eternal God created a temporary home for man on earth, and through His Son He is preparing an eternal home for His children (John 14:1-3). Sadly, the goodness of God has been spurned by man's sinfulness, and the good earth has been spoiled by man's iniquity. It evoked God's wrath on mankind, making the earth suffer too, yearning for the day of complete renewal (Rom. 8:18-22).

Moses compares man's short life to a few hours sleep, a fleeting dream, a leaf in a stream, withering grass, a grieving sigh, and a bird flying by. God gives and takes the life of every generation and makes them return to dust. With the resurrection, He will again make them all return—either to a life of joy with God or to a life of horror away from God (Dan. 12:2, John 5:28-29).

For the eternal God, a thousand years feel like a day. However, one day can be like a thousand years to God, the apostle Peter pointed out (2 Pet. 3:8), for God can do much more in one day than man can accomplish in a thousand years. Because of this difference in heavenly and earthly calculation, Moses prayed for the wisdom to use our short life span wisely.

In view of the fact that we will all return to dust, Moses beseeches God to return to us in mercy before our short lives are wasted. Moses has highlighted God's wrath and punishment—even for the sins we are not aware of—but at the end of his prayer, he turns his eyes toward God's mercy: *"Return, O LORD! How long? And have compassion on Your servants."*

He prays that God will bless us in the morning (in our youth) so that we may gladly walk in God's ways for the rest of the day (the rest of our lives). He is pleading with children to give their hearts to God early in their lives so that their short lives will have meaning for God's kingdom. Then the glory and beauty of the LORD will be evident to them, and He will bless and establish the work of their hands and minds. That is what we hope for as we grow older: that our accomplishments, however small they might have been, will outlast our lives, which went by all too soon.

A prayer: Help us to bring children to You and not block their way.
A thought: How wisely do I invest the limited time I still have left?

326. The Shadow of the Almighty
I will openly say, "In God I trust!"

<table>
<tr><td>

November 21

~ ~ ~

Psalm 91

</td><td>

The unnamed writer of this psalm marvels at the protection of the Almighty. He lays down the conditions for enjoying this safety, describes the perils of the believer with seven metaphors, and paints God's help with three images.

</td></tr>
</table>

He ends the psalm with God speaking of three things the believer must do and seven ways in which God cares for His child.

To enjoy God's protection, believers must make God's presence their dwelling place where they live and feel at home (v. 1, 9). Occasional visits to God in times of need are not good enough. God must be the steering wheel of our lives, not a mere spare wheel. The "secret place" reminds us of the inner room Jesus spoke of, where we are alone with God and where we don't try to impress anybody (Matt. 6:5-6). Quality time with the Almighty is as refreshing as the shadow of palm trees for the weary desert traveler. Believers not only dwell in God's presence, but they also testify openly about it (v. 2).

The perils for believers are manifold: traps, pestilence, terrorism, arrows, destruction, war, and the devil, who is in the New Testament also pictured as a lion and a serpent (v. 13, 1 Pet. 5:8, Rev. 20:2). Amid all these adversities, believers enjoy God's protection. The poet compares it to the safety a hen offers her chicks, the protection provided by armor to the soldier, and the invisible but real intervention of guardian angels (this verse was misquoted by Satan in Matt. 4:6).

Then the poet's praises are taken over by God's own affirmation of His loving-kindness toward those who know, love, and trust Him. In addition to the three metaphors used by the poet, God now names seven more ways in which He cares for His children. He delivers them, sets them on high, answers them, stands with them in trouble, honors them, gives them long (eternal) life, and bestows salvation on them.

While the poet wishfully alleges that no trouble will come near believers (10), God realistically mentions that He sometimes does allow believers to get into trouble (15), but that He is with them in that trouble, just as He was with Daniel in the lion's den and with his friends in the fiery furnace.

God led the poet to correct himself, qualifying his opinion on both the dangers and the protection. God's Word must be read in context. We must compare scripture with scripture to come to the whole truth. Without that, verse 10 can make people think that believers should not have problems.

A prayer: Father, I want to dwell in the safety of Your presence.
A thought: Do I allow God to correct my views?

327. Palms and Cedars
They flourish even in old age.

Psalm 92 contrasts believers with unbelievers, especially with regard to their insight into God's works and wisdom and into man's success and prospects. Believers want to thank God with prayers, praises, and music for His mercy and faithfulness, for His power and wisdom displayed in creation (v. 1-5).

November 22

~ ~ ~

Psalm 92

Wicked people do not understand the high intelligence behind the fine balance in the cosmos. Their prosperity is as short-lived as that of flourishing grass (v. 6-7), but the long-term success of believers is like the faithful fruitfulness of palm trees and the enduring power of cedars (v. 12-14). God's enemies will surely perish, but God will rule forever (v. 8-9).

The poet uses extremes to portray the privileges of believers: They are as free as the wild buffalo and as dedicated as the anointed high priest (v. 10). Fresh (virgin) oil was used for the lamps in the Holy Place (Ex. 27:20), and holy oil was used to anoint and consecrate the priests (Ex. 30:22-33). In both cases the oil symbolized the work of the Holy Spirit (Zech. 4:1-6, Luke 4:18).

Believers need the fresh anointing of the Spirit every day to practice the Spirit's main gift of love (1 Cor. 13), as well as His individual gifts of service (1 Cor. 12). Then they will prevail over their chief enemy, the devil (v. 11).

Anchored in God's Word and at home and in God's house, believers flourish like the palm trees of Jericho and like the cedars of Lebanon (v. 12-13). The fruitfulness and strength of these trees increased as they matured. Likewise, believers can continue to be fruitful and strong in spite of the aging process. *"Therefore we do not lose heart",* Paul said, *"Even though our outward man is perishing, yet the inward man is being renewed day by day"* (2 Cor. 4:16).

Whether you yourself are near or in old age, or whether you care about somebody in that phase of life, take heart with the poet of Psalm 92 that senior believers *"shall flourish in the courts of our God. They shall still bear fruit in old age; they shall be fresh and flourishing"* (v. 13-14).

This blessing is not primarily for their own enjoyment but to serve God, *"to declare that the LORD is upright; He is my rock, and there is no unrighteousness in Him"* (v. 15). Senior believers have thrown off the senseless burden of rebellion against God. From their own experience they know that God's way is the best way and that God's time is the best time. Instead of bumping their heads against closed doors, they wait for God to open the right one at the right time.

A prayer: Father, make me a palm and a cedar in Your church all my life.
A thought: Do I seek the Spirit's fresh anointing every day?

328. The Cry of the Oppressed
Rise up, O Judge of the earth!

November 23
~~
Psalm 94

Psalm 94 was probably written in a time when an evil king in Judah (like Ahaz or Manasseh) assembled around himself a corrupted upper class that oppressed the nation with a perverted justice system that favored the rich and abandoned the poor (v. 20). As the gap between rich and poor is still increasing in many countries today, this psalm is just as valid now as when it was written.

The poet voices the groans of the oppressed by crying out to the LORD God, the Judge of the earth to whom vengeance belongs (Rom. 12:19), to punish the proud perpetrators of God's law. In desperate frustration the question on everyone's mind is repeatedly asked, *"How long will the wicked triumph?"* (v. 1-3).

The corruption of the wicked is evident in their thoughts, attitudes, words, and deeds. They break and afflict people, especially the needy like widows, orphans, and strangers who were protected by the Law of Moses. The wicked boast openly about their deplorable methods and insult the God of Jacob by callously saying that He neither sees nor cares about their evil practices (v. 4-7).

By simple logic the poet calls the culprits to order (v. 8-11). They don't realize how stupid their reasoning is. Humans were created in God's image. He who created our hearing and sight can hear and see far better than we. He who disciplines nations does punish, and He who teaches man has knowledge. God knows how limited man's thoughts really are. In his first letter to the Corinthians (3:20), Paul quoted this verse to persuade this church not to think too much of their Greek philosophy.

The poet thanks God for the instruction coming from His Word and from tribulation. He then reassures the oppressed that God will not forget or forsake His chosen people. He will eventually reinstate a justice system that is based on righteousness and they will be part of it (v. 12-15).

The poet shares his own experience with his audience. He too wondered who would stand up for him against the oppressors. He testifies that God's help saved him from death many times. When he slipped, Yahveh supported him. When he was devoured by anxiety, God calmed him down (v. 16-19).

A political and justice system *"which devises evil by law"* is so obviously against God's will that He will definitely eradicate it. He will judge them harshly for shedding innocent blood (v. 20-23). Was there ever a time when so much innocent blood was shed as now? The Judge of the earth stands ready.

A prayer: Lord, give us the courage to stand up for Your values and justice.
A thought: In what ways are we guilty of the sins addressed by this psalm?

329. Salvation For All
Do not harden your hearts!

Psalm 95 begins with a powerful call to worship, but it ends with the sad record of Israel's disobedience to that call. Psalm 96 brings good news to the Gentiles: They can come and take what many in Israel have rejected. It is a prophecy about the Great Commission given by our Lord to take the gospel to the ends of the earth (Matt. 28:18-20, Acts 1:8).

November 24
~ ~ ~
Psalms 95, 96

In Psalm 95, David (Heb. 4:7) enthusiastically calls his people to worship the LORD with song and music, with joy and thanksgiving (v. 1-2). For David, who danced in front of the holy ark when it entered Jerusalem, worship was not a somber, long-faced business but a time for celebration. Yes, he did bring his sorrows to the Lord as well, as is evident in many of his psalms, but for him communal worship should be dominated by praise.

As reason for rejoicing, he points to the wonderful works of God in nature (v. 3-5), a theme taken up again at the close of the next psalm (v. 11-12). Then he returns to the call to worship, words which every church can repeat: *"Oh come, let us worship and bow down; let us kneel before the LORD our maker, for He is our God, and we are the people of His pasture, and the sheep of His hand"* (v. 6-7).

That is what Israel should have done. Instead, they hardened their hearts in the wilderness and many times after that. David did not know of the apostasy that would eventually lead to Israel's and Judah's exile. The writer of the letter to the Hebrews quotes Psalm 95 to warn the Jews not to make the same mistake as their ancestors had made (Heb. 3, 4). The psalm ends with the sad words, *"I swore in My wrath, 'They shall not enter my rest.'"*

In complete contrast, Psalm 96 opens with the joyful invitation, *"Sing to the LORD, all the earth!"* It proceeds with words that seem to be taken straight from the New Testament: *"Proclaim the good news of His salvation ... Declare His glory among the nations, His wonders among all peoples"* (v. 2-3). The difference between the LORD and other gods is pointed out to the Gentiles (v. 4-6), and then "the families of peoples" and "all the earth" are called to worship the true God, Yahveh, because He reigns over the entire world (v. 7-10).

All the nations have to join creation in glorifying the LORD (v. 11-12) for He is coming to judge the world and all its peoples. All who rejected or ignored God's salvation will be judged with righteousness, and those who accepted God's salvation will worship Him with joy forever.

A prayer: Lord, I will help carry Your good news to all nations.
A thought: Where is my heart hardened against God or against people?

330. Praising and Practicing
God reigns through faithful believers.

The recurrent theme in Psalms 95 through 100 is that the LORD reigns over Israel, over the nations, and over nature. The "holy, holy, holy" of Psalm 99 is followed by the jubilant call to worship in Psalm 100. God wants to reign through devoted rulers; therefore, Psalm 101 records a code of conduct for God-fearing leaders.

The first "holy" of Psalm 99 (v. 1-3) is linked to the nations. Surrounded by cherubim high above the peoples, the LORD God of Zion reigns over all creation. The nations should tremble before Him and praise His holy name.

The second "holy" (v. 4-5) should be uttered by Israel. God gave His Law to His chosen people to show them what justice really means. He taught them to treat all people equally before the Law and to practice righteousness that is in line with God's Word. Israel too should praise His holy name.

The third "holy" should be written over history. While Psalm 95 records the disobedience of Israel, Psalm 99 records the ways of faithful people like Moses, Aaron, and Samuel. It is stressed several times that they called upon Yahveh, and He answered them because they obeyed Him. God disciplined His people when they sinned, but He also forgave them when they repented. The faithful also praised God's holy name (v. 6-9).

Psalm 100 gives a universal call to worship. All should come and serve the three times holy God (Isaiah 6:3) with joyful singing. Yahveh, the God of Israel, is the only God. He is our Creator and our Shepherd—He has gathered us to be His flock. It suits us to enter His house with praises and thanksgiving. His mercies endure forever and His goodness for all generations.

The religious beliefs and actions described in Psalms 99 and 100 have to be brought into practice in everyday living, from the highest official to the lowest worker. In Psalm 101, David lays down a code of conduct for himself and for all righteous rulers.

God-fearing leaders honor the LORD (v.1). They act wisely and stay blameless, also in their private life (v. 2). They do not covet the wrong and avoid people who do (v. 3-4). They do not mingle with people who slander or despise others (v. 5). They employ faithful and blameless people (v. 6) and fire liars and cheaters (v. 7). Every morning they set their minds against the wicked and cut evildoers off from the city of the LORD (v. 8). God reigns through them.

A prayer: Lord, please, endow our leaders with faithfulness and integrity.
A thought: Is my daily living in line with my worship? Do I walk the talk?

331. The Triumph of Praises
Remember all God's mercies.

This superb song of praise has become a favorite in communal worship and has been taken up in the thanksgiving part of the Lord's Supper. David starts and ends this psalm with a powerful call to himself to praise Yahveh. He doesn't use the familiar "hallelujah" (directed

> November 26
> ~ ~ ~
> Psalm 103

toward a group), but "baraki Yahveh" (directed toward himself): *"Bless the LORD, O my soul; and all that is within me, bless His holy name!"*

Worshipers spur themselves to praise God full out, not holding back. The self-motivation is repeated, and the reason for jubilation is added: *"Forget not all His benefits."* The blessing God bestows on each of us personally is the main driving force behind our jubilant praises (v. 1-2).

David might have penned this psalm after severe illness. He lists the personal blessings he received, starting with forgiveness—which makes all other blessings possible. In the believer, spiritual healing may precede physical and emotional healing. When we don't wait too long, many of the destructive consequences of sin can be replaced by the rejuvenating influence of a sound, God-pleasing lifestyle (v. 3-5).

The psalmist then shifts the focus to Yahveh's blessings on His people. He freed them from the oppression of other nations many times. Through Moses, He revealed His Law to Israel, but they were often disobedient. In spite of that, God was patient and forgiving. He did not give them the full punishment they deserved and forgave them when they repented (v. 6-10). This releases a threefold crescendo of praise: His mercy and compassion are boundless (v. 11-13).

In the second section, man's temporality (v. 14-16) is contrasted with God's eternal love for those who stay true to Him (v. 17-18). The threefold metaphor about man's short-lived physical existence (dust, grass, and flower) is overshadowed by the threefold image about the long-lasting spiritual benefits of faithfulness (fear, covenant, commandments).

Yahveh's rule over all creation (v. 19) gives rise again to a threefold glorifying crescendo (v. 20-22). Sinful man can't do it properly; therefore, the mighty angels who execute God's will, the heavenly hosts who do His pleasure, and God's mighty works in creation are all called to burst into praises to the almighty Yahveh—who also wants to be our tender, caring Father. When David envisages this scene of the praising hosts of heaven, he joins them with his own small but sincere voice: *"Bless the LORD, O my soul!"*

A prayer: Holy Spirit, teach me to praise with even more devotion.
A thought: There is no space for sulking in such a praising atmosphere.

332. God is Glorified by Creation
You renew the face of the earth.

November 27

~~~

Psalm 104

While Psalm 103 glorifies God for salvation, Psalm 104 praises Him for creation. Though it does not follow the same sequence as Genesis 1, it does refer to the main elements: light and darkness; firmament and earth; sea, land, and plants; son and moon; sea life and birds; land animals and humans.

God is described in poetical terms. He is closely associated but clearly differentiated from creation. Light is His garment, the heavens His curtain, the clouds His chariot, the wind His path, and the angels His servants (v. 1-4). The separation of sea and land then comes into focus (v. 5-9). At first, the planet was totally covered by water. By God's word, the crust of the earth was so altered that some parts rose to form land and other parts sank to form sea. In spite of the continuous pounding by the waves, the land has prevailed.

God cares for His creation (v. 10-18). By evaporation, masses of fresh water rise from the oceans, drift as weightless clouds to land where they condensate to sustain plants, animals, streams, and fountains. We can see wildlife drinking from brooks; we can hear the chatter of birds in trees around the pools. In spite of ongoing death because of sin, all life-forms are continuously replenished by feeding and procreation. Man and beast live out of God's hand (v. 27-30). When He gives, they thrive; when He holds back, they die.

In His merciful generosity, God gives much more than bare necessities. He provides enough for good enjoyment too: *"Wine that makes glad the heart of man, oil to make his face shine."* Of course, God's gifts are only beneficial when they are enjoyed in moderation. The storks in the trees, the goats on the hills, and the hyraxes on the cliffs are less likely to overindulge than man.

The earth's 24-hour spin around its own axis exposes most of its surface to life-giving sunlight, while it also regulates the balance between work and rest (v. 19-23). The earth's yearly orbit around the sun supplies the benefits of four seasons to its entire surface. The moon regulates the tides for countless creatures in the tidal zone, and it also serves as a month-counter for man.

The sea with its great variety of living creatures is not overlooked by the poet. Mankind is again seen as part of creation (v. 24-26).

His overview of creation makes the poet burst out into jubilant praises toward the One who made it all. He prays that his own meditations be acceptable to God and that the wicked be removed from God's good earth.

A prayer: Lord, O Lord, great is Your name on all the earth!
A thought: Do I deprive myself from the inspiration of nature?

333. God's Role In Success
Do we honor God for His mercies?

The positive and negative in Israel's history are highlighted by Psalm 105 and 106 respectively. God's mercies make up the positive side, and Israel's shortcomings fill up the negative side. This viewpoint corresponds with the Christian perspective that the good in our lives can only be ascribed to God's grace and that the bad comes from the interaction between man's sinful nature and the devil's temptations.

November 28
~~~
Psalm 105

</div>

Psalm 105 starts with a call to remember God's goodness and to testify about it continuously (v. 1-6). God's people should convey to all the nations the true knowledge of God that they have received. They must urge the nations to seek the LORD, the only God—a call urgently repeated three times.

The focus then shifts to the patriarchs, Abraham, Isaac, and Jacob (v. 7-15). They sojourned as foreigners in a land God had promised to their descendants. They had to survive by faith in this promise. Although they were few in number, God protected them against harm and told local kings, *"Do not touch My anointed ones, and do My prophets no harm."*

God provided for Jacob and his household during a severe drought by allowing Joseph's brothers to sell him as a slave to Egypt (v. 16-25). After many hardships, God made Joseph ruler in Egypt so that he could care for his family. There they became a nation in the next four centuries.

After Yahveh had defeated the gods of Egypt with plagues they could not resist, God called Moses to lead Israel out of bondage to the Promised Land (v. 26-36). They left Egypt with many gifts from their former oppressors, who were glad to get rid of them. God lead them through the wilderness by a pillar of cloud by day and a pillar of fire by night. He quenched their thirst by water from a rock, and He stilled their hunger by birds from the sky and by bread from heaven (v. 37-41).

God helped them to conquer the Promised Land (v. 42-45). The cup of iniquity of the inhabitants of Canaan overflowed, and they lost their privilege of staying in God's land (Gen. 15:16, Deut. 9:4, Lev. 25:23).

Psalm 105 makes it abundantly clear that it was God—and not their own cleverness—who provided for Israel, from the calling of Abram to their settling in the Promised Land. People in all walks of life eagerly take credit for successes. Deep in our hearts, however, we know that success is the result of many factors that come together, a process that we cannot fully control.

A prayer: Father, my success is the result of Your blessing.
A thought: Am I shy to recognize openly God's role in my success?

334. Heed History!
History can liberate or incarcerate.

<table>
<tr><td>

November 29
~ ~ ~
Psalm 106

</td><td>

How did Israel respond to all God's mercies listed in Psalm 105? Very poorly indeed, according to Psalm 106 (see Ps. 78). Although there were good times under some of the judges and some of the kings, these times became shorter and fewer until the majority were so corrupt that God

</td></tr>
</table>

expelled them from the Promised Land and sent them into exile.

The psalm begins by praising God for His majestic mercy and by praying for His forgiveness and for the restoration of Israel (v. 1-5). The poet proceeds with confession of sins, for that is where forgiveness begins. He admits that his generation has sinned just as their ancestors. He refers to the ungrateful attitude immediately after they had seen God's powerful miracles in Egypt and had been freed from their slavery (v. 6-7, Ex. 14:10-12).

In spite of their bad attitude, God made a path for them through the sea and let their enemies drown when they pursued them (v. 8-12). They praised the LORD for the rescue but soon afterward lost faith again when the going got tough in the desert. God filled them physically but starved them spiritually—a sad situation that still exists in our materialistic age (v. 13-15).

The poet does not stick to the chronological sequence of events. The rebellion led by Dathan and Abiram (v. 16-18) is recalled before the episode of the golden calf (v. 19-23), and the idolatry on the plains of Moab (v. 28-31) is described before the strife at Meribah (v. 32-33). Nevertheless, all these sins are seen as part of Israel's bad response to God's mercies. More than once God wanted to destroy them, but Moses, as a type of Christ, stood in the breach for them with intercession, and God spared them (v. 23).

Two of their most unacceptable sins, from God's viewpoint, were their refusal to take the Promised Land (v. 24-27), a mistake that cost them forty years in the wilderness, and their mixing with the nations in Canaan (v. 34-43), which led to idolatry and to the exile.

The psalm concludes with the prayer that God would gather Israel from among the Gentiles and bring them back to the Promised Land (v. 44-48). The poet makes it clear that this would only become a reality through the mercy of Yahveh and for the purpose of glorifying Him. Recently, Jews have returned in great numbers to their land, but the turning to God in great numbers still has to be realized. The spiritual return, not the physical, is God's priority.

A prayer: O God, let the failures of the past correct us in the present.
A thought: God's history lessons can help me make better choices (1 Cor. 10:11)

.

335. Distress Calls
Gratitude for salvation

Psalm 107 records distress calls in four types of crisis: "desert," "prison," "disease," and "storm" situations. Though the desert may include Israel's wandering in the wilderness and though the prison may include Israel's exile, diseases and storms are so universal that one senses that probably all four situations point to human calamities and not to Jewish troubles only.

> November 30
> ~ ~ ~
> Psalm 107

Desert situations (v. 4-9) represent all circumstances where people feel lost, abandoned, homeless, hungry, and thirsty and where they yearn for the fulfilling of their basic needs, whether physical, emotional, social, or spiritual.

Prison situations (v. 10-6) stand for those situations where people feel trapped by their own wrong choices. They feel imprisoned in a dark dungeon and there is no ray of hope that things will soon get better. Guilt, shame, and anger (toward God, self, or others) may be part of this somber experience.

Disease (v. 17-22) represents affliction that taps the strength of body, mind, feelings, willpower, or faith. This situation may also be the result of one's own mistakes, but many "diseases" strike without warning. Appetite for food and zest for life disappear, and death looks like the only option.

Storm circumstances (v. 23-32) can catch people unaware in their daily work, just as a storm can unexpectedly fall on a ship and its sailors. All one's knowledge and experience seem to be worthless against uncontrollable forces. A sense of powerlessness is part of all four crisis experiences.

The poet weaves two refrains through each of the four situations. First, there is the repeated distress call and answer, *"Then they cried out to the LORD in their trouble, and He saved them out of their distresses"* (v. 6, 13, 19, 28), followed by the call to thanksgiving, *"Oh that men would give thanks to the LORD for His goodness, and for His wonderful works to the children of men"* (v. 8, 15, 21, 31).

Then the poet changes his style and concludes his song by affirming the omnipotence, justice, and mercy of the LORD (v. 33-43). Because of people's wickedness God can turn their fruitful land into a desert, and likewise, in His mercy, He can turn a desert into a garden. He can disgrace princes and exalt paupers. The wise and the righteous notice Yahveh's wisdom and justice in His dealings with humanity and praise His name for His loving-kindness.

The message of Psalm 107 is clear: Whatever trouble you are in, come to the LORD for help and show your gratitude with your voice and lifestyle.

A prayer: Thank You, God, for answering my distress call.
A thought: How can I thank God practically for His deliverance?

336. The Rejected Stone
became the cornerstone.

December 1
Psalm 118
It is the middle chapter of the Bible, and the middle verse is
Ps 118:8.

Parts of Psalm 118 (v. 5-24) resemble David's style (see Ps. 18:28-42). The beginning and the end of the psalm might have been added after the temple had been built by Solomon. It was probably sung as an antiphony by the Levites on the one side and by the procession of worshipers on the other side (v. 1-4).

Various groups in the procession take turns to identify themselves with king David's struggles. They agree with him that human help and support is often futile—real help comes from the LORD (v. 5-9). Another group continues and recalls the battles of King David against the enemies of Israel until he had subdued them completely (v. 10-13). A third group reaffirms that David's victories came from Yahveh, the God of Israel. They repeat three times that the "right hand of the LORD" gave them victory and freedom. The enemies tried to destroy Israel, but God used that animosity to establish them (v. 14-18).

Then all join their voices to request entrance into the sanctuary to worship God with thanksgiving for His salvation (v. 19-21). Their attention is focused on King David, who first had been rejected by Saul and his army but who was later hailed as king by all Israel (v. 22). In this, David was a type of Christ who would also be rejected at first but who will return as King of kings: *"The stone which the builders rejected became the chief cornerstone"* (Matt. 21:42, Acts 4:11).

Again this marvelous change of history is ascribed to God's power and mercy, giving rise to jubilant thanksgiving: *"This is the day the LORD has made; we will rejoice and be glad in it"* (v. 23-24). It is still a popular song of praise.

The Levites then open the gates and invite the pilgrims into the temple to bring their sacrifices (v. 25-27). Together the Levites, priests, and pilgrims conclude the worship by praising and exalting God, whose goodness and mercy endure forever (v. 28-29).

Christians often also go through the cornerstone experience. Sometimes the world not only rejects the gospel, but usually it rejects and ridicules Christians too. When Christians keep on trusting in God and persevere in their testimony in word and deed, God brings about a change of heart in their audience. Then the rejected stones once again become the cornerstones of that society. Workers and converts can then all sing in full force, "This is the day the LORD has made; we will rejoice and be glad in it!"

A prayer: LORD, Your goodness and mercy endure forever.
A thought: Do I feel and act like a rejected stone or like a cornerstone?

337. Your Word Is The Truth
God and man communicating

The middle chapter of the Bible (Ps. 118) is preceded by the shortest chapter and followed by the longest one. Psalm 119 is an alphabetical prayer: Every group of eight verses begins with one of the 22 letters of the Hebrew alphabet. All verses (except for 99, 122 and 132) refer to God's word using eight synonyms alternately.

> December 2
> ~ ~ ~
> Psalm 119 (a)

The name Yahveh appears 24 times to clarify that the psalmist refers to His word. The psalm depicts the relationship between God and worshiper. While each verse refers to God speaking to the believer, the whole psalm is also a prayer—the believer speaking to God. The two are communicating.

Like the book of Proverbs, there is, for the most part, no logical link between one verse and the next. However, verses can be linked to different themes that surface repeatedly. Some verses refer to the *mind*, some to *feelings*, some to *actions*, and others to evil *enemies*. We devote one lesson to each of these themes.

The psalm starts with the statement that Yahveh's word is good for us. The first benefit it brings is to give insight and understanding. The psalmist asks the LORD to open his eyes that he may see the wonderful things in His word (v. 18). The phrase, *"teach me"* occurs ten times in this prayer. The psalmist either asks or thanks for *"understanding"* nine times. The best known testimony in this prayer regarding God's guidance is verse 105: *"Your word is a lamp to my feet and a light to my path."* God's word made the psalmist wiser than his enemies, yes, even wiser than his teachers and the elderly (v. 98-100).

In addition to understanding, God's word has to be memorized and meditated on: *"Your word I have hidden in my heart ... "* (v. 11), *"I will meditate on Your precepts, and contemplate Your ways"* (v. 15), *"... I will not forget Your word"* (v. 16). When he remembers God's judgments, it comforts him (v. 52). Having meditated on God's word day and night (v. 97, 148), he comes to the conclusion that *"The entirety of Your word is truth ..."* (v. 160, John 17:17).

Consequently, he feels compelled to bring God's word to others: *"I will speak of Your testimonies also before kings, and will not be ashamed"* (v. 46). Even in the presence of his enemies, he gets his wisdom from God's word (v. 23). When he strays like a sheep, he hopes that the Good Shepherd will find him (v. 176). Therefore he decides, *"My lips shall utter praise, for You teach me Your statutes. My tongue shall speak of Your word, for all Your commandments are righteous"* (v. 171-172).

A prayer: Father, Your word is the truth.
A thought: Do I feed my mind every day with God's word?

338. God's Word Gives Joy
Your law is my delight.

The composer of Psalm 119 not only appreciates the enlightening effect of God's word on his mind, but he also sings about its stimulating effect on his emotional life. He describes how God's self-revelation elevates him from the deepest depression to the highest gratitude and jubilance.

The psalmist confesses that God's judgments sometimes fill him with raw fear (v. 120); therefore, he remains humble and respectful in his contact with God. When he becomes aware of his own insignificance and loneliness, God's word saves him from self-pity (v. 19, 54, and 141).

God gives him hope in affliction: *"You are my hiding place and my shield; I hope in Your word"* (v. 114, also 49, 81, and 92). God saves him from dangerous people and situations: *"I cry out with my whole heart; hear me, O LORD! I will keep Your statutes"* (v. 145-148, also 51-52). God's word cheers him up when he feels depressed or anxious: *"My soul clings to the dust; revive me according to Your word"* (v. 25); *"My soul melts from heaviness; strengthen me according to Your word"* (v. 28, also 107, and 143).

Having been pulled from the pit of bad circumstances and bad feelings (see Psalm 40), he has reason to rejoice in God and in God's mercy toward him: *"Your testimonies are my delight and my counselors"* (v. 24); *"At midnight I will rise to give thanks to You, because of Your righteous judgments"* (v. 62); *"How sweet are Your words to my taste, sweeter than honey to my mouth"* (v. 103); *"I rejoice at Your word as one who finds great treasure"* (v. 162).

The psalmist affirms nine times that he finds *"delight"* in God's word and at least ten more times that he finds some kind of enjoyment from it: *"I will delight myself in Your commandments, which I love. My hands also will lift up Your commandments, which I love"* (v. 47-48); *"Your testimonies I have taken as a heritage forever, for they are the rejoicing of my heart"* (v.111); *"Seven times a day I praise You, because of Your righteous judgments"* (v. 164).

The Bible can improve the mood of believers when it shifts their attention away from the problems right onto God. When they realize how great their God is, they realize how easily the Almighty can solve their problems. When people did that when they asked Jesus for help, He called it "great faith" (Matt. 8:10, 15:28), and when people focused on the problem and not on Him, He called it "little faith" (Matt. 14:31). The author of Psalm 119 was led by the Spirit to show us how God's word can change both mind and heart.

A prayer: LORD, Your word lifts me out of the pit.
A thought: Do I feel better after reading the Bible? If not, why not?

339. Practical Faith
Walking on the right path

Good **insight**, supported by positive **mood**, may spur the **will** into action. The composer of Psalm 119 realized that God's word had to go beyond thoughts and feelings to be fruitful—it had to inspire righteous deeds. Many verses in this psalm point openly or subtly to the practical lifestyle of the believer.

December 4
~~~
Psalm 119 (c)

A positive lifestyle starts with a change of heart that makes the person turn around, away from sin and toward God. The psalmist emphasizes that God takes the initiative to bring about this conversion: *"Before I was afflicted I went astray, but now I keep Your word. It is good for me that I have been afflicted, that I may learn Your statutes. I thought about my ways, and turned my feet toward Your testimonies"* (v. 67, 71, 59).

The author of Psalm 119 urges young people to seek this change of heart and lifestyle early in their lives: *"How can a young man keep his way pure? By living according to your word"* (v. 9, NIV). It is by **walking** on God's path daily (v. 35) that the benefits of God's word are really manifested in one's life; therefore, one should pray each day, *"Direct my steps by Your Word, and let no iniquity have dominion over me"* (v. 133).

This dedication to God must not be occasional but continuous: *"Your word I have hidden in my heart, that I may not sin against You. I shall keep Your law continually, forever and ever. You are my portion, O LORD; I have said that I would keep Your words"* (v. 11, 44, 57).

This attitude and lifestyle imply that one often has to make a decision and deliberately turn away from temptation: *"I have restrained my feet from every evil way, that I may keep Your word"* (v. 101). The main reason for that is love and respect for God as a person who sees all my actions: *"I keep Your precepts and Your testimonies, for all my ways are before You"* (v. 168).

It is easier to stay on the narrow way when one stays in the right company: *"I am a companion of all who fear You, and of those who keep Your precepts. Depart from me, you evildoers, for I keep the commandments of my God!"* (v. 63, 115). Sometimes the wrong company will even set you up to fall into temptation: *"The wicked have laid a snare for me, yet I have not strayed from Your precepts"* (v. 110). In New Testament language it means, *"Put on the Lord Jesus Christ, and make no provision for the flesh, to fulfill its lusts"* (Rom. 13:14). In all Paul's letters he explains that we are saved by grace, and then we do good works out of gratitude.

A prayer: Help me to stay on Your path by what I think, feel, say, and do.
A thought: How can I reach the world without sinking to its level?

340. Surviving Attacks
The believer's enemies

The believer whose mind, feelings, will, and actions are continuously empowered by God's word will inevitably run into opposition. This hostile onslaught may come from within or from without. The age-old trio (flesh, world, and devil) operates here too.

First of all, the author of Psalm 119 fears the enemy from the inside, his own sinful nature called "flesh" in the New Testament. He asks God to prevent him from wandering from God's commandments (v. 10). Satan knows that he will not succeed if he urges us to do a terrible sin to start with. He starts by luring us into small mistakes—either neglecting the right or doing the wrong. By increasing the sin gradually, he keeps the conscience asleep. Therefore, Hebrews 2:1 urges us to "heed the things we have heard, lest we drift away." The psalm ends with the admission that the author has indeed wandered off like a sheep, and he longs to be found by the Good Shepherd (v. 176).

There are specific sins he tries his best to avoid, like lying (v. 29, 163), coveting (v. 36), and the sins of the eye: looking at sinful things (v. 37).

The enemies that are incited by Satan to attack the believer are identified by this psalm as princes (v. 33, 161), the proud (v. 21, 51, 78, 85), the wicked (v. 53, 61, 119), evildoers (v. 115), deceivers (v. 118, 158), and those who ignore God's law (v. 126, 136, 139, 150).

The author sees these people as enemies of God and of himself. They speak against him (v. 23), mock him (v. 51), lie about him (v. 69), accuse him falsely (v. 78), and try to catch him in their snares (v. 110). The psalmist complains that he is incessantly persecuted by his enemies (v. 84-87); they dig pitfalls for him and wait to destroy him (v. 85, 95). They close in on him (v. 150), bind him (v. 61), and oppress him (v. 121, 134).

Because he stays on God's side by embracing God's word, God saves him from evil people. God flushes them out and discards them like dross (v. 119). They do not have part in God's salvation (v. 155).

The dividing line between those who stand with God and those who are against Him runs through Psalm 119 too. For believers, God's word enlightens the mind, inspires the heart, empowers the will, and gives victory over the internal and external enemies. In contrast, the enemies of God and of believers experience the opposite: a blinded mind, a hardened heart, an evil will, and eternal horror without God's presence.

A prayer: Help me to stand with You in spite of Satan's attacks.
A thought: Can I handle rejection and persecution?

341. Divine Protection
Pray for real peace.

Psalm 120 describes the yearning of Israel for Jerusalem while in a far-off region; Psalm 121 voices their prayer for a safe journey to the temple; and Psalm 122 depicts the jubilant praises of the pilgrims when they have arrived in the holy city. In Psalm 84 we see the same three phases of the pilgrimage to Jerusalem (323).

| December 6 |
| ~~~ |
| Ps. 120 - 122 |

Psalm 121 has endeared itself to travelers, but it is also applicable to life's long journey. Whether pilgrims came from north or south, from east or west, they had to go through some hill country before they reached Jerusalem. As they looked up to the hills, their eyes were drawn higher up to the sky and clouds, yes, also to the LORD who made and sustains it all. They know that He is the only One who can procure a safe journey. They will not even stumble on the road or fall prey to robbers, day or night, because Yahveh is their keeper—and He neither slumbers nor sleeps.

Verses 7 and 8 make this psalm universal. Just as God protects the pilgrims on their way, so He protects the believer against all evil. Only God can protect both body and soul from the moment you leave your home until you return safely. He will do it continuously if you ask Him.

In Psalm 122, the pilgrims eventually stand on Jerusalem soil. Their eyes take in the impressive buildings and fortified walls. In silent awe they ponder for a while the importance of this place for their nation. Here all the tribes assemble, united by their faith in the one God, Yahveh. From this place the country is governed by the dynasty of King David, who was appointed by God.

Then the silence is broken by the jubilant praises and prayers of the pilgrims. They urge one another to pray for the peace of Jerusalem—not only for the mighty walls and buildings, but also for all people who love the city. Each individual joins in the jubilation: *"For the sake of my brethren and companions, I will now say, 'Peace be within you'... May they prosper who love you."*

However important the city might be for the nation, the pilgrims realize that it is the temple and God's presence in the temple that really make Jerusalem uniquely great. That's the real reason for their pilgrimage: They have come to worship God in His house. This is what each and every sanctuary should be—a meeting place between the one true God and His children. Jesus made this reconciliation between God and man possible with His atoning death, resurrection, and ascension.

A prayer: Jesus, please give us peace with God, others, self, and nature.
A thought: What kind of peace have I been praying for?

342. Freed from the Snare
God rescues His children and cares for them.

Again, three psalms form a unity. Psalm 123 and the first part of Psalm 124 describe the oppression of God's people, the latter part of Psalm 124 records their liberation, and Psalm 125 tells us about the destiny of believers and unbelievers.

Israel and the church not only endure the contempt and scorn of the world (Ps. 123:3-4), but their very existence is sometimes threatened by vicious enemies who want to devour them as a predator devours its prey or engulf them as a forest fire and a giant wave overwhelm their victims (Ps. 124:1-5).

In these perilous circumstances, they look up to God for mercy and guidance as slaves in ancient times looked up to their owners for merciful care and instructions (when the slaves behaved well) or for merciful discipline and punishment (when the slaves erred)—"So our eyes look to the LORD our God, until He has mercy on us. Have mercy on us, O LORD, have mercy on us!" (Ps. 123:1-3).

God rewards their trusting dependence with a miraculous rescue. He makes the predator hesitate, and the prey escapes. He makes the snare of the hunter fail, and the little bird flies off (Ps. 124:6-8). All believers who have been freed from enslaving sin—Satan's snare—can sing from their hearts: "The faithful LORD Himself has set us free. The snare has failed, the bird sings in the tree. We have been saved like a bird from a snare. The only God—all flourish in His care—He is our Savior, He has set us free."

Psalm 125 paints a picture of those who were saved by God. They stand firmly like Mount Zion. As this mountain is surrounded by other mountains, so God's children are surrounded by God's loving care (v. 1-2). Even when they suffer affliction, God will see to it by the work of His Spirit in the hearts of His children that they are not controlled by wickedness (v. 3).

The prayer concludes with the request that God will do good to those who trust and love Him and that He will punish the wicked for their iniquity. When God answers this prayer, one of the results will be that Israel and the church will have peace instead of scorn and persecution.

The church in all countries should join in prayer for Christians and Jews who suffer severe persecution and who live in mortal danger. These psalms show that God wants us to turn to Him in such tribulation and lift one another up before Him in faithful supplication. He will surprise us time and again by destroying wicked snares with sincere and faithful prayers.

A prayer: Father, save Your children by smashing Satan's traps.
A thought: Has my freedom made me forget God's persecuted people?

343. From Tears to Joy
Those who sow in tears shall reap with joy.

Psalm 126 is a jewel about joy in spite of hardships, about hope in spite of setbacks. For seventy years in exile, Judah had been mourning the loss of Jerusalem, the temple, and their freedom as a nation. Many of them had been seeking forgiveness for the sins that had caused this catastrophe.

> December 8
> ~ ~ ~
> Psalm 126

When they got the fantastic news that King Cyrus had given them permission to go home, they could hardly believe it. The dream of return was just as incredible as the nightmare of exile. They laughed and cried, sang and danced for pure joy—joy against the backdrop of a terrible tragedy (v. 1-2).

Even the Gentiles rejoiced with them and recognized that this miracle could only have been brought about by their God. *"The LORD has done great things for them,"* they said, and the Jews confirmed it wholeheartedly, *"The LORD has done great things for us, and we are glad"* (v. 2-3).

Verse 4 can be translated as *"Bring back our captives"* or as *"Change our fortune"* (NIV), in the same way that the dry wadis in the Negev are changed into streams in the raining season. The first translation points to the past and asks that all the captives may eventually return. The second translation points to the future and the immense problem of rebuilding a devastated country.

In the past during the exile, they had sown with tears, and in the future they will do so again. However, the hope is kindled in them that their present sowing with tears in their country will bring the same joyful harvest as their sowing with tears had done in Babylon (v. 5).

They realized that this experience had a wider application. It is true for all people: When you proceed faithfully with your duties, albeit with tears many a time, you will be rewarded in the end—just as the farmer who toils with plowing and sowing will eventually enjoy a rewarding harvest. The personal experience had become a universal truth (v. 6).

This psalm brings hope and encouragement to those who labor in difficult circumstances. This truth has also been experienced by parents, teachers, preachers, missionaries, and all who work on the invisible fields of the soul. Don't allow hardships and setbacks to bring your good work to a halt. Persevere in faith—faith in the caring, almighty God—and as sure as day follows night you will bring in a harvest on God's time. His time is the best time; His path is the best path; His method is the best method.

A prayer: Father, please turn our tearful toiling into a joyful harvest.
A thought: Where do I have to resume plowing and seeding?

344. Part of the Family
When success is a blessing

The "songs of ascents" (Ps. 120-134) are pilgrim songs. Although they had been written at different times in Israel's history, they were probably bundled after the exile to be used by pilgrims on their way to the temple in Jerusalem. Thus psalms of David and Solomon are among them.

We looked at Psalm 127 from Solomon's point of view when we studied his life (191). Now we view it from the pilgrim's perspective. The temple was rebuilt by Zerubbabel from 520-516 B.C., and Jerusalem was restored by Nehemiah ±445 B.C. These building projects were accompanied by vicious threats from surrounding enemies, as well as with apprehensive hesitation among the Jews themselves. They proceeded by trusting God and by confessing their dependence on Him: *"Unless the LORD builds the house, they labor in vain who build it. Unless the LORD guards the city, the watchman stays awake in vain."* Long after the temple and the city wall had been completed, pilgrims still said these words when they approached Jerusalem.

This truth is then expanded to their daily living—all their hard work will be in vain without God's blessing (v. 2). This thought shifts their focus from God's house to their own home and family. They recognize that their children are wonderful gifts from God. Children are like arrows in a warrior's quiver— the more one has, the better one can defend oneself against the problems of life (v. 3-5). Farms and businesses were family enterprises in those days.

This idea is resumed in Psalm 128. When one trusts and serves the LORD, He will bless one's labor and family life. The table will be laden with produce from the fields and garden. The mother will be like a fruitful vine. The children will look like young olive trees all around the table. The father will look at these riches he has received from God and thank Him from his heart (v. 1-4).

Then the attention shifts back to Jerusalem and to the temple on Mount Zion. The pilgrims pray that the eternal One who dwells in the Most Holy place on the ark of the covenant will continue to bless them all the days of their lives so that they will be privileged to see their grandchildren. When Yahveh grants them these prayers, then Israel is truly blessed (v. 5-6).

Psalms 127 and 128 weave faith, work, and family together into an organic unity. Worship is not only practiced in far-off Jerusalem—it saturates the daily activities back home too, in both home and work.

A prayer: Father, make us aware of Your presence in all we do.
A thought: Do I honor God for His blessings on my work and family?

345. Inner Peace
created by God's redemption

Psalm 129 tells about Israel's physical suffering under foreign nations. Their spiritual bondage because of sin and guilt is the theme of Psalm 130. Liberation from both physical and spiritual enemies leads to the inner peace described in Psalm 131.

December 10

~~~

Ps. 129 - 131
</div>

In Psalm 129, the leader of the group of pilgrims starts singing the first line, *"Many a time they have afflicted me from my youth,"* and the group then joins him by repeating this tragic fact that Israel has been persecuted by other nations through the ages.

Their suffering is seen as flogging, and their lacerated backs are compared to furrows ripped open by a plow. Then the metaphor shifts to the harnessed animals pulling the plow. God has unyoked them like oxen, and they don't have to toil for others anymore (v. 1-4). They pray that those who hate Zion— its people and its God—may die soon like grass sprouts on a flat roof, without leaving any offspring. May these enemies never hear or receive the harvest time greeting of blessing (v. 5-8).

Their physical oppression and liberation draws their attention to their need to be saved from the spiritual bondage of sin and guilt. Like David in Psalm 40, they see themselves in Psalm 130 as crying out to God from the bottom of a deep pit or crevice where they are hopelessly stuck (v. 1-2). They confess to God that they have nothing to offer for their salvation—if God pulls them out, it would be a deed of pure grace from His side (v. 3-4).

They realize that they cannot be demanding; they have to wait on God to work His salvation on His time. However, they keep on yearning for His forgiveness just as guards on night watch look forward to daybreak when their watch and its dangers will be over. The new day symbolizes the new era for the person who has been forgiven by God (v. 5-6). The psalm closes by encouraging Israel to seek the LORD's merciful forgiveness (v. 7-8).

Psalm 131 paints the picture of a child sleeping in its mother's arms (v. 2). Note that it is not a nursed child but a weaned one. It has gone through the difficult weaning process—learning to love its mother for her person and not for her milk only. The child no longer complains, but has fallen asleep in the arms of the mother. Likewise, the pilgrims have found rest and contentment in God's presence. They have been relieved from their physical and spiritual burdens. What they need now is not earthly riches and honor but closeness to God. That is the main goal of their pilgrimage to the temple in Jerusalem (v. 1).

A prayer: Open my eyes for Your blessings and fill me with contentment.
A thought: Have I found peace after being weaned from my favorite pleasure?

346. The Living Temple
of the eternal Priest-King

<table>
<tr><td>

December 11

~ ~ ~

Ps. 132 - 134

</td><td>

The pilgrim songs conclude with a hymn about the love between God and man (Ps. 132), a hymn about the love among fellow believers (Ps. 133), and a farewell song between those who served in the temple and the departing pilgrims (Ps. 134).

</td></tr>
</table>

If we take Psalm 132 literally, we would be faced with several inexplicable problems like the following: David's desire to build a house for God and God's promise to build a "house" (dynasty) for David are here described as **oaths** taken by both of them, while they are not described as such in the historical record (2 Sam. 7, 1 Chron. 17). Moreover, both oaths would have been in vain because David was not allowed to build the temple, and his descendants ruled as kings only until 586 BC when Jerusalem was destroyed.

These "oaths" (or solemn undertakings) refer to much more than the interactions between God and David regarding a building and physical offspring. The Old Testament shows **God's unfolding plan of salvation**, which would be completed by God's Son, who would become a human being born from the lineage of David. The dealings between God and David point to the centerpiece of the Bible: salvation in Christ.

Like David, we should eagerly support God's living temple, consisting of saved sinners (1 Cor. 3:16, 1 Pet. 2:5). In this temple, the Spirit of the eternal One dwells (John 14:23). Jesus is the priest-king who sits on David's throne forever (Ps. 110, Luke 1:32-33). The word for "Anointed" in verses 10 and 17 is "Messiah." Believers are the "royal priesthood" (1 Pet. 2:9) who are clothed with righteousness and salvation, the saints who shout with joy (v. 9, 16).

Psalm 133 shifts the focus onto the loving care that believers show to each other: *"Behold, how good and how pleasant it is for brethren to dwell together in unity!"* Jesus phrased it this way, *"By this all will know that you are My disciples, if you have love for one another"* (John 13:35). The love in Christian fellowship is as refreshing as dew on a dry land and as unique and sacred as the oil that was reserved for the anointing of the priests (Ex. 30:22-33, Lev. 8:12).

Eventually the pilgrims have to return to their homes, far or near. In their farewell hymn, they urge the priests and Levites who remain in the temple service to fulfill their duty with such devotion that it will be to God's glory. The priests and Levites answer by blessing the departing pilgrims in the name of the LORD, the Creator and Sustainer of heaven and earth.

A prayer: Increase our love for God, neighbor, and church.
A thought: Am I excited to be part of God's living temple?

347. God's Mercy Endures Forever
The art of constructive repetition

Practice makes perfect. To stay in top form in any activity, one has to engage in a lot of sensible repetition— whether the activity is physical, mental, emotional, or spiritual. Like other history psalms, Psalms 135 and 136 improve our memory about God's power and mercy by using the tool of repetition.

December 12
~~~
Ps. 135, 136

Both psalms recall God's greatness and goodness in nature and in history, and both psalms show the incomparable superiority of the true God over the false gods. In Psalm 135, the covenant name of God (Yahveh) is repeated 17 times to make it clear who the true God is, and in Psalm 136, it is repeated 26 times that *"His mercy endures forever."*

It is feasible that these psalms were used in different parts of worship. The leader recites Psalm 135 on his own, and when he goes through the same truths again, the congregation joins in by responsively repeating, "His mercy endures forever" after each statement that the leader makes. When these kinds of repetitions are made with reverent awe for God's Person and Presence, the truth is positively engraved on the mind, heart, and will.

In Psalm 135, God's greatness as Creator and Sustainer is highlighted by referring to heaven and earth, sea and clouds, and lightning and rain. Psalm 136 also refers to His wonders in heaven and on earth and adds the blessings God stored up in the sun and moon.

While Psalm 135 recalls in five verses Israel's liberation from Egypt and their conquering of the Promised Land, Psalm 136 describes the same events in fifteen verses, reiterated by the refrain, "His mercy endures forever."

God's supremacy over lifeless idols is humorously and thoroughly worked out in Psalm 135:13-18; therefore, Psalm 136:2-3 only affirms shortly that Yahveh is God over gods and Lord over lords.

Psalm 135 starts and ends with a call to the priests and Levites who serve in the temple to praise the LORD, referring to Israel only once. In Psalm 136, the whole congregation is participating in the praises by repeating the refrain. When they hear each statement about God's greatness and goodness, they repeat in grateful awe: "Amazing grace, amazing grace! His mercy endures forever!" If you find the repetition in worship services boring, maybe you should look at it from the perspective of the musician or sports person, practicing those vital movements over and over again.

*A prayer: Lord, motivate me on the inside to keep on practicing.*
*A thought: Have I imprinted God's mercy into my mind and soul?*

# 348. Rebels Without Insight
## They wanted to be a curse, not a blessing!

<table>
<tr><td>

December 13

~~~

Psalm 137

</td><td>

The contrast between Psalms 136 and 137 is amazing. Psalm 136 overflows with joyful gratitude for God's blessings, while Psalm 137 boils over with bitter hatred because of God's discipline. When the Bible describes how Abraham, Moses, and David sinned, it shows us what we should NOT do. Psalm 137 serves the same purpose.

</td></tr>
</table>

The composer begins by describing how depressed Israel was during the exile. They sat down and wept. Their sorrows made them passive. Not once did the psalmist try to answer the obvious question: Why are we in Babylon? If he had, he would have admitted that their persistent idolatry, in spite of many warnings by many prophets, was the real cause for their exile.

They showed their passive aggression by hanging their harps openly on the trees—by not storing them away. They made their obstinate refusal to sing publicly known. They argued: We cannot rejoice in adverse circumstances, and we cannot praise God in a foreign country. They forgot that David praised God with psalms even when he was in distress (Ps. 27, 40), and that Abraham worshiped God in a country where he sojourned as a foreigner (Gen. 12:8, 13:18). The Creator of heaven and earth is not limited to national borders: *"The earth is the LORD's, and all its fullness"* (Ps. 24:1). They missed the opportunity to testify for God in Babylon—as Daniel and his friends had done.

Then their real motives and attitudes came to the surface. They grieved for their personal and national losses, not for the harm they had done to God's kingdom. They put a curse on themselves if they would forget Jerusalem. Was exalting Jerusalem first priority? Should they not rather have started to worship God instead of idols? The prophet Ezekiel lived among them in Babylon and complained about the same attitude (Ezek. 14:1-6).

They had reason to complain about Edom's gloating attitude, as Obadiah had done (260), and about Babylon's harsh methods, as Habakkuk had done (249). However, the author of this psalm ignored the fact that God used Babylon as His rod to discipline Israel. Therefore, Jeremiah had urged them to pray and work for a prosperous Babylon (256).

But, alas, they did not find peace in God's rod and staff as David had done in Psalm 23. Instead, they cursed that rod and by implication, the Hand that used it. Instead of becoming a blessing to the nations, as God had promised Abraham (Gen. 12:3), they prayed for a curse on the nations. They needed new hearts (Jer. 31:33, John 3:3).

A prayer: Lord, help me to see Your discipline as a blessing in disguise.
A thought: Have I blamed others for the consequences of my own mistakes?

349. Finding Peace
in God's loving knowledge, presence, and power

The style of Psalm 139 resembles that of David, but the Hebrew used is of a later era. Maybe this wonderful psalm of David was "translated" into a younger form of Hebrew for the benefit of a later generation—just as the New International Version of the Bible is in today's English, while the old King James Version is in the English of several centuries ago.

> December 14
> ~~~
> Psalm 139

David marvels at Yahveh's perfect knowledge of him—his thoughts, words, and actions are known to God even before they happen (v.1-6). Because of David's sinful nature, God's omniscience makes him uneasy, but when he considers fleeing from God, he realizes that he cannot escape God's omnipresence—not in heaven or hell, not in east or west, not in light or darkness (v. 7-12).

Fleeing to the past or to the future would not help either, for God was with him from the moment of conception. This made David aware of God's omnipotence. When he was still an embryo, consisting of undifferentiated stem cells, God was working on David's body, soul, and spirit. Even at that point, God already knew what kind of person he would become and what God had in store for this future king (v. 13-16). Is it necessary to add anything about today's disregard for the rights of the embryo and fetus?

David is dumbfounded about the thinking of such an omniscient, omnipresent, omnipotent Being. If God controls all the cells in all creatures—not to speak of the universe out there—then God's thoughts must be more numerous than the grains of sand on earth. Instead of fleeing from this God, David surrenders to Him. Knowing that this one true God, Yahveh, is in full control, he sleeps peacefully, and when he awakes the next morning, he still feels safe in God's caring presence (v. 17-18).

When one becomes aware of how wonderful God is, one cannot help to become aware of man's sinfulness too. David distances himself from the wicked in the strongest terms and takes his stand with God (v. 19-22). But when he does so, he realizes that he is not blameless either. He needs to be examined, tested, and purified by God: *"Search me, O God, and know my heart; try me and know my anxieties; and see if there is any wicked way in me, and lead me in the way everlasting"* (v. 23-24).

David needed forgiveness and to get that, he needed a Savior. Only through God's Son can we have peace with this awesome God.

A prayer: Lord, help me to find peace in Your knowledge, presence, and power.
A thought: How can I help those who are still trying to run away from God?

350. Believers versus Terrorists
David shares his strategy with us.

Since the violence committed by Cain against Abel, some people have been terrorizing others in many ways: by sharp words and by nasty attitudes, by mean backstabbing and by open violence, by disguised assassins and by invading armies. At the start of the twenty-first century, terrorism has taken on new forms on an unprecedented scale.

When David describes his terrifying persecution, we sense the same nagging fear as caused by current terrorism. David saw them as "evil," "wicked," and "violent." Their sharp tongues and poisonous lips stir fear into the hearts of populations; they spread their nets of terror along the roads to catch people in their traps (Ps. 140:1-5). Dictators and terrorists have massacred many and have scattered their bones into mass graves (Ps. 141:7).

To protect themselves from these predators in our time, people have "imprisoned" themselves behind high walls, steel bars, and expensive security systems (Ps. 142:7). Bodyguards and armored cars are in high demand. People are learning to stay vigilant for any suspicious package or movement. We can cry out with David in agony, *"Attend to my cry, for I am brought very low"* (142:6). *"My spirit is overwhelmed in me, my heart within me is distressed"* (143:4). *"Answer me speedily, O LORD; my spirit fails!"* (143:6).

David takes refuge with Yahveh (141:8) and pours out his heart before his heavenly Father (142:2). Although he feels very lonely and deserted, he knows that God will not forsake him (142:4-5). In these circumstances one must keep one's own side clean. David asks God to guard his words and deeds so that he will not sink to the level of the terrorists (141:3-4).

David needs council to survive the onslaught of his enemies. He prefers the honest criticism of true friends above the tricky advice of those who serve the enemy (141:5-6). Above all, David longs for God's guidance, *"Cause me to hear Your lovingkindness in the morning, for in You do I trust; cause me to know the way in which I should walk, for I lift up my soul to You"* (143:8).

David prayed, *"In Your mercy cut off my enemies, and destroy those who afflict my soul; for I am Your servant"* (143:12). The answer came in Psalm 144—stop complaining and make war against the terrorists (v. 1) for they are only human (v. 3-4) and God is on your side (v. 2). We must prevail against tyrants and terrorists lest they take over and rule. People in their grip have to be liberated and restored into a free, orderly, dignified society.

A prayer: Help me to keep up the fight against Satan and his helpers.
A thought: Will terrorists relent if we get soft on terrorism?

351. Victorious Yet Alert
A safe environment for family and daily business

After Saul's death, David became king over Judah at age thirty, and 7½ years later he was crowned king over all twelve tribes (169). When he had dealt with the inside enemies, he realized that he and his people would never have peace until their outside enemies had been subdued as well (173). In Psalm 18, he describes in poetical language

> December 16
> ~~~
> Psalm 144

how God had helped him conquer all his enemies (174). Psalm 144:5-7 uses the same metaphors to paint the same victories.

As in Psalm 118, David recognizes that God made him a great strategist, showing him how to fortify his own strongholds and when, where, and how to attack his enemies with great success (Ps. 144:1-2). That made him aware of the vulnerability of the once powerful enemies who had terrorized him and his nation (v. 3-4). When we look at the same words in Psalm 8, it is clear that David also stayed aware of his own insignificance in God's great universe.

David praises God for his victories (v. 1-2, 9-10), yet he repeats a prayer for deliverance from treacherous enemies (v. 7-8, 11). The reason for this apparent contradiction is the practical fact that a country can never let down its guard. In spite of the victories of the past, enemies and terrorists will never stop trying to undermine a prosperous country. Although David had subdued his enemies, he had to stay alert because his enemies had proven themselves to be unreliable. They distorted the facts, and their right hands (with which they made an oath or with which they shook hands to close a deal) were hands of falsehood.

When Israel's safety was secured by God through David, they could proceed with their daily task of bringing up their families and managing their farms and businesses (v. 12-14). David watched with gratitude how his own children, and those of family and friends, developed from babies to young men and women who were healthy in body, soul, and spirit. As the trimming of trees and vines, as well as the carving of statues, is a time-consuming job, so is the right upbringing of children and the forming of their characters. But what a joy it is to parents when those children become the backbone of society.

Blessed are those who can live in such an environment. They cannot do it without God's help. Therefore, blessed are those who know, trust, love, serve, and praise the one true God, Yahveh. The Bible does not hesitate for one moment to make this seemingly "politically incorrect" statement.

A prayer: Lord, teach us how to be more than conquerors (Rom. 8:37).
A thought: Do I cover all bases in my spiritual life too?

352. Wisdom vs. Folly
Wisdom is a process.

December 17
~ ~ ~
Proverbs (a)
Teaching and
Learning

We will conclude this study with psalms of praise, but for now we make a detour to the wisdom literature of the Bible. Some more wisdom for the holiday season is not out of place. When we studied the life of King Solomon, we took a quick look at his proverbs (189). Others also contributed to the book of Proverbs (22:17, 30:1, 31:1).

The Proverbs emphasize repeatedly that true wisdom comes from God (1:7, 9:10). God uses certain channels to get His wisdom to us, such as His Word (13:13, 16:20) and the nuclear family (6:20-21). There we learn the basic rules of life—what is good or bad for us, as well as for others.

It is stressed right through the book of Proverbs that wisdom has to be taught by the older generation and it has to be learned by the younger generation. The learning process starts with acquiring **knowledge** of facts. Gradually the child develops **insight** into the interconnection of the facts and how that affects his/her life.

This explains the many why questions of children. In this way they discover the **virtues** of life—making the right choices to obtain the right consequences. This learning process has to be continued throughout life so that wisdom will be imprinted on the whole personality (3:1, 4:25-27). People whose knowledge and insight lead to right conduct have wisdom. Those who do not translate their knowledge to insight and to virtue are fools. Even parents and teachers may fall into this trap (9:7, 28:10).

Because wisdom is conveyed by communication, Proverbs stresses the impact of our words on others. Words can heal or hurt (12:18), build up or tear down (10:11, 15:4), clarify or confuse (9:7), and direct others in the right or wrong way (11:9, 12:6). Wars can be won by the words of the wise (21:22). Just as important as it is to speak the right words at the right time (15:23), so it is to keep silent at the right time (11:13, 13:3). Proverbs discourages gossip—scattering the kind of words that does nobody any good (16:28).

Proverbs eagerly advertises the fruits of wisdom (2:9-22) and solemnly warns against the consequences of foolishness (1:20-32, 26:1-12). Usually, society honors a wise person and despises a fool. The wise enjoy material and spiritual riches while the fool shoots himself in the foot time and again. The next lessons elaborate on the positive effects of wisdom on various aspects of life. The Index on Proverb Themes in the Appendix gives more information.

A prayer: Lord, You give wisdom to those who ask You for it (James 1:5-6).
A thought: How do my knowledge and views affect my lifestyle?

353. Diligence vs. Laziness

It is wise to work.

According to Proverbs, diligence is one of the most important virtues spawned by wisdom. And of course, the lack of wisdom causes laziness. The logic of this viewpoint is obvious: Lazy farmers don't produce food, and lazy workers don't earn wages to buy food (13:4, 16:26, 28:19). If lazy people end up hungry, then it must be wise to roll up our sleeves, do an honest day's work,

December 18
~~~
Proverbs (b)
Diligence

</div>

and feed our families and ourselves (27:23-27). We can assume that the same rule can be applied to our spiritual food: If we lazily neglect Bible reading, prayer, and church, we will end up with spiritual hunger.

Proverbs shames our occasional laziness by sending us to the ants to learn from them (6:6-11). Look at them! They are so tiny—how much brain can there be in those minute little heads? But are they industrious! If we compare their size to their speed and strength, they must be the best sprinters and weight lifters. In spite of their gigantic efforts, they still have time to touch each other.

Another object lesson about laziness is to have a good look at the garden of the lazy person (24:30-34). The untidiness, weeds, and disrepair of the fence are enough to spur us into action and get our yards in order.

As zeal without knowledge achieves nothing (19:2), planning our schedule is essential for progress. When we use times of high input well (like seeding and harvesting), we can enjoy the times of low input better (10:5, 12:11, 20:4). Working wisely includes following through. To stop halfway is like putting food on the fork without putting it in your mouth (19:24). Too much sleep, talk, and daydreaming block the way to success (14:23, 19:15, 20:13, 21:25-26). Fear and negative thinking can stand in your way too. Some people talk themselves out of success because of low self-esteem and the fear of failure (22:13, 26:13-14).

Proverbs warns against the unrealistic expectation of getting rich quickly (23:4-5). It is better to make steady progress with hard work (13:11). That is the kind of résumé that employers look out for (12:24).

When Proverbs praises hard work, it does not support "workaholics." We are admonished not to trust in our hard work, but to trust in God. We can't know or control all the factors needed for success. When we pray for God's guidance and provision and gratefully honor Him with our tithes and offerings, He will bless our efforts and fill our barns and tables (3:5-10). Jesus affirmed this approach in the Sermon on the Mount (Matt. 6:25-34).

*A prayer: Lord, help us to trust and obey.*
*A thought: Am I diligent or lazy in my spiritual life?*

# 354. Generosity vs. Stinginess
## The diligent can afford to be generous.

December 19
~ ~ ~
Proverbs (c)
Charity

The Bible maintains a close link between work and charity: *"He who has been stealing must steal no longer, but must work, doing something useful with his own hands, that he may have something to share with those in need"* (Eph. 4:28 NIV). It is therefore not amazing that Proverbs encourages both diligence and charity.

The main motivation for helping the needy is that God cares about them. If we neglect the poor, we insult God and arouse His anger (14:31, 22:22-23). This is especially true if we ignore those who are heading for destruction: *"Deliver those who are drawn toward death, and hold back those stumbling toward slaughter. If you say, 'Surely, we did not know this,' does He who weighs the hearts consider it? He who keeps your soul, does He not know it? And will He not render to each man according to his deeds?"* (24:11-12). We may apply this to genocide, starvation, epidemics, and to lost souls on their way to hell.

Therefore, it is important that we don't delay our help when we can help (3:27) and that we don't shut our ears for the cry of those in need (21:13, 28:27). We should rather be forgiving toward the mistakes of others and have compassion on the poor (14:21). When we share food with them, we lend to God (19:17), and He will repay us when we are in need (22:9).

That is another good reason to help others—we benefit from it ourselves. It makes one feel good to do good (11:17). Moreover, it activates a "natural" law of God's kingdom—when we share God's blessings, they increase: *"One man gives freely, yet gains even more; another withholds unduly, but comes to poverty. A generous man will prosper; he who refreshes others will himself be refreshed"* (11:24-25, NIV).

Proverbs encourages us to practice this policy even to animals (12:10) and to our enemies (25:21-22). Paul quoted this passage in his letter to the Romans, *"If Your enemy is hungry, feed him; if he is thirsty, give him a drink; for in so doing you will heap coals of fire on his head"* (Rom. 12:20). This policy should be applied not only by the individual, but also by the state (29:14).

Our generous approach toward the needy should include holding back on litigation (3:30, 24:28, and 25:8-10). Unfortunately, human rights are sometimes practiced in a very selfish way with the emphasis on *my* rights instead of protecting the rights of others. Being able to ignore an injustice is seen by Proverbs as a characteristic of the wise (12:16, 17:9). Indeed, the real spirit of charity continues to give even when it hurts.

*A prayer: Generous God, help me to be generous toward others.*
*A thought: Do I keep on giving even when it is apparently not appreciated?*

# 355. Joy vs. Anger
## Overcome evil with good.

The fiercest enemy of charity is anger. While Proverbs promotes charity keenly, it has to oppose anger firmly. It does so by showing the penalties of anger and the benefits of its alternatives. Anger and its consequences are baggage that nobody can afford to drag along on life's narrow way.

The roots of anger may go back to one's childhood, but more recent events may cause a buildup of frustration and irritation that only needs a spark to set off an explosion. However, Proverbs does not go into the causes of anger. Its viewpoint is: Whatever the causes, get rid of anger or it will destroy you.

A short temper is linked to the belief that it is okay to get angry, that it is one of one's human rights. This leniency toward anger gives it easy access. And once you get angry, the anger pops up easier for the rest of the day. When anger gets the pinky, it wants the whole hand. Proverbs advises to get rid of that short fuse. It destroys happiness (14:17, 29; 19:19, 29:22).

Because of man's sinful nature, some people provoke anger deliberately with gossip, allegations, innuendos, or insults. They look for a fight and are shocked when they get one. Proverbs reminds us of the bitter fruits of such behavior and advises us to refrain from playing with this fire (17; 14, 19; 18; 3, 6, 7; 26:20-21). Proverbs even urges us to break company with short-tempered people, lest their ways rub off on us (22:24). Instead of harboring bitterness and seeking revenge, Proverbs encourages us to trust God and to promote goodwill with kindness and gifts (15:1, 20:22, and 21:14). These gifts have no strings attached to them; bribes pay for illegal favors. Proverbs detests bribes because they pervert justice (17:23).

The alternative for anger is calmness of spirit (17:27, 22:11, 29:8, 11). The secret is to brush insults aside (12:16) and to be patient with the shortcomings of others (14:29, 16:32, 19:11, 25:15).

Inner joy flows from a choice, the choice to maintain a positive attitude toward life and toward people: *"He who is of a merry heart has a continual feast"* (15:15), *"A cheerful heart is good medicine"* (17:22 NIV), and *"A heart at peace gives life to the body"* (14:30 NIV). This attitude can be contagious: *"The light of the eyes rejoices the heart, and a good report makes the bones healthy"* (15:30).

When we heed the wisdom and experience preserved for us in Proverbs, we will not get tired of replacing bad moods with good ones. It pays.

*A prayer: Lord, help me stay friendly and helpful in all circumstances.*
*A thought: Do I sometimes give the devil a foot in the door?*

# 356. Virtues and Vices
### Playing safe or taking chances

December 21

~~~

Proverbs (e)
Morality

Just as Proverbs links wisdom to diligence, charity, and joy, so it does with morality. For Proverbs there is no doubt about it: The wise stick to a moral lifestyle; fools do not. Proverbs emphasizes this truth in general terms (2:12-15, 4:10-17) but also gives examples like honesty, moderation, and sexuality.

Chapter one takes off with a warning against theft and robbery (v. 10-19). Lying, cheating, and deceptive body language are also rejected (6:12-15). Faulty scales, representing all dishonest business, are strongly condemned (11:1, 20:10, 23). False witnesses (19:5, 9) as well as unjust judges (17:15, 18:5, and 24:23-25) violate divine justice and human rights.

Proverbs rejects gluttony for it may ruin relationships and productivity (21:17, 23:1-3, 6-8). The disastrous effects of alcohol abuse are painted in vivid word pictures to illustrate this folly (20:1, 23:20-21, 23:29-35, 31:4-7). The danger of addiction is suggested by pointing to the probability that the drinker may seek the euphoric effects of alcohol repeatedly in spite of severe after-effects.

Sexual immorality receives much attention in the first nine chapters. The same tragic scene is described five times over: how a young man is seduced by a lustful, married woman. This apparently one-sided approach might not have been considered strange in the tenth century B.C. The Law addressed the male (Ex. 20:17) as the leader of the family, but it was applicable to all in the home. Likewise, Proverbs addresses "my son," but it goes for "my daughter" too.

The only safe sex (physically and morally) the Bible supports is between husband and wife. To prevent corruption of their religion, it was forbidden for Israelites to marry people from other nations (Ex. 34:12-16, Deut. 7:3-4). Rahab and Ruth were exempt from this rule because they accepted Yahveh as their God. Marriage adaptations are tough enough—marrying outside one's culture and faith may make it even more difficult. Paul addresses this issue for Christians in 1 Corinthians 7 and 2 Corinthians 6:14-15.

The argument that women did not have any rights in biblical times is not quite true. Some rights of women were covered in the Law (Lev. 12, 18, Num. 5, 27, 36, Deut. 21, 22, 24, and 25). Women like Sarah, Rebecca, Leah, Rachel, Rahab, Deborah, Ruth, Hannah, and Mary played a major part in Israel's history. The next lesson shows that Proverbs, too, has a special message in store for women.

A prayer: Lord, help me to stay morally wise and responsible.
A thought: Do I sometimes water down my ethical principles?

357. Love vs. Lust
The fulfilling experience of true love

Solomon was a great lover. He was so fascinated by women that he just couldn't get enough of them. Eventually he had 700 wives and 300 concubines. Although many of these relationships served the purpose of strengthening political ties with neighbor countries, Solomon did know the overpowering joy and excitement of falling in love with one specific woman. His Song of Songs testifies to that (Lesson 361).

> December 22
> ~ ~ ~
> Proverbs (f)
> Marriage

He advises his students to experience the joy that young married couples have, a joy so deep and satisfying that it can last a lifetime (5:15-20). He contrasts this long-term, satisfying, body-and-soul oneness of the married couple with the brief, guilt-producing physical encounter with a harlot (5:1-14). As in his Song of Songs, Solomon reaches for metaphors from nature to describe the tender fondness and fondling of the young couple.

Solomon knew that marriage was more than basking in thrilling love. From the wonderful unity of marriage, the wonder of life emerges. A baby is born who needs the parents' loving care and later their patient instruction and discipline. Solomon urges his students to take the instruction of their parents seriously and to see it as preparation for real life (1:8-9, 6:20). He spurs them on to become good parents themselves too (13:24, 19:18, and 23:22-25, 29:17).

The role of the mother in bringing up the children did not escape the eyes of the wise king. He was convinced that a good wife and mother is a marvelous gift from the Almighty (18:22, 19:14) and a crown to her husband (12:4). She builds her husband and children up and doesn't tear them down (14:1).

King Lemuel's mother compliments Solomon's wisdom on the value of a good wife and mother with the famous poem on a virtuous woman (31:10-31). Her husband trusts her because of her benevolent influence on the whole household. She is diligent in caring for her family and servants with food and clothes. Her good deeds go far beyond her home—the needy also enjoy what she prepares. In spite of her busy life, she finds time to enjoy herself with crafts. Her children and husband love and honor her. For them, she's the best. Her beauty is much deeper than good looks. She supports others with wisdom and kindness. Her personality excels because she trusts in the LORD.

In comparison with the virtues of the good woman, Solomon's criticism of some other women is not too bad (11:22; 19:13; 21:9, 19; 22:14, 23:26-28).

A prayer: Dear God, bless all girls and women, wives and mothers.
A thought: Do I show courtesy, consideration, and appreciation to my family?

358. Modesty vs. Pride
The true and false sense of security

December 23
~ ~ ~
Proverbs (g)
Self-esteem

State and private riches crested in Israel during the reign of King Solomon (1 Kings 10:14-29). The wise king realized the danger of materialism and warned his people against a false sense of security. He also knew that in a time of plenty, many try to look wealthy while in reality they could ill afford to compete with the Joneses. He pruned this snobbery relentlessly with sharp proverbs.

Although the well off think their riches will protect them like a fortified city (10:15, 18:11), those who trust in riches will fall (11:28). The rich often become victims of blackmail while the poor are spared this ordeal (13:8). People are discouraged to get rich quickly because riches can suddenly fly away like a bird (23:4-5; 28:20, 22).

Those who try to look rich, but in fact aren't (13:7), are chastised repeatedly by the "better" statements. It is better to be poor and have a servant than to honor yourself and have no bread (12:9) and better to have little and fear God than to have treasures with a lot of trouble (15:16). It is better to have a simple meal with love than a banquet with hatred (15:17) and better to eat dry bread in peace than to take part in a feast with strife (17:1). It is better to have little with righteousness than a large income with injustice (16:8) and better to be humble with the lowly than to share profit with the proud (16:19).

Proverbs identify the real problem behind false security: pride. The rich are wise in their own eyes, but the poor see through the charade (28:11). God hates pride (6:17, 16:5), so when people become proud, their fall is imminent (16:18, 18:12). Pride is a sin (21:4) and leads to shame (11:2).

Because false security is unreliable and because pride leads to destruction, Proverbs urges us to humbly trust in the Yahveh, the God of the Bible: *"Trust in the LORD with all your heart, and lean not on your own understanding"* (3:5) because *"There is a way that seems right to a man, but its end is the way of death"* (14:12, 16:25). The humble are wise (11:2) and enjoy God's grace (3:34). They don't pose as wise people (12:23), but when asked, they give good counsel and are honored (29:23). Jesus referred to Proverbs (25:6-7) when He said that we should not arrogantly take the best seats, lest we be embarrassed (Luke 14:7-11).

By contrasting wisdom and folly, diligence and laziness, generosity and stinginess, joy and anger, virtues and vices, love and lust, modesty and pride, Proverbs clarifies the issues in a wise and stimulating way.

A prayer: Lord, help me to understand deeply in order to teach simply.
A thought: Am I on the right side of the line regarding these issues?

359. A Ray of Hope
amid depressing circumstances

Lamentations just before Christmas?! Not quite. We will focus on that marvelous passage of hope and praise in the middle of Jeremiah's laments. Likewise, Christ's birth was God's bright light of grace breaking through the dark night of sin and all its consequences on this planet.

December 24
~~~
Lamentations
3:21-26

Jeremiah poured out the sorrows of his heart in five poems shortly after the destruction of Jerusalem and the temple—the place where he lived all his life and where he fulfilled his ministry of calling the nation back to God. They did not listen and they paid a terrible price: Their country was devastated by war and most of them were taken captive to serve as slaves in Babylon. Jeremiah was allowed to stay behind with the poor. While he sat amidst the ruins, he gave expression to his grief and that of the nation by writing Lamentations.

Amid the sickening destruction of all he had loved, amid the depressing realization that his life's mission had failed, could there be any positive thought to soothe his pain, any ray of hope to comfort his weeping soul?

Yes! In the midst of the misery in him and around him, Jeremiah shifted his gaze for a few moments from the material to the spiritual, from temporary things to the eternal God. Instantly his laments changed to praises: *"Through the LORD's mercies we are not consumed, because His compassions fail not. They are new every morning; great is Your faithfulness"* (3:22-23). It became one of the favorite songs in the church: "Great is thy faithfulness! Great is thy faithfulness! Morning by morning new mercies I see." *

The comforting Holy Spirit ensures believers that the sun keeps shining although it may be temporarily blocked out by dark clouds. In this spirit Paul and Silas sang hymns of praise after they had been beaten up and jailed in Philippi. And God rewarded the faith He had instilled in them by setting them free from prison and by leading the jailor and his household to Christ (Acts 16:22-34). Therefore, Paul wrote to the Romans that in spite of severe persecution we can keep on praising God because nothing can separate us from the love of God that He bestows on us through Christ (Rom. 8:35-39).

Jeremiah knew that it would take 70 years from the destruction of the first temple to the dedication of the second. Therefore he stressed, " ... one *should hope and wait quietly for the salvation of the LORD"* (3:26).

A prayer: Lord, keep my eyes on Your faithful mercy so that I can wait in hope.
A thought: Do I forget about the sun when I'm under a dark cloud?

* Text: Thomas O. Chisholm, 1923, Tune: William M. Runyan, 1923

360. The Salvation of the LORD
The real meaning of Christmas

<table>
<tr><td>
December 25
~ ~ ~
Isaiah 7:14, 9:6
Micah 5:2
</td></tr>
</table>

For most people with a Christian background, Christmas is a time of goodwill that they want to share. For some, however, it is a time of grief and loneliness amid rejoicing crowds due to painful circumstances or memories. To enjoy Christmas freshly and deeply, we have to shift the focus from self to God, as Jeremiah did, and *"wait quietly for the salvation of the LORD"* (Lesson 359).

Yeshua (Jesus) means *salvation of the LORD*. He is the essence of Christmas. If our gifts, decorations, and festivities point to the salvation of the LORD and make us appreciate our Savior and our salvation anew, then our Christmas is a thrilling success. If not, our "holiday season" is just that, another holiday.

What does the Bible mean by "the salvation of the LORD"? It is the salvation of sinners, planned by God the Father, executed by God the Son, and applied in our hearts by God the Spirit. God promised it already in Genesis 3:15. He demonstrated this salvation by symbols such as Noah's ark, Israel's liberation from Egypt, and by the rituals commanded in the Torah.

God the Son became a human being, Jesus Christ, to fulfill His Father's plan of salvation. He lived a sinless life in our place, He paid our sin debt in full on the cross of Calvary, He rose from death with a resurrected body, He ascended as Savior to the right hand of His Father, and He sent the Holy Spirit into the hearts of those who accepted Him in faith as their Savior.

This is "the salvation of the LORD" we should seek and celebrate at Christmas time. Isaiah prophesied that a virgin would bear a Son and that He would be called Immanuel, meaning "God with us." The angel Gabriel told the virgin Mary that she would become pregnant by the Holy Spirit and that her baby would be called the Son of God (Luke 2). Joseph was told in a dream to call Him Jesus (Greek) or Yeshua (Hebrew). Isaiah said He would also be known as Wonderful Counselor, Mighty God, Everlasting Father, and Prince of Peace. Isaiah's co-pastor, Micah, predicted that this eternal Ruler would be born in Bethlehem, the town of King David, the ancestor of Jesus' parents.

Whether Christmas is for you connected to past or present trauma or not, you can experience the true meaning of Christmas by looking at the sacrifice God made to save you from eternal doom and to bring you into the eternal feast He has prepared for all who accept His Christmas gift—the price His Son paid to set us free. Then you may indeed say, "Blessed Christmas!"

A prayer: O God, let me experience from now on the salvation of the LORD.
A thought: How can I keep and increase this blessing?

361. Lyrical About Love
Preparing for the ultimate wedding

Solomon's Song of Songs is a poem about love in the idiom of Israel three millennia ago. The metaphors used to express the mutual affection and adoration of the young lovers are strange to our ears. Today a young lady will probably not take it as a compliment when her neck and nose are described as towers. In spite of the awkward

December 26

~ ~ ~

Song of Songs

wording of a different culture in a different time, one senses the strong and genuine attraction the two people have for each other.

Interpretations of this poem vary from liberal to conservative. Taking into account that it is part of God's Word, one would be safer to take a moderately conservative approach. Then it cannot be denied that there is a strong emphasis on the physical characteristics of the man and woman in this song. Going into the "garden" and enjoying its fruits may point to the thrilling physical closeness and kisses (1:2, 2:6, 4:11) of the young lovers. However, there are sure signals that this closeness did not include premarital sex. The refrain appeals to the daughters of Jerusalem not to awaken love before it is ready. The way the brothers protect their young sister (8:8-9) supports this interpretation, as do other passages (4:12, 7:13, 8:6).

Amid the admired physical qualities there is also a continuous yearning for each other as persons. Solomon admitted that this woman was very special to him and that she rose far above all the women in his harem (6:8-9). And for her part—she went through a nightmare experience when she thought that she had lost him (5:6-8). Behind their mutual physical "chemistry" is a strong emotional bond of caring that would not tolerate any harm to the loved one.

The Old Testament points to the Messiah; therefore, we can safely assume that God did not put this song in His Book just to tell us something about the love between a man and a woman (compare Ps. 45). In the New Testament, Christ and the church is compared to a groom and a bride respectively (Matt. 9:15, 22:1-14, 25:1-13; Eph. 5:22-33; Rev. 19:7-9, 21:2). Solomon wrote the Song of Songs to tell us about his true love; God let him write it to tell as about the yearning love between Jesus and those who are saved by His redemptive work.

When we read the Song of Songs again from this perspective, we can only bow in awesome wonder that He loves us so much that He declares us spotless (4:7). And we can proclaim to the world about Jesus, *"He is altogether lovely. This is my beloved, and this is my friend"* (5:16).

A prayer: Heavenly Groom, we yearn for our reunion with You.
A thought: Am I completely "in love" with Jesus?

362. Telling the Good News
of God's goodness and power

December 27

~ ~ ~

Psalm 145

More than any other Old Testament believer, David emphasized the importance of telling others about the goodness of God. He practiced that himself by composing and singing his psalms and leaving them as a written testimony about God's grace to the entire world.

In Psalm 40, David describes how God pulled him out of the pit of despair, and how He put a new song into his mouth. He concluded, *"Many will see it and fear, and will trust in the LORD ... I have proclaimed the good news of righteousness in the great assembly; indeed, I do not restrain my lips"* (Ps. 40:3, 9).

The Law of Moses had the same purpose, especially the seven feasts of Israel. Passover and Unleavened Bread commemorated their liberation from Egypt. First Fruits and Pentecost, at the start and finish of the grain harvest respectively, reminded them of God's goodness in nature. Trumpets and Atonement focused on God's forgiveness for repentant sinners. The Feast of Tabernacles pointed to God's care for their ancestors in the wilderness, and it was also a jubilant conclusion of the fruit harvests. Moses admonished Israel to teach the Torah, including Israel's history, to their children (Deut. 6:4-9).

Psalm 145 proceeds with this tradition of David and Moses. It urges each generation to convey to the next generation the facts about the good things God has done to them and to their ancestors (v. 4). We are encouraged to tell this good news in such a way that it will stimulate discussion (v. 5-7)—just as people talk enthusiastically about the good news of the day.

David spurs us on to talk about God's patient love and forgiveness (v. 8-9), about His majesty and glory (v. 10-13), about His power to provide and to save (v. 14-16), and about His faithfulness to answer prayers (v. 17-21).

When you feel frustrated about unfulfilled ideals, think and talk about what Jesus suffered to pay your sin debt, and praise Father, Son, and Spirit for the salvation God accomplished for you. Behold the colors of trees and grass, flowers, and sunset, and listen to the voices of loved ones and to the sounds of nature, and praise God for His majesty and glory in creation and for giving you the senses to enjoy it with Him.

Think about the many things, great and small, that God provides every day. Think about the many prayers He has answered in a crisis. Praise Him for His infinite goodness and power and for His yearning love that He has patiently spent on you and by which He has brought you into the fold. Hallelujah!

A prayer: O God, I praise You for who You are and for what You do.
A thought: Do my celebrations glorify God or myself?

363. Hallelujah!

Praise the LORD for His compassion.

In the last five songs of the book of Psalms, the mutual yearning between God and man reaches a glorious peak. These psalms glorify God, not man. However, God is invisible; therefore, the focus is on His works rather than His person. And His works include mankind and creation.

December 28
~ ~ ~
Psalm 146

"Hallelu Yah" is a command to a group: "You people, you must praise the LORD." The singers of Psalm 146 make it personal, each commanding his/her own soul to praise the LORD. Their intention is to keep on praising God as long as they live (v. 1-2). It is not a passing feeling but a lasting devotion.

To emphasize that they glorify God, not man, the singers ridicule the limitations of man. One cannot even trust the promises of princes because they may be dead before they become kings (v. 3-4). It happened to Absalom.

In contrast with man, God is eternal and almighty. He made and sustains heaven and earth. He knows the facts and the truth. Blessed is the person who has chosen the God of Jacob as his helper. The phrase "God of Jacob" is used 25 times in the Bible (KJV). Jacob here means Israel. If Jacob meant "cheater," then Israel would not have identified themselves by that name nor would they have dared to call Yahveh the "God of Jacob."

The mercy of Yahveh is highlighted by listing **His acts of compassion** toward the less fortunate. He provides justice to the oppressed, food to the hungry, freedom to prisoners, sight to the blind, courage to the depressed, protection to strangers, and care to orphans and widows (v. 7-9). It is reiterated five times that the LORD does this. This passage reminds of Isaiah 61:1-2, which was read by Jesus in the synagogue at the beginning of His ministry (Luke 4:16-21). Jesus showed God's true nature (John 1:14-18, 14:9).

Psalm 146 ends with the reaffirmation that God will reign forever, as it was said in Psalm 145:13 already. That is a second call to the wicked (v. 9) to make peace with God and to avoid destruction. God's patience with sinners is in itself a manifestation of His compassion: He does not want sinners to perish, but He wants them to be saved (John 3:17, 2 Pet. 3:9).

Psalm 146 spurs us on to praise God for His compassion. When we observe His many deeds of love to the afflicted, we cannot respond in any other way than to glorify Him for His love—without which we all would have perished. Therefore, praise the LORD, sing hallelujah!

A prayer: God, I was saved by Your compassion.
A thought: I can improve my mood by praising God for many blessings.

364. Praise God

for His healing and restoration.

December 29
~ ~ ~
Psalm 147

The reason given by Psalm 147 for praising God is His work of restoration in Israel and in nature. The two themes alternate and are sometimes intertwined. When God brought the exiles back to their land, He also blessed them with good seasons and harvests.

Verses 2-6 underline the fact that it is Yahveh who brought the Jews back and who inspired them to rebuild Jerusalem. He nursed and healed their emotional wounds. The almighty God who knows the stars by name and controls them in their orbits had lifted up the humbled Israel and cast down the wicked nations who oppressed them.

God cared for His people as faithfully as He cared for His creation (v. 7-9). He brought the clouds and rain and gave grass on the hills to feed the animals that do not store up in barns (Matt. 6:26). God is not impressed by the power of the flesh but by the strength of faith and obedience (v. 10-11). Praise Him with voices and with musical instruments!

Once again the focus shifts to the returning exiles. When they had rebuilt Jerusalem under Nehemiah, they thanked the LORD, the God of Zion, for this achievement. Their safe borders and fortified city were symbols of God's care and protection for them and their children (v. 12-14).

Moreover, God's blessings in nature secured their crops and livestock when they had to start from scratch. Apart from spring and summer rains, God stored up water for them during winter in the form of snow, frost, and hail on Mount Hermon. When they needed that water later, God let the ice melt and fresh water trickled down to brooks and fields (v. 15-18).

Likewise, God stored up many blessings in His Word that He had given only to Israel in Old Testament times (v. 19-20). However, they should have passed it on so that they could have become a light to the nations (Is. 49:3, 6). When the Messiah came, He opened up the streams of God to the whole world. God's life-giving streams are now available to all who thirst for them (John 7:37). Jesus reconciled the yearning God with yearning humanity.

Although Satan brought disease, decay, and destruction into the world, God used it to show His compassion through healing and restoration. After the destruction of Jerusalem and the temple, Israel appreciated them even more when they were restored. Likewise, when a drought is broken, people enjoy the restored environment even more. Illness helps us to appreciate our health anew. Having been lost makes being saved all the more wonderful.

A prayer: Heal us and our land, O God, and fill us with jubilation.
A thought: Have I embraced the blessing of my crisis and of my restoration?

365. Heaven and earth
praise their Creator.

The words and melody* of Psalm 148 have made it one of the favorite songs of the church. Old and young pull out all the stops when they joyfully affirm in song, "And His glory is exalted, far above the earth and sky."

December 30
~~
Psalm 148

It is a true creation song. Although the angels, universe, and earth are spurred on to exalt the Creator, it is as if the psalm also makes us listen to the song that the entire creation is singing already.

We can only try to imagine what it must sound like when millions of angels sing with perfect voices and in perfect harmony to the glory of their Maker, whom they willingly serve with devoted love (Matt. 6:10, Heb. 1:14). They have no doubts about the existence and qualities of God as we sometimes have, so they sing the song of creation with complete commitment and dedication.

The stars, sun, and moon make no sound that we can hear, but they paint the mountains and valleys, the seas and lakes, with a symphony of color that is beyond description. Our strongest telescopes only recently have begun to pick up this color symphony from far off galaxies. And because God wants us to enjoy His universe with Him, He has put earth in such a position that we can see some of the wonderful stuff out there even with the naked eye.

The next part of the creation choir that falls in is the small but beautiful planet earth. An amazing variety of oceans and lakes, hills and meadows, plants and flowers, land and sea animals, young and old people all sing in their own way the song of creation. It pleases God's yearning love.

The psalm mentions three heavens (see 2 Cor. 12:2): the heavens of the angels, of the stars, and of the clouds. The distant rumbling of an approaching thunderstorm is sweet music to the ears of people in a drought-stricken area. And after the clouds have refreshed the earth, a choir of frogs, insects, and birds joins with rippling streams to sing the glory of the Creator.

What does this mighty chorus of heaven and earth sing about? First, they praise the Creator for their very existence, *"for He commanded and they were created."* They were created with an awareness of their surroundings, and each enjoys life according to its nature and capability. Second, there is an intuitive awareness of the One who made them and sustains them, and they praise His name—Yahveh. His glory is exalted, far above the earth and sky.

A prayer: Lord, I want to stay part of this cosmic choir.
A thought: Would you rather believe the angels or the atheists?

* Melody by William J. Kirkpatrick (1838-1921)

366. Praise or Lament?
How will I end this year?

After Psalm 148, the song in which the entire creation takes part, Psalm 149 zooms in on Israel and the church. Psalm 150 then concludes this book by giving us once again the wide-angle view of heaven and earth—God's entire creation praising Him with voices and instruments.

The "assembly of saints" (v. 1) includes "all His saints" (v. 9). Old and New Testament believers are together in one place. The true Israel is called upon to rejoice in their Maker and King with song, music, and dance. It is only possible for those Jews who have accepted God's salvation in Christ: *"For the LORD takes pleasure in His people; He will beautify the humble with salvation"* (v. 2-4).

Thanksgiving for salvation is never out of place. Even when believers wake up in the middle of the night, they may praise God for His greatest gift—the gift of eternal life (v. 5-6). Parents, imagine how the Father must have felt to give His only Son to suffer and die for the sins of humanity—would you do that for others? Imagine what Jesus suffered in our place—would you stand in for others like that? Amazing grace!

Suddenly the joyful celebrations change to somber tones. God's sword has two cutting edges: Those who accept God's grace in Christ are cut loose from their burden of sin and are welcomed to the heavenly feast, but those who reject or ignore God's salvation are cut loose from God's presence forever. By proclaiming the gospel, all believers handle this two edged sword of God (v. 6-9, 2 Cor. 2:14-16).

However, the Book of Psalms does not end on such a tragic note. In Psalm 150, the focus shifts back to those who are saved and will sing God's praises forever (see Rev. 5:8-14). From the sanctuary, the psalmist zooms out so that we can see the whole picture again: Everything that has breath praises God in full force for His mighty works in the heavens and on earth. The chorus swells as one group of instruments after the other joins in.

Each of the last five psalms begins and ends with "Hallelujah!" Ten hallelujahs to end the year, ten times "Praise the LORD!" to end this study of the Old Testament. Though Israel failed many times, Yahveh kept yearning for their genuine trust and love. He sent His Son to make that possible for Israel and for the world. *The Yoke of Yeshua* tells the whole story about Jesus. When God sees and hears the fruit of His Spirit in us, praising Him from the heart, He smiles with joy.

A prayer: Praise the LORD! Sing hallelujah!
A thought: With whom can I share this book?

Appendix

Other studies by the author

Jesus, The Full Report, 2001, reprinted as **The Yoke of Yeshua**, 2005. A daily devotional on the entire life of Jesus Christ, based on a harmony of the four gospels.

Web Site: www.messiah-study.net
In addition to excerpts from the books, new studies are posted here from time to time.
Feedback can be sent to author@messiah-study.net

Maps

For Bible Atlas Online go to:
www.anova.org/sev/atlas/htm/index.htm

Some Bibles like The Thompson Chain-Reference Bible
have maps at the back of the book.
It may give the reader a better understanding
of the locality and the topography of places.

Peace With God

What's the problem?

We all struggle with the burden of guilt. Some guilt burdens are heavier because the mistakes may be larger or the conscience may be stronger. When the burden becomes unbearable, we try to throw it off with denial, excuses, blaming, accusing, and by seeing ourselves as victims.

We may fool ourselves and others, but we can't fool God. He sees right through us and knows exactly how big our sins and guilt are. He can waste us right now ... but then he proposes a deal.

What's the deal?

The good news is that God loves sinners though he hates sin. He looks on us with compassion. He knows we cannot pay our own sin-debt; therefore, He made a plan to bail us out—a plan so costly that we cannot pay for it, only receive it as a free gift.

In God's courthouse, justice is applied differently. When we plead "not guilty," we get the maximum sentence for our sins because "*If we claim we have not sinned, we make him (God) to be a liar*" (1 John 1:10 NIV).

When we plead "guilty," God's Son steps in and offers to pay our debt in full. He does not force us—we must ask him. When we do, we are freed from our debt and punishment, but we are bound by a code of honor that compels us to show our gratitude to our Savior as long as we live. We have exchanged the old boss, Satan, for the new boss, Jesus. We are no longer slaves of a tyrant but children of a caring Father. That's a good reason to rejoice every day.

How was this deal made possible?

God created human beings to manage this planet: He put them in the Garden of Eden "*to work it and take care of it*" (Gen. 2:15 NIV). As custodians, humans are accountable to the Owner of this planet. To protect man against evil, God put up a moral boundary for them. If they would stay inside that boundary, they would thrive; if they would step over that boundary, they would wither and die. We still face this choice. Like the first humans, we all fail this test, and we face the same consequences. "*All have sinned and fall short of the glory of God*" (Rom.3:23, also Ps. 14:3, Is. 53:6).

In his justice, God could not leave sin unpunished; yet in his love, he could not leave man unsaved either. So he asked his Son to pay the price of our sins, so that he could set us free: "*For God so loved the world that he gave his one and only Son, that whoever believes in him shall not perish but have eternal life*" (John 3:16 NIV).

When Jesus suffered on the cross, God's justice and love merged in Him. Therefore the Bible says, "*God made him who had no sin to be sin for us, so that in him we might become the righteousness of God*" (2 Cor. 5:21 NIV) and "*For the wages of sin is death, but the gift of God is eternal life in Christ Jesus our Lord*" (Rom. 6:23 NIV).

How can I get in on this deal?

We like to be in on good deals and out of bad ones. Here's the best one you'll ever get—peace with God, with yourself, with others, and with nature.

The **first step** is to believe that God exists, for "*Without faith it is impossible to please God, because anyone who comes to him must believe that he exists*" (Heb. 11:6 NIV). Maybe you do believe that God exists; otherwise, you wouldn't be interested in making peace with Him.

The **second step** is to believe the Bible's message of salvation, for "*Faith comes from hearing the message, and the message is heard through the word of Christ*" (Rom. 10:17 NIV). Maybe you do believe the Bible's message of salvation; otherwise, you wouldn't be reading this message. If you feel the need to make peace with God through his Son, you can be sure he is calling you: "*Cheer up! On your feet! He's calling you*" (Mark 10:49 NIV).

The **third step** is to **ask Jesus** to forgive your sins and to change your heart so that you can live a new life to His honor. By surrendering yourself to Christ, *the* Savior becomes *your* Savior.

When you have made this commitment, you can know for sure that Jesus has saved you because of **his word of honor**: " ... *whoever comes to me I will never drive away*" (John 6:37 NIV) and "*I tell you the truth, whoever hears my word and believes in him who sent me has eternal life and will not be condemned; he has crossed over from death to life*" (John 5:24 NIV).

How do you know that Jesus accepted you when you came to him? Answer: "**He said so**; he gave me his word of honor." Where? "In John 6:37— whoever comes to me I will never drive away." Can you slip out of Christ's hands and end up in hell? He gave us his word of honor that he will not allow that to happen: "*I give them eternal life, and they shall never perish; no one can snatch them out of my hand*" (John 10:28 NIV).

How do I proceed from here?

The new life you have received from God is like a small tree you have planted. Just as the tree needs food, moisture, and sunlight to grow, so you need the "food" of **God's Word**, the "moisture" of **fellowship** with other believers, and the "light" of God's presence experienced in quality time with

Him in **prayer**. If one of the three is missing, the tree will wither, and so will you. When all three are present, you will grow and become stronger and **bear fruit**.

Yes, we cannot only take energy in; we must also send energy out. We must do something useful for the Lord and for others. A wise man once said: Always testify for the Lord; use words if necessary. He meant that our deeds speak louder than our words. Saved sinners must always try to make life around them better. They must try to prevent harm to others and try to do good to others—at home, in the workplace, on the road, and in all walks of life. They must practice the Great Commandment of love (Matt. 22:36-40).

By FAITH we enter into God's kingdom. By FAITH and LOVE we live as citizens of that kingdom. God's indwelling Spirit enables us to do that. Jesus compared our contact with him to the contact between the vine and its branches (John 15). In contact with Christ (the vine), we (the branches) are filled with his power so that we can bear fruit. *"The one who calls you is faithful and he will do it"* (1 Thess. 5:24).

~~~~~

Bible books and corresponding lessons

Bible books   ## Lessons

Bible books	Lessons
Genesis	1-37
Exodus	38-73
Leviticus & Numbers	74-92
Deuteronomy	93-99
Joshua	100-112
Judges	113-126
Ruth	127-133
1 Samuel	134-164
2 Samuel	165-184
1 & 2 Kings } 1 & 2 Chronicles}	185-258
Ezra	275-280
Nehemiah	283-284
Esther	285-286
Job	287
Psalms	288-351 362-366
Proverbs	352-358
Ecclesiastes	192-193
Song of Songs	361
{Christmas	360}
Isaiah	233, 235, 237-239, 244-246, 274
Jeremiah	252-259, 273
Lamentations	359
Ezekiel	268-272
Daniel	261-267
Hosea	236
Joel	226
Amos	229
Obadiah	260
Jonah	230
Micah	240
Nahum	248
Habakkuk	249
Zephaniah	250
Haggai	276
Zechariah	277-278
Malachi	281-282

The prophets are studied in the time they lived.

Lessons and corresponding scripture

Lesson	Scripture
1. Touched By Life	Gen. 1:1-25
2. Touched By Love	Gen. 1:26-29, 2:7-9
3. Touched By Discipline	Gen. 3
4. Choices and Consequences	Gen. 3:7 - 4:12
5. Grace Amid Catastrophe	Gen. 3:15, 3:21-24, 4:6-15
6. Two Kinds Of People	Gen. 4:17 - 6:4
7. Miracles Amid Decadence	Gen. 6 - 8
8. A New Deal	Gen. 8:20 - 9:17
9. The Birth Of Nations	Gen. 9:18 - 11:9
10. The Promise	Gen. 11:27 - 12:10
11. A Blessing Or A Curse?	Gen. 12:10-20
12. The Broad And Narrow Way	Gen. 13
13. Abram Becomes A Blessing	Gen. 14
14. Grace And Faith	Gen. 15
15. A Dangerous Detour	Gen. 16
16. A New Beginning	Gen. 17
17. A Caring Host	Gen. 18:1-15
18. A Caring Intercessor	Gen. 18:16-33
19. Compromised Believers	Gen. 19
20. A Promise Fulfilled	Gen. 20, 21:1-7
21. God's Timely Provisions	Gen. 21:8-24
22. The Sacrifice	Gen. 22
23. The Closure Of A Tested Life	Gen. 22:20 - 25:28
24. God's Promise Endured	Gen. 25:22 - 28:9
25. Finding Our Niches	Gen. 27:41 - 28:22
26. Blessings Amid Hardships	Gen. 29 - 31:18
27. Great God, Small People	Gen. 31
28. Jacob Becomes Israel	Gen. 32
29. Two Surprised Brothers	Gen. 33
30. Sorrow Upon Sorrow	Gen. 34 - 35
31. Favoritism Breeds Hatred	Gen. 37
32. Character And Conduct	Gen. 38 - 39
33. Trust And Work Ethics	Gen. 39:1-6, 20-24
34. Dreams And Reality	Gen. 40 - 41
35. Facing The Truth	Gen. 42 - 43:14
36. Facing The Person	Gen. 43:11 - 45:8

Themes in Proverbs

Wisdom vs. folly

God is the source of wisdom 1:7, 2:5-8, 3:5-12, 9:10, 9:22-31, 11:30, 16:3

fruits of wisdom 2:9-22, 3:13-26, 4:6-19, 6:22-23, 8:3-36, 9:11-12, 13:14, 13:20, 14:8,

fruits of foolishness 1:22-32, 5:3-14, 13:16, 20, 16:22, 26:1-12

parents 1:8-9, 4:1-5, 4:20-5:1, 6:20, 13:1, 24, 15:5, 19:18, 23:13, 22-25, 29:15, 17

learning process 1:2-9, 2:1-4, 3:1-4, 4:1-9, 20-27, 5:1, 6:21-23, 7:1-2, 9:7-10, 12:1, 13:18, 15:12, 22, 31-32, 16:22, 18:15, 19:2, 20:18, 22:6

wisdom seekers 9:7-9, 10:10, 12:1, 15, 13:1, 18, 20, 14:6, 33, 15:5, 12, 14, 31-33, 17:10,

word-power 10:10-21, 31-32, 11:12-13, 12:6, 13-14, 17-18, 25, 13:2-3, 14:3, 15:4, 7, 15:23, 16:20, 23-24, 18:20-21, 21:22-23, 25:11-12, 15, 29:8

peer pressure 1:10-19, 2:12-15, 14:7, 18:24, 22:24-25, 24:21, 27:17, 28:7

wisdom personified 1:20-33, 8:1-9:6

Diligence vs. laziness

diligence 10:4-5, 22, 12:11, 24, 13:4, 11, 14:4, 23, 16:26, 18:9, 20:4, 13, 22:13, 24:30-34, 27:18, 27:23-27, 28:19, 31:10-31

laziness 6:6-11, 10:26, 12:24, 27, 13:4, 19:15, 19:24, 20:4, 20:13, 21:25-26, 22:13, 24:30-34, 26:13-16, 26:13-16,

Generosity vs. stinginess

charity/goodwill 3:27-35, 11:17, 24-26, 12:10, 14:21, 31, 17:4, 19:17, 21:13, 22:9, 22-23, 24:11-12, 25:21-22, 28:27, 29:14

pledging is dangerous 6:1-5, 11:15, 17:18, 20:16, 22:26-27

Joy vs. anger

anger 12:16, 14:16-17, 29-30, 15:1, 18, 28, 16:27, 32, 17:9, 14, 19, 27, 18:3, 6-7, 18-19, 19:11, 19:18-19, 20:3, 22, 21:14, 22:10-11, 24- 25, 24:28-29, 25:15, 26:20-21 , 29:8, 11, happiness 13:9, 12, 14:30, 15:13, 15, 30, 17:22

Virtues vs. vices

wicked vs. righteous 11:3-31, 12:2-7

dishonesty 6:12-15, 17-19, 10:2, 6, 11, 22, 11:1, 3, 18, 17:8, 20, 23, 19:5, 9, 22, 20:10, 23, 17, 21, 20:23, 21:6, 22:5, 27:5-6,

gluttony 21:17, 23:1-3, 6-8

inebriety 20:1, 23:20-21, 23:29-35, 31:4-7

immorality 2:16-22, 5:3-14, 6:24-7:27, 9:13-18, 23:26-28

Love vs. lust

marriage 5:15-20, 27:8, 31:10-31

adultery 2:16-22, 5:3-14, 6:24-7:27, 9:13-18, 23:26-28

women, recognition 11:16, 12:4, 14:1, 18:22, 19:14, 31:10-31 women, criticism 11:22, 12:4, 14:1, 19:13, 21:9, 19, 22:14, 23:26-28

Real vs. false security

false security 11:28, 12:9, 12, 15:16-17, 27, 16:8, 19, 17:1, 18:11, 19:1, 4, 6, 21:9, 19, 23:4-5, 25:24, 28:6, 11, 20, 22,

modesty 3:34, 10:14, 19, 11:2, 12:23, 13:10, 29:23

pride 6:17, 11:2, 12:9, 13:7, 15:16-17, 16:5, 8, 18-19, 17:1, 18:12, 21:4, 24, 22:2, 25:6-7, 26:23-28

wisdom versus smartness 3:5, 12:5-6, 15, 13:18, 14:12, 16:25

Justice vs. injustice

authority 16:10-15, 28:12, 15-16, 28, 29:2, 4, 14, 16,

justice 16:10-15, 17:15, 23, 18:5, 17, 19:5, 9, 28, 20:21, 21:15, 26, 21:6, 28, 22:8, 28, 23:10-11, 24:23-25, 25:8-9, 29:7

gossip 10:18, 11:12-13, 16:27-28, 17:4, 18:8, 20:19, 26:20-27, 29:20

What God loves and what He hates

God's law 12:3, 28, 13:6, 13, 14:27, 34, 15:9, 33, 16:20, 19:16, 23, 20:9, 28:4, 5, 7, 9, 13, 29:16, 18

God hates these 6:16-19, 11:1, 20, 12:22, 15:8-9, 26, 16:5, 17:15, 20:10, 23, 21:27,

God punishes sin 5:21-23, 13:13, 21:12,

God rewards goodness 3:5-12, 10:3, 11:30, 12:2-3, 13:6, 13, 14:26-27, 34, 16:6, 20, 19:23, 21:3, 22:4, 23:17

~~~~~~~~~

Consulted Resources

Commentaries

Bakker, F.L. (1955): *"Geschiedenis Der Godsopenbaring, Het Oude Testament"*, Kok, Kampen.

Church, Leslie F. (Ed.) (1961): *"Commentary On The Whole Bible By Matthew Henry"*, Zondervan Publishing House, Grand Rapids, Michigan.

Ellwell, Walter A. (Ed.) (1989): *"Baker Commentary On The Bible"*, Baker Books, Grand Rapids, Michigan.

Geldenhuys, J. N. (Ed.) (1958): *"Die Bybel Met Verklarende Aantekeninge"*, Verenigde Protestantse Uitgewers, Kaapstad.

Ridderbos, J. (1952): *"De Kleine Profeten"*, Kok, Kampen.

Scroggie, W. Graham (1956): *"Know Your Bible - A Brief Introduction To The Scriptures"*, Volume I, The Old Testament, Pickering & Inglis, London.

Study Bibles

Hayward, Jack W. (Ed.) (1995): *"Spirit Filled Life Bible For Students"*, NKJV, Thomas Nelson Publishers, Nashville.

Kohlenberger, John R. (1987): *"The Interlinear NIV Hebrew-English Old Testament"*, Zondervan Publishing House, Grand Rapids, Michigan.

Thompson, Frank C. (1983): *"The Thompson Chain-Reference Bible"*, NIV, Zondervan Bible Publishers, Grand Rapids, Michigan.

Vosloo, Wil & Van Rensburg, Fika J. (1993): *"Die Bybel In Praktyk"*, Nuwe Vertaling, Christelike Uitgewersmaatskappy, Vereeniging.

Lexicon

Davidson, Benjamin (undated): *"The Analytical Hebrew and Chaldee Lexicon"*, Samuel Bagster and Sons Limited, London.

Geography

Bible Atlas Online: www.anova.org/sev/atlas/htm/index.htm

Grollenberg, Luc. H. (undated): *"Atlas van die Bybel"*, Nasionale Boekhandel, Kaapstad.

Van Deursen, A. & Meima, G. (1953): *"Beknopte Bijbelse Aardrijkskunde"*, Wolters, Groningen.

Wright, George E. & Filson, Floyd V. (1953): *"The Westminster Historical Atlas Of The Bible"*, SCM Press, London.

Hymns and Creeds

Brink, Emily R. (Ed.) (1988): *"Psalter Hymnal"*, CRC Publications, Grand Rapids, Michigan.

Encyclopedia

Grosheide, F.W. & Itterson, G.P. (Ed.) (1956): *"Christelijke Encyclopedie"*, Kok, Kampen.

Encyclopædia Britannica (1975), Helen Hemingway Benton Publisher, London.

www.britannica.com

Electronic Media

Logos Bible Software 2.0 (1995).

Subject Index

U

Unleavened bread 46
Ur 10,
Uriah 176

W

Water from the rock 51,
Weeping 35, 302, 312,
Widows 201, 215
Word of God 95, 100, 251, 255, 284, 295,
300, 322, 337-340
Work ethics 33
World evangelism 297, 315, 329,
Worship, true 293, 310

Y

Yearning for God 307, 323, 341

Z

Zadok 181, 185
Ziklag 161, 162, 164
Zion 171, 309
Ziphites 157, 160, 161

Printed in the United States
38699LVS00003B/7-69

9 781420 874709